THE PROGRESSIVE UNDERGROUND

KEV ROWLAND

Vol 4

Edited and scanned by Kevin Rowland
Typeset by Jonathan Downes
Cover by Martin Springett

First edition by Gonzo Multimedia 2022

c/o Brooks City,
6th Floor New Baltic House,
65 Fenchurch Street,
London EC3M 4BE
Fax: +44 (0)191 5121104
Tel: +44 (0) 191 5849144
International Numbers:
Germany: Freephone 08000 825 699
USA: Freephone 18666 747 289

© Gonzo Multimedia MMXXII

All rights reserved. Without limiting the rights under copyright reserved above, no part of this publication may be reproduced, stored in or introduced into a retrieval system, or transmitted, in any form of by any means (electronic, mechanical, photocopying, recording or otherwise), without the prior written permission of both the copyright owners and the publishers of this book.

ISBN:

Dedicated to my incredible wife Sara as without her support, I would never have been able to spend so much time writing about music.

It is also dedicated to my amazing daughters Nicola, Elizabeth, Hannah and Amanda, who grew up thinking that having a dad stuck at a computer all the time, while playing strange and often unusual music very loudly, was the normal thing to do.

Foreword

Hello there! Let me open this book by giving my personal thanks to each and everyone of you who have chosen to read this book, as there aren't too many of you around anymore. As I'm far from being a spirited youngster, I still remember fondly when we had to buy magazines to read music reviews in order to get suggestions about what music we should possibly desire to get more engaged in, and I can recall the days when being a music reviewer gave you a position of considerable influence. Alas both me and Kev are too young to have ever been able to get into such a position ourselves, but I suspect Kev has read as many stories as I have read about how music reviewers were treated back in the day.

These days, writing music reviews is a task executed by everyone that cares to do so, and often by people with strong opinions and perhaps not as much of a factual or objective foundation as the reviewers had in yesteryear. Reading music reviews has also become a more narrow field, as a growing amount of people rely on YouTube, Spotify, Amazon and similar services and their algorithms to guide them. So those who take the time to appreciate the art of the written word and the descriptions given by someone with a strong emotional attachment to the art of music - this as opposed to music as a means of mere entertainment - is something to be appreciated. Hence why I thank you all for taking the time to read this book. The art of the music review is a dying art, and as I dabble in reviews myself I appreciate everyone that supports it.

Kev has chosen to call his series of books "The Progressive Underground". Personally I think I would have gone for "The Chronicles of Kev Rowland, the prog reviewer". This due to having a slightly dry sense of humour as well as referencing another piece of art from a slightly different field of the arts, but also one I suspect many of the readers of this book will be familiar with. That the reference will be recognized by many of the artists that have been covered by Kev's words here and is from a field generally associated with progressive rock is fitting too I think, and the fact that this particular piece of art can be as demanding as some of the material Kev has written about in this book makes it a good fit too I think. So for me, this series of books will always be internally referenced in that manner. As I know Kev hasn't restricted himself to merely covering progressive rock, I expect a similar series of books covering genres such as jazz, folk and metal to be forthcoming in the next few years. If Kev has the capacity to compile them that is.

What most people reading this book will not realize is just how much of a mammoth task it is to compile the material for such a book as this one: Tracking down cover art in decent quality for albums released in a limited edition, often with digital files only sent for review, can be daunting. Even in this digital age. And as this book covers material released at more or less the dawn of the digital age, or at least in the early morning hours, the availability online for some of this material can be scarce. If I should guess from a position of some knowledge, I would guesstimate that each page of this book has taken around two working hours to assemble. Possibly a bit more. It is a case of getting the information, text and cover art, reading through the text and looking for any spelling and grammatical errors and correcting them, then setting up the book page using set parameters to ensure that everything looks good on each and every page. And then to error check for anything to move out of place when the final file needs to be prepared for printing. It is quite the mammoth task, and much more work intensive than what most people can imagine.

The time period covered in this book is an interesting one. The years from 2008 to 2013 represent the years when physical music sales really started to decline, a decline that started in the year 2000, and now increasingly being replaced by digital options. Initially by Apple Music and their iTunes Store, which had really started taking off at this point, and with Spotify launching in 2009 music consumption gradually became more of a digital only experience for a growing amount of people in this time period. The artists started to move their own independent sales from Myspace to these and other established platforms, and when Bandcamp appeared in 2008 this became an increasingly important tool for artists and later on also labels to control their digital existence and presence, and one increasingly used for promotional purposes too.

While many reviewers would still get the majority of their promos in physical shape in 2008, by 2013 the majority of the promos would be digital ones. Unless you were a very established reviewer whose voice still had a commercial impact that is, or you had a personal attachment with an artist, a label or a PR firm that found the cost of sending you a physical copy was still worthwhile. I suspect Kev may well write a book about these and other tendencies he has observed and been a part of in the three decades and a bit that he has been an active supporter of the art of music. If he should find the time for it, and have the interest to do so.

While not as interesting for those that have read to this point of the foreword I suspect, it was in this time period where I got to know Kev too. He knew about me due to my role for a website called progressor.net, while I didn't know who Kev was at all at the time I have to admit. We first started talking with each other at a site called Progarchives, and while we both pretty much quit that site for different reasons some years back we kept in touch, and have established a friendship over the years that also goes beyond the field of music. Which is why I was given the honor of writing the foreword of this book.

I've never been a man that has had problems with words, other than probably using too many of them. But I will start concluding this foreword with the same words that I opened them with: Thank you for reading this book. Some of you will make many new discoveries while reading through Kev's reviews. Many of you will fondly recall albums forgotten about. Some of you will agree with Kev's opinions, some of you will disagree. I suspect that just about everyone reading through the entire book will encounter a multitude of artists you have never heard about, and some of you will read about albums by artists you know but with albums you didn't know about at all. And I suspect all of you who have bought this book or been given it as a gift have a profound love and affection for music as one of the creative arts. Just like me and Kev. So thank you again for reading, and I wish you a happy experience reading onward from here and getting to the important parts of this book.

Olav M. Björnsen, Norway
November 2021

The Progressive Underground Vol 4

Introduction

When I first started thinking about compiling my progressive rock reviews and interviews into a book, it was always planned that it would contain my writings from the years 1991-2006. That was when the mass media's contempt for the genre was at it's height, and included the days when the internet was either non existent or in its infancy, while personally it neatly encompassed the years when I was running Feedback fanzine in the UK. I was involved with Feedback from its earliest beginnings as a newsletter for Mensa's Rock Music Special Interest Group in 1988, before becoming secretary myself in 1990 and running it until we emigrated to New Zealand in 2006. So the concept was always to compile a single book, which soon became an issue when the text amounted to more than half a million words. The single book concept no longer worked as it was too large, so it was suggested that instead it should be broken into smaller sections, and include all the album artwork. This resulted in The Progressive Underground Volumes 1-3, which really is one large book, divided into more easily digestible chunks.

The positive reaction was more than I could ever have imagined, and it was wonderful to feel I had shone a light on a dark period for progressive rock music. I got back to normality (whatever that is), knowing I had accomplished something special, but was soon being asked questions by many artists, namely "when are you going to print my reviews?" or "why isn't my album in the book?". My response always was that TPU Vols 1-3 were over a specific period of time, from 1991-2006, and the reason they were not included was because that particular piece of writing had been later. However, it did start me thinking. The older writings were hard to pull together as I only had that in hard copy fanzines, but all my more recent scribblings were in electronic form, so just how difficult would it be to compile another one?

It took longer than I thought it would, but at last here is the fourth volume in the series, this time compiling my progressive rock writings from 2008-2013. Unlike Vols 1-3 this is complete, in that it has the full alphabet of A-Z, plus the interviews I undertook at the time. There are no live reviews included, as back then I knew very little about the New Zealand scene, and virtually no international progressive rock artists can find our country on a map let alone actually play here. Maybe that will change in Volume 5, but that is off in the future...maybe.

2006 saw us emigrate from the UK to the other side of the world. As part of that, I made the decision to stop running Feedback and instead spent more time away from the computer to discover the opportunities available to us in this incredible country. I told every label and PR company to remove me from their mailing lists, told all the bands I was no longer involved, and started listening to music I wanted to, as opposed to what I was having to due to a looming deadline. I got away with it for nearly eighteen months.

This volume sees an introduction from Olav M. Björnsen, and comments on the rear cover from Thierry Sportouche and Jerry van Kooten. Between us we have more than 100 years of writing about progressive rock music, and one reason for us all still going is that there have not been enough new people coming into the scene who are prepared to keep pumping out the reviews week after week, year after year. Consequently it is incredibly hard to drop away, as I discovered when bands and labels kept contacting me and saying "I know you don't do this anymore, but would you please mind writing a review?".

I slowly succumbed, writing the odd one here and there, then somehow found myself as a collaborator on ProgArchives, working behind the scenes with Olav before we both moved on and I eventually joined him at Progressor.net (one of the oldest continually running progressive rock sites in the world, launched in 1998) where we can both be found to this day. My writing volume slowly increased, my name started to appear on lists once again, and even though I was living in New Zealand it didn't matter as promos were now being sent out most commonly as downloads so geography was no longer a constraint. This means that although my reviews used to concentrate on certain countries that was no longer the case, while my style also changed as I was no longer writing for the same group of people getting a magazine on a regular basis, as my reviews were now appearing in multiple places worldwide.

As I write this at the end of 2021, I can honestly say I am as involved with a music scene as I was 30 years ago, except back then it was concentrated on one genre and now it is geographic as my main focus these days is on bands and labels in Aotearoa. But, prog is never far away, and I still write hundreds of reviews on the subject every year.

I truly hope you enjoy discovering yet more bands and albums which are new to you. Use this as a guide, a way of seeking out wonderful music which has been overlooked for no other reason than being the "wrong" genre. Prog never died, it just went underground.

Read on, I hope you enjoy it.

Kev Rowland, New Zealand
November 2021

Album Reviews

ACID RAIN
THE DESCENDING LINE
This 2009 album was the debut full-length release from Argentinean outfit Acid Rain, with a line-up of Sebastian Fernandez (vocals), Fernando Culen (guitars), Andres Blanco (keyboards, vocals), Ezequiel Gimenez (bass, vocals) and Martin Magliano (drums, percussion). Musically these guys are great, a strong melodic pomp mixed with prog – sort of Styx crossed with Dream Theater, with a high level of obvious musical virtuosity combined with great hooks that mostly make this an album to die for. I say 'mostly', as there is one bit that just doesn't fit, namely the lead vocals. Sebastian does have a good voice, with a strong range, but he is way out of his musical league here. His vocal style has much more in common with Dan McCafferty (okay, that is a little unfair – he's not quite that gravelly) than James LaBrie, much more hard rock than prog.

The result is an album that is great on many levels, with guitar and keyboard interplay to die for and a great rhythm section, but it just fails at the final hurdle. This is a band that I would like to hear a lot more from, and they could actually make it as an instrumental outfit. It is powerful and certainly impressive – and hopefully we will hear much more from them in the future.
Oct 2011

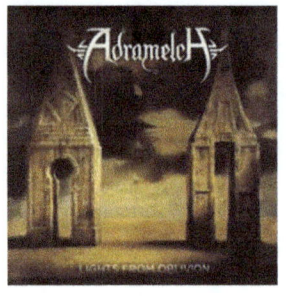

ADRAMELCH
LIGHTS FROM OBLIVION
If ever there was a band that doesn't like to rush things, Italian proggers Adramelch has to be it. Their debut came out in 1988, but they split up soon afterwards. The lead singer Vittorio Ballerio and guitarist Gianluca A. Corona decided to create a new version of the band in 2004, primarily to record songs that they had written before the original split, and the follow-up 'Broken History' came out in 2005. So now, only seven years since the release of their second album (this came out in 2012 but I have only just come across it), and the same line-up from the last album have stuck around to record a third. These guys are coming towards prog from the areas of hard rock and metal, but also bringing in melodic rock as well. The result is an extremely well-crafted and constructed album that is going to appeal to fans of many genres. Imagine Savatage combining with Porcupine Tree, City Boy and Uriah Heep and you may just come close to what these guys are all about. Twin guitars and a very strong rhythm section (hats off to bassist Maurizio Lietti who provides some incredible runs when the mood requires it) means that this is an album that hits the spot on so many levels. It is easy to listen to and enjoy from the very first play, and the more attention it gets the more rewards it gives out. It has now got me wondering what the other albums are like, and just how long we may have to wait for the next one! Not for those who really want crunching riffs, as they certainly are no Threshold, but if well-crafted music is what you are after then look no further.
Jun 2013

AFTER...
HIDEOUT
'Hideout' is After...'s second album, being released in 2008. Here is a band that have been paying close attention to fellow Polish Progsters Riverside as well as Porcupine Tree, Pink Floyd and Parallel Or 90 Degrees. In other words, we have some great symphonic prog with strong vocals and guitar lines all being melded into a glorious whole. Yep, I like this one. A lot. This is all that I want from a progressive rock act – when I am after comforting prog that I don't have to think about too much (as opposed to Art Zoyd etc). It may not do anything dramatically new, and doesn't voyage through uncharted waters, but what it does it does very well. It is like being wrapped in a warm security blanket, all snuggly and comforting. It is music to listen to in the harsh nights when all you want to do is to sit in front of a roaring log fire with a decent brandy and relax. There are some wonderfully delicate keyboards, and "Fingers" is a sheer delight with lead vocalist Krzysiek Drogo getting the emotion and timbre just right. The gently distorted guitars near the end of this, and the climactic build is just wonderful. There are some reviewers who are always looking out for the band that is breaking new territory – and while that is fine and good, I also want music that hearkens back to something that in many ways is familiar. When I listen to Triumvirat I may think

of ELP in many ways, but so what? This is a great album and is one that many progheads will thoroughly enjoy.
Oct 2011

AHLEUCHATISTAS
HEADS FULL OF POISON
Ahleuchatistas (AH LOO CHA TEES TAS) is now Shane Perlowin (guitar/ bass) and drummer Ryan Oslance – originally a trio, this is the seventh album from the band that was founded in 2002. For the curious the name comes from two words, "Ah-leu-cha" (a Charlie Parker song) and "Zapatistas" (a revolutionary movement which started in Mexico in 1994). To say that the music is as unusual as the name, is something of an understatement. The music was recorded live, with just a few overdubs from Shane where he was providing more than one instrument at a time, and the result is something that is quite inspired, albeit not exactly easy listening.

This is an instrumental odyssey into the unknown, and for many this will be a journey that they will not wish to embark upon, but if you have a need to expand your musical boundaries then this may be just the thing. Free jazz is just a starting point, and with obvious nods to Art Zoyd and Can they have brought together textures from all over the world. Ryan must be worn out at the end of each gig as his percussion rate is phenomenal, while Shane moves easily from fuzzed out droning guitars to single string attacks on an acoustic where I am amazed that he doesn't break strings with regularity given the ferocity and tempo. If he was playing chords instead of single notes and turned it up, then this would give most thrash bands a run for their money. There is also a lot of Eastern influences at times, with some songs sounding almost Japanese in style. Each track is very different, but to enjoy this leave your preconceptions of what music should sound like at the door and settle down to something that will challenge your ears. There won't be many who will relish playing this to be honest, but those who do will be richly rewarded. This is the first time I have heard the band and I have read that in the early days they sounded a bit more like Beefheart – some further investigation is in order methinks.
Sep 2012

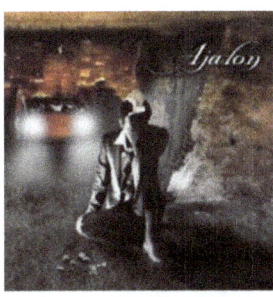

AJALON
THE GOOD PLACE
It took four years for Ajalon to follow up their highly acclaimed 'On The Threshold Of Eternity', of course Randy George has been working quite a lot with Neal Morse during that time so perhaps they can be forgiven. As before the band are a trio (multi-instrumentalist Randy George, vocalist Wil Henderson and drummer Dan Lile) but they also use guest musicians which gives the sound a far more layered and complex flavour that it would otherwise. The artwork on the

CD and booklet are wonderful, the playing is superb and the production really polished, so why is it that I can't bring myself to fall in love with it? I think the reason is that to my ears it sounds too much like prog by numbers – let's put together all the elements of American prog that everyone enjoys so much and release it as an album.

The first time I played the CD was on headphones and I found myself drifting away and that shouldn't be the case when the attention should be centred just on the music. There is one joyous beacon of light on the album, with "Lullaby of Bedlam" standing head and shoulders above the rest where everything comes together in a slighter harder and boisterous fashion, and with the bass and keyboard combining with the keyboards and drums to show that the band can be a force.

This isn't a bad CD, far from it, and there will be many who will enjoy it, but for the most part this is just too cloying and suffocating for my own personal tastes.
Apr 2010

AKIN
THE WAY THINGS END

Formed in 1998 in Lyon (France), Akin were heavily influenced by Anathema, The Porcupine Tree and Opeth. Their first demo was positively received, and they consequently signed with Sacral Productions for 'Verse' in 2001 and 'Forecast' in 2003. Both were very well received in France and assisted in them getting the gig to open for bands such as Within Temptation, Dark Tranquility, Epica and others during 2002 and 2003. There then followed a long period of inactivity from the band and it was only in 2009 that they got back together to work on 'The Way Things End' which was released by Progrock Records in 2011.

I wonder why the band took such a long break, as if the earlier albums are anything like this then they literally have the world at their feet. Although bands like Legend have never gained the attention they deserved, over recent years symphonic metal/prog bands fronted by female singers with a great range have been coming very popular. In many ways Akin remind me especially of Within Temptation, and also Epica and Nightwish (the Anette Olzon version, not Tarja Turunen). This is powerful music with great interplay between all of the musicians, often coming from a metallic area but they also use a string quartet to bring an additional edge to proceedings and whatever the band is doing behind her, singer Adeline Gurtner is more than up to the task. This is a great album that should find a lot of fans. It is also possible to go to Bandcamp and listen and purchase their earlier works.
Sep 2012

AKPHAEZYA
ANTHOLOGY IV (THE TRAGEDY OF NERAK)
Just to get a couple of things out of the way, firstly this isn't an anthology and this is actually their second album and not their fourth. This French outfit came together in 2002, with Stephan H. Zag-Zero (guitars/concept-story), Nehl Aelin (vocals/keyboards), Loic Moussaoui (drums) and Stephane Béguier (bass) and have been working on this album for the last couple of years. There are some songs such as "Utopia" that are just strange (much in the vein of some of System of a Down's quirkier moments), whereas others are a little (but only a little) more straightforward, but the only debate to be had here is whether this is prog metal, symphonic metal, or avant-garde metal? To be honest, who cares? This is complex music played with passion and aggression yet always with stacks of melody and often some great piano to provide a little lightness.

The production is stunning, but when one looks a little closer at the credits it is hardly surprising as it was recorded and mixed by S.Biguet (Trepalium, klone, Comity...) and mastered by Brian Gardner (Down, Lamb of God, Queen, Suicidal Tendencies, QOTSA etc.). There are times when Nehl reminds me of Candia from Incubus Succubus with her good clear vocals, but she is adept at many different styles which is just as well given what is going on with the music. It can be acoustic and gentle one minute then strident and domineering the next, truly progressive as it moves through lots of different styles and emotions – but always with a metal base. This is heavy stuff, and needs to be played at a high volume, but if you enjoy music that is both heavy and moving in different directions then this should be on your player.
Sep 2012

ALBION
THE INDEFINITE STATE OF MATTER
I was sorting through my music the other day and was surprised to come across a cassette release of this band's debut album, now the best part of 20 years old: I hadn't realized that I had been aware of them for so long. This is their first album for five years, and they are now down to being just a trio with guests, which in many ways is somewhat surprising given that the rhythm section has been outsourced as it were. But, it has to be said that in many ways this feels much more like a solo album than it does a band release. There are times when the guitar wails poignantly, and there are times when Jerzy even dares a riff, but this appears to be very much the album of keyboard player Krzysztof Malec. There are a couple of long instrumental numbers on here, as well as long instrumental passages, which in itself is rather surprising given that Katarzyna Sobkowicz-Malec has such a wonderful voice.

A friend of mine asked to borrow this album but soon returned it with the comment that it was just too boring and single-natured for him, and while I may not necessarily agree

with the statement I fully understand where he is coming from. An issue I have with some extreme metal bands is that they forget the importance of contrast, so tend to not have enough lightness to emphasis the heaviness and here the reverse is true. The album is crying out for some crunching guitars and more dynamic solos, as otherwise it is running the risk of falling into the background. That is not to say that this is a bad album, not at all, but where Jerzy throws in the Gary Chandler-style leads it demonstrates just how good this could really be. Solid as opposed to spectacular.
Mar 2013

ANATHEMA
WEATHER SYSTEMS

If you visit the Top 2012 albums in www.progarchives.com you will find that currently this album sits inside the Top 20 and if you visit the Top 2012 albums in www.mlwz.pl you will find that this is number one! So, a very highly rated album by lots of people, and one that I enjoyed playing a great deal. But, and you of course realized that there was going to be a "but", this isn't prog music people…There is some wonderfully delicate piano and gorgeous acoustic guitar, with outstanding vocals, but this has more in common with Coldplay than anything else. True, there is the odd hint of Muse, but is this really a progressive album at all? Well, that's an easy one to answer, as this is more pop and cheese than prog but in many ways it is a very special album indeed.

Play a song, virtually any song on the whole album, and you will be taken aback by the sheer majesty of what is happening in front of your ears. But, it is like a rather rich cheesecake, the odd slice can be savoured and thoroughly enjoyed but if you eat the whole thing then you will be rather unwell. If I dip in and out of the album then I get a great deal out of it, but when I play it from start to finish, I find that I am always fed up by the end and am looking for something a great deal heavier to reset my ears. But love it or hate it, this is definitely worth investigating.
Mar 2013

ANDEAVOUR
ONCE UPON A TIME

The roots of Andeavour can be traced back into the 80's when guitarist Steve Matusik was in a metal band called Damien Steele, a local covers band from Erie Pennsylvania. Steve was writing original material but keeping it to one side. In 1993 he played this material to bassist Doug Peck, who had also been in Damien Steele. He liked what he heard and put words to Steve's music and also took on the role of singer. Needing a drummer, he thought of Steve Starvaggi who he had played with in Loudhouse, and Andeavour were born. Chris Rodler (Drama, Leger De Main, RH Factor) had been watching these guys were doing and realised that they were struggling in the live environment with Doug trying to sing, play bass and keyboards all at the same time so he offered his services as keyboard player, and also had his own recording facilities and label.

In 1999 the band released their debut CD 'Once Upon A Time' to great acclaim – fuelled by a strong performance at Powermad '99. It was the second bestselling album in PMM's catalogue and in 2008 talk of the 10th anniversary led to the album being remixed and remastered. The result is a very clean album that shows a band very much in the prog metal mould, probably more Fates Warning than Dream Theater, more hard rock Rush than metal Threshold. To be honest, the band they remind me most of in many ways is Winter, but as they only released one mini-album on SI Music (if you ever see it grab it – just awesome) I doubt that they could have been a major influence. This is an incredibly enjoyable album, one that takes the best of all of the above-mentioned bands and bringing it together in an extremely melodic whole. Chris takes more of a back seat than I have normally heard from his work, here he is acting to bringing it all together as opposed to acting as a major soloist in his own right, and the feeling overall is that this is very much a band playing songs as opposed to just a vehicle for a group of musicians to show how clever they all are.

The one small niggle that stops me from acclaiming this as essential is that I am not 100% convinced of the vocals – I get the impression that Doug is on the very limit of his ability, and sometimes the strength and pitch isn't quite there, but for most of the time he is bang on. But when he keeps within his own boundaries this really is a joy to listen to.
Oct 2011

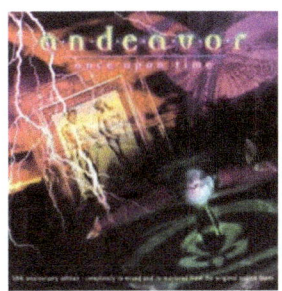

ANDEAVOUR
THE DARKEST TEAR
So, with the band talking about the 10th anniversary of course the conversation soon turned around to recording a new album. Chris had left the band some years before but was more than happy to stay involved as producer and to ensure that the album could be recorded and released. He also ensured that the artwork for both this and the reissued debut were tied together, and they were released at the same time. In many ways this is the stronger of the two releases – the band have stayed true to their progressive influences but here have moved much more into hard rock. The songs have far more impact, with the whole band apparently way more focussed and intense. Doug's vocals have improved tremendously in the intervening years, and with the removal of keyboards the band use space to much greater effect. The result is a progressive hard rock (certainly not metal) album that contains heavy classic Rush influences but in a more progressive manner.

It is hard to define, but the band seem more relaxed and ready to play and the material feels far tighter. The debut is an enjoyable album, but this one is superb. It is of no surprise to me at all that this is a recommended album by DPRP – I wholeheartedly agree. If you want melodic progressive hard rock, strong in every aspect, then you need this.
Oct 2011

ANEKDOTEN
CHAPTERS

Anekdoten are one of those bands who prove that the term 'progressive rock' really does cover a huge area of music. While there will always be some comparisons with King Crimson, their instrumentation and background and bringing in of some folk roots will always mean that they stand apart from the crowd. They came together in 1991 as a quartet comprising Nicklas Barker (vocals, guitar, Mellotron, Moog), Peter Nordins (drums, percussion), Jan Erik Liljeström (vocals, bass) and Anna Sofi Dahlberg (Mellotron, organ, Moog, Rhodes, cello, piano, vocals) and five studio albums later it is still the same four people. The use of a very strong rhythm section providing support for hard rock guitars and two Mellotrons (along with cello) means that this is a very powerful band indeed. This two CD set brings together songs from their last three albums on CD1 along with a new recording (which features Per Wiberg of Opeth) while CD2 contains music from the early years along with unreleased demoes etc.

The music is often challenging, never content to sit within any expected norm, yet also manages to have an immediacy and depth that brings the listener in as there is always more to investigate and discover. The music twists and turns with a vibrancy and depth often missing from many bands. It is clear with great production, each instrument can be clearly heard and defined yet it is the combining of all of these elements that make it such a tour de force. If you have not come across the music of Anekdoten before (and if that is the case, then you should be ashamed of yourself and rush out and get 'Vemod' immediately) then this is a great way to discover more. And of course, if you already know the band then you realise that this is an essential purchase. The set is in a nice digipak with good artwork and a booklet with details of where every song has been taken from, players etc.
Apr 2010

ANTONIUS REX
HYSTERO DEMONOPATHY

I was playing this album in the car the other day, taking my sixteen-year-old to school, and as she got out she told me exactly what she thought of the music and ended it with "it sounds as if someone is being killed!". I told her that I agreed with some of what she said, but that this was a 5* album if I had ever heard one. The more I have played this the more I have enjoyed it, and it now makes me wonder what I have been missing out on as this is the first of their albums that I have come across. These guys have been around for a very long time, based around Antonio Bartoccetti (guitars, vocals, bass) and released a number of albums in the 70's before coming back in 2005 and this is their fourth since then. Antonio is joined by Rexanthony (vocals, keyboards, synths, piano, digital drum, orchestra), and Monika Tasnad (whose contribution is listed as 'medium') plus special guests Florian Gorman (acoustic drums) and singers Laura Haslam, Vladimir Leonard and Svetlana Serduchka.

Just a short playing of some of this album would inform the listener that here we have an Italian prog act that is working in the same area as the mighty Goblin, and that the screams and effects work hand in hand with the music to create a soundscape that is beautiful, horrifying, complex, simple, dark and threatening all at the same time. At times the guitars are really in your face, but at others it is the orchestration. It really is an incredible piece of work that will be unsettling for some, as this is not the sort of prog that you would take home to play for your mum. This is music that is designed to be dark and to provide a very real edge to proceedings. Cinematic and visual, this is a stunning piece of work.
Jul 2013

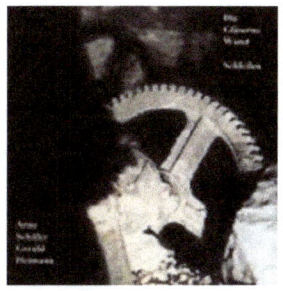

APOGEE FEAT. GERALD HEIMANN
DIE GLÄSERNE WAND & SCHLEIFEN
This album contains material from 1988 – 1989, before Arne Schäfer became involved with Versus X. Apogee has always been intended to push the boundaries of what could be accepted as prog, so Throbbing Gristle and Kraftwerk have as much influence as VDGG or King Crimson. On this double CD set he is joined by vocalist Gerald Heimann, and while all the vocals are in German there is an English translation of the lyrics in the booklet. I really wasn't sure what to expect from this release, as although I have albums by all four bands mentioned above in my collection – how would it all fit together? Also, I noticed that the five songs on disc one (and the first song on disc two) were all described as movements of the same piece. Now, when someone states that it is a movement they raise the stakes as normally movements are associated with classical music – so just how good is this? Well, to be honest, not very. There are some sections where it is really very good, but that is overweighed by the times when I was wondering just how much longer it had to go on. Some of the keyboard sounds being used are incredibly dated, even allowing for the fact it was recorded more than 20 years ago. There are times when it reminded me more of some of the worse elements of electronic music that was around twenty years ago – but there again I don't believe that I am the intended audience as this is part of a series of releasing some of Arne's archives, so there must be people out there who are demanding this. To me this just sounds like a series of demo recordings that I am unlikely to listen to again.
Sep 2012

ARABS IN ASPIC
PICTURES IN A DREAM
Now, it doesn't take much to get me confused, but at the moment I'm not actually sure what the name is of this band. According to their Facebook page they are Arabs in Aspic II, but according to the label they are Arabs in Aspic. The cover art doesn't show the band name, and I was sent this as a download so I don't have a physical copy to look at. I have no idea where the band name (whichever one it is) actually comes from, apart

from thinking that it must have something to do with a certain King Crimson album, so maybe it's fortunate that the name is so unusual. Mind you, one has to wonder about the name altogether, is it likely to upset someone in the current climate? Maybe, but these Norwegians have been together for more than 15 years now and this is their fifth album so they're not exactly newcomers. But, this is the first album of theirs that I've come across which shows how easy it is to miss out on great bands, even with the internet.

They say that their main influences are Sabbath and Wetton-era King Crimson, but there is also the requirement to mention how important psychedelia and plenty of early prog bands are to these guys. This is chunky prog that definitely hearkens back to forty years ago and makes no excuses for that whatsoever. It is controlled, with really heavy elements which threaten more than appear, with special guest singer Rune Sundby (from famous Norwegian 70's proggers Ruphus) doing a standout job. While the guitars are heavy, the drums are dramatic, and there are loads of Mellotron and Hammond on this.

The result is something that those into heavier 'classic' prog that is very much geared towards the Seventies sound will enjoy a great deal. I did.
Jul 2013

ARCHANGELICA
LIKE A DRUG
Archangelica were formed in Poland in 2004, releasing the two mini-albums 'Archangelica' in 2007 and 'Where Are You Now?' in 2009. During that period they moved on from their original Anathema influences to something that was more melodic and immediate, without losing all of their emotional roots. They have also made quite a few personnel changes, with founder and keyboard player Darius Ojdana leaving his own band: in fact only guitarist Maciej Engel (who also provides keyboards on this album) is there from the band that recorded the debut. The rest of the line-up is completed by James Kolyada (bass), Chris Sałapa (vocals), Arek Gawdzik (guitar) and Peter Brzezicki (drums) while guest Natalia Matuszek provides some incredible additional vocals to add more layers.

I have played this album numerous times now, and am still at a loss as how to quite describe it. There are some wonderful guitars, but it's not really prog metal, while there are times when it is quite emotional and dreamy yet definitely isn't trance (which is one of the words they actually use themselves to describe their music). In some ways it is almost neo-prog, but that isn't quite right either and the best I can come up with is Jadis crossed with Anathema with plenty of influences from Shadowland but there again I could be wrong. All of the vocals are in English, and it is a wonderfully polished and incredibly vibrant and immediate album that I have enjoyed immensely. Complex without being complicated, simple and harmonious, this is a delight.
May 2013

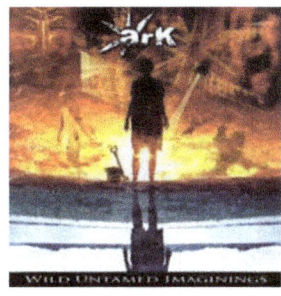

ARK
WILD UNTAMED IMAGININGS
OK, time for a history lesson – so pay attention as I might ask questions later. Ark came into being in 1986 with Ant (vocals & flute), Pete Wheatley (lead guitar), Steve Harris (guitar synth), Steve's brother Andy Harris (bass) and Gary Davis (drums) – note no keyboards, somewhat unusual for a prog band. In 1988 Andy left and was replaced by John Jowitt (yes – that John Jowitt, now known for IQ, Arena, Jadis, Frost* etc).

After a mini-album 'The Dreams Of Mr Jones' and the 'New Scientist' EP (both well worth searching out – they are currently stored with the rest of my vinyl but I do seem to recall a photo of Mr Jowitt with hair on one of them...) they toured with the likes of IQ before John left in 1990. The band kept working and released more material and gigged hard but by 1995 it was all over.

Or was it? In 2009 Steve Harris got in touch with John and the idea came about of a new album highlighting the best of Ark combining old songs and new, and before they knew it there was virtually a full reunion as Tony and Peter jumped at the chance with the line-up completed this time with Darwin's Radio drummer Tim Churchman. Now, I can hold my head up high and say that I was into Ark before John had joined IQ – and god knows how many years I have had the vinyl, but it is great to hear some of these songs again in a much cleaner setting. The production is all that one would expect from a release of 2010, but the music dates back to the time when neo-prog was covered by fanzines and spread by word of mouth – no internet back then. So, is the music still relevant today? Hell yeah, this was a band that never got the acclaim that they deserved even within prog circles. For years they have been remembered not for songs such as "Gaia" and "New Scientist" but as the band that John was in before he became famous. Thankfully that wrong has now been corrected – Ark are back and I for one am truly thankful. Essential.
Oct 2011

ART CINEMA
ART CINEMA
This album was Robin Taylor's first release of 2008, his 25th album, but under a different name. This was quite a different project for him as although the instrumental passages were still important this involves far more musicians and lyrics. The line-up for this album was Robin (guitars, keyboards, percussion), Jytte Lindberg (primary lead vocals), Louise Nipper (lead and backing vocals), Michael Denner (guitars), Bjarne Holm (drums), Carsten Sindvald (saxophones), Flemming Muus Tranberg (bass), Jon Hemmersam (guitars) and Pierre Tassone (violin). This album sees Robin head far more into progressive territory, yet still with the restraint and use of space that is such an important feature of his music. Michael is there providing just a hint of menace, but again he is very much part of the band and in many ways fits into this role better than he did in the previous release. This is more of a songs-based album than the others, with less jazz stylings (although it is never too far away) and is a real coming

together of styles with prog combining with music that in some ways is almost New Age. This is an extremely mature release in that there is a feeling of there being nothing to prove, all those involved know their part and are happy with it. This is music that the listener needs to go towards and to discover – it will not be rammed down the throat of all and sundry but instead will be enjoyed by those lucky enough to hear it. The vocals are pure and clear, working well with a musical backdrop that at times can be quite minimalistic. It is the arrangements that make this album, simple statements showing the music does not have to be overblown to be technically clean and beguiling – there is almost a sterility reminiscent of some of Roger Eno's work, yet at the same time there is a warmth and comfort that welcomes all.
July 2009

ARZ
TURN OF THE TIDE
ARZ is a duo from Portland, Oregon, comprising guitarist/singer Steve Adams and drummer Merrill Hale who met while they were members of a Yes tribute band called All Good People. ARZ was originally the name used by Steve as a one-man band where he recorded all instruments himself, and he then brought in Merrill to assist with the fourth album, 'Solomon's Key'. After that album he and Merrill decided that they wanted to record an album they could perform live, and they devised a way of doing this using MIDI and samples etc but after some feedback from fans they decide instead to record the best album they could and not worry about the live part just yet. So back into the studio they went and created an album that can only be described as majestic. Merrill is a great drummer who cites Barriemore Barlow and Danny Carey as his major influences but given the way that he hits those skins and drives the music along it is obvious that he has been listening to Portnoy a great deal and his touch also reminds one of Palmer. He never overpowers Steve but provides him with an incredible foundation that allows him to build and build with multi-layered riffs and keyboards or sometimes just simple chords and melodic vocals, whatever is right for the moment. This is modern progressive music that is immediate, structured, and climactic. It has the complexity, yet somehow maintains a simplicity and naivety that draws the listener in every time. As I said before, this is majestic, in every way.
Oct 2012

ASIA
XXX
So here we are, some 30 years on from the debut, and the four original members continue their reunion with another album. Back in 1982 I was studying for my degree and I played their debut to death – for me every song was a triumph, and I knew the words to all of them and would happily sing along. So when I was sent this album to review I was really looking forward to it: it's a real shame that it doesn't live up to all my expectations.

John's vocals are as strong as ever, and of course the musicianship is second to none, but it is the quality of the songs themselves that somewhat let the band down. The choruses are repeated too often and the song structures don't allow for the brilliance of the players to really come through. Of course all the harmonies and hooks are there, but there is a feeling that this has been created for radio airplay in America and in that context it could work as there are some catchy moments and it does work well when being played in a car, but in many ways this is an opportunity lost. Well produced and well played, this is an AOR album with a few prog tendencies that is for diehard fans only.
Sep 2012

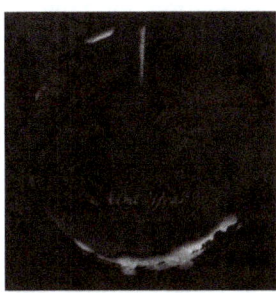

ATMOSFEAR
ZENITH
This is the third album from German prog metal outfit Atmosfear. They're not exactly prolific as they have been around 15 years – but given that this was released nearly two years ago and I'm only just writing about it I'm hardly able to cast stones. The press release uses the word "soundscape" when discussing their style, and that is a great way of describing it. When people hear the term 'prog metal' they either think of crunching riffs combined with strong keyboards and vocals (a la Threshold) or a band that can do absolutely anything and get away with it as not only are they all virtuoso musicians but they keep coming back to hard rock/metal at least some of the time (Dream Theater – yes I know that is a vast under-representation for them but you get the drift). But these guys have connections with, but are totally different to, both of those, and sit within the genre but in many ways are totally separate from it. The band name was obviously chosen with some care, as this is extremely atmospheric metal, and it has an edge that is much more than just the complexity of the instruments and the wonderfully clear vocals. Yes, there are parts that remind me somewhat of Savatage, but they are only sections in songs as opposed to complete pieces. I read one review on the web where they basically asked what on earth this band had been doing to get this far and not been picked up and praised by the prog scene and I know where he is coming from. This is progressive metal of the very highest quality, and anyone who enjoys melodic rock that is easy to listen to and full of hooks yet has a presence that takes it to a new level really ought to search this out.
Nov 2011

JEFF AUG
LIVING ROOM SESSIONS
This is Jeff's fourth solo album, and it grew out of material he has been working on as part of Anne Clark's album 'Smallest Acts Of Kindness'. He then took these and rearranged them as instrumentals for solo acoustic fingerstyle guitar. I have been racking my brains to try and think who he reminds me of, and at times he is like a more intense Gordon Giltrap while at others he is definitely Nick Harper as he shreds his acoustic. To say that

this guy can play is something of an understatement. There are not many people who are prepared to open for Allan Holdsworth, but Jeff happily tours with him (which in turn says something about Allan's own confidence in his abilities).

None of these songs outlive their welcome, they are full of melody and pleasure and then are gone again. The only thing to really do is just put the CD on again and enjoy the experience. As the title suggests it was recorded with little or no studio trickery, just a man and his guitar sat in a living room (belonging to pianist and composer Murat Parlak) and playing away. The CD also contains videos for two of the songs, and as part of the promotion for the album he set a new world record of playing six gigs in six different countries in 24 hours and lived to tell the tale. Well worth investigation for fans of acoustic guitar, you won't be disappointed.
Oct 2009

JEFF AUG
WEDDING SONG
This is Jeff's fifth solo album, and since the last one it's been 3 years, 1 world record, 2 tours, 4 European tours with Anne Clark, 1 tour as support for Soft Machine and countless solo headline performances across the U.S. and Europe. To promote the new album, Jeff Aug completed a full-on European tour in one day, nine concerts in nine countries in 24 hours. In May he is back out on the road performing solo dates as well as supporting Allan Holdsworth – it could be said that Jeff doesn't like to sit around getting bored...

One of the areas of music that I just don't listen enough to is that of acoustic guitar - there are just not enough hours in the day to play everything I want to, so when I first stumbled across Jeff, I was both grateful and pleased as here is a musician of incredible virtuosity and skill that somehow makes extremely complex music both interesting and compelling, and enjoyable for all of that. This is music at its' most pure – just a man and his guitar, no overdubs or messing about with additional instrumentation (there is piano on just one song) or vocals. I am a huge fan of Richard Thompson, and I can see some elements of his work in Jeff's, particularly in the driving "Still In The Hedge". At times there is some of the wistfulness of Gordon Giltrap, and I know that some commentators have likened him to Al Di Meola, but all I can really say is that I totally get what this man is about and really enjoy hearing him play. Highly recommended
Apr 2012

THE AVENGERS
ON A MISSION
This is the debut album by a jazz-fusion supergroup that has been put together by Uruguayan guitarist Beledo, with Adam Holzman (keyboards), Lincoln Goines (bass) and Kim Plainfield (drums). It would take too long to list all of the people these guys have played with, but just mentioning Miles Davis and Dizzy Gillespie should be enough to

The Progressive Underground Vol 4

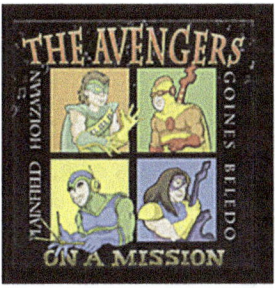

get you paying attention. I was playing this in the car the other day waiting for one of my daughters, and when she returned, she was dismayed to find me with my eyes closed, moving gently to the music, and asked me if I was okay. I was more than okay; I had been taken to a different world altogether. Sometimes an album just grabs hold of you and refuses to let go, transporting you through time and space to a dimension where nothing else matters apart from the music, and that is very much the case here.

I can't explain what this album does to me, whether it is Beledo's incredible fluidity or the way that Adam can switch between supporting roles and lead in his own right, or that the band just seem to be so incredibly tight. The photo of the band in the booklet shows them all facing each other as they record – no messing about here, this is all about interaction and a band actually being in the studio at the same time. We have all heard stories of drummers recording their parts and then disappearing until it is time to hear the final playback (read Peter Criss's biography), but this album is organic and warm as everyone knows their part but plays not as an individual but very much as part of the band.

Adam was Miles' keyboard player when they recorded 'Tutu', and on this album we find a version of "Portia", which of course also appeared on that work. The instrumentation is now somewhat different and Beledo and Adam make this very much their own. This is an absolutely stunning piece of work, and fans of jazz-fusion need look no further.
Aug 2013

AYREON
THE THEORY OF EVERYTHING
So there I was listening to this album, and I found that I was extremely intrigued by some of the keyboard passages as some of them sounded like Wakeman, but others were a direct Emerson lift, so it got me wondering just who was playing on this. So I investigated and my jaw hit the floor, as not only was Arjen Anthony Lucassen providing some of the keyboards (it is his concept after all so he can do what he likes), but he had been joined by Rick Wakeman, Keith Emerson and Jordan Rudess! Talk about having the heavyweights of the keyboard world involved! To then notice that Steve Hackett was providing the lead guitars was just the icing on the cake, there can't be many times when these guys have all played on the same album.

Ayreon has always been renowned for having some of the finest singers involved, and for this one Arjen has restricted himself to just seven, none of whom have previously performed on an Ayreon album. From the symphonic side we have Marko Hietala (Nightwish) and Tommy Karevik (Kamelot), while Cristina Scabbia (Lacuna Coil) and JB (Grand Magus) represent the metalheads. There are two relatively unknowns in Michael Mills (Toehider) and Sara Squadrani (Ancient Bards), while the line-up is completed by none other than John Wetton (I haven't got room to list all of the major bands he has been with, so let's just say King Crimson and leave it at that).

No science fiction story here this time, but rather how two parents deal with their savant child and the ramifications of that approach. The double CD set is broken into 42 songs, and is approximately 90 minutes long, and there are some astounding passages of music within this while the vocals are stunning. But, there are times when it doesn't quite come off, and this is mostly when Arjen is trying to force the lyrics to fit in more of the storyline and it is just doesn't seem to scan as well as it should. There also isn't enough melodic repetition of ideas within the whole for it to work seamlessly as a complete piece of music, with many of the songs being very short indeed. While there are times when this is sheer brilliance, I found that when comparing it against Clive Nolan's 'Alchemy' which was also released this year, it doesn't contain the same level of continuity and travel. However, it is still an incredible piece of work and something that I have found myself returning to time and again. I was a little surprised to see that Ian Anderson wasn't involved as Jeroen Goossens has obviously been playing close attention and some of his playing contains exactly the same attack and inflections that one would expect from the master.

Overall this is a big album, with big ideas and a huge sound that is complex and incredibly powerful but somehow just hits short of the masterpiece level. It is still an wonderful album all the same.
Nov 2013

AZAZELLO
MEGADREAM

Many years ago, I was lucky enough to be sent a copy of Azazello's third album, 'Black Day' and I was mightily impressed. A while later I was sent a copy of their seventh album and again I really enjoyed it. So, when I saw that Kerry Kompost had guested on their newest album then I knew that I had to grab a copy. Unfortunately, drummer Vladimir Demakov, passed away in December of 2011 so he never got to hear the fruits of his labours, but he would be pleased to know that his mates had done him proud. Led by multi-instrumentalist Alexandr Kulak, along with Vladimir Kulak (keyboards) and Yan Zhenchak (vocals), this is a band that apparently have no understanding of boundaries and are happy to play whatever pleases them, so if that means coming across as Metallica on one song then all power to them. These guys can really riff when they want to, with more than a hint of Voivod about them, but they are way more than just a fancy metal band and bring in folk and more overtly progressive influences to create something that isn't quite Western, not quite Russian, but always interesting and compelling, much in the way that Dream Theater used to be, but with more instrumentation (the violin is particularly effective)

Kerry is not the only guest on the album, with Misha Ogorodv (Pierre Moerlen's Gong) and Bill Berends (Mastermind) also making their presence felt. I was fortunate one night

to catch Mastermind in concert, and by the end of the gig my jaw hurt as it had been hanging open most of the night in awe. Those guys can play, really play. That is the same for all those involved here, as we morph and move all over the place, but a special mention should be made of "Run In Parallel (Leo)" which is the first time I have heard a happy baby over the top of an acoustic guitar! This is an album with real depth, and the more I have played it the more I have enjoyed it. Yet another outstanding release from Azazello, well worth discovering.
Sep 2013

BATISFERA
SOLAR WIND – THE INNER CIRCLE
As soon as this arrived, I couldn't wait to get it onto the player as this screams class. The care that has gone into the booklet is incredible with the lyrics and artwork combining in 28 pages to provide an experience all on its' own. Unfortunately, I know nothing about the band, but assume that the trio is Russian (with a couple of guests). Musically this is incredibly complex and hearkens back very much to the Seventies and obviously brings in influences from Yes, King Crimson and a host of other British prog bands. There are six main songs, stretching from nine to fourteen minutes in length, with short transition pieces in between.

But and it is a big 'but', these guys should have stayed as an instrumental group. One of my daughters walked in when I was playing this, looked at me, and said "this guy can't sing". Oleg Anurin is a great keyboard player, but he also feels that he is Jon Anderson in the way that he goes for long notes, scats down etc, and he really isn't. Having played this a few times I don't feel that I am being unfair, but it hurts me so much to say it as the rest of this album is just so good! There are some great instrumental passages with Oleg and Mike Zonov (guitars) swapping licks and Mike Heifets (drums) really driving them along. So this is a work of great ambition which achieves on so many levels yet really lets everything down on the vocals. If the guys had brought in a singer or had even delivered this album as an instrumental work then everyone would be singing it's praises and I really regret that I can't.
Nov 2012

BEAM-LIGHT
BEAM-LIGHT
Now, somewhere in the shed is a box (well in fact there are many boxes), and in that particular box is this CD. But, as I don't have the CD itself to hand and have no press release either I would normally turn to the internet for more information, but in this endeavour I have failed miserably. There seems to be virtually nothing out there on this - I mean, I have tried the usual suspects (Sea of Tranquility, DPRP, Prog Archives, Rate Your Music, Last FM etc.) but this 2008 (okay, I got that much

from RYM) album seems to have passed everyone by, which is both a mystery and a real shame. The reason it hasn't gained more plaudits is probably because this was released on the Polish label, Lynx Music. Now, they have released some great music over the years – most notably Milennium and of course the MLWZ triple CD compilation which every proghead must own – but even they have only written a few lines on their website, in Polish of course, on this album.

Why has this gone missing in action? It certainly isn't down to the quality of the music, but probably more that it doesn't really fit into pigeonholes. Certainly most progheads will say that this shouldn't be considered as such, as it has more in common with Kate Bush and Tori Amos than Genesis and Gentle Giant – yet there is a combination of fragility and delicacy that I have found intriguing. The delicate female vocals are always at the edge, waiting to break and crack, and are always centre stage with a very restrained backing which could just be keyboards, gentle percussion or even a full band – but they are always in the background. This is an album that needs to have full attention paid to it – unless it is placed centre stage it will just disappear and that would be a crime as this really is a wonderful piece of work. There is a strange melancholy, even when the music is upbeat, and it is compelling. The lyrics are in English, so there is no excuse for not trying to find out more about this superb album.
Dec 2011

BEARDFISH
THE VOID
Beardfish are another Swedish band that have decided that 2012 is the right time to produce something that is a little out of the ordinary, well for them at least. This album may start with a gentle spoken introduction (care of Andy Tillison of PO90 and The Tangent), but then is off with some crushing riffs which isn't exactly these guys' normal style. We are treated to some great melodic neo-prog that at times is more metal than rock, but always with a great amount of melody and vocals. This is prog that at times is much more direct than many may be used to, and in fact moves away from what some people consider to be prog at all, but it is always class, solid class. They may be more Radiohead and jagged edges than Floyd and a warm blanket, but the result is something that is both enjoyable and extremely accessible the first time it is played.

There will be some who have thrown their hands up in horror of Beardfish actually progressing in a musical sense, but isn't that what it is all about? True, the guitars at time have a wonderfully fuzzed out distorted sound that one would associate more with Kyuss than Yes but who cares? This is an album that should pick up fans who would not normally touch anything associated with the word 'prog' and all power to the guys for moving into what is for them uncharted territory. Hopefully they will not lose the people who bought the previous six albums, and there is still plenty on here for the 'traditional' Beardfish fan to enjoy with loads of different styles throw into the mix.
Sep 2012

BELIEVE
THE WARMEST SUN IN WINTER
For some strange reason, although I have Believe's debut album 'Hope To See Another Day', which came out in 2006, I haven't heard any of their other releases until this their fifth studio album. Now, given that I have always enjoyed Mirek Gil's work (I am a huge fan of Collage, with Satellite not too far behind) that is a massive oversight on my part, and something that I will definitely need to do something about, and having now played this album a great deal just adds additional emphasis to that as this is superb. Laid back, with an almost Camel-esque feel to proceedings, this is a band where some songs seem to contain just one long guitar solo behind the vocals as Mirek provides incredible emphasis. There are times where he is more Gary Chandler than Andy Latimer, and his impact and contribution to this album cannot be understated.

This is all about atmosphere and melody, and contains some wonderful individual performances as each person adds their own finesse and skill to what is a beautifully crafted and polished album. Karol has a wonderful voice, and Konrad is a fine keyboard player who adds complex layers, but there is no doubt that this album belongs mostly to Mirek whether he is wrenching yet more sustain or simple almost Eighties style staccato notes out of his instrument. This is an album that is accessible the very first time it is played yet has hidden depths and it is only with repeated playing that the listener truly gets the most out of it. This really is the full package, as the well presented booklet containing the lyrics (all in English) fits neatly in the digipak, and the music more than stands up to the quality of the presentation. Believe are yet another great Polish progressive rock band at the top of their game.
May 2013

BENESSER
THE START OF SOMETHING NEW
Apparently, Robert Olsson (bass, lead vocals), Henric Hermansson (guitar) and David Olsson (drums) grew up in the same area of a small town in Sweden, and by the age of nine they decided that they were going to form a band together even though at the time only two had instruments. That was back in 1998, and some fifteen years after the event they are here with their debut album. One has to admire the tenacity it has taken to get to this point, as most people have no idea what they really want to do when they are nine years old, let alone pursuing it like these guys obviously have. The biography mentions influences such as Coldplay, Rush, Black Country Communion and Subsignal, but to be honest there is just one name that you need to know, Muse.

To say that these guys have been influenced by Muse is like saying that the pope is Catholic. True, they have tried to put in some slower sections that contain much more restraint, something like Coldplay without the keyboards, but it is obvious where their hearts really lie. Robert Olsson has a great voice, and he can get incredibly high when he wants to, but for the most part this is about building emotion with powerful layers and crunching guitars. Given that they have played together for more than half of their lifetimes it is no surprise at all that they are incredibly tight, and that there is a real purpose to what they are doing.

If you enjoy Muse and are looking for something that has been influenced by their earlier material, then look no further as this is for you.
Jul 2013

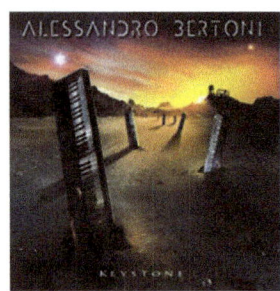

ALESSANDRO BERTONI
KEYSTONE
This is the debut solo album by keyboard player Alessandro, who previously was with Aphelion, and for this he has been joined by guitarist Brett Garsed, Ric Fierabracci on bass and Virgil Donati on drums. The album was produced by Derek Sherinian (ex-Dream Theater), who also gave Alessandro access to his own keyboards at Beachwood Manor Studios. The result of this is an incredibly warm fusion album that brings together four wonderful musicians, mixing jazz with progressive rock and the odd hint of metal in a manner that is seamless throughout. One of the things I really enjoyed about this is each player is a master of their craft, but they all allow the others to take centre stage when the time is right and no one person hogs the limelight. Indeed, Alessandro lets the others take so much credit that it seems much more like a band than a solo project. The way that he interacts with Brett on "Megas Alexandros pt. 3 - To the Ends of the Earth" is an example of how to use Hammond chords sparingly but to incredible effect. Ric employs fretless bass, which allows him not only to slide and play additional effects but provides an incredible warm glow to the whole album, while Virgil of course has nothing to prove. He has been at the top of his game for years and although he is content to provide some basic backing for much of the time, he also knows when to provide additional fills and power to give the music that little bit more emphasis.

Alessandro wanted to have the songwriting in the centre first and foremost, so that listeners would concentrate on that instead of the virtuosity of those involved. While of course one can never move away from the fact that these are all masters, the result is an album that is incredibly enjoyable, and much more than just a contest in "look how clever I am". Derek's production should also get a special mention as he has allowed the guys to breathe, move and meld, yet kept everything clearly separate while also bringing it all together in harmony. This is wonderful stuff.
Nov 2013

BEYOND THE LABYRINTH
CASTLES IN THE SAND
There are times when I feel guilty, and this is one of those as this album was released in 2008 yet it is towards the end of 2011 that I am writing about it. I can only apologise for

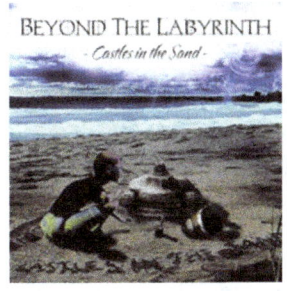

tardiness, and I am trying now to catch up on everything that I should have reviewed yonks ago. This was the follow-up to 'Signs', an album I really enjoyed, and yet again guitarist Geert Fieuw has delivered an extremely strong set of songs. The band is completed by Jo de Boeck (vocals), Genry Versteken (bass), Bruno Goedhuys (drums) and Danny Focke (keyboards) and they lay their wares clearly out for all to hear – this is a band that enjoyed the Eighties and Nineties and saw no reason at all for their music to reflect anything else. Think Savatage, Uriah Heep and Queensrÿche with possibly some of their harder AOR cousins and you may get a feeling of what this is all about.

Yes, the band are not English or American (in fact they are Belgian) and it means that Jo has a slight accent but is that a problem? It may be for some but the last time I looked both Scorpions and Helloween were still managing to do very well for themselves, and so should these guys. During the lead up to this album they had toured in support to bands as diverse as Riverside, Jon Oliva's Pain, Doro and Sonata Arctica and I am sure that the metalheads and progheads all enjoyed these guys immensely. This is a powerful hard rock album with more than a nod to AOR and prog and one that all lovers of classic rock should get immediately.
Oct 2011

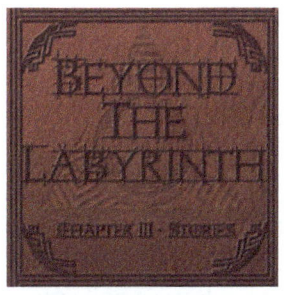

BEYOND THE LABYRINTH
CHAPTER III - STORIES
The third BTL album came out in 2011 with a slight line-up change from the last, for this the band were a four-piece with songwriter Geert Fieuw providing keyboards as well as guitar with the departure of Danny Focke. There is also a new drummer in Michel Lodder, while Jo de Boeck (vocals) and Gerry Verstreken (bass, vocals) are still here from before. Like their previous works, this is an extremely polished hard rock album with progressive undertones – with Savatage and Heep right at the forefront of influences. Jo's singing appears to be even stronger, and the whole band are really kicking. Since the recording of the album, they have added a second guitarist in Mark Wenkin which I find an interesting move, as I presume it means that in the live environment Geert will be playing either guitar or keyboards depending on the song – but it means that they will be able to have a heavier attack when they need it, something that is going to be very powerful indeed.

Beyond The Labyrinth are easily the best Belgian hard rock band I have ever come across, but now is the time to stop thinking of just their own country as these guys have proved that they have the songs and the musical ability to go all the way. They have been playing festivals as well as support earlier this year for bands like Pagan's Mind, and lovers of melodic hard rock need to check these guys out. Superb.
Oct 2011

BIG BIG TRAIN
THE UNDERFALL YARD

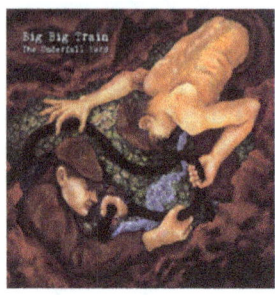

I am always going to have a soft spot for BBT, as they were the first band ever to send me something to review that I hadn't paid for. That was a cassette (those were the days) of early demos that they called 'From The River To The Sea', and these songs were later re-recorded and formed the basis of their debut CD in 1992. They have never been exactly a prolific gigging band, but I did manage to capture one of their gigs many moons ago and we used to see each other at concerts and stayed in contact for years. So, onto their sixth album which features a new line-up for the band. Founder members Gregory Spawton and Andy Poole are still there, although they have a new singer in David Longdon. The current line-up also features drummer Nick D'Virgilio (Spock's Beard) and guitarist Dave Gregory (ex-XTC).

In fact, BBT have changed quite a lot from the band they were in the early days in that Greg and Andy now very much take the role of arrangers, bringing in the correct musicians to do justice to Greg's songs. So, here we have Francis Dunnery (It Bites) providing additional guitar while Jem Godfrey (Frost*) assist on keyboards as well as Jon Foyle on cello. Dorset prog stalwart Rob Aubrey (IQ, Transatlantic, Asia, Galahad) mixed the album, and he has managed to provide a great overall clarity of sound, although it is incredibly layered.

Many years ago, Greg walked up to me in a pub, and asked me what I thought of the new album (I think 'English Boy Wonders') and he quickly realised that I wasn't overly enamoured, and he shouted out "You don't like it!" I tried to explain that I felt that there was nothing wrong with the album, but that it wasn't BBT to my ears. Twenty years on from the first time I heard BBT I can honestly say that yet again this sounds nothing like the BBT I knew then, but now I can say that I like it. Okay, I really like it. Okay, it is easily the best album they have ever released and has catapulted them past most of their contemporaries.

This album is a delight from start to finish – and must be in every prog lover's collection. There is depth, there is clarity, a pastoral beauty, and a restrained very English feel to proceedings. Progressive music really doesn't get any better than this, and the harmonies and use of instrumentation is just brilliant. Another album that has taken me nearly two years to review, I challenge any proghead not to play any single minute of this album chosen at random and not fall in love with it immediately.
Nov 2011

BIG BIG TRAIN
ENGLISH ELECTRIC PART ONE

Over the years I have listened to countless thousands of CDs, but Big Big Train were the very first, so I have always maintained a close interest in what they are doing. There have been one or two line-up changes over the years, but Greg (now on bass, keyboards) and Andy Poole (keyboards, production) have been there from the beginning, and singer

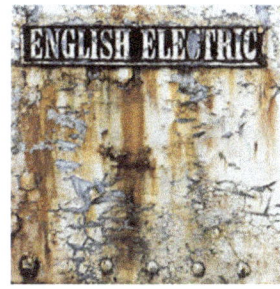

David Longdon (plus mandolin, keyboards, flute etc) who joined in 2009 has been a real find. It is these three that have written all of the songs, but since 2010 they have been joined by guitarist Dave Gregory and some drummer called Nick D'Virgilio. Yes, the ex-Spock's Beard and current Mystery sticksman is also a key member of this band.

One word screams out all the time that this is playing, and that is "Maturity". The band have changed immensely since those early days and have produced an album that is huge and the reason for that is the control that pervades everything that is happening. I was playing this while out in one of the paddocks and I was trying to think who it reminded me of, and the closest I can come to is Marillion combined with Chris Rea but that has much more to do with the way they have approached the construction and composition as opposed to the musical direction.

Many people will say that this isn't a prog album, but so what? That really depends on your personal definition of prog, but given the use of additional guests and instruments where else does it really fit? On a personal level, when I heard the flute, I immediately asked myself if Martin Orford (IQ/Jadis) had become involved in the music scene again as I know that he had contributed to past BBT albums. Well, I was wrong about the flute as that is by David, but Widge does provide some backing vocals – it was a huge loss to not only UK prog but to music when he decided not to continue so hopefully there will be more to come.

This is a part one album, with the second to follow in March, and to be honest I can hardly wait. To my old, jaded ears this is stunning – and when I received that cassette all those years ago I could never have imagined that one day I would be listening to anything as powerful as this. This is essential for any lover of good music.
Aug 2012

A BIG GOODBYE
SOUNDS & SILENCES PT 1
This is the debut album by American trio A Big Goodbye and was released in 2011. Now, that is bad news as it means that I missed it when it first came out, but the good news is that the next one is due very soon! This is the first in a three-album series, with the overall theme on this one being about emptiness. Lyrically it deals with relationship struggles, particularly "The Great Divide". The final song on the album, "Memories" is also the longest at fourteen minutes. This is about the main character, who having killed the woman who betrayed him is now contemplating killing himself. Together they had a child called "Autumn", which will be a song on the next album. The story has deliberately been chopped about so that it is not in sequence, rather like Saga's "Chapters".

So, for their debut they decided that from the off it was going to be a trilogy, and if that isn't a strong statement of self-belief, how about the music they have pulled together to accompany the words? The band itself is comprised of multi-instrumentalist Matt Glisson, his brother Andrew on drums and singer Daniel Mills plus three guests, Adam Cambria (sax), Joseph Castleberry (trumpet) and Paul Boatwright (trombone). Yep, here we have a prog band that have brought in a brass section. If that wasn't enough, how about complex math-rock sections where they come across as Protest The Hero, combined with complex prog metal where they are Dream Theater, or dramatic acoustic where musically (if not vocally) they are Roy Harper. Often all in the same song! Daniel has a strong clear voice and sometimes it is only his vocals that are keeping it all together as the band splits and changes in a myriad of different directions. If you want a dramatic emotional rollercoaster of a prog album, then this is it.

There is no doubt that this is one of the most exciting debuts I have ever come across. Roll on the next one!
Jul 2013

THE BLACK NOODLE PROJECT
ELEONORE
I first heard from singer/guitarist Jérémie Grima back in 2005 at the time of their second album 'And Life Goes On..', and we were in regular contact for a while but lost touch after I moved to NZ. That may explain why it is only now that I am writing about this their fifth album, from 2008 (since this they have released a CD/DVD live set, another studio album, and a double disc of early demoes – these are busy boys). Anyway, The Black Noodle Project have long been one of my favourite French prog acts and this was an interesting departure in many ways as before this album was recorded keyboard player Matthieu Jaubert left the band and wasn't replaced. The line-up therefore was just Grima, Anthony Leteve (bass), Sebastien Bourdeix (guitars) and Fabrice Berger (drums) – yep, no keyboards.

Now back in Feedback #83 I said that the music was "where Pink Floyd has been crossed with Roine Stolt in a way that makes for an album that is extremely enjoyable and open". I also said that it was the finest French prog album I had heard since Minimum Vital's 'La Source'. So, with no keyboards it was obvious that this was going to quite a different sounding album to what I had come across before. The CD is a concept story of a small girl who lives in the forest with her parents and when they die she reads all of the books in the attic (of course) trying to find a way to get her parents back, but she finds a mysterious tome and the story starts there. Musically this is a dark album, with some heavy passages, but incredibly there is also a large amount of space, and it is very much a band album with some wonderful interplay between the guys.

Somehow TBNP have managed to still provide what is very much a prog album, as opposed to a prog metal album, with a strong storyline and performances. There are still some elements of Stolt in the guitarwork, but overall, this brings in much more Porcupine

Tree and even The Pineapple Thief.

This is yet again a great album – I just need to get hold of the others now. The website is available in both English and French, and is well worth a visit
Dec 2011

THE BLACK NOODLE PROJECT
DARK & EARLY SMILES
When I was first in contact with Jérémie Grima back in 2005 I wasn't aware that he had already released an album under the guise of The Black Noodle Project called 'Dark Smiles..", but it was really a collection of demos to gain the attraction of record labels. It did the job as he was soon working with Musea and put together a proper band to record the music, and hence their album 'And Life Goes On..' was released. Fast forward a few years and it was felt that the time was right for a double disc compilation of the demos that formed that album plus more, so the result is a two CD set of cuts from 2003 – 2005.

One has to say that they do not sound at all like rough versions as these could all have been released in their own right. Back then I asked Jérémie what his main influences were, and as well as citing the obvious Pink Floyd he also pointed to The Gathering and to movie soundtracks. He stressed that he wanted to be thought of as a musician that could use just a few notes to convey emotion as opposed to thousands and mentioned Slash and Tommy T. Baron (from Swiss metal act Coroner).

As with all of TBNP's albums, there is a wash of symphonic keyboards a la Floyd but the guitar cuts right through all of it in an extremely heavy manner, providing a dynamic all of it's own. It may be too rocky for fans of Floyd, but for me this really hits the mark. This is prog with a passion, and this should not be viewed as a set that is only of interest to those who are already fans but instead is a great way to start listening to them as these two discs show a band that even in their very early days were hitting the ground running. These guys are easily my favourite current French prog act.
Sep 2012

THE BLACK NOODLE PROJECT
READY TO GO
In many ways this is one of the most diverse albums that TBNP have come up with yet. There are still the Pink Floyd and Porcupine Tree influences, but the guys have also turned it up a little more so that the intensity and guitars have that little more edginess than usual. There may be some who think that this is going to be an ethereal and delicate album as suggested by the album artwork, and indeed there are some numbers that are in that vein, but this is again an album that brings the term 'rock'

crunching back in at the right moment. Jérémie sent me this album to listen to at the same time as the collection of demos, and it is interesting to compare the two and see how the band have changed since those early days. Undoubtedly the biggest change is the in the confidence of all those involved, and this in itself allows the band to spread their wings without going too far.

The band do not try to hide their influences, but they are the starting point and not the end product. They have matured and the result is yet again an extremely solid accessible album that all progheads will enjoy.
Sep 2012

THE BLANK ATTACK
THE BLANK ATTACK
The Blank Attack came about when Jon Wobesky (bass, cornet) and David Kirkdorffer (guitar) decided that it was time to put together a project. David wanted a departure from the ambient scene he had been working in, and Jon saw the opportunity to take a break from his horn duties with Reverend Glasseye. They started writing material with a drum machine but decided that they needed a more human element so brought in David Ross (previously of Girl on Top). But they still needed a frontman, and who better than Adam Crary? Adam had previously fronted the incredible Specimen 37, who to my ears are easily one of the best prog bands to come out of the States in recent years, but as that band had gone on hiatus, he was looking for an outlet.

I've really been trying to think of the best way of describing this album, but for the most part the best description is probably a stripped down Hawkwind, with elements of punk in the abrasive guitar attack. Opener "Tally Ho! (Quick! Back to the Tardis!)" is just wonderful, as any song containing three exclamation marks in the title is always going to be. But one of the most incredible is the reworking of "Ain't No Sunshine". My initial reaction when I heard it was that it was post-nihilistic punk, but on reflection I'm not sure what that means. How about Lou Reed doing a version of this on 'Metal Machine', with some Stooges thrown in for good measure? What makes this really incredible is that while the guys are providing this stripped-down metallic version of the song where often it is only the bass that is following the original note structure, Adam is providing wonderfully clear and melodic vocals over the top. It is the clash between the two totally different styles that really makes this worse – and my poor abused ears prefer this to the original!

This is an incredibly bouncy album, one that always makes me move when I play it, and yet again I bemoan that state of the record industry when music as good as this will be ignored in favour of the latest plastic creation. Solid gold from start to end.
Jul 2013

BLIND STARE
THE DIVIDING LINE

Blind Stare started as long ago as 1999, but through the years there have been line-up changes, problems with record labels etc (including all of the band having to undertake national service at one point) so it has taken a lot longer than anyone imagined for them to get to this their second album. Mind you, many could argue that it was worth the wait as this is a strong release in the melodic/death/symphonic/prog metal style. There are a few times when for some reason the keyboard sound is quite Eighties and doesn't really work, but for the most part this is a good combination of keyboards and guitars (even some delicate piano) with good hard edged vocals (although both Eino and Jaako also contribute clean vocals which provides strong balance).

There are definitely some power metal moments as well, while the main influence is probably Children of Bodom but the band are bringing a great deal into the overall mix. While not totally indispensable, this is a good album that is well worth investigating further.
Sep 2012

THE BLUE PROJECT
ADRIFT

Back in 1993 the Italian band The Bel Am released an EP called 'Eternal Carmine' and then promptly disappeared without trace. Now, some twenty years later, their singer Maria Cristina Anzola has joined with Davide Borghi (Albireon, Ekra) to create The Blue Project. Before you ask, there is no 's' on the end of 'Blue', whatever LastFM may think as they autocorrect it. These guys are here not looking at the blues as a basis for what they are doing, but instead are creating something that is new, existing, otherworldly and at times quite disturbing. What we have here are the marrying together of an incredible female soprano with soundscapes that are sometimes gentle and ambient, lulling the listener into believing that they are listening to New Age, while at others it is jarring and contains noise and other aspects that are far more threatening and surreal.

There are times when I am reminded of the classic Italian prog horror band Goblin (who I saw in concert last week here in NZ, can't believe it!). Like Goblin, these guys have the knack of creating something that on the surface is delicate and gentle but emotionally it is far more than that and definitely has a much darker side. An album that can be listened to on many levels, this is far more complex than the simple use of vocals and musical textures may lead one to believe. Riccardo Spaggiari of Ataraxia guests on "The Glass Child", and all in all this is an album that is both different and well worth investigating.
Jul 2013

THE BOB LAZAR STORY
(sic)

When I was asked to join the Crossover Team on PA I had many email conversations with the team leader, Marty, who asked me if I knew that it was possible to search for band by country and provided a link. I wasn't aware, so immediately went off to have a look at NZ as we aren't exactly a prog hotbed down here. I commented that some bands were probably missing from the list but was surprised and pleased to see that there were some active bands around, which is how I got in touch with Matt Deacon. In 2004 he released an album under his own name, which was more ambient but with some prog leanings, and he felt that if he was going to release something that was very different then perhaps, he should use a pseudonym, so due to his interest in UFO's he chose the name Bob Lazar (a controversial figure in the scene who claims to have worked with extra-terrestrial technology). The first time I played this I was just blown away, as here is another artist unknown to me (and many others), who is bringing together elements of Zappa with Seventies progressive music in a guitar-driven album that is impressive to say the least. Matt is a wonderful guitarist with great feel, and is happy to use acoustic or electric, whatever the requirement is for the piece, and will bring in heavier elements or jazz as the mood strikes. Most of the drums on this album are a machine, but isn't as intrusive as it could be, and Matt brought in some mates to act as session musicians so that it has more of a band feel. There are times when it blasts into something avant-garde that could have come straight from the Art Zoyd playbook, and I love it.

There is a real melange of styles throughout this album, with the only constant being Matt's guitar, which is often, although not always, driving the proceedings forward. He has an incredible fluidity to all that he does, and I am sure that if he was based in the UK or America as opposed to down here in NZ then he would be really well known within the scene. He provided me his own views on the songs, and they are worth repeating.

"Levers Of Doom" – Acoustic intro over feedback fades in to main section of eastern tinged melody, back to acoustic, then heavy outro.
"ThreeFourFaster" - Reworking of tune from first album. Heavier, faster. With theremin. This one has been # 1 in the all time guitar charts on garageband.com(Experimental Rock) for the last year.
"Double Turn Double Safe" – Heavy, heavier, then country.
"Heavy Sandwich" – Groovy first section, then acoustic solo, then outro section with monster sax solo.
"Greengold" – My ode to Spirulina. Percussive intro, grinding odd time riff, keyboard feature, space out then key solo and guitar solo outro.
"Son of Six" – Another old tune reworked into a more acoustic feel. I really like this one.
"The Progressive Adventures Of Foodstool" – Weird and wacky, several different directions explored in one song.
"I Didn't Get Anything Off That" – Epic outro, building from humble beginning featuring Tanya Didham on spoken word stream of consciousness.

All in all this is a wonderful album that those into Zappa style inventive guitar driven prog seriously need to investigate.
Aug 2013

THE BOB LAZAR STORY
THE SILENCE OF PEREZ DE CUELLAR
Matt followed up the 2006 release of '(sic)' with this EP (another UFO reference in the title) the following year. No drum machine here (and in fact there are two drummers credited). This album is even more Zappa-esque than the previous one, with some wonderful bass/guitar/drum interplay as each musician is in perfect sync with the others. There are also some delicate vibraphones in the background at times, which also adds to the feel. This EP is more controlled than the previous one, with a seeming less spontaneity and more thought and layering. Matt has also ensured that everyone has their chance to shine, and there is a wonderfully poignant bass solo in "My Hand Looks Like A Brontosaurus" which is followed by some multi-layered guitars that takes it all to a new level.

In many ways this is music that is incredibly complex, yet in others it is quite simple as it is all about clean lines and demarcation while bringing everything together in a wonderfully warm and non-clinical manner. There are times when everything is almost gentle in its' approach, while at others it is a collision waiting to happen as the notes are flying everywhere yet it always maintains the patterns so that everyone comes through unscathed. This really is instrumental progressive jazz-influenced Zappa-influenced music as its' very best.
Aug 2013

THE BOB LAZAR STORY
SPACE ROOTS
In 2009, Matt had the next album almost 95% written when he had to return to the UK for an extended period, so all writing and recording stopped until he returned to NZ in 2012. At this point he got together all the music from the various places it was stored, got in a friend to undertake all the basswork, and put together an album. It is thematic in the sense that it has a long track followed by a short one, the result being that the album contains some 19 songs in the end. In some ways it isn't as consistent in its' approach as the others but given how the album came together it is really not at all surprising. Again, we are treated to some wonderful instrumental numbers where I found that I ended up in a world where I really wanted to stay for a while. This is music that definitely benefits from being played on headphones so that there are no distractions and all of the nuances (such as a simple acoustic guitar drop in for just one bar) are there to be heard. The only positive about not coming across Matt before is that I was able to hear all three of his works in one go, the downside of course is that I am now

hungry for more. He is a wonderful guitarist with some great eclectic ideas, and fans of Zappa and music that is made by real musicians really do need to hear this asap. Available, as are the others, as downloads from various places such as Bandcamp as well as CDs from his website, below is his own guide to the album

"It's Thirteen" (03.08)
From "The Aranui Sessions" recorded in June 2009. Clunky, quirky and heavy. Like your mother.

"Synthyer" (0.07)
Short but sweet.

"Two Vowels Contemplate The End Of The World" (05.26)
Longest track on the CD. Goes through several changes. No wanky prog solos.

"Fuhdstewl" (00.24)
Short but sweeter.

"Instant Jedi" (02.27)
One of the very few guitar solos features in the midst of another track from "The Aranui Sessions".

"Rawk" (00.16)
Heavy, synthy, short. Drums by Chris Jago, who once played in goal against Robbie Fowler.

"Mr Weiner Pants" (02.54)
My old Headmaster used to wear his trousers very high. Lots of gear shifts in this one. Third track from "The Aranui Sessions".

"Techno Bert vs The Klezzies" (00.41)
Eastern Europe meets game show meets Knight Rider on steroids.

"Alive In The Mullet Zone" (3.00)
Fearsome drums from The Jago. Riff-Tastic first half, Jazzy bit, then best solo ever by me. Someone once told me an old song of mine sounded like YYZ by Rush, so the last 4 notes pay homage to the end of that song.

"Deadbiking Trilogy" (04.49)
This one took ages to write. All synth for the first 2 parts, then multi layered guitar outro. Will be the hardest for rock fans to get into, but almost my favourite tune on the disc.

"Late Night Guitar" (00.42)
Four guitars, nowt else.

"Henry Kissinger Must Diet" (02.36)
The last of "The Aranui Sessions". Starts in 9/4 and morphs into mellow jazz before

heavy ending.

"Lou Reed's Haemorrhoids" (00.10)
Lou Reed's Haemorrhoids have more talent than Lou Reed.

"Rawk II" (03.22)
Heavy and synthy with a beautiful bass interlude from Fud.

"Death To The Meat Whores" (00.12)
Short but Swede.

"I Haven't Touched Your Dog, Mate" (03.53)
Honestly, I haven't. Mellower tune to break up the madness, although there is a heavy break in the middle.

"Widdly Diddly" (00.25)
Sequenced oddness.

"Glass Eyed II" (03.04)
Written to a pre-existing drum track. Heavy, jazzy, clunky.

"Siren" (01.15)
Thereminty. Mellow closer.
Aug 2013

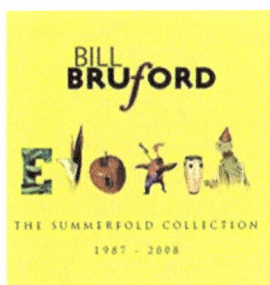

BILL BRUFORD
THE SUMMERFOLD COLLECTION
This double CD brings together music from 12 albums released on the label between 1987 and 2008, 22 songs in all. Those looking for progressive rock workouts should turn their attention to the companion Winterfold release as what we have here is jazz in its' truest and many forms. While there have been important jazz drummers since the scene started to be made available in a recorded format, Gene Krupa being of course the most notable, there is no doubt that in recent times Bill has made a claim to being the most important player in the scene. This is not only due to his playing and songwriting, or his ability to bring together great musicians, but also due to the history he brings with him. Many people have been turned onto jazz who originally were fans of his from his progressive rock days and have followed him on the journey and stayed the course.

Prior to this collection I had heard little of the output from this label, but the collection has been put together with care, showing the many sides of Bruford and his take on the genre. There are big band arrangements through to more simpler bands set ups, although still providing the complexity and spontaneity that this music needs. The booklet is extremely informative and in many ways, this is the perfect introduction to the jazz side

of Bruford and certainly has led me to want to find out more.
Oct 2009

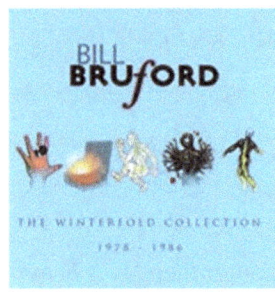

BILL BRUFORD
THE WINTERFOLD COLLECTION

This single CD compilation is the companion to the Summerfold collection. While that concentrates on 1987 – 2008 and 12 releases, this is 1978 – 1986 from six albums. With musicians such as Allan Holdsworth, Jeff Berlin and Patrick Moraz on board there is no surprise that here is music of the highest order. Although not fully jazz, there are still huge elements of that within the progressive style that is on display. What impresses me so much about this album is that Bill doesn't feel the need to be at the front over-riding the rest of the guys. This feels very much a band as opposed to a drummer with some hired guns to provide the melody. The impression is that improvisation was taking place in the studio, with musicians all on the same wavelength and it is certainly no surprise that from this he moved more and more into a 'pure' jazz style.

Of the two sets this is probably the one that will be most accessible to those who may not normally listen to jazz, but in reality they are both essential listening and a great guide to the music of someone who to many will always be associated with prog giants such as King Crimson or Yes. The booklet is well written, extremely informative with plenty of photos.
Oct 2009

DEWA BUDJANA
DAWAI IN PARADISE

Moonjune boss Leonardo Pavkovic has a real love for Indonesia, and also for the music of the country. Although I have yet to go there myself, I do have some Indonesian friends and just from talking to them I understand how important music is to the people. Leo wants to ensure that he does all he can to publicise great music, and I know that he feels that music from Indonesia deserves a sub-label within his own roster and from what I have heard to date I totally understand why that is the case. This is the fifth solo album from Dewa Budjana, who may just well be the finest fusion guitarist you have never heard of. He may start the album with some strange sounds being pulled from his guitar, but he can shred with the very best of them while also at times just using simple nuances to take a number to a whole new level.

Leo describes this album as "ranging from the bold and adventurous to the gracefully elegant, Dewa's playing bounces from the frantic urgency of a Fripp or McLaughlin to the organic intimacy of a Metheny or Towner with equal ease and fluidity. Previously unexplored waters are navigated with an adroit leisure, as his bountiful skills as both a composer and improviser are clearly on display. His international debut is chocked full of surprises, and it's elegance and repose belies the enormity of the album's ambition. This is progressive jazz and world music of the absolute highest order, and a "coming out party" for one of its best-kept secrets."

Personally, I am just blown away by the quality of the music on offer: if ever anything should ever be called fusion, then this is it as he moves from avant-garde to folk influences to progressive to melodic jazz to anything and everything that takes his fancy. What impressed me so much with this album is that while it is his name on the cover, Dewa is more than prepared to take a back seat and let others shine while he just adds some poignant touches. There are a whole host of other musicians involved, but some that should be mentioned are Grammy-winning artists drummer Peter Erskine (Weather Report; Steps Ahead) and multi-instrumentalist Howard Levy (Bela Fleck & The Flectones), the renowned Indonesian jazz keyboardist and producer, Indra Lesmana, his Indonesian contemporary, celebrated pianist Ade Irawan, and the late legendary jazz bassist, Dave Carpenter.

When I played this the first time around, I kept trying to think of one word that I could use to describe it, and while "masterful" and "incredible" are words that certainly fit, the one that makes the most sense to me is "beautiful". This album sums up why I stay involved with the music scene, and why I spend so many hours sat in front of a keyboard, because if it wasn't for being sent this to review I would certainly never have found it on my own. Essential.
Apr 2013

DEWA BUDJANA
JOGED KAHYANGAN
This is Dewa's sixth solo album to date, and while he may well be a bona fide pop star in his home country with his band Gigi selling millions of records, he is still relatively unknown outside of his native Indonesia. With this, his second album for the international label Moonjune, surely that will soon change. The album title translates to "Dances of Heaven", and if you are at all interested in jazz fusion that is the place to which you will be transported when listening to this. On this album he has been joined by Larry Goldings (organ, piano), Bob Mintzer (tenor and soprano sax, clarinet, bass clarinet), Jimmy Johnson (bass) and Peter Erskine (drums) as well as singer Janis Siegel guesting on the one number with vocals.

The musicians didn't see Budjana's charts until the day of the recording, and the first take was the only rehearsal they had with the second or third take ending up on the album. Recorded in just a single day, this is pretty much a full live recording, which makes it even more incredible. Dewa has strong understanding of the use of space and harmony, as well as discord, and combines all the elements to make an album that takes the listener

by the hand as opposed to bashing them over the head. There are whole passages where Dewa is notable by his absence, letting the rest of the guys take his music on a journey and he joins in with wonderfully fluid Metheny/McLaughlin style at just the right moment. It is a wonderfully restful album, one where time and space disappears and is replaced instead by a world filled with harmony, delicacy, and restrained power. Every piece is a classic in it's own right, while the restraint of everyone involved in the vocal "As You Leave My Nest" is superb. The digipak opens up to provide three pages of notes, written by John Kelman, which definitely add to the overall experience. This is an essential album to anyone who enjoys wonderful music, whatever the genre.
Dec 2013

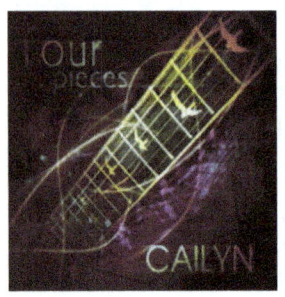

CAILYN
FOUR PIECES
This is the third album from multi-instrumentalist Cailyn Lloyd and is an interesting fusion of classical and progressive rock music. As the name of the album implies there are just four songs (total running length just under forty minutes), and each of the first three are adaptations of famous classical pieces – the most well-known probably being Dvorak's "New World Symphony" which is used in the second piece, "Largo". The final song of the four is a piece that she says was mostly inspired by Debussy, but also by Chopin and Schubert. Yes, it's pretty safe to say that here is someone who knows her music. It is an instrumental album, with the main melody instrument normally (but not always) a multi-tracked guitar which at times manages to come across very Brian May.

Although the drums are electronic, in this case she was playing an electronic kit as opposed to drum machine and the difference between this and a drum machine is like chalk and cheese. Cailyn has a great touch on the guitar, and there is a real sense of affinity of the melding of the styles - in many ways it gives the impression of being a 'grown-up' album. It would be easy for this to fall into the trap of coming across as background music, but the simple remedy is to play it just a little louder and to give it the time and concentration that it deserves. This is a delight.
Nov 2012

CAMELIAS GARDEN
YOU HAVE A CHANCE
Now come on, music like this just doesn't get released these days. It's 2013! Didn't anyone check the calendar? Imagine Cat Stevens mixed with early Genesis, Yes, Al Stewart and possibly just a little Gentle Giant and you may get somewhere close to understanding what this wonderful album is like. It is a summery burst of sunshine, where it is all about great music and plenty of acoustic guitars with swathes of keyboards to boot. It is fragile yet strong, modern yet extremely vintage and the result is

something that is like a breath of fresh air to these poor abused ears of mine.

This Italian trio is led by Valerio Smordoni (lead and backing vocals, MiniMoog, keyboards, piano, harmonium, acoustic guitar, tambourine and Taurus Pedals) and he is joined by Manolo D'Antonio (acoustic and 12-string guitar, electric guitar, classical guitar, ukulele and backing vocals) and Marco Avallone (bass, synth bass, Taurus Pedals and percussions) plus a few guests to provide some additional timbres. It really is a thing of beauty, and I only hope that we are going to be hearing a great deal more from them as this progressive/folk debut is a delight.
May 2013

CARMEN
FANDANGOS IN SPACE/DANCING ON A COLD WIND
Many years ago, I became very interested indeed in Jethro Tull, and spent far too much money building a collection of singles and albums from all over the world. However, there are only so many versions that I wanted of 'Living In The Past' so took then as my guide Terry Hounsome's wonderful 'Rock Record' and started looking for material by groups featuring ex or future Tull members. I soon managed to discover the wonderful Wild Turkey, as well as Paris, Aviator etc but it was when I picked up The Gods that I held in my hands the first material featuring John Glascock. He had replaced some guy called Greg Lake (whatever happened to him?) and was rhythm partner to Lee Kerslake (later Uriah Heep, Ozzy etc) and I saw that according to the bible he was later in Chicken Shack, and then in an outfit called Carmen.

Although I never managed to get the Chicken Shack album, I did obtain the debut by Carmen, which had appeared on Regal Zonophone, 'Fandangos In Space'. I fell in love with the album so much that I devoted many resources to getting as much material by Carmen as possible. I even had a letter published in Record Collector where I asked for more information – I asked them to print my full details and I was contacted by various people with items for sale (including a promo poster for the debut, singles and even a white label!), one of whom was David Rees. For those who don't know, Dave was the founder of 'A New Day' – the Jethro Tull fanzine, and at that time I knew him quite well. He had also seen my letter and asked me if I would feel able to write a review or feature on Carmen to appear in 'AND', which duly came to fruition in #17 (I think). That was the first time I had ever written about music and was what gave me the inkling that I might just like doing so again if the opportunity ever arose.

That same article then appeared in the very first issue of Feedback, and it seems strange to me that all these many years and literally thousands of reviews later I now have the chance to write about Carmen again. The albums had been issued on CD previously, by Line in Germany in the Eighties, but those were very basic releases and the first track on 'Fandangos' has the intro missing so I normally went straight to the vinyl when I wanted to play them. I have no doubt that 'Fandangos' is easily the most played vinyl record in my collection, so to be able to now have this and their second on my iPod is wonderful.

Carmen billed themselves as the world's first flamenco rock band, incorporating not only music but dance in their performances. Originally formed in 1970 it wasn't until they left the US for Britain in 1973 that they started to make their presence felt, so much so that their first two albums were produced by Tony Visconti and released on Regal Zonophone. The line-up on these (and their final, third, album 'The Gypsies' which was only released in America, on Mercury) was David Allen on vocals/guitar, his sister Angela on vocals/ Mellotron and dance, Roberto Amaral vocals/vibraphone/dance, John Glascock bass/vocals and Paul Fenton on drums. Paul only joined the band when they arrived in the UK and later turned down a gig with Wings as he had so much confidence in the band.

I have never managed to see the 'Midnight Special' performance with Bowie which gained them so much exposure, but every time I play their music I 'see' them in my mind. This is extremely visual, with some of the numbers featuring pounding footwork and dynamism while at times they can be gentle and almost dreamy. Personally, I have always felt the music to be extremely open and something that can be played and enjoyed on first hearing, and it is no lie when I say that whatever song I am playing is my favourite. Since I first started listening to these albums more than twenty years ago, they have often found their way back to my player, and unlike many albums from this period (73 and 74 respectively) I don't feel that they have aged at all.

They incorporate the styles and flavours that David picked up from his parent's flamenco restaurant where he had been appearing from the age of four yet bring that into a modern era so that while there are still plenty of acoustic guitars there is also room for the rock element and plenty of passion and soul. This is music that has a depth and vitality that is missing from many bands that have sold countless millions of albums, and I have often wondered why this band never gained the success they so richly deserved.

One day I am going to sit and catalogue all of the reviews I have written over the years, which runs into the thousands, but I can honestly say that of all the music I have spent time attempting to describe it is Carmen that in many ways is the most important to me, not least as it was the first time that I ever tried to convey my musical impressions into words.

There are two bonus songs contained on this two-disc set and I fervently hope that there is enough interest for Angel Air to decide to also release the third album on CD. Carmen toured with Tull, with John then joining as Jeffrey Hammond Hammond's replacement in time for 'Too Old To Rock 'n' Roll' which also featured Angela as a guest. He will probably be best remembered by many for performing on the classic Tull albums 'Songs From The Wood' and 'Heavy Horses', before passing away from heart problems having played on just a few of the 'Stormwatch' numbers, but to a lucky few he will also be known as one of the members of the best flamenco rock band the world has ever seen and heard. Carmen.
May 2007

CARMEN/WIDESCREEN
THE GYPSIES/WIDESCREEN

And then if that wasn't enough, I heard that Angel Air were also releasing the third album plus the first new material from guitarist David Allen for many a year. 'The Gypsies' wasn't released in the UK at the time, something I still don't understand, as this isn't a weak album of a band soon to break up but a powerful follow on from the first two. By now the band were tour veterans and were taking on some external influences (including of course Tull with whom they had most recently been playing). All five members of the band were confident singers and while the flamenco stamping may not be as to the fore here, there is no doubt where the roots firmly lie. The two bonus songs are both interesting. The first of these is a song that was released on a single but has never been available elsewhere, "Flamenco Fever". This is one of the singles that I paid extortionate money for years ago but am now glad that I did as what can be heard on the CD has been remastered from my own copy, not that you can tell from the sound quality, which is superb. The second song is a new recording from Widescreen with Angela singing, "Only Talking (For John)" which is very personal, very moving.

And so, onto Widescreen. This is a new project from David where he has been working with Steve Legassick, Laurence Elliot-Porter and Julian Ferraretto. This is music that shows David going back to his roots, with an instrumental acoustic album that portrays both his classical and flamenco guitar skills. It is at times gentle, and at others racing yet he is always in control as he evokes the images of Spain. Carmen fans will also be pleased to hear his new take on the title of the second album which is now very different indeed to what it used to be like.

I know that Widescreen have been playing with Buena Vista Social Club recently and I hope that these releases and the live work spur David on to make more recordings in the near future as this is very enjoyable indeed.
May 2007

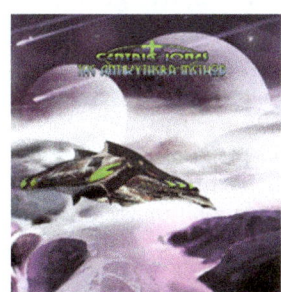

CENTRIC JONES
THE ANTIKYTHERA METHOD

Centric Jones are a duo comprising Chris Fournier (guitar, bass, keyboards) and Tobe London (drums, keyboards) and assorted guest musicians including singer Laurie Larson. Chris originally became known in the prog scene in the Nineties with Fonya who released albums on both Kinesis and Musea and has been working under the Centric Jones label for ten years, with Tobe joining for their last album 'Foreign Tea'. Although this is very much a project as opposed to a group, Chris and Tobe worked these songs for nearly two years playing and refining before recording to ensure that they were as organic as possible. In Laurie they have a singer in the style of Lana Lane who can soar to the heights when required, providing calmness to the complexity and almost frantic music that is sometimes taking place.

Stylistically this is quite a hard band to pin down, as while they have obviously been influenced by King Crimson these guys have also brought in elements of Tangerine Dream, Ozrics and Yes. In fact, there is a cover version on the album of "Then", taken from 'Time and a Word'. I'm not quite sure of the reason for doing this as it doesn't bring anything dramatically new to the piece, but if you enjoyed the original then you will also like this. Tobe has a very busy approach to drumming, even using rimshots if that is the right thing to do, and this definitely takes the music to new heights – especially when it is in a section when the keyboards are the main instrument as while there can be long held-down swirling chords from Chris, Tobe keeps driving it along. The album does sound a bit dated at times, but overall is a very solid effort and is worth looking out for.
Sep 2012

IL CERCIO D'ORO
DEDALO E ICARO

It is always interesting to find a band that makes others such as Credo to appear incredibly active when it comes to releasing albums. These guys started their career in the Seventies, releasing some singles etc., but not actually releasing a proper album until after they reformed in 2008. Now here we are only five years after that, and they are back with their second. So, when the comment is made that these guys sound as if they should be back in the Seventies then there is a lot of truth contained within, as they were! Truly, this album firmly belongs squarely within the Italian progressive rock movement as we have plenty of Hammond organ and Mellotrons to go with the rest of the keyboards, and an approach that certainly does sound as if it belongs from forty years ago.

But there are a few things that make it stand out as being part of the current scene and much of that can be laid at the feet of bassist Giuseppe Terribile who provides an incredibly fluid and warm sound to the bottom end. It is his bass that really pins all the others together, whether it is a dramatic piano/keyboard solo or some plaintive guitar, it is the bass which makes it whole. Martin Grice may only be a guest on this album, but his use of flute and sax on different numbers need to be commented on as each time it is dramatic and totally changes the punch of the song.

There are times when it is reflective, but for the most part this is progressive rock that while hearkening back in many ways to a time gone by, is also driving forward with a passion. Harmony vocals and strong melodies just strengthen the proposition, that this is an Italian prog album that needs investigation.
Aug 2013

THE CHANT
A HEALING PLACE

The Chant is a seven-member Finnish band based in Vantaa and Helsinki comprising Mari Jämbäck (keyboards, piano), Ilpo Paasela (vocals), Markus Forsström (bass), Kimmo Tukiainen (guitar), Roope Sivén (drums), Pekka Loponen (guitar, vocals) and Jussi Hämäläinen (guitar, vocals). This is their third album, and I think I'm going to have to go back and investigate the others as this is a highly polished affair indeed. The artwork gives a small clue as to the type of music being employed, as this is incredibly atmospheric – and according to which reviewer you read they are either a metal band or a prog act. Me, I plump for the latter.

True, there are elements of Anathema and Katatonia in what they are doing, but not nearly as metallic as either and they have more in common with Porcupine Tree and Riverside. Did you notice in the line-up that they have three guitarists? I'm not sure what they are doing for most of the time as the guitar sound is minimal, but obviously form part of the layers that comprise this mostly fairly depressing sound. Their music is like a blanket that cocoons the listener but providing none of the comfort that one would expect. There is little angst, and little overt emotion, yet the end result is compelling and intriguing. If I was going to pick a fault with the album is that the songs do somewhat tend to run into each other and by the end of it you won't remember any of the tunes or lyrics. But all in all, this is an interesting piece of work and if you enjoy the genre or any of the bands mentioned above then you need to find out more.
Oct 2012

CIRCLE OF ILLUSION
JEREMIAS – FORESHADOW OF FORGOTTEN REALMS

This is an album that is going to have two quite different responses. There are those who are going to rave about it (I was approached by someone who told me that I had to listen to this as these guys were the new Haken!), and there are others that will feel that in many ways it is just too clever for its' own good. Guess which camp I fall into? This is an album that I have enjoyed less, the more I have played it, and I am sure that this is because instead of seeing this rock opera as an incredible piece of art I instead see it as an opportunity missed. That the three singers are wonderful vocalists, that the songs are incredibly structured and well played is never in doubt, but there are just too many forms and styles of music being brought in that I just don't like.

There are times when this crosses into funk and disco, and that annoying music you used to get in the cinema when they were about to play the adverts. It can come across as really cheesy 70's pap, but there are other times when the jaw just hits the table when listening to the speed and interplay between all those involved. These guys can really blast it out, in perfect unison, and when they soar then this is just stunning. But, and it is a fairly big but, they just bring in all these other elements that for me really drop the album

instead of lifting it. Highly arranged and incredibly well played, this should be a 5* review, but it isn't. I realise that I am probably in a minority of one, but then that's nothing unusual. I would love to rate this more highly as there is so much promise within it, but there are also huge chunks where the Vegas lounge is just too much for me.
Nov 2013

CITIZEN CAIN
SKIES DARKEN

I first came across Citizen Cain in 1993 when their debut CD was released by Dutch label SI Music, but in truth they had already been active for some time before that, appearing on the famous compilation 'Fire In Harmony' back in 1985. I was immediately taken by the Gabriel-esque vocals of Cyrus, and the way that the band managed to evoke the spirit and feeling of early 70's Genesis but had brought them into the 90's. I was hooked. Over the years there were some line-up changes, and gradually the output slowed with the last release being 'Playing Dead' in 2002. Like many I never really thought that there would be another album, although I kept in touch with keyboard player Stewart Bell and often asked the question. So, it was both delight and trepidation last year when I heard that the band were recording again. I mean, after all this time was it going to be any good?

When the disc arrived, I opened the booklet to see who was involved, and could see just three names – Cyrus, Stewart and Phil Allen. Annoyingly for me there are no details about who played what, and who (if any) were the additional musicians involved. The Citizen Cain website is still under construction, and the Festival Music site just lists releases so neither are helpful in this regard. I did find a few details on one site where it states that Stewart provided drums as well as keyboards, Cyrus provided bass (as he did in the early days of the band) and vocals and Phil provided guitars. There is a very simple reason as to why this bothers me, as we need to give credit where credit is due as this is an absolutely stunning piece of work. To put it bluntly, this is one of the finest prog albums you are ever likely to hear.

Put it in the player and immediately the listener is taken aback by the complexity and interplay of the introduction to "The Charnel House". The maelstrom of notes and complicated inter-rhythms gives way to delicate piano and vocals, and one of the most Genesis-like passages of the whole album. Already the listener is deep inside the world of Citizen Cain, and with less than three minutes on the clock there has been musically a lot to digest. The interplay between the musicians, and particularly the way that the melodies and counterpoints are chased and are at times heavily structured and dense, contrast greatly with the simplicity of other phases of the music. And all of this within one song! Stewart's keyboards are a revelation, bringing together a multitude of sounds and styles, often layered, and he would need to be an octopus to be able to replicate this in a live environment. By the time I got to the end of this album I felt that I had been taken on an incredible musical journey, one with a richness and passion to match anything I have heard in recent years. The only sane thing to do after listening to this is put it back on.

The more I have played it the more I have fallen into the spell. So, it took 10 years for this one, when's the next?
Jul 2012

CITIZEN CAIN
GHOST DANCE
Over the years I have had to cull my collection various times, so the filing cabinets full of press releases and band information had to go (although I did keep my complete files on certain bands), as did many of the CDs. But I kept every photo I was ever sent, along with every cassette. Many of those bands are no longer with us so these tapes are sometimes the only thing left to remind me of what might have been, but here I am now playing a remastered version of a CD that I previously was unaware of (apparently it was released on Mellow at some point), which in turn is of a tape that I was originally sent by Stewart Bell twenty years ago. The CD contains the same track listing as the tape, which was subtitled 'The Original Citizen Cain 84-87'. It isn't easy to track down a biography of the band from these early days, but luckily I have also never thrown out any music books so by referencing the first issue of 'The Progressive Rock Directory' (written and published by David Robinson who now runs Festival Music which has released this) which came out in August 1992, I am pleased that my recollection of events is right (for a change).

Citizen Cain were originally a trio, forming in 1984 with George Scott (now known as Cyrus or Xyrus) providing bass and vocals, Tim Taylor (guitar and keyboards) and Gordon Feenie (drums, keyboards and flute). Interestingly, Tim and Gordon were previously both members of Not Quite Red Fox who turned a pre-Marillion Fish down as a frontman because he didn't have enough presence! Over the next three years Citizen Cain gigged a lot, especially in London at The Marquee and started to gain a reputation as a slightly different sounding band due to the way that the bass is often a lead instrument. They had one song on the famed 'Fire In Harmony' compilation, but had to split up after Cyrus was in a car crash that left him unable to play bass. After he returned to Edinburgh, he then met up with the guys who would then form the basis for a new group, who went in a more symphonic and overtly early Genesis direction.

So, history lesson out of the way, what is this album like? Well, remember that it isn't actually an album as opposed to a collection of songs as they only officially released the one song during their existence. But, given that this originally was a set of low-key recordings from the Eighties it stands up well against the other material from the time. Yes, Cyrus has a distinctive voice that makes many think of Gabriel, but these guys sound nothing like Genesis with a bassline and approach that is quite different. I would be interested to hear what they sounded like in the live environment, as keyboards are an important aspect although not essential, and I am sure that Tim switched between the two during a gig as Cyrus is often playing lines that are far more than just backing. This was a powerful prog trio and one can only wonder what they would have achieved if the accident hadn't taken place.

Some people have been quite disparaging about this album which is a real shame as I believe that it definitely has its place in the prog canon. It is something that I have really enjoyed playing, but just remember that this was early days for the band and in many ways, it is totally different to the style they developed in the Nineties. So, although some may feel that this is only one for completists I would instead say that while not essential it is a damn fine listen and something I have enjoyed playing again after quite a while.
Aug 2013

CITIZEN CAIN
RAISING THE STONES
Here we have the third album from Citizen Cain (not the fourth as some would have you believe), some three years after 'Somewhere But Yesterday'. There had been quite a change in line-up as well, with the band now reduced to just a duo of Cyrus and Stewart Bell. There are no details of who plays what, just that they performed everything themselves apart from lead guitar on one song which was played by Andy Heatie. As with all five reissued albums, it has been remastered and there is a subtle alteration of the artwork, but the track listing is as the original with no additions. In many ways this is one of the band's darkest pieces of work, as they strike their own path and move somewhat away from the early Genesis feel into something that is more brooding and powerful. The bass is now much more to the fore, and taking on a greater lead role, while Stewart's keyboards have grown both in stature and layers.

The word that keeps coming to mind when trying to describe this album is "power", as although they are now reduced to a duo this is very much a band firing on all cylinders that challenges the notion that prog musicians should just sit back and not worry too much about the rock element. That is definitely disproved here as these guys belt it out, yet still have loads of time changes, switches and moves through numerous styles and designs. By this time in their history Stewart and Cyrus knew each other well, and how to work together, and more than 15 years after the release of this album they are still producing great music. Festival Music have reissued the first five albums in a remastered form, and now couldn't be a better time to discover the incredible symphonic prog of Citizen Cain.
Aug 2013

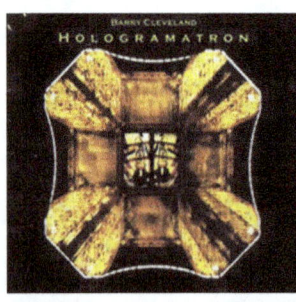

BARRY CLEVELAND
HOLOGRAMATRON
On this his fifth album, which was nominated for a Grammy in 2010, Barry has responded to contemporary social, political, and even spiritual realities, and has produced a modern-day "protest album" that draws inspiration from a musical continuum spanning art rock, psychedelia, avant-metal, ambient, global fusion, trance, and fun—with two early-'60s pop covers tossed in for kicks. He has brought

together a fine group of musicians to assist him in producing his vision, so while he concentrates mainly on guitars of various types including synth guitars, this also involved his long-time collaborator Michael Manring (they were both members of the improvisational quintet Cloud Chamber), drummer and percussionist Celso Alberti (Steve Winwood, Airto Moriera), and pedal-steel guitarist Robert Powell (Peter Gabriel, Jackson Browne), along with "avant-cabaret" vocalist Amy X Neuburg, and guest vocalists Harry Manx and Deborah Holland (Animal Logic). Additional musicians include Turkish electro-acoustic guitarist Erdem Helvacioglu, percussionists Gino Robair and Rick Walker, and Michael Masley (also from Cloud Chamber).

I have played this album numerous times, each listening giving me even more, but for some reason the same question kept going through my brain, "How on earth am I going to write about this?". It is complex yet simple, cutting edge yet mainstream, prog and jazz and pop and rock. I mean, what on earth is going on? Years ago, I read a very wise review, where the critic said that he was fed up of trying to fit music into pigeonholes and that in future he was going to put music into just two categories, namely "good" and "bad". Well, this definitely fits in the former and if anyone feels that it fits in the latter then I feel sorry for their musical tastes. I suppose one could describe it as art-rock, and Fripp has obviously been an influence, but musically it is all over the show. As with every recording he is involved with, Manring's warm fretless bass is a key to the overall sound seemingly at the heart of all the layered complexity. This is such an easy album to listen to musically, with melodies in abundance, and a surprise around every corner. One of these has to be the version of "Telstar" which is just wonderful as the Sixties song is taken into a new age. Barry has written some books on Joe Meek and obviously this is his homage.

This is a great album, one that I have enjoyed playing immensely. Highly recommended.
Jan 2013

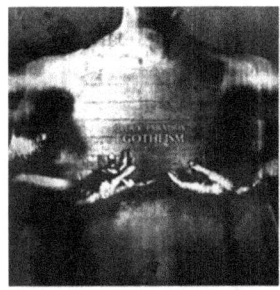

CLOCK PARADOX
EGOTHEISM
The beginnings of Clock Paradox can be traced back to 2009 when Antti Karhu (The Man-Eating Tree) and Jyrki Hiltunen (Impish, Rectum) decided to join forces. They knew that they wanted to stretch the normally accepted definition of death metal into a more progressive area and when they were joined by drummer Jani Kuorikoski (Depth Beyond One's, Joint Depression) they started recording material. During this period they were looking for a bassist so that they could gig, and in came Timo Tyynismaa (Komi Bell) which allowed them to move forward. After a while Antti felt that he needed to concentrate on guitar, so the final piece fell into place when Jouni Koskela (Abysmalia, Vermivore) arrived.

'Egotheism' is their debut full length album, and they have already proved that they are different to the norm even before putting it on the player, as this is a concept album – how many death bands have done that? It describes a psychopath's views on himself, other people, and life in general in a diary-esque fashion. The soundtrack for this trip into the deepest reaches of the human mind is based on the progressive wing of traditional death metal where a brooding atmosphere is merged with solid compositions.

It contains the edginess and heaviness that the genre demands, yet at the same time there is a smoothing of the edges, not taking away any of the power but instead emphasising the dynamics. Although it must be said that Clock Paradox are more melodic, in many ways they remind me of The Axis of Perdition in their approach and the result is an album of depth and power. If you want your metal to be heavy but also to allow you to think then this is something that needs to be investigated as it is one of the finest progressive death albums you are likely to come across
Oct 2012

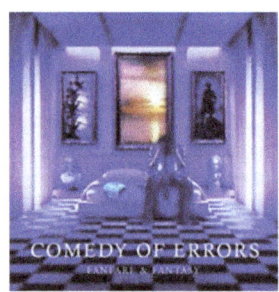

COMEDY OF ERRORS
FANFARE & FANTASY
Listening to this album makes me think of the Monty Python sketch where the old codgers are all comparing their childhood days and how the kids of today didn't know how well off they were. I first came across Comedy of Errors in the early Nineties, by which time they had already released some cassettes and were making a name for themselves in Scotland. But looking back twenty years it is hard to imagine that no-one, and I mean no-one, in popular media were writing about progressive rock, and the only way to find out what was going on was by going to gigs, buying fanzines, writing letters, and talking to others in the scene. Yes, this was the time before the internet existed, and most of us didn't have email either. Back then I was spending quite a bit of time with Mark Colton (then just ex-Casual Affair, followed by Freewill, and now for many years Credo) which not only did wonders for my alcohol intake but ensured that I listened to some bands that otherwise I wouldn't have heard of. I am pretty sure that Graham Younger and the fanzine 'Blindsight' had some impact as well, while Keith Richardson also has plenty to answer for and between the three of them, I got to hear one of C of E's albums quite a lot, and in particular the song "The Student Prince, Part 1".

Faced with the almost impossibility of getting media coverage outside of fanzines, it is no surprise that C of E faded away given that they were toiling at their craft in Scotland, which has never been widely known for their prog scene (yes, I know Fish is Scottish, and Pallas did make an impact while Abel Ganz also made an impression) and back then it was hard for prog bands to exist outside of the South, and in particular London. The underground scene was very insular and only those 'in the know' were privy to some stunning music and live performances.

But, thankfully the band are back in business with originals singer Joe Cairney, keyboard player (and songwriter) Jim Johnston and guitarist/bassist Mark Spalding being joined by drummer Bruce Levick and new member John Fitzgerald who has joined on bass but was too late to play on this album. Rob Aubrey was given the task of mixing and mastering this album, the second since they started playing again (I haven't heard the first). I was emailing Artur of MLWZ recently and said that I had yet to play this CD and he told me that I was in for a real treat when I did, so it soon made it to the player, and I was transported. The only accurate description of this album is neo-prog, with loads of classic Marillion references, but that isn't really a surprise given that they would have had very similar influences themselves. They manage to come across as Gryphon in one number, while Kansas also have their impact, but all in all this is Comedy of Errors and I love it.

Great vocals? Check.
Harmonies? Check.
Musical hooks and interesting songs? Check.
Great musicianship throughout? Check and double check.

When it comes to the end of the year this album is going to be up there with Big Big Train for the number one slot in my mind. It just doesn't get much better than this.
Apr 2013

COMEDY OF ERRORS
DISOBEY

When I reviewed C of E's most recent album (the incredible 'Fanfare & Fantasy') I happened to mention that I hadn't heard this their 2011 debut, so both Joe and Bruce kindly asked if I would like a copy. Daft question really. I still have some trouble realising that this is a debut album when they were a band that I knew about in the early Nineties, yet by then they were already pretty much defunct, so what on earth gave them the impetus to get back together again? Original members Joe Cairney (vocals), Jim Johnston (keyboards, additional guitars and backing vocals) and Mark Spalding (guitars and bass) brought in drummer Bruce Levick for the album (he has since joined) and even convinced Hew Montgomery to help out as well. But, this is way more than just some old guys (yes I can say that as I am one as well) getting together and messing about; these guys mean serious business.

There is no way that a band that has been apart for more than twenty years should be able to get together and produce an album that screams quality from start to end, it really does beggar the question "where have you been?" Loads of bands came and went during the 80's and 90's, but I can't think of any that disappeared for such a long time before coming back with a neo-prog album of such epic proportions. While Marillion is an obvious influence, I would also point to Grace and Credo on some numbers, although Gryphon does definitely have an impact as does Kansas.

This is everything I want from a neo-prog album, from harmonies and melodies through to strong keyboards and punishing guitar lines. To finally have their classic "The Student Prince" on CD is just a huge bonus to boot: so glad that they brushed that one off and gave it the performance it deserved. All in all an incredible album that progheads will savour.
May 2013

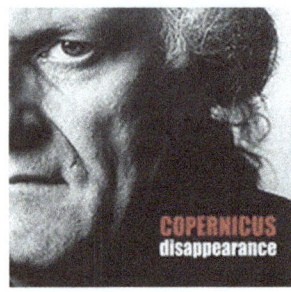

COPERNICUS
DISAPPEARANCE
This is the 12th album from performer-poet Copernicus, and was recorded on November 2nd 2008. On that day he gathered together a large ensemble of improvising musicians, led by long-time musical director Pierce Turner (keyboards). It is free form, it is chaotic, but there is a strange and eerie passion that makes it quite compelling to listen to. Copernicus orates as opposes to speaks, and I can imagine him with wild eyes in the middle of a storm of his own creation, the wind and rain striving to stop him. But he has a presence, so that even when his voice is little more than a whisper it demands to be heard and is the centre of the universe.

This is music that you will either love or hate – there is no middle ground. It is Beefheart taken to the nth degree, music that is at the very limits of that definition, but somehow I find it hard to turn it off once it has started playing. Is this music even sane, or something that is taking the listener into new areas of their own mind? I don't know, but do know that I have never heard anything quite like it.
Nov 2011

COPERNICUS
L'ÉTÉRNITÉ IMMÉDIATE II
You're going to have to bear with me on this one, as to say I am confused myself is something of an understatement. If I have my facts right, after the release of 'La Eternidad Inmediata' in Ecuador in 2005, Copernicus performed 25 concerts all over the country with a show that was very faithful to the original album. The concerts were always performed in Spanish, but as recording costs were very low in that country Copernicus decided to rerecord the original. Once that was completed, he then revisited the album, recording vocals in different languages and releasing them as different albums. So, the one we have here is the one with the vocals recorded in French, hence the title 'L'Éternité Immédiate II.' But what is even more confusing is that the title of the album does not reference 'II' anywhere. Still with me? Leo from Moonjune has been working with Copernicus on reissuing albums, and apparently, he prefers the French version, which is why this has now been made available again.

There is a booklet with the digipak, lyrics, and notes, but of course it is all in French, which isn't a lot of help to me, so instead I'll concentrate on the music. This is also quite different to what I would normally expect from this artist, as while it is still jazz and avant-garde, there is a warmth and delicacy often missing from the albums I have heard from him. Normally he is wild and abrasive, very much in the face of the listener, commanding the band as if is the centre of a whirlwind but this seems to be much more thought out and directed. Maybe that is due to having just played a series of concerts, and then of course re-recording vocals in different languages, but whatever the reason this seems to be a far more structured and controlled approach than I would normally expect. In fact, it was such a surprise that it took a while for me to really get into this album, but musically this is quite superb with some wonderfully restrained playing from those involved.

Copernicus is always going to appeal only to a small audience due to his very nature, but if you haven't come across him before then this may actually be a good place to start as it isn't nearly as provocative as some of his albums while Cesar Aragundi (guitar), Freddy Auz (bass), Newton Velasquez (piano, synthesizer), Juan Carlos Zuniga Lopez (drums) and Matty Fillou (saxophone) are a heck of a band – all brilliant musicians in their own right.
Dec 2013

COPERNICUS
WORTHLESS!
A few years ago, I reviewed, 'Disappearance', and back then I asked questions such as "is this music even sane, or something that is taking the listener into new areas of their own mind?" I still don't have an answer, but he is back now with his latest work (I missed the intervening 'Cipher and Decipher'). As before, he provides words while 14 musicians improvise at the direction of Pierre Turner. Unusually, this time he also has another singer in Sari Schorr who definitely provides another facet to proceedings. I know that Copernicus is not something for the mass market, as he mixes poetry and passion with avant-garde into something that is Beefheart in an asylum, Zappa with any sense of melody and constraint squeezed out.

Over the years I have trained my ears and mind to understand music that many people wouldn't even define as such. It is only in the last few years that I have started to really discover Art Zoyd, Can, and many other artists that some people will never enjoy listening to. It's a bit like eating vegetables, when young most people only like peas and carrots, it takes a while for the palate to mature and to be able to enjoy Brussels sprouts and broad beans. Copernicus is like that. Listen to him with a closed mind and you will only hear a discordant cacophony, but if you have an open mind then you will find something that is strangely compelling, something that has to be played through to the end. The strange thing about this album is that "What Is Existence" starts with a guitar gently playing "Go Tell It On The Mountain" and that is strangely jarring with what else is happening.

Not for the fainthearted, and definitely not for those who only like peas and carrots. It comes with an informative booklet as well.
Aug 2013

CORVUS STONE
CORVUS STONE

My understanding is that this band came about when the three main musicians, Colin Tench (guitars), Petri Lemmy Lindström (bass) and Pasi Koivu (keyboards) found each other through Facebook, and they recorded most of the album before some other members came into the fold, which is one of the reasons why it is mostly instrumental. Before I started writing this review, I thought that I would have a perusal of what others have been saying about it on PA. I don't normally look until afterwards as I don't want to be influenced by others, but I was intrigued to understand just how much of a minority I was going to be in. And yep, there are a lot of people who really like this, and it is currently #33 in the Top 2012 charts. But there are also quite a few people who feel the same as me, which is that it is perhaps a little too disjointed and fractured at times for its' own good. I have no idea how the songs were written, but we can go from crossover prog to something that is far more intricate and Zappa-like to sometimes go through fusion and into RIO, which can make it confusing for the listener.

There is no doubt that the three of them are wonderful musicians, with Petri providing some incredible fretless bass lines, Pasi having a wonderfully delicate touch, and Colin being an amazing guitarist, no matter what style they are working on, but it doesn't always work. At one point I was reminded of the story Rick Wakeman told of him telling every member of his band that they were going to start with a different song the next night, so when they all started playing it wasn't exactly what was expected. Each of them was a professional but none of them were working together and that was the feeling I had here, but on only some of the songs, and that is why I found this an incredibly frustrating album to listen to.

It is very long for a single CD, a fraction under 80 minutes, and there are times when this is nothing short of sheer genius, but there are others when the listener just shakes his head and asks what one earth is going on. I have to confess that I smiled when I heard the snippet of "Smoke On The Water: inside "Moron Season", and again when "Oh Well" turned up inside "Scary Movie", and the latter is one of the standout songs on the album for me as it could easily have come from the masters of horror prog themselves, the mighty Goblin. The more I played this album the more I liked it, but consequently also the more I felt that there were some things wrong with it. I mean, a drum solo on a studio album in 2012? Come on, we weren't that fond of them in the Seventies (unless you were John Henry Bonham of course).

I had a long hard think about the grading I gave to this album, as there are many times when it is at least 4*, and others when I can only give it 2* at best, so 3* is probably fair. But if I put this onto my iPod and only played the songs I liked then it would be 4/5. So, this is one when it really does pay to listen to it before purchase so give it some plays on Bandcamp and then either download or pick up the CD that contains a 16-page booklet.
Nov 2013

A COSMIC TRAIL
II: MISTRAL
From the title it probably comes as no surprise to hear that this is the second album from this German instrumental prog act, following on from 2010's 'The Outer Planes'. Apparently that CD is now completely sold out, so if you want to hear their music you are going to have to plump for this one. The label characterises them as a progressive metal act, and although I can see why they are stating that, given that the guitars can riff and blast away at times, but for a large part of the album they are far more atmospheric and about the feel and emotion. They paint a fairly bleak soundscape, with little in the way of warmth, which is reflected in the black and white artwork to boot. Apparently they work to the mantra of producing music that is "widescreen cinema for your ears" and I get that, as this has a big sound which feels that it is out in the open landscapes as opposed to being constrained inside a tiny room.

Their music is obviously influenced by elements from rock, prog, metal, jazz, folk and soundtracks and they bring in twists and changes that create a distinctive atmosphere. However, there are times when one feels that they have slightly lost their sense of direction, and it isn't as vibrant and compelling as it could have been. It is always interesting to hear a fully instrumental prog album, and while not essential it certainly contains enough elements and ideas to make it worth seeking out.
Jul 2013

COSMOGRAF
THE MAN LEFT IN SPACE
'The Man Left In Space' is the fourth album from Comsograf, which is actually a solo project by multi-instrumentalist Robin Armstrong who provides guitars, keyboards bass and vocals and utilises additional guests to fill in the sound. So for this album, the guests are Nick D'Virgilio (Spock's Beard/Big Big Train), Dave Meros (Spock's Beard), Matt Stevens, Greg Spawton (Big Big Train), Simon Rogers, Steve Dunn (Also Eden), Lee Abraham (The Lee Abraham Band), Luke Machin (ex-The Tangent) and Dave Ware. It is a concept album that explores the themes of aspirations, achievement and travails that the quest for success sometimes brings by depicting these within the constructs of a failed space mission.

It is an ambitious project in many ways, and one that took me a long time to warm to. There are times when the music is just too polished, too sanitised, that I found myself drifting away and it took some effort to keep coming back. But the more I played it, the more I discovered the underlying layers and the complexity that is intriguing and not nearly as clinical as I first imagined. At times it is very Floydian, at others Muse and at yet others RPWL, yet there is a deftness in some of the lead guitar and keyboard lines that definitely lift this out of the ordinary. If I had written about this having only played it once or twice it would have received just 2/5, but although I do have some issues with having a song called "Beautiful Treadmill" this album has moved up to be 4/5. There is a clarity and crispness in the production that belies the fact that it was recorded at a home studio, with the guitar and bass on "The Vacuum That I Fly" being a case in point.

If you enjoy strong neo-prog with powerful guitar lines then this is definitely worth further investigation.
May 2013

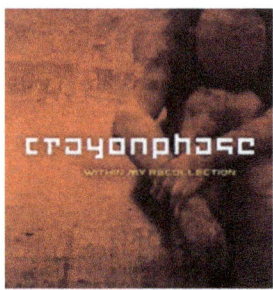

CRAYON PHASE
WITHIN MY RECOLLECTION
This is the debut album from German band Crayon Phase, who describe their music as being "located somewhere between Neo Prog and New Art Rock, between epic and 13/8, between rock out and listening closely. The music reflects a wide range of sounds and atmospheres: sometimes melodic and playful, then back to hard rock, sometimes epic, sometimes dynamic, often complex and tricky, but also straightforward and intuitive." They state that they are influenced by classic bands such as Genesis and Yes through Marillion and Saga, up to Spock's Beard and Porcupine Tree. When the album first started I was convinced that I was listening to an instrumental act, and was somewhat surprised when vocals made their presence felt, some four minutes into a six minute song.

It didn't take much longer for me to wish that Frank Wendel had stuck with providing additional vocals and that the band had indeed stayed as an instrumental, as although some of the keyboard sounds being used are more than a little dated at times, I felt that the band just sounded so much better when he wasn't singing. There are instances when he is trying to cram just too many words into a line – it may have scanned well in German, but that doesn't mean that it will do the same in English. Also, there is something about his vocals that I just can't take to, and having played this album a few times to be able to write about it I sincerely doubt if I will ever listen to it again.
May 2013

CREDO
AGAINST REASON
In another lifetime (or at least it seems that way now), I was talking to singer Mark Colton one day (previously of Casual Affair and then with Freewill) and he told me that he had been approached to also join another band, then called Ad Hoc. The name soon changed to Chequered Past, and then to Credo and the band started to make their presence felt on the London circuit. Mark's 'main' band Freewill folded and he put all of his energies into Credo who signed a contract with Cyclops and soon released their debut album 'Field of Vision'. Back then I was very involved with the band, attending most of their gigs and trying to publicise them in any way that I could.

It became apparent that keyboard player and main lyricist Mik Stovold wasn't going to be the right fit going forward, and Shadowland (and now Landmarq) keyboard player Mike Varty came on board and this was where the band really started to get traction. While drummer Paul Clark and bassist Jim Murdoch provided the solid background, guitarist Tim Birrell and Mike Varty lifted Credo to new heights while Mark was the consummate frontman. But although the band were improving all the time, writing great music and having storming gigs, all was not well. It transpired that Mark was seriously ill, and at one point was only a few hours from death, while Paul was also having some issues. This meant that the band while working behind the scenes, seemed to have gone dormant to many prog lovers minds.

Mark started singing with a folk rock band where he met drummer Martin Meads, and when Paul announced he was leaving, Martin was the obvious replacement. It was the new line-up that released 'Rhetoric' only eleven years to the day from the debut. During the intervening years myself and Mark has located to different parts of the country, so I wasn't so up to date with the material but the album blew me away and I did manage to see them play again before I moved to the other side of the world.

And so, onto the third album. I haven't seen the band play live for more than five years, so this was all new to me. Mark had been raving about it, so it was with some trepidation that I put it on the player. Straight from the opening of "Staring At The Sun" I was captured and enthralled, and everything that I had planned to do for the next 69 minutes was placed on hold. The band may be accused of playing neo-prog, but what's wrong with that? I like neo-prog! I was lucky enough to be heavily involved in the UK prog scene in the early Nineties, and while it could be argued that this belongs to that time it is way more polished and musical than most of what was coming out then.

This really is a musical tour de force – it is everything that a prog fan could want and much, much more. I have always previously viewed Mark as more of a frontman than I have as a vocalist, his passion onstage is what lifts the band and the performance. While he is often likened to Fish I feel that it is an unfair comparison – there may be similarities but his range and intonation are quite different. However, my view has now changed as having heard just about everything he has ever recorded (including much that has never reached the public domain) I can categorically state that this is easily his best performance ever. The control and pitch are superb, and the rest of the guys have also stepped up considerably. Tim Birrell has been their secret weapon since the very beginning, one of the finest guitarists ever to grace a UK prog stage (if you don't believe me then search out "A Kindness?" from their debut and imagine how much better that was live) – and here he is using a controlled restraint as he links with Mike to provide incredible interplay. Martin and Jim provide the bedrock, which allows Mike and Tim to really stretch out. If you want to listen to just one minute of how good this album is then start playing about two minutes into "Insane" and the next sixty seconds provides everything you could ever wish to hear from this style of music.

Credo's best album to date? Definitely. My favourite prog album of the year? Oh yes. Any regrets? Yes, I'm the other side of the world so haven't heard any of this being played live. If you enjoy progressive rock music, melodic rock, neo-prog, art rock, or any

of the other labels that get bandied about then you owe it to your ears to get this. It doesn't get any better than this.
Oct 2011

CROWNED IN EARTH
A VORTEX OF EARTHLY CHIMES
This album had a few things going for it before I even put it on the player. Firstly, it was released by Black Widow, one of my favourite labels, and I just loved the artwork, which reminded me a great deal of the music of the Seventies. This is the second full-length album from the guys (and at 47 minutes is 12 minutes longer than their last album), and multi-instrumentalist Kevin Lawry and drummer Darin McCloskey have been joined by Brian J Anthony on Mellotron. Note the important distinction there: he doesn't play keyboards plural, but Mellotron singular. That is already enough to get many proghead's pulses racing, as if just one instrument was seen as being key to the Seventies prog sound, then that would be it.

There are only five songs, but three of them stretch out to more than ten minutes, so I settled back to enjoy an album that promised to bring together influences from the likes of Black Sabbath, Cathedral, Reverend Bizarre, Camel, King Crimson, Black Widow, Ancestors, Electric Wizard and Atomic Rooster. Well, maybe not quite. There are parts of this album that do gel together very well, but there are others where it is way too workmanlike. The vocals just aren't powerful enough, and while the guitar sound is beautifully rich and dramatic, with some nice Mellotron overlays, there just isn't enough going on to fully maintain my interest. When I look at Umur's review on MMA of their previous album he says "the music is rather dull though and lacks power and conviction. The songs aren't especially memorable either. There's nothing really bad here either though, the material just comes off mediocre.". Now I haven't heard that album, but pretty much it can be said for this one. It is okay, but really nothing more than that.
Jul 2013

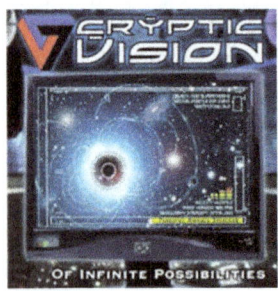

CRYPTIC VISION
OF INFINITE POSSIBILITIES
There are some bands that seem to fly under the radar, even in the progressive underground, and I have always been mystified as to why Cryptic Vision aren't far more well known. It certainly isn't down to lack of musical ability, songs, hooks and prog timings as these guys have all of the chops. They may not be the most prolific when it comes to releases but the same can be said of most of the bands in the genre. However, after a five-year gap they are back with the conclusion to the trilogy 'Moments Of Clarity In A World Of Infinite Possibilities'. The five guys behind Cryptic Vision are main songwriter, drummer, guitarist and keyboard player Rick Duncan, vocalist Todd Plant (Eyewitness, Millenium), keyboard player Howard Helm (Zon,

Refugee), bassist Sam Conable and guitarist Tim Kesse but they have also brought in some guests in the form of David Ragsdale (Kansas), Gary Schutt, John Zahner, Shawn Bowen, John Leblanc, Mike Carello and Carrie Preston.

The note density and complexity is off the scale, while intricacy and harmony vocals are also the order of the day. It is almost as if Spock's Beard and Gentle Giant have combined forces with Kansas and Presto Ballet to produce something very special indeed. This is prog that is very much for today but also looks back with loads of references to great bands of the past that have somehow been melded together into something that is just incredible. It is immediate, with a very American feel, yet it also has incredible depth and the more that it is played the more the listener will get from it. I remember that before I left the UK I played one of their albums virtually non-stop in the car, and even back then I couldn't believe that this wasn't a name familiar to all progheads. If you enjoy prog, and you must do otherwise you wouldn't be reading this, then you owe it to your ears to investigate further.
Sep 2012

CYNIC
THE PORTAL TAPES
Although this may appear to be a 'new' album from Cynic, it is an album that is now more than 15 years old. Back in 1993 the band released the wonderful 'Focus' where they mixed metal, jazz, and prog in a way that some people fully understood while others didn't, and it has to be said that their record label probably fell into the latter camp and didn't promote it as they should have done. Now, if you are only aware of the recorded history of the band you probably think that following the debut, they didn't do anything until the widely acclaimed sophomore 'Traced In Air' which came out in 2008 following their reformation, but you would be wrong. Following a lot of touring to promote 'Focus' the band split up, only for Paul Masvidal, Sean Reinert and Jason Gobel to get back together for a new project called Portal. To complete the line-up, they brought in Chris Kringel and Aruna Abrams, the latter to provide a female lead/ harmony vocal as they went for a different musical and vocal approach. They recorded a demo album, but nothing ever came of it until now – strangely there is no mention of the album or the project on the band's website, but at long last we have the opportunity to hear it.

What is interesting about this album is that while it would have surprised a lot of Cynic fans if it had been released at the time, it now sounds incredibly relevant to both what Cynic are doing and to the music scene in general. The twin vocals work extremely well, while of course the intricate musicianship is just what one expects from these guys. The addition of Chris Kringle has made quite a difference to their overall sound as he plays fretless instead of fretted bass, and that adds a very different warmth and feel to the sound. The way he bends notes and gently moves around the music provides extra dynamics and lots more depth. Some of the songs are almost radio friendly with Aruna's vocals being quite like Tracy Hitchings, relaxed but with clarity and range.

I still find it hard to think that this album was recorded as a demo in the Nineties, and that it has taken until now for it to be released. It is not nearly as heavy as Cynic could be back in the day, with far more atmosphere and light within the shade, and is something that progheads need to search out much more than metalheads with prog and jazz elements often taking centre stage.
Oct 2012

DAEMONIA
DAWN OF THE DEAD/ZOMBI
This band is the creation of Claudio Simonetti, composer and keyboardist of Goblin, who are best-known for their contributions to the soundtracks of the films directed by Dario Argento. I was fortunate enough a few weeks ago to see Goblin play in front of a showing of the classic 'Suspiria', and it was just awesome! Here he has got together some younger musicians to assist him in revisiting some Goblin numbers and giving them a fresh sound. Originally released in 2006, it now contains three bonus numbers, one of which is for me the absolute highlight of the whole piece. There is no need to know the original songs here, as Claudio has treated them afresh and these are new arrangements which capture the bombast and gothic darkness that make Goblin such a powerful live act.

Some of the songs sound as if they have been lifted straight from a horror set, while others are somehow even more dramatic with a menace and presence that is quite incredible. "At The Safari" contains some incredible percussion that threatens and drives, while others can be lighter in manner yet always with a brooding atmosphere which is Italian prog at its' very best. Although it does have to be said that the honky tonk of "Torte In Faccia" does seem somewhat at odds with the rest of the album.

Towards the end of the Seventies, I was intrigued by Sky's version of Bach's "Toccatta and Fugue", which even made the charts in the UK. But that is a mere lightweight compared with Daemonia's "Toccata e Fuga" which takes the song to a far more dramatic and powerful level. It sounds a little quick to me, but the overall effect is stunning with the melodramatic keyboards combining perfectly with the chugging metallic monster that is the rest of the group. This album is definitely well worth investigating.
Jul 2013

DANTE
THE INNER CIRCLE
Dante was founded in 2006 by keyboardist Markus Maichel and guitarist Markus Berger who had been friends since school. It was at a Dream Theater show in Munich that they decided that they really ought to start working together in a progressive vein and from then started working on sessions in Markus's own studio. It soon transpired that what

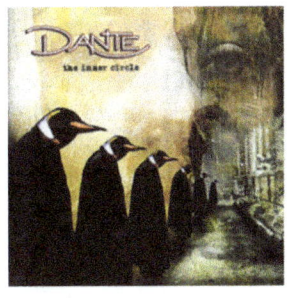
they were doing was starting to turn into something special so vocalist Alexander Göhs, a close friend of Maichel and the singer of Berger's former band Twelve was asked to join the recording sessions to get a better idea of what the songs could sound like. He soon joined the band as a full-time member and the line-up was completed by drummer Christian Eichlinger, who not only shared his passion for progressive music, but also had experience with complex arrangements. The resulting album is something of a masterpiece in so many ways. It is unusual these days for a prog band to release such a stunning debut without first being picked up by a 'major' (okay, I use the term loosely) label.

Yes, there are a few – but they don't happen very often, and it has been a long time since I last heard an independent debut from a totally unknown band that has impressed me so much – probably Spock's Beard or Discipline. There is huge depth in this recording, loads of different styles and sounds and while they can be termed 'prog metal' on some numbers this band has way more in common with the actual 'prog' field. Berger can really crank out the riffs when he wants to, but he also lets Maichel take centre stage in the musical front – so either of them can be powering onwards, supporting the other as the need arises, or taking a more restrained approach altogether.

This is a great rock album, not really neo-prog, but with some elements of that combined with a hard-edged approach and complex arrangements and layered instruments and melodies that result in something that is both powerful and simple, easy to listen to but never easy-listening. Alexander has a vocal style that is well suited to the band, more of a rock singer than a prog singer; it really works. They even put in a 'short' ballad that is less than four minutes long, and extremely powerful with a delicate arrangement, and then to show they understand their prog roots they end with one that is nineteen minutes. Well worth discovering
Nov 2011

DANTE
SATURNINE
Given the quality of their debut, it was no surprise that for the follow-up, released in 2010, they had signed to one of the largest labels in the genre. By now the band had been augmented by a bassist, Michael Neumeier, who had joined Dante when they started playing live. This album is basically a continuation of the debut – why change a winning combination? There is bombast, there is a delicacy and emotion, complex arrangements yet also a simplicity to some of what they do. They may have started life at a Dream Theater concert, and indeed they have taken on some of those influences, but they are no way a DT clone. They obviously pay attention to bands such as Porcupine Tree and Yes, as well as some elements of Genesis right up to Neal Morse.

Yet again this is a great album, and one that I have enjoyed playing immensely but I did find that this time I felt that there were times when Alexander was struggling. He is a great singer when allowed to be more emotional and controlled such as on slower pieces, but when the band is rocking out, he allows himself to push his range and control and it doesn't always work. That being said, this is an album that I really enjoyed playing, although possibly not quite as much as the debut. But this is still very much a new band, and I hope that we soon get to hear the third instalment of what promises to be a long and fruitful career. If you enjoy prog that knows how to mix it up with slow and fast, emotional, and bombastic, then this would be worth searching out.
Nov 2011

DAYMOON
ALL TOMORROWS
Although this is a debut album, the roots of the band actually go back a long way, and this could easily have ended up being classified as a solo album from Fred Lessing (guitars, flute, recorders, keyboard, vocals, and ethnic percussion). He has been joined on this by André Marques (acoustic and electric drums, and incidental vocals), Adriano Dias Pereira (clarinet, flute, melodica, keyboard, sax, percussion, and vocals), Paulo Catroga, (keyboards and vocals), Nino Mar (bass guitar), Joana Lessing (keyboard, percussion, and vocals, Rodrigo Caser (electric guitar), Mark Guertin (bass guitar) and Davis Raborn (drums). Although there are a lot of musicians, and I did read somewhere that they added their parts and sent them back to Fred to weave into the musical whole as opposed to recording together, the feeling is that of a group as opposed to a project. Musically this is heavily rooted in the Seventies, with large elements of classic Genesis and Gryphon, but it is somewhat let down by the vocals. They are somewhat of an acquired taste and that combined with the very regressive prog sound results in an album that shows promise but ultimately doesn't really deliver. Much has been made in some quarters about the fact that this band is from Portugal which isn't normally thought of as a prog hotbed, but personally it doesn't matter so much to me as to where a band are from as it does to how they sound. This isn't a bad album but having written about it I somehow can't see myself playing it again.
Mar 2013

DAYMOON
FABRIC OF SPACE DIVINE
It is probably fair to say that I wasn't incredibly impressed with the last album by these guys, but when I saw that the subtitle for this one is "Ramblings on Darwinistic monotheism and the history of the universe – inspired by the works of Stephen Baxter" I was more than a little intrigued. Daymoon realistically are less a band and more a project, with multi-instrumentalist Fred Lessing very much to the fore, and there are a few songs where it is just him and one other, although there are also plenty

where there are many contributors. Musically and stylistically, this is incredibly varied and complex, and it is no wonder that on the rear of the digipak are the words "Thank you for supporting non-commercial music!" One of the reasons for the album being so varied, is that Fred actually started work on this back in 2000 and it wasn't completed until 2012, so it has been a very long road to get to this point.

Musically this seems to take its' influences from just about everywhere, mixing Western and Eastern, rock and jazz, electric rock instrumentation with woodwind, and then putting it together in a way that should never make sense, but somehow does. It is an album that does take a lot of work to really get into just because there is so much going on, and it keeps splitting into new areas and tangents, and can be incredibly complex (or gentle and simple with just acoustic guitar and Mellotron).

Lyrically this is also complicated, bringing up lots of ideas and concepts, but contained in the booklet are the lyrics (and the all-important details of who played what), there are also detailed reasonings behind each song and what Fred is trying to convey. The result is something where the listener gets the most of the experience by going through the booklet whilst playing the album, and concentrating on both. This should never be background music; one just won't get the best out of it.

This is progressive music that really is refusing to see any barriers, and the album is one of the most diverse I have come across.
Jul 2013

DEAD HEROES CLUB
A TIME OF SHADOW
You have to feel a little sorry for these guys – I mean, not only do they play progressive rock (which has to be probably the most critically despised form of music in the world), but they also come from Ireland which is a country that doesn't exactly have a great history in these matters. But one of the most important bands ever to come from Ireland could be called progressive – namely the mighty incredible Horslips – so maybe there is a chance for them after all. Of course, prog music and fantasy artwork has always gone hand in hand so by getting Ted Nasmith, the official illustrator for the Tolkien estate, to get involved was definitely a good move. So, to be an Irish progressive rock band makes them a rarity, and originally this was an unsigned release that they put out on their own so these guys obviously have plenty of passion and belief, and the main reason for that is simple. This is bloody good.

This is music that obviously has its' roots in the Seventies, but really it has way more in common with the bands that were making their presence felt in the early Nineties. There are links with Citizen Cain (and therefore Genesis) and with the much-missed (by me anyway) Belfast proggers Winter, and Hammond-style keyboards can never fail to be a hit either. There is plenty of melody and great lyrics, with vocals that have a real presence, and loads of time signature moves and changes in emphasis and musical

dominance. This is the sort of music that I used to be sent a great deal when I was first getting involved with the underground scene in the early Nineties, and I had forgotten just how much I had missed it. Once this has finished, I think that I will have to play Galahad's 'Nothing Is Written' – I'm just in the mood. This is an album that looks backwards as well as forwards and is something that progheads will play time and again – a sheer delight.
Jan 2012

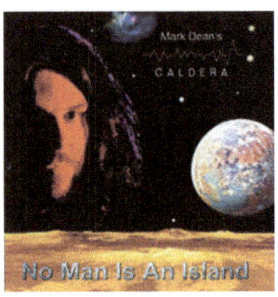

MARK DEAN'S CALDERA
NO MAN IS AN ISLAND

I have been in contact with Mark quite a lot recently concerning Tim Morse's latest album, and it was during one of these exchanges that I mentioned that I hadn't heard his own album which he then kindly sent along. I seem to have been writing quite a lot about multi-instrumentalists recently, and here is yet another example. Over five years Mark recorded every note, sang his heart out and of course also engineered and produced it. This doesn't sound like a solo effort, but that of a band who are in perfect harmony with each other. Some of the songs are very heavy indeed, but there is such a mix that there is something here for everyone.

The song "Do I Care" is a typical example. It starts off with some extremely heavy almost doom-laden riffs before breaking into something that I can only describe as being some of the best Living Color that I have heard in years. Normally solo musicians start on keyboards or guitar and fail at either vocals or by using a drum machine, but Mark knows the importance of 'real' drums in a rock context and more than proves himself to be a fine drummer – although only he will know if they were recorded 'live' or had many hours of rerecording and splicing to get it right.

But that's the point, it is right. In fact, this is a very enjoyable hard rock album with progressive tendencies. You may have to have eclectic tastes to get the most out of it, but I do so that's fine with me. Well worth investigating.
Sep 2012

DEAFENING OPERA
BLUEPRINT

This is the second full-length album from Munich band Deafening Opera, following on from 2009's 'Synesteria'. Although it is available through Bandcamp it is also available as a properly released CD, which is what I have. The first thing that really strikes the listener is just how polished this is, which both takes the edge off the heaviness but also provides additional emphasis where required. They describe themselves as a cross between Porcupine Tree and Riverside, but there are also plenty of elements of City Boy, 3rDegree and more in an album that is both restrained and in your face, full of Seventies influences yet very much for today, clean and simple yet complex and layered: all at the same time. The first time I played this it brought a smile to my face and each time I have listened to it that has just got bigger.

It is an album that brings in so many influences that different people will classify them in different ways: PA has them marked as 'Heavy Prog', MMA has them as 'Hard Rock' and my personal view is that they are Crossover with elements of Prog Metal. But really, who cares what we call it? In simplistic terms there are just two types of music, good and bad, and this definitely falls into the former.

When there is a need for the music to crunch it does just that, but where it needs to be more restrained then yet again it hits the mark. This is a wonderful album, and if you want something that is polished and dynamic while packed full of great songs then this is for you.
Nov 2013

FRANCIS DÉCAMPS
REVISITE CARICATURES
Ange was formed in late 1969 by brothers Christian Décamps (vocals) and Francis Décamps (keyboards) who were later joined by guitarist Jean-Michel Brézovar, bassist Daniel Haas and Gérard Jelsh on drums. The band has become recognised as one of the most important ever to come from France, and indeed is still active although Francis parted ways with his brother in 1995. But why so much information on Ange when this is a solo album by Francis? Well the reason for that is quite simple, this is a full re-recording of the 1972 debut Ange album which forty years on finds Francis providing most of the instrumentation as well as the lead vocals. According to PMA the original album is rated at 3.82, but I have never heard it (in fact I don't think I've heard anything by Ange to be honest), so I can't provide any comparison, only what I think of this as it stands.

Probably the biggest issue for me is that I am a typical pom and only understand English, and this album is not only in French, but I also get the impression that the lyrics are extremely important given the focus that is provided on the vocals. That then leads to the next issue, I don't think that Francis is a very good singer although there is no doubting his keyboard skills. There are flashes when this album really works, but for the most part I found this a struggle. No doubt there will be plenty of people who will explain that I don't know I am missing, but while there are sometimes when I convince myself that this is worth 3 *'s, I know in my heart that it is only worth 2 as the biggest thing it has going for it is that it is less than 40 minutes long.

Not something to which I will be readily returning.
May 2013

The Progressive Underground Vol 4

DEEEXPUS
KING OF NUMBER 33

DeeExpus were formed in 2007 when guitarist and multi-instrumentalist Andy Ditchfield met up with singer Tony Wright, and they decided to put a band together. However, they found that they worked together well and instead of forming a complete outfit just brought in a few guests to assist and 'Halfway Home' was released in 2008. A band was formed for the live shows, and then in 2010 it was time to start on the second album. It was about this time that Mark Kelly became involved and joined the band as a full member – of all the Marillion guys it is Mark that has produced the least amount in terms of additional projects, so it shows that he was keen on what he had heard. His keyboards are also much more than just an added extra, as his runs and interplay on "Maybe September" reminded me why I first fell in love with his other band thirty years ago. The line-up here has been completed by John Dawson on bass and Henry Rogers on drums (while none other than Nik Kershaw provides lead vocals on 'The Memo').

This certainly doesn't sound like only the second album, as it is a hugely polished effort moving from riffs to gentle piano and through a gamut of neo-progtastic moves. There are areas of extreme delicacy such as gentle piano, fretless bass and acoustic 12-string on "Marty and the Magic Moose" before Andy lets fly with a great guitar solo and the band brings it all together. If you enjoy bands like IQ and Galahad, then this is something you need to seek out. Mark has had to take a temporary break from the band so he has been replaced for live work by Mike Varty (Credo/Landmarq/Shadowland) as they support Marillion on their UK tour.
Sep 2012

DEEEXPUS
HALFWAY HOME

Having enjoyed their second album so much, it only seemed right and proper to go back to the debut to see how that stacked up. Given that it was released in 2008 I am just a little behind the curve but given the size of the prog scene here in NZ I'll forgive myself. As with their second album here is a band that is full of maturity and power – it just doesn't seem that they have been around for such a short period of time. This is all about great songs and musicianship, combined with powerful production and stacks of hooks. There is enough complexity for any proghead, with melodies and countermelodies throughout while at the same time the vocals lines are easy to get involved with. It is an 'immediate' album, one that can be listened to for the very first time with a smile on the face, and when it comes to an end the only sensible thing to do is to put it on again and get even further immersed in their world. They have been compared by many to Porcupine Tree, but while I can see that as an influence these guys are way more than just copyists with nods to Gentle Giant and Marillion among the mix.

One of my favourites is by far the shortest song on the album, "One Day", which is a gentle piano and acoustic guitar instrumental duet that demonstrates that beautiful music doesn't always need words, or great length. In contrast, the album closer and title track belts in at more than 17 minutes with wonderful complex rhythms and guitar lines at the beginning that cries out Mr So & So. In fact, my only complaint at the end of playing this album is that the lyrics in the booklet are just too hard to read! They may fit on two pages on font 5, but some of us are getting on a bit now…

Seriously, this is a great album from a band who, at this time, were more a project than a group. If you have yet to come across DeeExpus then you owe it to your ears to investigate this great British band.
Oct 2012

FREDDY DELIRIO
JOURNEY
Freddy is best known for being the keyboard player in historical cult band Death SS, the singer of the hard rock band H.A.R.E.M. as well as being a producer and sound engineer. This album mostly dates to 1992, with three songs added and the whole thing then remastered and reissued last year. This is very much a solo effort, so of course that means a drum machine, which doesn't belong in any recordings as far as I am concerned, so we are already off to a bad start. Musically Freddy has obviously been heavily influenced by Rick Wakeman as opposed to more dreamy material such as Jean Michel Jarre. This certainly makes the album much more in your face and hard hitting than otherwise, and he even brings in some Hawkwind-style space effects when he feels the need.

But sometimes the gimmicks get just a little too much and actually detracts from the main thrust of the music. Also, some of the keyboard sounds that he utilises would have seemed a bit dated in 1992 (too Eighties), let alone now, which means that some of the songs just haven't aged very well. The end result is an album that contains some interesting pieces and some good playing but not enough to make it essential.
Jul 2013

DELTA SAXOPHONE QUARTET
DEDICATED TO YOU BUT YOU WEREN'T LISTENING
As I have got older, my listening tastes have got even broader so that as well as searching out genres such as progressive rock, I am educating myself in the joys of other luminaries such as Frank Zappa, John McLaughlin and Soft Machine. What has that to do with this review I hear you murmur? Well, this album is a tribute to the last of those three – with 'Dedicated To You But You Weren't Listening' containing three improvised numbers that have been inspired by the Softs (particularly Hugh

Hopper – who guests with them on one of his own compositions), and the rest being their versions of numbers recorded by the band between 1969 and 1976.

I have to confess that I hadn't heard of DSQ before being sent this release (it came out in 2007), but they were formed in 1984, and even though they have been through some personnel changes it is therefore no surprise that these guys know what they are doing. The very best tribute albums are those that can musically stand in their own right and add something new to the music – as opposed to just being clones of the original (which in my opinion is totally worthless), and this is definitely one of these.

I can listen to this album all night – the interplay of the saxophones is stunning, and when it is all over then I can go back and revisit the originals and see what the inspiration was for it all. If you enjoy jazz, or music that is different, or are just an old Softs fan at heart then this is indispensable
Nov 2011

DIALETO
THE LAST TRIBE
Oh. My. God. What we have here is yet another awesome band that have been uncovered by Leonardo, this time from Brazil. This instrumental trio comprise Nelson Coelho (guitar), Jorge Pescara (touch guitars) and Miguel Angel (drums) and in many ways are quite unlike anything I have come across before. Apparently, this band originally formed in 1987, but were on ice for a long period before getting back together in 2006, after which they released a couple of albums. Last year original bassist Andrei Ivanovic left, to be replaced by Jorge who instead plays touch guitar, and this is their first album since then. What makes these guys so unique, is the way that they are bringing together so many different styles and forms of music in a way that is progressive, instrumental, heavy, and containing so many influences that one doesn't really know where to start.

So, with an instrumental trio it isn't unusual for there to be plenty of jazz structures and tendencies, and that is indeed the case. But there are times when these guys move from 13/8 into standard 4/4 without missing a beat and suddenly, we have shredders that are moving the music in a very different direction indeed. It is slow, it is reflective, it is hard, it is in your face. Miguel is the one person attempting very hard to keep the others in line, as Jorge is not averse to providing a secondary lead line, very different to what one would expect to a 'normal' bassist (although he can also hunker down when the time is right). But Nelson is a real star, with a wonderfully fluid touch that is reminiscent of the great Allan Holdsworth, yet often much more in the face in the style of Satriani.

This album could only ever be described as progressive, yet there are only the three instruments on show, which just goes to show what can be delivered by those who totally have mastery and understanding of what they need to achieve. This may be their third album in recent years, but the first to get a full international release, and I know that we

are going to hear a great deal more from these guys. Just stunning.
Aug 2013

DISCIPLINE
TO SHATTER ALL ACCORD

I can't remember when or how I first heard of Discipline, but let's just say that it was it was somewhere in the Nineties. Back then I was stunned by the quality of the music that these guys were producing, and 'Unfolded like Staircase' should be in every prog lover's collection. But that was their last studio album and came out in 1997. Since then, there has been some live releases (if you can find a copy of 'Progday '95' on which they feature then grab it), but nothing new from the band. Singer Matthew Parmenter has released some superb solo albums, but when it came to light that the band were reforming in 2008 for NearFest the question would be would they stay together? Thankfully the answer to that is a resounding "Yes!" and Matthew (voice, Mellotron and keyboards), Jon Preston Bouda (guitar), Mathew Kennedy (bass) and Paul Dzendzel (drums) have released a new studio album at last.

Only five songs (but one of these is more than 24 minutes in length), and two of these have appeared previously (in live versions), but I am very much in prog heaven. It is quite hard to describe the music of Discipline – they always remind me of classic Genesis but actually sound nothing like them at all, while it is possible to hear elements of King Crimson, VDGG and a host of others but with some strident and at time almost discordant guitars.

Progheads aren't always the best at saying what they think about music, but the review of this album that appeared on www.dprp.net is a delight – in that Brian Watson says about the epic 'Rogue' "this is perhaps Jon Preston Bouda's finest hour. There's a fluidity to the playing that is truly a joy to behold. If this song was a girl, I would not only ask it out. I'd marry it. I mean her. Yes, I love this song." It seems a tad picky that he gave the album only a 9/10 and I'm sure that this was because he doesn't think that it is quite as good as 'Unfolded'.

To be honest I'm not so sure – this is prog with an edge, music that demands attention. It can never sit happily bubbling along in the background like Genesis, Floyd, or Moody Blues. 15 minutes into 'Rogue' and the shrieks are genuinely un-nerving. There are long instrumental passages that allow everyone to shine and at the end of the album there is only one thing to do. Take a breath, put on the kettle, and play it again. Only this time just that little bit louder. If this album doesn't deserve maximum marks then nothing does. Sheer brilliance.
Jan 2012

DISCIPLINE
CHAOS OUT OF ORDER

There are a few things that must be mentioned right at the beginning of this review, and the first is that at the time of recording Matthew was underage and Jon and Woody were just 17. Yep, what we have here is the original 'Chaos Out of Order' which was released in 1988 as a cassette, plus an additional song from 1987, enhanced as opposed to remixed as the original tapes weren't up to the task so there have been some very minor tweaks here and there. Personally, I have been after this for years but have never been able to find a copy, which probably has a lot to do with Matthew never being happy with it and after the initial production of cassettes ran out it was not re-released. It took another five years before they produced 'Push & Profit', and another four after that for 'Unfolded Like Staircase', after which there was no more. Now, I firmly believe that Discipline are one of the finest progressive bands to come out of the States in the Nineties, and I have searched out live albums and compilations, and when the band reformed for the amazing 'To Shatter All Accord' in 2011 I was overjoyed. But there was still that niggle, just what did 'Chaos Out of Order' sound like?

Many years ago, I can remember chatting with Martin Orford, asking if IQ would ever reissue 'Seven Stories Into Eight', and at that time there was absolutely no plans to do so, but it was an album that many fans wanted to hear, no matter what it was like. Of course, they later did make it available, along with a complete re-recording, and it was warmly received. But what about this one? Matthew has provided plenty of sleeve notes, along with the lyrics etc, but it is obvious that he has some reservations about making this available again after all these years, and in some ways I can understand why.

If this album was viewed on its own without knowing anything about its' history or the age of those involved, then it is quite possible then it wouldn't get the most favourable review in the world and a listener may believe that all of Discipline's album are similar. But if you already know their music then this is a delight in so many ways. Even at such a young age the guys are demonstrating their musical dexterity and handling of complex layers and stylings. There is also a naivety in what they are performing, demonstrating promise while also showing the simplicity of youth. I was surprised at just how much I kept being reminded of Todd Rundgren when I played this, as he isn't an artist that I normally associate with these guys, which shows just how far they had to go to reach their true identity.

If you have yet to hear all the other Discipline albums, then gently walk away as this has not been made available for you. But, if like me you have never been able to get enough of their music and have for years wanted to hear this material then it is essential.
Sep 2013

DISPERSE
JOURNEY THROUGH HIDDEN GARDENS
When I first saw the album cover, I was fairly convinced that what I would be hearing would be a doom album, so to say I was somewhat surprised when I put this on and realized that here was yet another top quality Polish prog act is something of an understatement. Apparently, the band made their breakthrough when they supported Riverside on a national tour, and it was from there that they were invited to record this their debut album which was released in 2010 but has only just come to my attention. Poland seems to have way more than their fair share of great prog acts, and on the basis of their debut Disperse should soon be gaining the same sort of attention that is normally reserved for Riverside, Quidam, Millenium and the like.

For the most part this is prog metal, but with large amounts of neo-prog thrown in for good measure. It is hard to pick out a highlight from the album as it is so good throughout, and while the guys are all strong musicians it is the guitar of Jakub Żytecki that really takes this to the next level. They say that they are heavily influenced by bands as diverse as Cynic, Toto, Portal, Aeon Spoke, Planet X, Devin Townsend, and Allan Holdsworth, and they certainly manage to capture the fluidity of Holdsworth's guitar solos. There is loads of atmosphere on this album, and the result is something that is polished and packed full of emotion. Given that this is now two years old we can only hope that there is a new album due sometime soon.
Dec 2012

DIVERSION VOICE
UNDERWATER
Do not adjust your set, the album cover is in 3-D which means that without the glasses it does look a little strange, a bit like the music contained within. This is the debut album from Russian jazz/psychedelic/prog group Diversion Voice, and an interesting listen it is as well. Comprising Matvey Ushakov (guitar), Ilya Bolkisev (saxophone, electronics), Dmitry Krasov (guitar, percussion), Ivan Dorokhov (bass) and Alexey Kryuchkov (drums) these guys are really mixing it up. Just when the listener feels that they have a handle on what is going on they move in a different direction so that there is always a great deal to take in. At times they are a dance act, at others they are pure jazz, at time dark and others light. The music can be light hearted or extremely deep as they bring in Floyd, Canterbury scene, Porcupine Tree, Ozrics and a whole host of others to create a sound that is beguiling and invigorating all at the same time. Intrigued? Well, the best bit about this is that you can now get this album for free, gratis. The guys have made it available as a free download so why not visit their site (thankfully it is available in English), have a look around, and then get a copy for yourself? If you enjoy jazz prog with hints of the above-mentioned bands then you need this.
Nov 2012

DORIAN OPERA
NO SECRETS

Here is the debut of yet another Prog Metal band, this time from Germany, with the CD being released on the Russian Mals label, home of keyboard player Andrew Roussak's solo album. This is prog metal that really comes alive during the instrumental passages where they often combine differing classical styles with the metal, creating a sound that is truly progtastic. But I did find that at times the vocals aren't as strong or as melodic as they might be, while at others they are wonderful (possible quality control issues?). Also, to me the production wasn't as clear cut as it could have been so that there are times when the music is a little muddy. So, it is fairly obvious that I don't like the album then? Um, wrong. This is actually a really good debut. While the guys obviously know how to rock out, Roussak has a fine touch on the piano, and it is the judicious use of runs on the piano that perfectly complement what is going on in the maelstrom. This is an album that does grow on the listener and the more one plays it the better it gets! Yes, there is room for improvement in many areas but this album should gain the band a strong following within the genre and I look forward to the next release with some interest.

Oct 2009

DOUBT
MERCY PITY PEACE & LOVE

This is the second album from the trio of Alex Maguire (keyboards), Michel Delville (guitar, Roland GR09, samples) and Tony Bianco (drums, sequencer) and was recorded live in the studio over two days (more than six months apart) in 2011. Although it is instrumental throughout, this is in fact a concept album deriving its inspiration as much from William Blake's visionary aesthetics (the title is taken from the poet's "Songs of Innocence and Experience" – and Blake is thanked in the credits along with Stravinsky and Sen. Bernie Saunders) among a diversity of 20th-century musical icons. One of these icons is Hendrix, and I am sure that he would have enjoyed the raucous, loose yet tight interpretation of "Purple Haze" that appears here; while instantly recognizable, it has been ripped to pieces and then reconstructed with loads of fuzzed guitar and a chaotic approach that is just wonderful.

But they can go from one extreme to another so from a blasting rock out we can go to something quite gentle and reflective with Alex controlling the proceedings with some finesse and beautifully dated keyboard sounds. This is an album that is completely timeless as although it brings in influences from modern acts such as Tortoise it goes back to the invention of the Sixties and combines it with some over the top 70's histrionics. It is only the sound clarity that leads one to the conclusion that this is a work of today as opposed to something from 40 years ago. This does take some perseverance, just because the styles they are using are often very diverse, but the listener is rewarded.

Jan 2013

DRUCKFARBEN
DRUCKFARBEN

If you're a proghead and you don't own this album, then you need to correct that immediately and with due haste. 'Nuff said. Oh rats, I probably need to write more than that. Okay, the band with a very strange name are not German at all but are Canadian, and this is their debut release They have all known each other for a long period of time and finally got a band together four years ago and at their debut live show their first number was "Close To The Edge". Yep, it's a given that these guys can play. I mean they can really play. What they have done here is taken the classic influences (Gentle Giant, Yes, King Crimson, ELP and have brought in Colosseum, Allan Holdsworth, Hatfield & The North among others) and have then just had a blast.

The first number is "ELPO" and is a keyboard-led instrumental. I mean, given that this a band that had a great singer who even opens an album like that? I was sent this as a download so hadn't read the booklet so when I started playing it I just presumed that it was an instrumental act. We move through the influences mentioned, plus more, as Druckfarben take us on a journey that contains great vocals and stunning musicianship. The only real question I have is how can I convince more people to investigate this? They are already recording their second album and are working on a live DVD release to boot. This is a brilliant album, well worth five stars, and one that I already love immensely. You need to visit their website and play some songs and then decide if you feel the same way.
Nov 2012

DYNAMO BLISS
DAY AND NIGHT

If ever there was a band that defined the sub-genre 'Crossover prog' then it this Swedish trio, who mix pop and prog in equal measures to create something that is beautiful, exciting, enthralling and engaging in equal measures. There is a really clean sound to this as it brings together music in a way quite similar to that of their artwork. If you want to listen to this as a progressive rock album then there are plenty of layers and intricacies to discover, but if you want to just view this as beautifully crafted melodic power pop then there are plenty of hooks. To me this brings together the very best of the Seventies and Eighties but updates the sound for today. Some reference bands would be 10CC ('Deceptive Bends' era), City Boy and ELO with Styx and even Jean Michel Jarre also making an appearance.

This really is an album that is totally accessible and enjoyable the very first time it is played, and from there on in it just keeps getting better. There are times when spacey keyboards take centre stage, but at others it is the bass, or acoustic guitar, or lush vocals, or, well you get the idea. It is fresh, it is fun, it is a bloody fine album.
Nov 2013

DYONISOS
AGES HIGH
Before I go any further, I need to confirm that I do have the title correct – this is 'Ages High' – not 'Aces High'. This is Dyonisos and not Iron Maiden, although it appears that virtually every web reviewer can't read either the label website or the CD cover itself, never mind. So, once you get over the shock that this isn't the latest compilation by everyone's favourite HM band, you can sit back and relax in this album by Dan Covan. Of course, Dan is American, his stage name is that of the Greek god of wine and madness, vegetation, and the theatre, and he is signed to a Russian record label. I'm glad I've managed to clear that up...

This isn't the first time I have come across Dyonisos, as I reviewed his debut, and this is his third (and since this album he has released a fourth) and yet again I find myself enjoying it. This is an unusual album in that it never really seems to sit in any particular style, but rather happily moves around – following whatever is the correct path. To my ears it sits mostly in the happy style of late Seventies rock but just when I feel that I am getting a handle on it off it goes again. "Passage To Evermore" is a case in point with some great layered guitar solos and rock ethic that suddenly goes full pelt into 'Animals' style Floyd. Just wonderful.

This is an album that is worth hearing, but while there are elements of Jadis and Camel (and maybe some Hackett) this isn't a prog album as such, just one that contains bits and pieces. It can feel a little disjointed at times, but when it works this really is a delight.
Dec 2011

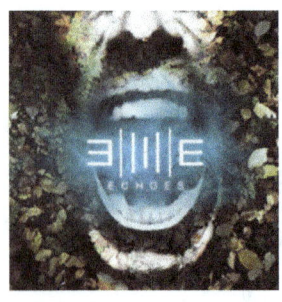

ECHOES
NATURE|EXISTENCE
I must confess that my knowledge of the Venezuelan music scene is pretty poor, in fact it wouldn't be a stretch to say that it is totally nonexistent, but at least I do now know one band that comes from there, and mighty fine they are too. Echoes first started to get attention for themselves in 2005 when they won the prestigious 'Alma Mater' Rock Festival and since then they have been playing as many shows and festivals in their own country as possible to hone their craft. This is their debut album, released at the beginning of 2010, and shows that these guys have a view of metal and prog that is going to gain them many friends in countries well outside of South America.

The press release says that it is a mixture of prog rock with math metal and loads of other stuff thrown in for good measure and I reminded myself that yet again I shouldn't read the press release before playing the album as how could that be right? One eaten humble pie later I can say that I totally get where that statement is coming from – there are bits and pieces, in fact whole passages, that could have come straight from the latest Protest The Hero opus, while at others the guys definitely show their prog inclinations. There is a section in "Despair" where they combine all of this with some great sax (care of guest Dave Duffus) that tries to bring all of their influences into a VDGG maelstrom, and it works oh so very well indeed.

This is an album that does benefit from being played very loud indeed, yet while there are huge metal elements there is no way that this could be confused with being a straight metal album. So okay it is prog metal, but much more in common with Dream Theater than acts like Threshold, and then not really like them either. Imagine Protest The Hero playing prog and that is the best analogy I can come up with, and as they are one of my favourite bands you can see how much I have enjoyed this. The vocals appear to be all guests, so it is probably no surprise that a) they are top quality and b) there are very long instrumental passages. But this is much more than fancy metal, as there is delicate piano, acoustic guitars, strings and so many other musical ideas to discover.

These guys are incredible musicians with great songs, and overall, this is an album that needs to be discovered at once if not sooner.
Jan 2012

EDISON'S CHILDREN
IN THE LAST WAKING MOMENTS

As with Druckfarben I was sent this to review as a digital copy, so hadn't seen the booklet when I started listening to it. Also, I hadn't undertaken any research so didn't know who was involved and was treating this as a totally new band. It was only afterwards that I realised that this was a joint project of Pete Trewavas (Marillion) and Eric Blackwood (Crimson) who then brought in various friends and guests (including the rest of Marillion, which is the first time they have all appeared on an album which doesn't have their name on the front). I was pleased that I had no idea who was involved as it means that my view of the album is untainted, and this atmospheric spacey Floyd-type prog is right up my street.

There are times when the drums are just too basic for my taste, but that is just a minor knock against what is a very fine album. Both Pete and Eric provide lead vocals, and while they may not be standout singers, they suit the music just fine and it really works. The production is top quality, and this is an album that definitely benefits from being played at night, looking out at the stars with a glass of fine malt at hand. If I had the choice of playing this or the latest Marillion album, then this wins hands down every time.
Nov 2012

ELECTRIC FORGIVENESS
ECHOES & BOOMS

Electric Forgiveness is a new band consisting of John Bundrick (The Who) and Jon Dawson (Third of Never) along with Jeremy on guitar and Tony Stiglitz on drums. Now, I am a huge fan of Jeremy, like Third of Never, and one of John Bundrick's solo albums is often on my CD player, but this just isn't an album that I have been able to get too excited about. Although I have been known to dabble a little with Tangerine Dream I have never inhaled and most of the electro progressive musos wash right over me. By having 'real' drums as opposed to programming and an electric guitar (too often in the background) they have at least taken some steps in the right direction but for the most part this feels like two keyboard players having fun in the studio, improvising, and bouncing ideas off each other and recording the results.

I am a huge fan of Wakeman and Emerson, and certainly enjoy Floyd a great deal, but to me this album doesn't contain enough in the way of strong material to keep it consistently interesting – there just isn't enough in terms of dynamics. This is very much music to be played in the background while doing something else and isn't something to which I will be readily returning.
July 2009

ELORA
CRASH

Elora came together in Marseilles in 2005, and after releasing an EP in 2010 they signed with German label Progressive Promotion Records and have now just released their debut album 'Crash'. I have no problem listening to lyrics in another language, as it allows me to concentrate on the overall feel and sound of the songs (I'm a typical pom, can understand Te Reo Māori just enough to sing the anthem and I know the odd word, but apart from that it's English all the way). But, here I think I must be missing out on something as I just don't 'get' this album as much as I think that I should. It's extremely solid crossover with loads of influences, notably Porcupine Tree and Pink Floyd among others, and the use of male and female leads, and harmonies is a nice aspect, but it is never really more than that.

If I try to dig into why I feel this way, I can only say that there is no real hook or melodic flow for me to really connect with the music, so it rather passes me by. At times very dreamy indeed, and almost New Age, there just isn't enough bite and edge for me to get excited about it. Possibly if I understood French then it might have more meaning, but this is like a snack as opposed to a full meal and leaves me wanting more.
Nov 2013

ENID
MUNSALVAESCHE
It's amazing how important a single word can be at times. If I put "The" in front of the band name, then I would be reviewing the classical prog group that has now been going for approx. forty years under the tenure of ex-BJH arranger Robert John Godfrey. But I didn't, and instead I am talking about the latest album from Robert Wiese, although when this started, I was getting confused between the two. A quick check and I could see that I had been sent this by Code666, one of my favourite extreme metal labels, yet this was all orchestration and delicate piano. What is going on? When Robert started singing on the second song "Legends From The Storm" I actually started searching the web as I was sure that there was something wrong with the download – but then riffing guitars and Gregorian chants mixed with Alestorm led me to believe that all was good, just confusing.

The album has been inspired by the medieval novel "Parzival", written by Wolfram von Eschenbach and the word "epic" is the only think that I can think of to describe it. Everything just seems so big! I have seen some reviews where this has been described as post-Black Metal, but as I don't know what that sounds like (apparently, it's what I am listening to), I'll come up with a different way to describe it: don't tell the metalheads, but this is a prog album. I don't mean neo-prog, or retro, or any of the other subgenres, but a good old fashioned rock album that is pushing boundaries and bringing together different genres and instruments in a way that makes total sense. Best not tell the progheads either come to think of it, as there is a lot on here that they won't like (those guitars really are heavy when they hit).

But if you like prog and metal, (but this isn't prog metal – that is something else again, don't you love pigeonholes?) then this is something to savour. It is almost cinematic in its' approach, and it would fit a vision of an arduous journey, so given that Parzival was looking for the Grail I would have to say that Robert Wiese has achieved what he wanted to with this album. If you hate pigeonholes as much as I do, then this is worth discovering.
Dec 2012

THE ENID
INVICTA
Twenty years ago, I went to see Galahad support Aerie Fairie Nonsense, which of course was The Enid under an assumed name, and RJG introduced himself to me by putting his arms around me and asking if I knew he was a poof? Now, that can make quite an impression on a lad, although it must be said that it didn't have as much impact as seeing him play piano later that night which was just astounding. RJG is one of those very few musicians who has always brought classical and progressive music together from the early days when he was working with Barclay James Harvest to

when he formed The Enid in 1974. Since then, the path has been complex and often tortuous, yet still he prevails. The current line-up features original drummer Dave Storey (although he, like Simon Nicol in Fairport, had some time off for good behaviour), guitarist Max Read (who has been there since '97), guitarist Jason Ducker (07), bassist Nick Willes (09), and new singer Joe Payne. It is interesting to see that the band now features a twin guitar attack as not many people would view them as a guitar-based band – as this is all about providing modern classical music.

There are a lot more vocals on this album than I am used to with The Enid, but at the same time it is also full of the styles and arrangements that one expects from RJG and the more I played it the more I was gradually drawn back into his world. In fact, there were times when I felt that I was being taken all the way back to "Raindown" from the classic 'Something Wicked This Way Comes' and this new album stands up very well indeed to what is widely regarded as one of their best works. This is a band that is probably only ever going to be appreciated by a relatively small audience as their music is seen as 'highbrow' or 'eclectic' even within the prog scene, but if you have never come across The Enid then this album is a great introduction.
Nov 2012

EPHEL DUATH
HEMMED BY LIGHT, SHAPED BY DARKNESS
It has been four years since the last Ephel Duath album, so when I saw that this was available, I was really excited as this experimental avant-garde Black metal band have always intrigued me and I have enjoyed what I have heard of their previous albums. The line-up this time was founder, guitarist and songwriter Davide Tiso, Marco Minnemann (Kreator, Necrophagist, Joe Satriani) on drums, Bryan Beller (Dethklok, Joe Satriani) on bass and Karyn Crisis (Crisis, Karyn Crisis Band and more importantly Tiso's wife) on lead, while it also includes some contributions from Eric Rutan (Hate Eternal), who also appears on two of the songs. Musically this is brutal stuff, which is also bringing in lots of different styles from death metal through to jazz, and touching on loads of stuff in between, but for me it just doesn't really gel. There is a fine line between being experimental and creating a new style of music and being experimental and creating something that in some ways in unlistenable, and there are times on this album where they straddle that line and times when they go crashing right on through. There is little in the way of continuity, and I found myself getting musically confused as to what they were trying to do, as while there are plenty of BM elements it all seemed too disjointed and angular, almost as if they were trying to be too clever for their own good. The one thing that I couldn't fathom at the end is where the fault is with the music or with my personal understanding of it. I listen to a great many forms of music, and have been known to enjoy Art Zoyd and Can, as well as plenty of free form jazz, but I just don't get this at all. It is difficult to listen to, both in terms of timbre and style, and possibly if I made more effort, then I would get more out of it, but it just seems too much like hard work.
Dec 2013

ETERNAL DEFORMITY
THE BEAUTY OF CHAOS
Eternal Deformity was founded in 1993, and originally started life as a doom band, but continually strived to push across boundaries and the five-year gap between 'The Serpent Design' in 2007 and this their 2012 release seems to have allowed them to do just that. Various discussions can be had on whether this is extreme prog metal, melodic symphonic death, or a combination of the two with black metal thrown in could last for days – it just shows how music often doesn't want to fit into the little boxes that we strive to put them into. The one thing I can be sure of is that here is something of epic proportions. Even on first play one realises that this is much more than just another album, and that there is something special contained within, and that feeling only grows the more time that is spent getting to know the music.

This is complex and complicated, where everyone has an important part to play yet is tight and incredibly heavy all at the same time. These guys refuse to conform to any expected norm so "Pestilence Claims No Higher Purpose" starts with a sublime piano introduction before all hell breaks loose and the band go mad. Within the same song there is a total change of direction with a small touch of doom and a different style of vocals. The atmosphere created in this one song is just incredible, as they twist and turn and use clean and gruff vocals to create a world all their own. It is possible to get lost inside this album; just play it loud and the world will pass you by. This is a stunning piece of work.
Mar 2013

EVERWOOD
WITHOUT SAVING
I must be honest and say that I don't know many bands from Hungary: the obvious exception for me up to now has been After Crying who have released some stunning progressive/art rock albums over the years – but with Everwood I am now wondering what else I might be missing from that country as this is just superb. However, unlike After Crying, one would be hard pressed to pick this as an Eastern European act as if I hadn't read the press release or seen the musician's names, I would have assumed that they were American. One more thing that you need to be aware of when playing this, is that to my ears it isn't prog – whatever the label may think. This is symphonic melodic metal/heavy AOR, with an emphasis on all the elements that one would expect from those genres. It is an album full of hooks, with great vocals and musicianship throughout and is totally accessible on the very first play. In fact, I was surprised at just how loud I ended up playing this as it is just so good that I kept cranking it up a little more. There may be just enough complexity within this for those who enjoy Dream Theater, but in truth this is more Rhapsody of Fire, Symphony X or a heavy Toto. Overall, it is a great album, with power ballads and rockers for all.
Oct 2012

FACTORY OF DREAMS
POLES
Multi-instrumentalist Hugo Flores first came to attention with his debut solo album in 2000, after which he formed Sonic Pulsar with whom he released two albums. From this he formed Project Creation (two more albums) and then in 2008 he felt inspired by vocalist Jessica Lehto to create new music outside of the style he'd been working in previously and formed Factory Of Dreams. Jessica started off by listening to metal oriented bands such as The Gathering, Within Temptation, Nightwish and Blind Guardian and from the age of 17 started writing her own material, obviously influenced by her earlier interests.

For this the debut, Hugo provided electric and acoustic guitars, bass guitars, synthesizers, additional drum arrangements and loops, percussion, sitar, 12 string guitar emulation; Chris Brown provided fretless bass while Jessica sings – like an angel. I have found it really interesting to see this reviewed on the web, obviously in some cases by people who have never listened to black metal (!!) yet feel that this is atypical. What we have here is a wonderful symphonic melodic rock band very much in the style of Within Temptation, with perhaps a tad Lacuna Coil. Jessica is a stunning singer, very clear diction, and great control, while Hugo is a consummate musician and songwriter so overall it is a great combination. If you enjoy this style of music, then this is definitely worth searching out.
Oct 2011

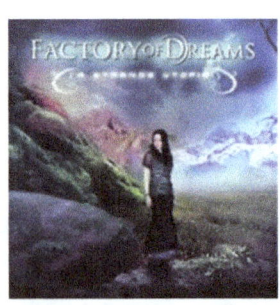

FACTORY OF DREAMS
A STRANGE UTOPIA
As with their debut album a year earlier, 2009's 'A Strange Utopia' features Jessica Lehto on the cover and lots more of her stunning vocals inside. I have always enjoyed multi-instrumentalist Hugo Flores' work, and in Jessica he has found the perfect counterpoint. He can indulge his love of complex layered music knowing that he has a singer who can rise to every occasion. This album is a continuation of the debut but is also a great deal more in every manner, 'Poles'^{2} if you will. In every area this album rises to greater heights, whether it be in the greater sense of drama, the greater feeling of symphonic goth, the over-arching passion and feeling, the heavier power chords or the lightness and deftness of touch. In fact, the only thing that I wasn't too fond of was some of the 'drumming' that is a little over the top and somewhat out of proportion at times (such as at moments in "The Weight Of The World"). There is even a guest in the form of David Ragsdale (Kansas, Salem Hill) providing delicious violin.

The production is very strong throughout, and Jessica is, well, just superb. She has to be one of the finest vocalists in this style of music (okay, in any type of music) and her musical collaboration with Hugo is superb. Fans of Within Temptation and gothic symphonic progressive rock need to find this without delay.
Oct 2011

FACTORY OF DREAMS
MELOTRONICAL

'Melotronical' is the third album by Hugo and Jessica and is a conceptual piece revolving around the evolution of an electronic Molecule into a living breathing Entity. This entity experiences several stages of life, goes through all emotions, love, hate, fear, happiness... The track list is arranged according to this evolution, and one can have a feel of each stage just by reading each song title, listening to the songs and lyrics. The finale starts with "Dimension Crusher", when all hope is lost and a new Universe is idealized through Reprogramming. Me, I just love the idea of taking the noun 'Mellotron' and turning it into a verb. The artwork for this album is far more dramatic than previously, and that fits in with the music which takes the last album and raises the intensity more than just one notch. In many ways it sounds as if Hugo has been tuning into Devin Townsend as when he rocks it out there is a real wall of sound that is so reminiscent of the mad Canadian's best work.

Hugo is also providing vocals here where the storyline suits, while Jessica doesn't allow the music to overpower her and manages to stay sweet and controlled, yet with emotion and passion. It is interesting to compare this with 'Poles' as in three short years the band have moved from something that is really enjoyable to something that is absolutely indispensable – quite a shift. Instead of being music that is worth searching out it is instead an album that belongs in every prog/symphonic/goth metal lover's collection. It is impossible to fault this album and of no surprise to me at all that of the five reviews posted on www.rateyourmusic.com, only one of them doesn't give it five stars. An awesome album – you owe it to your ears.
Oct 2011

FAIRCLOUGH & YUELL
MOMENTARILY

The line-up of this group is Peter Fairclough (drums & percussion), Hayley Youell (vocals & keyboards), Fred Thelonious Baker (bass) and Dave Bainbridge (keyboards, guitar & bouzouki). Dave is probably the best known of the four due to his excursions with Iona, while I have come across Fred where he has been working with Fairport's Ric Sanders, but the other two names were new to me. Apparently, Peter has appeared with Keith Tippett, John Harle, Ute Lemper, Mike Westbrook, The Bournemouth Sinfonietta and many others and has released four albums either solo or with Keith, while Hayley has performed with The British Expeditionary Force, A Certain Kind of Person & Tiny Little Secrets.

While many progheads may search this out just for Dave's connections, they may be a little surprised in what they find, as here we have a very polished jazz band that are bouncing ideas off each other with some finesse. The musicians are all that one wants from a jazz band, in that they are all consummate experts, and the bass lines in particular

are just sublime, while Hayley has one of those voices that is so very much at home in a jazz club. It isn't nearly as challenging as the jazz I personally like to listen to, but if you just want something that is polished and could easily hit on the airwaves this then just may be for you.
Oct 2011

SEAN FILKINS
WAR AND PEACE
Prior to this, his debut solo album, Sean had made a name for himself with both Big Big Train and Lorien, and so I approached this with some interest. There are also many guest musicians involved, including Gary Chandler (Jadis), Dave Meros (Spock's Beard), John Mitchell (It Bites, Frost) and Lee Abraham (Galahad) so given that I also like all these bands I thought that we may just be onto a winner here. It commences with the sound of a kettle boiling and then someone making a cup of tea while listening to a brass band playing "Jerusalem" on the radio. Yes, it's all very English in the extreme but I don't get it. My initial reaction was that Kiss did it much better at the beginning of 'Destroyer' many years earlier so why bother? But my initial reaction soon faded as we were flung headlong into "The English Eccentric" which moves from electric to acoustic guitar as the mood and style moves here and there. Sean has a great vocal style, and soon I was lost in the world and had almost forgiven him for the over-indulgent start.

The longest song on the album is "Epitaph For A Mariner", and it starts with a church organ and a young singer singing the first verse of "For Those In Peril On The Sea". As soon as I heard this, my feeling on the album took a major twist and I found myself listening intensely to what was going on. I was raised in a fishing community in the West of England, where not only do our churches have the standard Harvest Festival but also Harvest of the Sea. That hymn is something I sang many times when I was younger, as it was always a major part of the service when the community asked for the trawlermen to be watched over and brought back safe. Although not many fishermen were lost at sea, it always greatly affected the town when it happened. I found myself back in my youth, feeling very English (these days I am a proud Kiwi), and feeling that I was starting to understand the album and what Sean was attempting to achieve.

Overall, I feel he managed it, and the result is a prog album that is indeed very English in lots of ways, looking backwards and also forwards to the future and one that is well worth investigating.
Oct 2012

FINAL CONFLICT
RETURN OF THE ARTISAN
Back in another lifetime I was sent a cassette of the third album by a young neo-prog band, but unfortunately it was faulty and didn't play properly. I wrote to the band (email

didn't exist back then) and I was promptly sent a CD instead, the very first of the thousands I have received to review since then. Soon afterwards I saw them play at The Standard (I think with Landmarq, but maybe it was Mentaur?) where they then gave me my first t-shirt. So, Final Conflict have a special place in my personal neo-prog history and when I started writing reviews again after some time away, Andy Lawton was one of the ones I contacted to inform them of the fact. Andy then kindly sent me their latest album, which is what I am playing now. From those heady days of the early Nineties only Andy and Brian Donkin remain, but it is not only the membership that has changed as while I enjoyed the early albums ('Quest' is well worth tracking down) the guys have undertaken a major step change.

While the twin guitars and vocals are still important, what we have now is a band that is polished and in total control, ensuring that they provide an edge to the music so that while the keyboards of Steve Lipiec are incredibly important it is the guitars that shine against the backdrop. The rhythm section also adds to the overall sound as Barry Elwood often maintains a lead melody line while the rest go off on tangents, and Henry Rogers' drumming provides an additional depth. While he is happy to maintain the beat and keep everyone on the straight and narrow, there are also times when he provides powerful fills and touches that takes the menace to a new level. He is a very 'heavy' drummer, none of this arty-farty stuff; he hits the kit hard and ensures that everyone knows that this is a rock band first and foremost.

There have been quite a few bands from the late Eighties/early Nineties who have been delivering the goods over the last eighteen months, and Final Conflict are up there with the leaders of the pack. Hard-edged neo-prog with hints of Camel, Marillion, Winter and IQ, this is an album to savour.
Jun 2013

FLESHGOD APOCALYPSE
LABYRINTH
These Italians first became known when they released their debut two track demo in 2007, which then got released as part of a 4-way split. In early 2008 the band started to perform live in the Italian and European underground scene supporting bands like Behemoth, Origin, Dying Fetus, Hate Eternal, Suffocation, Napalm Death etc. At this time, they were known for their work as a brutal death metal band, but soon started to move into a more symphonic area, combining the brutality with choirs and orchestras. In 2011 Francesco Ferrini, the pianist and orchestrator who had worked with the band from the beginning, joined as full-time member which enabled them to have even more grand symphonic arrangements on 'Agony', while 'Labyrinth' takes it to a whole new level.

Somehow, the combination of a death metal band at full power with an orchestra also giving its' all enhances the brutality and rawness, as well as providing a very different dynamic. There are moments during this album when the listener just must take a step back in awe as the combination of choirs, strings, brass and metal with death growls is incredibly powerful. If ever music could be described as being totally 'over the top' then it is this.

The mixing and mastering work of Stefano "Saul" Morabito is just stunning, with everything perfectly balanced. In fact, the only real concern I have about this is how on earth are they going to be replicate this in a live environment? Brutal, symphonic, powerful, amazing. This is one of the finest metal albums you will come across this year, whatever the sub-genre.
Sep 2013

THE FLOWER KINGS
BANKS OF EDEN
And so The Flower Kings are back with their first album in four years, although most of the guys have been busy in other projects in the intervening time. I must confess to a love/hate relationship with the band, as while they have consistently produced great music over the years, there have also been times when they need to take a hatchet to their work and undertake some serious editing. I have only managed to see them in concert once but must admit to being suitably impressed and my then eight-year-old daughter sat on the stage at Roine's feet entranced by what was going on. There has always been a nagging feeling at the back of my mind that I ought to love everything TFK do without reservation, as they are mining a type of symphonic prog I have always enjoyed, but against that I also had the view that Roine's solo album which gave the group the name was actually superior to anything the group had managed to achieve.

So when this arrived to review I was more than a little cautious – a quick glance at the track listings showed me that although most of the songs were of the roughly six minute mark, opener "Numbers" was more than four times that length. So even before putting it on I already knew what it was going to sound like – wrong. To my ears this is easily the finest thing that TFK have ever achieved – there is a sense of direction that I haven't heard before. Even "Numbers" feels like a fully constructed piece without the meaningless noodlings I had come to expect. This is an album where everything is right. It is hard to put it into words, but if like me you felt that they really hadn't managed to come up with the goods then that is no longer the case. From start to finish this is a proghead's delight and I only hope that we don't have to wait so long for the next one.
Sep 2012

THE FLOWER KINGS
DESOLATION ROSE

Back in 1994 (wow, nearly 20 years!) I received a CD in the post by A Swedish musician called Roine Stolt. At the time I hadn't heard any Kaipa (since rectified) so I had no idea who he was, but the title track of that album was on my player repeatedly. He soon formed a band of the same name, and since then I have followed their career with interest. There was a time when in the prog world it seemed that they could do no wrong, but I got to the point where I no longer looked forward to new TFK albums turning up as I felt that they had become self-indulgent and needed a lot of editing which they weren't receiving. For me the turning point was 'Adam and Eve', which was easily their best album for many a year, and I was lucky enough to catch them on tour with that album (it was also the first gig I ever took my youngest to, she was 8 and still has the t-shirt).

So, would this be a continuation of the wonderful work they have been undertaking recently, or a return back to the bad old days? The first clue is in the track listing, with just one lengthy number, and that is only 13 minutes, which is just getting warmed up for The Flower Kings. The whole album is under sixty minutes in length, and the last two numbers only just get to six minutes when joined together! But for me it works, it really works. This is symphonic prog with a purpose, gone are the meandering never ending solos and passages where the band had seemed to have lost their way, and instead we have progressive rock music that has a direction and clear intent yet has lost none of the power and impact. These guys are incredible musicians, with great vocals and harmonies, and now they have added into that mix some powerful songs that work on all levels. I gave the last album five stars, and it has taken a lot of internal debate as to whether this is as good or should be marked slightly less. But the crunching riffs in "Dark Fascist Skies" really grabbed me, along with some great piano and lyrics. Yep, this is their second five-star album in a year. Let's hope they keep it up.
Dec 2013

FORGOTTEN SUNS
INNERGY

This 2009 album was the first in five years for these Portuguese proggers and saw a change not only in lead singer but also in their direction. When they first started these guys were heavily influenced by bands such as Marillion, but it is obvious that they have more recently been listening to Dream Theater and possibly Threshold which has meant that their music has become somewhat darker and heavier. Apparently in between 'Snooze' and 'Innergy' they opened for bands such as Fish, The Flower Kings and Pain of Salvation but if any of these now influences their musical style it is the last. This is prog metal that is on a roll – it flies with an exuberance not often heard with many bands, and it pervades the album. This is a joy to listen to – a real delight. Where there needs to be complexity it is there, melody always, but if there is a requirement for a simple crunching chord then these guys definitely deliver.

If you have heard the earlier albums, then all I can say is that while they were good works, they didn't show just what these guys were capable of. There are still some longer numbers that allow the bands to spread their muscle, but with nothing above 13 minutes there are no real epics. If you enjoy your prog heavy and metallic, with loads of symphonic soaring vocals then this is for you. And if you don't think that you like prog but listen to symphonic rock such as Therion then this album happily straddles the pigeonholes and is something that is definitely worth seeking out.
Jan 2012

41POINT9
STILL LOOKING FOR ANSWERS

You just have to read the band biography, as it is one of the best that I have come across in years. *"41POINT9 came about in a dark, cobweb filled corner of Bob Madsen's mind. One day whilst navel gazing, he thought to himself, "My, there's a lot of lint in there." Err..... umm.... scratch that..... what I meant to say is..... he thought to himself, "If its unlikely I'll ever make money making music, then I'm just gonna make music that I want to hear and that I enjoy making" With that decided, he went back to wondering why the lint was blue when he was wearing a red sweatshirt.......*

A few months later Bob (who plays bass by the way) tried to put together a band that would just be about having fun and writing the type of music that got the blood pumping, with songs that told stories and didn't skimp on the musical ideas and musicianship. At first he tried using local players to form the band, but that didn't quite work out so well. Then he remembered his old friend and former vocalist and founding member of Enchant - Brian Cline. Brian had done some great work on a Jazz album of Bob's and the two had had such a good time, it seemed like a no-brainer to work together again. He called Brian, begged, whined and cajoled until Brian finally acquiesced and agreed to become part of the band. Reportedly there are some photographs in a safety deposit box somewhere, that when Brian was reminded of their existence, tipped the odds in favor of his joining the band.

Next up, Kenny Steel joined the band. Fresh out of a recovery program for addicted metal heads, Kenny added the missing ingredient that Brian and Bob so clearly needed. Namely, he knew what the heck he was doing musically while Bob (and to a lesser extent Brian) were pretty clueless in this department. Kenny is the man with the fingers,... no, I mean it...... he actually has ten of the little things and they seem to know what to do most of the time. He routinely convinces them to do amazing things on guitar and keyboard and in the process helps out immensely when Bob and Brian paint themselves into a musical corner. So there you have it, the core of 41POINT9 was formed. This group of misfit musicians started writing music and having a blast doing it. Along the way somehow they convinced Nick D'Virgilio and Jimmy Keegan of Spock's Beard Fame to lend their prowess at smacking things to the album project. The world is just lucky they usually smack drums rather than random strangers. (however when they read this bio, Bob may get smacked a bit!)

After completing 7 of 9 songs for their debut album entitled "Still Looking For the Answers"- the project was picked up by Prog Rock Records and the album was released in early 2011. Unfortunately it is unclear whether Prog Rock Records really know what they have gotten into yet, however, the ink is dry on the contracts and all concerned are excited to see where this new collaboration of band and record company will lead. Damn the torpedoes, full steam ahead! and by the way, Bob is still confused about that blue lint........"

The album? Oh yeah, almost forgot about that. I really enjoyed the mix of Jadis with some more poppy elements, so much so that I have been playing it quite a lot. It doesn't really fit in with what most people believe progressive rock should be, as it is often too laid back and mainstream, but also too progressive to fit in with the radio crowd. In an ideal world this will be accepted with open arms as I really liked it, but it may fall between different camps of musical thought which could cause it issues. I know that the band had already been rejected for inclusion on ProgArchives (because I checked, and then asked if they could be), which is a shame as to me this is crossover that works really well indeed.
Sep 2013

THE FRACTURED DIMENSION
TOWARDS THE MYSTERIUM

The Fractured Dimension is a trio consisting of Jimmy Pitts on keyboards /piano, Jerry Twyford on bass, and Alex Arellano on drums/percussion. Pitts and Twyford were members of avant-garde dark metal band Scholomance (The End Records), and Arellano was the drummer for the progressive metal band Power of Omens (Elevate Records). So, on the basis of the above it would appear that this is a metal band with progressive tendencies. Right? Wrong! Firstly, they brought in a host of other musicians as guests to enable them to bring more diverse sounds to the table, and then decided that their debut album would be a tribute to Alexander Nikolayevich Scriabin. He was a Russian composer and pianist who initially developed a lyrical and idiosyncratic tonal language inspired by the music of Frédéric Chopin. Quite independent of the innovations of Arnold Schoenberg, Scriabin developed an increasingly atonal musical system, accorded to mysticism, that presaged twelve-tone composition and other serial music. Apparently the first major example of this is the 5th Piano Sonata of 1907 – now you know!

This use of atonal and extremely complex music means that this album has way more in common with free jazz than what many progheads would normally listen to. The musicianship throughout is stunning both in its' complexity and note density. Some of the drum fills are just incredible – "The Mathematics of Divinity" is a great example of their

work. Compelling and melodic, yet also totally off the wall with phased electric guitars also making their presence felt. While Jimmy is often at the forefront of what is going on, as he is usually providing the lead 'melody', it is the rhythm section that really makes this jump. If you are lucky enough to enjoy bands like Art Zoyd or Can then I definitely suggest that you give this a try.
Jan 2012

FRAMEPICTURES
REMEMBER IT

There aren't that many progressive rock bands from Portugal, and it must be said that this one had a very unusual beginning. They were put together as a group of session musicians to provide the music for a well-known pop star, but after rehearsing together for six months without a sign of the 'star' they decided that they may as well go their own way. Initially they planned to be an instrumental act, but after a while they decided that a singer was needed and with Tiago Delgado on board as the frontman, they set to recording this their debut album which was released in 2010. There is a really fresh feel to the music, and while they are obviously all masters at their instruments, they don't force it, but rather go with the flow. For example, in "Call For Me" (second longest song on the album at 12 minutes plus) the focus is going to be on the drive and interplay of the keyboards, guitars and drums, but what makes it for me is the incredibly complex bass lines that are going on behind it all, adding that extra layer of musicality and adding to the melody without distracting from it. The band has been compared to Sylvan by some, and I would agree with that although there is more than a touch of Porcupine Tree, Fripp and even some Japan.

This is complex progressive rock music that is vibrant and somehow manages to maintain an intimacy and immediacy even though there is so much going on. It really does feel like a cool spring breeze, relaxing at times yet with a biting edge at others. And yes, they haven't shied away from the epic either with the stunning "My Will To Live" which closes the album at some 26 minutes – there is some great guitarwork on this one. Well worth investigating.
May 2012

THE FUTURE KINGS OF ENGLAND
THE VIEWING POINT

This 2009 album was the third from the Suffolk instrumental outfit, featuring Ian Fitch (guitars), Karl Mallett (bass), Simon Green (drums) and producer Steve Mann (also keyboards). This album is one that is as rooted in psychedelic and space rock sounds as it is in progressive yet is so damn well played that anyone who likes even one of these genres will need to hear this. There are times when the Mellotron is lush and gentle, with delicate piano set against it yet there are others when the guitars are dominating proceedings with ease. This is a band that can be gentle and reflective, or coarse and hard – often all in the same song. It really does bring to mind some of the styles of prog that was coming out of Germany in the early Seventies with Amon Düül II being definitely front of mind.

This is music that definitely belongs to thirty years ago, but somehow is still invigorating and dynamic today – a joy to listen to from start to end.
May 2012

THE GAK OMEK
NONRENORMALIZABILITY

I was looking at Robert Burger's website (which is an interesting exercise in itself), and came across a review that I wrote in Feedback #84 for his previous album 'Return of the All-Powerful Light Beings' where I said "It is possible to be taken into the world of The Gak Omek and question what is going to happen next and where the journey is going to lead but at all times it makes musical sense and isn't a voyage into self-indulgence." Hmm, quite a statement – so how does this 2010 release stack up against that? Pretty damn fine is the answer. Robert is very much a one-man band and has a strong idea of the style of music that he is going to portray and isn't afraid to use multi-layered keyboards and guitars to get there.

There are times when he steps out to the edge and toys with the idea of moving into RIO, but for the most part he investigates what Ozric Tentacles would sound like if they had a far harder element to their sound and concentrated mostly on what the guitar could do. Whereas OT is always a pleasant trip (if you know what I mean), there is an air of menace and danger with The Gak Omek that is more exhilarating. Yes, there are elements of psychedelia and space rock, but it is combined in a daring fashion that ensures that Robert has a sound all of his own. He is a wonderfully fluid guitarist, who brings in electronica and voices in a unique style. Yet again this is a great album, and I am pleased to hear that he is now embarking on his fourth as we need musical adventurers like him.
Dec 2011

GALAHAD
EMPIRES NEVER LAST

Those who have been (un)lucky enough to have followed my reviews over the last 20 years will know that I have long enjoyed the music from this Dorset-based band. 'Empires Never Last' is the most recent studio album which came out in 2007 but for reasons that I can't explain I haven't written about until now. For those who previously haven't seen my ravings about this group I do have to confess to some links: Stu has stayed at my house when I lived in the UK, my wife and I were at his wedding, and I wrote the introduction to one of their rarities compilations. Now I've got that out of the way I would like to just say that this is the best thing they have ever done – and given my penchant for many of their other albums I still can't believe that I am saying that.

This band has changed so much from the one that won the Radio 1 Rock Show Rock Wars all those years ago, who first came to the notice of many progheads at the same time with their debut CD 'Nothing is Written'. True, in Stu, Roy and Spencer they have the same singer, guitarist and drummer and keyboard player Dean Baker has been there for a while now (line-up completed by bassist Lee Abraham) but it is the maturity and depth of the band that is such a surprise. Okay, they have been building to this for a long time with each release showing another side of the band, but here it all comes together in a major tour de force. It may open gently enough with "De-Fi-Ance", but this really is just an introduction for the band to kick off blazing into "Termination". Second song in and already Galahad have the listener by the ears and the balls. From here it is a rollercoaster ride of power and emotion, the band kicking together and showing that prog can be a really strong and dynamic force in the hands of guys who really know what they are doing and what they want to achieve.

If the last thing you heard by the band was their wonderful 'Sleepers', then you need to do yourself a favour and see what this band have grown into since then. The fact that Dean and Roy have been asked to join Twelfth Night in this year's reunion gigs show just what others in the scene think of them. You owe it to yourself to get this album!!
Mar 2010

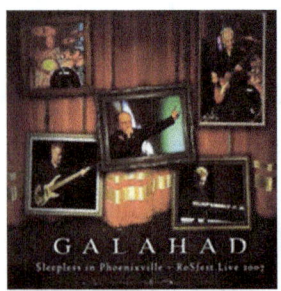

GALAHAD
SLEEPLESS IN PHOENIXVILLE
Through the years Galahad have often been linked with Poland, and for some reason of which I am not aware, it is through a Polish label that they have released this double CD digipak of their 2007 appearance at the American RosFest. Of course the main fare on offer is from 'Empires Never Last' and 'Year Zero', but we do get treated to a great version of "Bug Eye" from 'Following Ghosts' and two songs from 'Sleepers' with both the title track and the classic "Exorcising Demons" with just "Lady Messiah" from the very early days. Once upon a time I would not have been able to imagine a gig without "Room 801", "Richelieu's Prayer" and "Aqaba", but the band have moved on so much and now have such a depth of wonderful songs that obviously there just isn't room.

This is the strongest of their live albums just because of the material they have to offer as well as the tightness of the band. Roy plays with much more fire these days and Dean's attacking keyboards gives the band an edge that many others within the scene would love to command. While not forgetting the rhythm section who drive the band along, the main other factor in this band had to be Stu's vocals. He shows no sign at all of slowing down and from looking at the gigs coming up on their website obviously has no intention at all of doing so. He has always had great pitch and control and relishes performing in front of an audience, as anyone who has been lucky enough to see the band over the years will attest to. But here he is on top form, just listening to the final notes of "I Could Be God" shows his confidence and ability.

This album really does belong in any progheads collection and check the website for upcoming gigs. Lee is no longer with the band, but his replacement is none other than Neil Pepper who has been welcomed back into his old role.
Mar 2010

GALAHAD
IN A MOMENT OF COMPLETE MADNESS
So, here I go again. The first time I reviewed this album it was a tape (called 'In A Moment Of Madness') which was released in May 1989. By popular demand it was then reissued with additional tracks (and slight name change) on CD in April 1993, and it has now been reissued again with yet more additional material. So, what do I think of it more than 20 years since the original five songs were released? I love it. I always have. I heard this for the first time too many years ago to even think about and all of the songs are old friends. Just putting this CD into the player brings a smile to my face – how can anyone not love the sheer innocence of the early days of Galahad? The band that released 'Empires' is very different to the band that recorded these songs, albeit three of the five guys were on both. There is a joyous naivety of a band that had yet to record a CD, yet to appear on Radio One, yet to tour on both sides of the Atlantic. At least one number from the original five still appears in their setlist which shows just how strong the songs are.

Moving forward to 1993, the band re-recorded another three of their older songs – which was the first appearance with Galahad of bassist Neil Pepper who has recently returned to the fold to play with the guys again. In many ways this made the album more complete as not only was it now longer and more like album length, it closed a chapter.

But, now there's more!! Where were you on December 12th, 1992? I know exactly where I was, in a small village hall with condensation running down the walls watching two of my favourite bands, Freewill (I used to write their newsletter you know, those were the days...) and Galahad. Galahad subsequently released most of the concert as a cassette, and for some reason it has still to be released on CD, and three of those songs have now been added to this reissue. If you want to know what the guys sounded like eighteen years ago then here is your opportunity. This predates their official live album by more than three years and to me is a sheer joy as it was the time when I was seeing them play as often as I could.

I loved the cassette when I first heard it all those years ago, loved the initial CD reissue and love this one even more. If you ever wanted to hear what Galahad sounded like all those years ago then this is the CD you have to have.
May 2010

GALAHAD
OTHER CRIMES & MISDEMEANOURS

At the beginning of 1992 Galahad released a cassette-only compilation of rarities as 'Other Crimes and Misdemeanours'. It has now finally been made available on CD, subtitled 'An Erratic Musical History'. It is in a nice digipak format using the artwork from the band's only single release 'Dreaming From the Inside' (from 1987 – but actually isn't on this compilation, need to go to Part II for that). Here we have a band that was in a fluid state – although they did have the same lead guitarist and singer through this period, there are nine other musicians also forming part of the group at various times. Strangely, there is a far more cohesive element to this CD than one might imagine. Some of the songs (such as "Painted Lady", "The Chase", "Aries", "Welcome To Paradise") were re-recorded in later years while others such as the awesome (to my ears) "GSX" sank without trace.

It may be imagined that only die-hard Galahad fans will be interested in this, but actually anyone interested in the neo-prog movement from the UK should seek this out as there is way too much great music on this CD for it to just sit gathering dust, and all power to Polish label Oskar for getting it out there.
May 2010

GALAHAD
OTHER CRIMES & MISDEMEANOURS PARTS II AND II

Back in 1995 Galahad released a fan-club cassette, called 'Other Crimes & Misdemeanours II', which was then reissued on CD in 1997 including an introduction by yours truly. 'OCMIII' then followed in 2001 and now Oskar have made this available as a double CD digipak with a great booklet containing all the information you could wish for along with 40 minutes of additional music! If you wish to hear Galahad's only single (of which just 500 were pressed back in 1986) then this is the place. The two songs kick off proceedings which have been broken down into sessions, with the notes stating who was involved, where and when the recordings took place, and some history behind them.

Of the additional material, the 23-minute-long instrumental medley has reached some fame (Stu was ill and had to miss the gig) so it was great to hear it after all this time, along with an instrumental only version of "Lady Messiah". The bonus material on the second disc comprises a song called "The Pleasure House" that was recorded in 2000 and appeared on a concept album along with songs by other bands.

This is a wonderful release, packed full of information as well as great music, and I urge all fans of the band to seek this out at once if not sooner.
May 2010

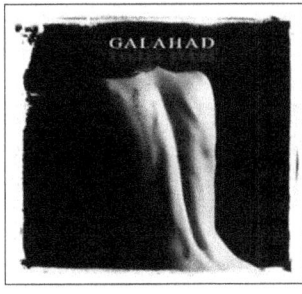

GALAHAD
BATTLE SCARS

Before I listened to 'Battle Scars' for the first time, I went back and played some of 'Nothing Is Written'. Incredibly that album is more than 20 years old, and back in the early Nineties I saw this band play many times. The line-up changed between that album and the follow-up, 'Sleepers', which came out in '95 – but some 17 years later four of the same five were involved with 'Battle Scars'. However, bassist Neil Pepper had left the band for a period and hadn't been back for long – it was an incredible shock to everyone that Neil was diagnosed as suffering from cancer, yet somehow, he made it through the recording sessions. The fact that he passed away in September 2011 at the age of just 44 leaving behind a widow and young family is something that many of us are still finding hard to deal with.

So, in lots of ways this was always going to be a hard album to review for me. Any opinion will always be subjective, no matter how objective the reviewer tries to be, and not only have I a long history with the band but I was aware that I really wanted this to be a great album, a fitting legacy as it were. But would it be?

As I said, before playing 'Battle Scars' I listened to 'Nothing Is Written' – when the band had won the Radio 1 Rock Wars and had been guests on The Friday Rock Show with Tommy Vance (those were the days). Back then they were young and dynamic, with much to prove. Here, all these years later they are not quite as young as they were, and in many ways are something of elder statesmen of the prog movement. But this is not a band to rest on their past achievements, as their last studio album 'Empires Never Last' amply proves. This is a band that is proud of what they have done previously, but also understand that they need to mature, and this is an album that shows that they have done just that.

In 'the new guy' Dean Baker they have a keyboard player with a huge palette and being able to bring to play many different sounds has enabled them to deploy different techniques to great effect. The title cut starts the album and the gentle choral and orchestral effects soon give way to a Freddie Mercury style chorus where Roy is finally allowed to crank up the guitar and deploy some strong riffs. Stu has always had a very melodic voice, yet he has managed to add just a touch of menace when the need arises which gives the song an extra edge.

Karl Groom's production, as always, is very polished and allows all the musicians to shine – this is complex stuff yet is brought together in a fashion that is immediate and melodic. It is music that can be enjoyed on first listen yet the more times it is played the more the listener will get out of it. Spencer and Neil locked in as if they had never been apart and this strong rhythm section allows Dean and Roy to run riot. I would love to hear "Reach For The Sun'" in a live setting as the impression is that this has been written so that they can really turn this up and blast out. There may be a few Ozric style keyboard sounds, but the star of this is the repeated riffing and the controlled passion.

Galahad in 2012 have produced an album that would be very recognizable to the people who used to go and watch them at Mr. Kyps in Poole yet is also very much the band that these days headlines prog festivals in Europe. At the very end of the album is a nod back to times past, as they revisit the title cut of their 1995 album 'Sleepers', and in many ways is quite different to the rest – showing just how much the band has changed. But it is great to hear it, as I for one always thought it contained Neil's best basslines and yet again, he proves what a great musician he was. Later this year Galahad will release another album, 'Beyond the Realms of Euphoria', which was recorded at the same time – it will be interesting to see just how that will compare as 'Battle Scars' is a winner on all counts.
Apr 2012

GALAHAD
THE CHRISTMAS LECTURE

I don't often review the same album more than once, but here I'll make an exception given that the last time I wrote about this was in 1993. Back then this album had been released on cassette, and until recently that was still the only format that this was available in (if you could find a copy anywhere). But the band have recently made it available to download from their site so now seems a good time to revisit it. But, before I even mention the album itself, it is necessary to put it into context.

Back in 1992, two brothers (one of whom was landlord of the village pub) were very much into prog and were getting fed up of having to travel for concerts– so the simple solution was to bring the bands to them. The village hall was literally the other side of the road to the pub, so why not approach some groups? They asked Galahad if they were up for it, and a short while later asked Freewill if they would be the support act – and so in July a group of us made our way to the sleepy village of Whitchurch not knowing what was going to be in store for us. I don't think the people of Whitchurch were ready for a load of progheads descending en masse (but some nice ladies did try to picket the hall), and it quickly became apparent to all that this was going to be a huge success.

So, in December that year there was a two nighter, the first night being headlined by Pendragon with Final Conflict in support, and the second night by Galahad, again with Freewill and openers this time being local folk-rock act The Morrigan. There was the opportunity that night for the bands to record to DAT, and both Freewill and Galahad availed themselves (I love the Freewill set – which has never been made commercially available). It was these tapes that allowed Galahad to release the live tape 'The Christmas Lecture'. Now, the band had only recently settled on the line-up of Stu, Roy, Karl, Spencer, and Neil, with Neil having taken over bass duties from Tim earlier that year, and Karl was also relatively new as he hadn't been involved with the previous year's 'Nothing Is Written'. But even though the hall was packed, these guys weren't going to show any nerves.

Stu told me before the gig that it was going to be a very special gig, and that they were going to being playing covers and some very old songs (but not 'Exorcising Demons' – looking back at the gig review I wrote at the time I felt that was a bad choice and that they should just have played a two-hour set...). You can't tell from the music, but all the guys were wearing Santa hats and Stu started the gig in full Father Christmas costume – that didn't last too long as this was one of the gigs where there really was sweat running down the walls. The feeling in the hall was electric, and Galahad appeared as conquering heroes. There may have only been a few hundred there, but boy did we enjoy it.

This is still one of my very favourite gigs, even after the best part of 20 years, and to hear these songs played with such enthusiasm and passion (and a certain naivety as well) is a delight throughout. "Room 801" was always a great song live, with much more depth and passion than the studio version, "Sleepers" was being aired some three years out from when it would eventually appear, they played "The Knife", "Clocks" and even treated us to the end of "One For The Record"!

If you weren't there that night (and most of you weren't, be honest) then you missed seeing one of our finest prog bands at their very best in front of a crowd that wanted a good time. The gigs in the village hall went on for a while longer (I still can't believe that I saw Steve Hackett play a full gig in a church hall!!) before moving out to the Community College, but after a few years it had all stopped which is a great shame. When my third daughter was born in 1993 my wife was wearing a Whitchurch Red House t-shirt, and the night before our wedding later that year was spent by me and "young" Mark Colton at that establishment having a few libations. Listening to this album brings it all back as if it was yesterday (first time I saw Threshold was in Whitchurch as well thinking about it, saw Jadis there, and Martin Orford playing IQ songs as a solo artist was just stunning) – if you have never heard it, or wondered why this little tape garnered so much attention at the time, then you owe it to yourself to get onto the site and order it for yourself.
May 2012

GALAHAD
BEYOND THE REALMS OF EUPHORIA

Whichever way you look at it, this has been an incredible twelve months for Galahad, with the release of this their second new studio album within that period, as well as a tenth anniversary reissue of 'Year Zero' and a double CD set of Whitchurch adventures from the Nineties. But on top of all of that is the loss of Neil Pepper, who passed away from cancer not long after the recording sessions for the album was completed. To say that everyone involved with the band has been on an emotional rollercoaster is something of an understatement, and yet they have kept it together and here is the latest part of the story.

Dean Baker has had a huge impact on the overall sound of the band since he joined, and nowhere is this more obvious than on the first number, "Salvation I – Overture". It is totally keyboard driven, with elements coming in from dance as well as Jean Michel Jarre, yet when Neil and Spencer join it takes on a new life and when Roy starts riffing it becomes obvious that this was a beat driven rock number all along. If ever there was a song that hearkens back to 'Deconstructing Ghosts', then this is it. If anyone may be concerned that the band has decided to become Pet Shop Boys (and it has to be said that there are elements of that on "Salvation II – Judgement Day") then don't worry as in many ways this is the heaviest I have ever heard the band, although part of that heaviness is due I'm sure to the lack of guitars in places so when they come crunching back they really hit home. I'm sure that Karl Groom must have had a smile on his face as he turned the faders up and allowed Roy room to breathe. What makes this song (and in fact the album) is the interplay between the guys. They are so tight that you feel that they are a multi-headed progbeast. There are times when Neil and Roy are providing incredibly quick complex runs that one just can't believe that this is two guys and not one – the note structures are immaculate.

Galahad have moved a long way musically over the years, but they still don't forget their roots. Today's prog test is what Genesis number is alluded to near the end of "Guardian Angel"? The song starts with a classic Roy riff, with Neil and Spencer driving it along until Dean takes control and moves it into another direction. Just near the end is the musical nod, which apparently was accidental on the part of Dean, but Stu and Karl heard the sound and knew here was an opportunity to bring a smile to the face of progheads. It only lasts a few seconds, but you'll know it when you hear it – not a steal at all, but a homage to one of the band's musical influences. I love this album, from start to finish – but something very special is the closing number. To celebrate their 25th anniversary Galahad decided to re-record a 'classic' for each album, so "Sleepers" appeared on 'Battle Scars' and here we have "Richelieu's Prayer". What makes this special is that Mark Andrews makes a recorded appearance with Galahad for the first time since 'Nothing Is Written', and the first time with Neil in Galahad. Mark originally wrote the song and was great friends with Neil and although they had played with each other in certain projects, they hadn't recorded together in Galahad as Neil joined after Mark had left. There is some extremely delicate piano on this, and they have managed to move it to a new level while retaining some of the original feel from 20+ years ago. This is a song that I always associate with a gig at King Arthur's Court (somewhere in another lifetime) where Stu passed out some party poppers to the usual suspects who he knew would be in the front row and asked us to all release at the same time when he sang "like a timebomb". It has always been one of my favourite songs and Stu shows that all these years on he has lost none of his range and his power and note control if anything has improved.

So, to sum up. This is one of the finest prog albums that you will ever hear, no matter what name is on the cover, and is certainly Galahad's finest work to date. The guys are all on top form, and Karl Groom has captured the very essence of the band and distinguished the instruments so that even when everything is blasting away there is still perfect clarity of what is taking place. I have been an advocate for the band for 20 years and know that I am always going to be biased. But I dare anyone to play this and not honestly give it top marks. Album of the year? I should bloody well think so.
Sep 2012

GALAHAD
WHITCHURCH 92/93: LIVE ARCHIVES VOL. 2

May 22nd, 1992, saw Galahad headlining again at The Standard, Walthamstow, this time with a five-piece Freewill (which only lasted a couple of gigs before moving to a four-piece) in support. It would have been auspicious in itself in that it was only a month since their last gig at London Astoria yet in between they had settled in a new bassist in Neil Pepper (Tim Ashton having moved to Japan), but what was also of interest was two shady characters in the audience (okay, there would have been lots of shady characters, me and Matt Ellis for starters...), Pete and Dave Martin. Pete was landlord of a village pub and thought it would be a great idea to hold prog concerts in the hall which was the other side of the street. And for the first gig they wanted the same bands from that night, Galahad and Freewill.

Now, no-one really knew what was going to happen, but on July 18th, 1992, a few of us descended on a sleepy village not far from Basingstoke. In the village hall there was corrugated cardboard over the windows to act as noise insulation, and it didn't really look like a prog haven. Could it ever be more than a one-off?

Being a contrary person by nature, I am going to review the second disc of this two-disc set first, just because I feel that is the right way to do it. This is an audio recording of the above gig, capturing the band in full flight. I had forgotten just how powerful a rock act Galahad are in concert; this was my third time seeing them that year and this disc brings it all back. The sound is really good all things considered, so I presume that it was recorded on DAT through the mixing desk as this is definitely not an audience recording. It is raw, it is powerful, it is dynamic, and shows the band just as they started moving away from 'Nothing Is Written' and towards 'Sleepers'. Only two 'new' songs were aired, "Dentist Song" and "Exorcising Demons", with the rest being from 'NIW' or earlier. This was one of the few times I heard them play "One For The Record", one of my personal favourites from 'In A Moment of Madness', but for many reasons the highlight of this set is "The Automaton". This was one of Neil's finest moments, he may not have played on the original but here he owned this song, not just because of the solo but with the different playing techniques he utilised which drove the attack. To be honest, I would be urging people to get this just to see what this band sounded like twenty years ago when they were still young and precocious. But what about the first disc?

The gig went well, lots of locals turned up, and it was obvious that this was the beginning of something special within the prog scene. More gigs took place at Whitchurch, including Galahad and Freewill (this time also with The Morrigan) back at Christmas. The following year they were invited back for their third appearance, this time with Shadowland in support, and this time it was recorded on video and audio. Lo and behold, that is disc one. Now, as this is a single camera the focus is on Stu, while Neil and Roy do also feature quite strongly but Karl and Spencer only appear on wide shots. It was never expected to be made commercially available but was for a private collection, so don't get this expecting multi-camera high definition. This is someone at the back of a very sweaty and loud group of people making a recording, and to be honest they have done a bloody good job. I'm not too sure about some of the effects deployed, but I am just glad that someone had the presence of mind (and the equipment, it wasn't cheap back then) to record the boys back in the day when Stu had hair……This saw a move towards newer material including "Sleepers", "Learning Curve" and "Before, After & Beyond" (and even a cover of "Sylvia"). Stu makes the comment that the next album will be out in 1998 the way it was going, he was wrong in that they got 'Sleepers' finally out in 1995 some two years after the gig but shows some of the frustrations they had at the time.

Overall, this is a great release, and for me brings back many great memories and for those who followed the British prog scene in the early Nineties I am sure that it will do the same. And if you weren't there then it just shows you what you missed.
Oct 2012

GALAHAD
YEAR ZERO 10TH ANNIVERSARY EDITION

It is safe to say that the end of the Nineties and into the Millenium was a trying time for Galahad. From the middle of 1992 until 1998 they had kept the same line-up, but in 1998 not only did they have to find a new keyboard player but also Roy Keyworth had left. Given that Roy was the only original member apart from Stu, this was quite a shock to everyone involved with the band and I clearly remember hours of conversation with Stu at the time. Luckily Roy returned the following year, and with new keyboard player Dean Baker on board they started work on 'Year Zero'. Galahad have never been afraid of pushing boundaries and had released albums as Galahad Acoustic Quintet and Galahad Electric Company, but here they stayed much more within the prog field but changed their approach.

This is their only concept album (so far), with one piece of continuous music broken down into fifteen digestible chunks (to make it easier for CDs) and they had clearly spread their musical wings. In fact, it takes until nearly halfway through the second track for the album to become recognisable as Galahad, as they are utilising the talents of Dean on keyboards to take the music in a new direction. He certainly brought a great many new sounds and effects to the band, some sounding much more like Hawkwind or Ozric Tentacles than Genesis! When Roy starts riffing it soon becomes clear that this is the old band with a lot of new ideas, which even allowed for John Wetton to sing a few lead lines, which certainly confuses the ear as he is quite different to Stu but was trying to sing in Stu's style.

It would be easy to fall into the cliché and say that this is the album where Galahad grew up, yet in many ways that is very true. They started with a clean palette and brought many new styles and colours to their sound, so many that at times it is hard to think that this was the same band that brought us 'Nothing Is Written'. Except of course it isn't. They had already been through a few keyboard players and bassists by then, and everyone was older, and that is reflected in the music that is far more mature and thoughtful. There is space, which allows the music to live and breathe.

That isn't to say that this is a sit back and relax mellowed out album, but rather one where ideas and energy have been allowed to flow and grow. "Charlotte Suite" is a short instrumental interlude and is instantly recognisable as Galahad, yet on the following "Haunted" it is only Stu's distinctive vocals that mark it out as being by them.

This is the tenth anniversary edition which is a double disc digipak, with the second disc containing a rare live performance of 'Year Zero' taken directly from the desk of a Galahad show at Mr. Kyps in Poole in 2003, by which time Neil Pepper had already left the band to be replaced by Peter Wallbridge. This is an interesting piece of history, and is fun to listen to, but is probably only going to be of interest to hardcore fans. Overall, this is a really nice set, and having listened to this album for the first time in a while I wonder just how many have overlooked this period of the band as this is a fine album. It marked the starting point of the journey that led to 'Battle Scars' and 'Feel Euphoria', and although the guys have been unable to have a stable line-up it was the 'Year Zero' members that recorded those albums. Worth investigating.
Oct 2012

GEKKO PROJEKT
ELECTRIC FOREST
This is a real hotchpotch of a debut album, and I love it. They ought to release "Black Hole" as a single as it is incredibly infectious, and I defy anyone playing this in the car not to be singing along to the chorus by the time it comes around for the second time. Now, singles are not something that one would normally think of with a prog band but one of the joys of this album is that if you don't like the style of the song you are listening to then don't worry as there will be another one along in a minute. There are elements of the instrumental "Cognitive Dissonance" that wouldn't sound out of place on a Weather Report album while Peter Matuchniak's guitar cuts through like Howe or Hackett but with more force.

This is mostly an instrumental album, and keyboard player Vance Gloster is credited as solo composer on most songs (and a co-write on two others) so it is not surprising that at times it can feel that the keyboards are taking over but these never last for long. Alan Smith has a great understanding of the way that drums can add to a song and at times he is very sparing, while at others he is dominating and bassist Rick Meadows isn't exactly a slouch either. There is a lot going on here, and musically it is all over the place with leaps in and out of fusion, jazz, and many other styles – but just think of it as a band pushing the barriers and just get into the groove. And don't forget to singalong to "Black Hole".
Sep 2012

GENS DE LA LUNE
ALORS JOUE!
This 2011 album is the second release from the band put together by Francis Décamps (ex-Ange), and there is a huge difference between this and the solo album which followed

the following year, as Francis should have stuck to his convictions and instead of going back over very old ground should instead have concentrated on the new material as this is a interesting piece of work. As with his other work, all the vocals are in French, but it isn't nearly as big an issue here as the music is just so powerful. This is classic 70's symphonic progressive rock with strong keyboards and guitars. The large use of extended Mellotron chords does mean that this could well have been released 30 or 40 years ago and it wouldn't have sounded out of place, so if Francis was attempting to recreate music from days gone by then he has achieved it.

The vocals are still an issue for me and provide a harsher edge which definitely gives them an edge, which is just too raw for my liking, and the production isn't nearly as polished as it could be, and the result is something that could well have been recorded live in the studio and it would have benefited from some additional finesse. But if I had to choose between this and the later solo album then this would win every time.
Jun 2013

GHOST CIRCUS
ACROSS THE LINE
This 2008 album was the second from multi-instrumentalists Chris Brown (from Tennessee) and Ronald Wahle (from The Netherlands) who 'met' in 2004 on a Neal Morse message board. In fact, these guys have never actually recorded in the same studio, but somehow have produced an album that sounds like a full band and not a project in any sense of the word. Chris provides vocals, lead guitar, rhythm guitar, bass guitar and keyboards while Ronald provides drums, percussion, keyboards, and rhythm guitar. Having 'live' drums makes all the difference to any band, and when these guys crank it up, they drive the music along. What makes this such a fine album is the sheer diversity of styles on play, so while they seamlessly move through symphonic prog, plenty of Moogs etc. they also bring in melodic hard rock and AOR-style vocals.

Melody is the heart of what they are doing, combined with a real sense of not wanting to stay within any particular style but instead going where the music leads them. This means that a Saga style prog epic such as "Holding On" has a great singalong chorus that will stick in your head and stay there. They even have a 25 minute plus song, and why not!? Accessible, fun, and full of balls, this is a great album.
Nov 2012

MICHAEL GILL
BLUES FOR LAZARUS
As one may surmise from the artwork, Michael Gill is a pianist/keyboard player/arranger and after some years of being in bands he has decided to promote himself as the main act

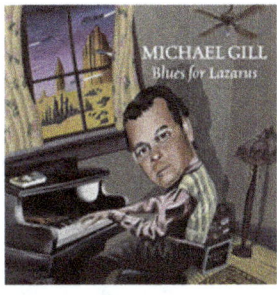
and this 2010 album is his debut effort. It is quite a mixture of style as he weaves a musical tapestry and has brought together musicians that have enables him to fulfill his ideas. He has a deft touch on the piano, but I found that I most enjoyed this album when he is in full flight – there are times during opener "Merlin's Journey" where it could almost be early Seventies Kansas. Sometimes the music and vocals don't really gel, such as on the title cut where the blues gravel vocals demand something a bit more definitive and dirty than the very sweet piano that accompanies it – true, the sax and bass do manage to put it in the right area somewhat, but overall the feeling is that it isn't quite right.

That aside, there are some strong moments on this album such as the evocative cover of Peter Gabriel's "Here Comes The Flood" which contains a perfect piano accompaniment to the stunning vocals of Callie Thomas. So, an album of contrasting musical styles and achievements, but worth seeking out with plenty of strong points.
May 2012

GILTRAP WAKEMAN
RAVENS & LULLABIES
It has been quite a while since I have heard new music from either Gordon Giltrap or Oliver Wakeman, so I was very intrigued indeed when I saw that this album had been released. Gordon is arguably Britain's finest acoustic guitarist, and his album 'Elegy' is so beautiful that it should be in every music lover's collection. Oliver on the other hand is probably more well known for being his father's son than for his own music, which is not right at all. The two albums he recorded with Clive Nolan are wonderful, with 'Hound of the Baskervilles' being indispensable, and the last album of his that I heard, 'Mother's Ruin', is also worth investigation. So, given what I knew of the background of these guys I expected to have an album full of acoustic guitar and piano/keyboard interplay and while there is some of that, there certainly isn't as much as I expected.

Although there are times, especially on the second disc, when it is just Gordon and Oliver there are others where it is a full band. Karl Groom has produced the album, and it is his Threshold colleague Johanne James who provides drums, while Paul Manzi (Arena, Oliver Wakeman Band) and Benoît David (Mystery, and of course he was with Yes when Oliver was with them) provide vocals, while Steve Amadeo is on bass. I have only really thought of Gordon as playing acoustic guitar, but he does also venture onto an electric while Oliver of course provides all manner of keyboards.

The album is fairly fractured in the sense that some numbers are beautiful instrumental duets while others are more band based and prog/AOR but instead of coming across as a jumble of ideas the result instead is one where each style stands up very much in it' own right but also provides a stronger emphasis on the others than it might otherwise have had. It is an album of delicacy and beauty, something that showcases the instrumental prowess of all involved without saying "look at me, aren't I clever?". Over the last few years, I have listened a great deal to Wakeman senior's work and was lucky enough last year to catch him at a piano concert here in NZ, and his style has obviously rubbed off on his son as there are times when Oliver's pianowork is just like his dad's, but it all adds to the joy of what is a wonderful album.

The version I am listening to has a second disc that contains some additional in concert and studio work and the in-concert material which features only Gordon and Oliver is what I expected the whole album to sound like before playing it, acoustic music that combines and interplays as two great musicians create something of beauty. Overall, this is a wonderful album, and I can only hope that they decide to take this journey further and record together again
Jun 2013

GLASS HAMMER
IF

Over the years the duo of Steve Babb and Fred Schendel have had a somewhat rotating door policy to musicians and styles, but here they have gone back to what many fans are going to love, namely classic progressive rock in the style of Yes. Now, it is in the style of as opposed to going out and copying what has gone before – and surely, they have been paid the ultimate accolade by that band, as not only has Jon Anderson appeared on a previous album but the vocalist on this 2010 release is Jon Davidson – who is currently the newest member of Yes, replacing Benoît David for the 2012 Australasian tour. Now, as I was lucky enough to see Yes in Auckland recently, I know just how good Jon D is in a live environment, so it is of course no surprise to hear him to be more than up to the task in the studio.

They may not have a Roger Dean cover, but in Tom Kuhn they have someone who again has prepared something in the style of as opposed to just rehashing something that came out thirty or more years ago. I read one review where a comparison is made between Glass Hammer and Citizen Cain and that makes quite a bit of sense – when CC was releasing albums in the early Nineties there was quite a lot of flak as it was stated that they were just doing what Gabriel had done with Genesis, but it has to be remembered that Peter had long left the band and the Genesis of 1992 wasn't anything like CC. Now, I really like 'Fly From Here' but this probably has more in common with the traditional Yes sound than that – and after 20 years GH still has the same two people at it's heart yet it took far less time than that for Chris Squire to go through two drummers, three keyboard players, two singers and three guitarists.

Anyone playing this or writing about this is going to compare Glass Hammer to Yes, but that isn't a bad thing. The question is not why does that have to take place, but more why on earth isn't this band better known and spoken about with the same reverence? This is a great album, whatever name is on the cover – if you like Yes then this is five stars and

essential. If you don't then don't bother, but it is your loss.
May 2012

GLASS HAMMER
COR CORDIUM
This 2011 release saw Glass Hammer as a four-piece, with additional guests. So, band leaders Fred Schendel (keyboards, guitars, vocals) and Steve Babb (bass, keyboards, vocals) were again joined by singer Jon Davidson and guitarist Alan Shikoh. Special mention should be made here of the artwork by Tom Kuhn, which is just stunning, even before the CD makes it into the player there is the feeling that the listener is in for something special and it must be said that the music doesn't disappoint.

Glass Hammer have always been heavily influenced by Yes (as well as Genesis, ELP and Camel), and having current Yes singer in their ranks will obvious strengthen those links, but this is much more than a band trying to recreate 70's glory days of someone else. True, there are times when the band do sound very similar, but there are plenty of others such as "Salvation Station" which is quite different indeed. Here there is liberal use of acoustic guitar, piano, swirling keyboards, punchy basslines (which have a very different sound to Chris Squire) and just the right amount of lead guitar to provide additional class. Then of course over the top of all of this are Jon's vocals. He has an incredible voice, lots of melody and control and a very pure clear sound. It is strange to think that he is a relative newcomer to GH, as it sounds as if he has always been there.

Like all great prog albums, repeated playing rewards the listener, and whereas some albums can feel very heavy and somewhat tiring this has a freshness and light that carries the listener along – so much so that during "Dear Daddy" I found myself smiling just because the music contains a real joy. Yet again Glass Hammer have released an album that belongs in every prog lover's collection, and I look forward to the next one with real anticipation.
Jul 2012

GLASS HAMMER
PERILOUS
This is the third album from the same GH line-up with Steve Babb (bass, keyboards, backing vocals) and Fred Schendel (keyboards, guitars, backing vocals) with Kamran Alan Shikoh (guitars) and Jon Davidson (vocals) along with Randall Williams sessioning on drums plus assorted guests. This settled line-up has assisted the band in quality while the borrowing of Jon for some other group has obviously aided the profile (I note that Glass Hammer are on the same cruise ship tour as Yes). GH have always put a lot of thought and care into their releases, so that the purchaser is already engaged before hearing a single note and the same is here again with great artwork and of course the booklet also contains all the lyrics.

Here we have a concept album (not unfamiliar territory for GH) which is based on what happens when we walk through the gates into the cemetery beyond and start a journey which can be 'Perilous'. The album kicks off with a string section, that leads into a fairly length instrumental introduction to "The Sunset Gate". This shows to me that Steve and Fred really know who their listeners are, and that they will be ready to spend the time and invest in what is going to be a great listening experience instead of looking for a quick fix hook or bridge. Long before the vocals started, the guitars and keyboards have struck an intense relationship with influences from classic prog bands abounding. An important thing to mention here is that while Glass Hammer have been influenced by the classic groups of the seventies, they are not just plain plagiarists but instead are doing something new while also casting a look back to what has gone before.

There is no doubt that Jon Davidson has a remarkably similar vocal style to Jon Anderson, that is why he has been chosen to replace him, but these guys are not Yes clones. One of the most effective songs on the album is "In That Lonely Place" which starts with classical guitar and vocals from Amber Fults which takes the music in a totally different direction and even when Jon joins in the duet he sings in a different way to normal. Yes, the Mellotrons come in to add backing but this is all about simplicity and context; prog does not need to be bombastic and multi-layered to be incredibly effective. Maybe now that Glass Hammer are gaining more recognition thanks to the Yes connection they will become well known to a much wider audience. This album certainly provides the basis for being able to do that.
Dec 2012

ANDREW GORZYYCA
REFLECTIONS – AN ACT OF GLASS

Andrew Gorczyca passed away in 2004, and his drummer brother Chris took it upon himself to complete this album – searching for the right musicians that could do justice to his brother's legacy. When you look at the people involved with this album, it is no surprise that it took so long with Spock's Beard and Enchant just some of the bands involved. The list is as follows:- Adrian Belew (guitars, vocals), Bryan Beller (bass), Nick D'Virgilio (vocals), Shawn Farley (bass, guitars), Chris G (drums, keyboards, percussion), Randy George (bass, keyboards), Andrew Gorczyca (vocals), Wil Henderson (vocals), Phil Keaggy (guitars), Mike Keneally (guitars), Ted Leonard (vocals), Dave Meros (bass), Rich Mouser (guitars), Rick Musallam (guitars), Ryo Okumoto (keyboards), Billy Oskay (violins), Greg Strickland (bass) and Marc Ziegenhagen (keyboards). Phew!

It is always problematic with so many musicians to get an overall band feel, but generally this has been accomplished. Musically, this is prog-lite mixed with AOR, and it feels much more like a snack than a four-course meal. Did I enjoy it? Certainly. Would I play it again? Probably. Would I play it repeatedly? And there's the rub – it is a fun album, and certainly there isn't anything inherently wrong with it, but is just a little too lightweight for me, not really proggy enough for that part of me that wants complex

music and not enough hooks for the Journey lover in me. It is certainly enjoyable and is worth hearing at least.
Oct 2011

ROB GOULD
THE BROKEN ROAD

This is the sixth solo album from Rob Gould (Fula, Ashtar) and contains guest appearances from members of both bands and is the first time that his solo works have included vocals. His pianowork reminds me a great deal of Roger Eno, with a simplicity and starkness that contain a bleak beauty. This is incredibly atmospheric and well-layered music that has elements of artists such as Mike Oldfield, Tangerine Dream, and even Pink Floyd. At times there are minimal notes or chord changes, but it all works incredibly well and is almost ambient at times. I did find that if I played it on headphones while doing something else that I often lost track of the music as it swept along without making much of an impression, but in the still of the night with just the stars and moreporks for company (if you don't already know they are our native owls with a very distinct call) then this is perfection on a disc.

There are some great vocals and guest musicians that add an extra element to this album, and if you enjoy your music to be thoughtful with a simple beauty then you can do no wrong with this. This is available directly from his website
Nov 2012

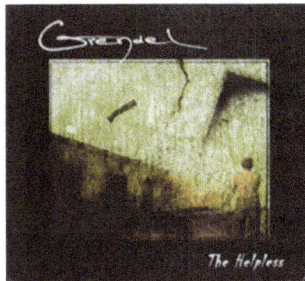

GRENDEL
THE HELPLESS

According to LastFM, there are nine bands with the name Grendel:-
1) Grendel is a harsh ebm artist from Netherlands.
2) Grendel is a melodic death metal band from Finland.
3) Grendel is a Polish progressive rock band.
4) Grendel is a black metal band from Italy.
5) Grendel is a black metal band from the UK.
6) Grendel is a power metal band from Spain.
7) Grendel is a black metal band from Germany.
8) Grendel is a split-up folk metal band from Estonia.
9) Grendel is a hardcore/avant-garde metal band from France.

Now, I think it is safe to say that eight of these acts are probably inspired by the monster of the same name from the saga 'Beowulf', and that the other took their inspiration from Marillion's song (which was about the monster – and still their finest work). So, can this Polish band bear comparison with Marillion, or any of the other prog greats?

I first played this album after listening to Glass Hammer – which was a bad idea as I

found myself comparing the two and it really is chalk and cheese. It is not that this is a poor album, and I have found more to like in it the more I have played it, but rather that it is rather uninspiring, and a pale washed out imitation of what prog can be like. That the guys can play, especially guitarist Sebastian Kowgier (who also provides vocals – in English) is never in doubt, but is this something to which I will be returning to time and again? The answer to that is sadly no. These guys concentrate on providing atmospheric prog but miss the mark and come out as Marillion-lite, and there are many more Polish bands that I would rather listen to (SBB, Millenium, Satelite, Votum, Quidam, Collage, Riverside etc.).
Aug 2012

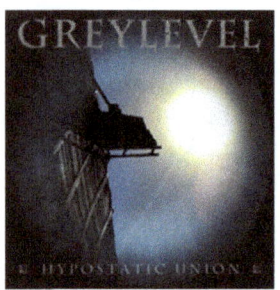

GREYLEVEL
HYPOSTATIC UNION
Between 2001 and 2005, Derek Barber (vocals, keyboards, rhythm guitars) was writing songs and recording them in a home studio, distributing them to family and friends. Then in 2005 he was joined by singer Esther Barber and guitarist Richard Shukin and together they worked on the material and released 'Opus One'. That gained them interest from ProgRock Records who signed them up and the group then expanded with the addition of bassist Davis Friesen and drummer Tyler Friesen, and it was the five of them that worked on the songs of the follow-up 'Hypostatic Union'. These guys made be Canadian, but they have much more in common with British prog than anything from their own country.

Imagine early Porcupine Tree mixing with Menel-era IQ and Pink Floyd and you may just get some idea of what this band sounds like. There is often a wall of sound, both vocals and music, yet although it is like a wave crashing over the listener, all the individual instruments and parts are still full of clarity and substance. The only thing that I found jarring is the use of Eighties style keyboard sounds which just didn't work for me, apart from making me think that I ought to play more music from thirty years ago. There is a melancholia throughout the album, yet there is a feeling also that there isn't as much depth as there needs to be, so overall it doesn't seem quite right.
Sep 2012

GUAPO
HISTORY OF THE VISITATION
There are times, just times you understand, when I question my sanity. Having now played this album a few times I wonder how can anyone enjoy listening to music where it is at the very edge of the definition? I can honestly say that I don't think that I would have listened to this all the way through when I was younger – like broad beans and Brussel sprouts this is something that is almost exclusively the preserve of those who are older and can savour the experience. The band has been

going for 19 years, and currently comprises drummer and founding member David J. Smith with mainstays Kavus Torabi (Cardiacs, Knifeworld) on guitar and James Sedwards (Nøght) on bass, joined by recent addition Emmett Elvin (Chrome Hoof, Knifeworld) on keyboards.

Now as soon as I see the name Cardiacs I sit up and pay attention and have also enjoyed what I have heard from Knifeworld, but it is fair to say that these guys understanding of music here (the label helpfully provides some references such as controlled chaos, atonal harmony, uplifting darkness, and beautiful destruction) is quite different to many. They seem to mix RIO with prog, and while King Crimson is an obvious reference it is possible to also bring Magma, Univers Zero, elements of Can, The Mars Volta etc. Easy listening this is not.

This instrumental album only contains three songs, and the first of these is twenty-six minutes long so it is heads down and see you at the end. There are large similarities with free jazz; never quite veering into that territory although reedmen Thomas Scott and Dave Newhouse from Maryland avant jazz-rock institution The Muffins are some of the guests taking part. The label describes this as "Sun Ra jamming with Stravinsky", and if that makes you believe that this can be hard work to listen to, yet ultimately rewarding, then you would be right. This will only appeal to a small part of the music buying public, but those who enjoy finding something different need to investigate further.
Mar 2013

GUERILLA TREE
MENTAL LEAPS
Sometimes it can be really hard to find out information regarding a band. True, it is generally a great deal easier now than when I first started writing reviews more than 20 years ago, but some bands don't make it easy. If you go to Guerilla Tree's website you will be able to watch a video of the song "Indocyanine Green" and details of how to obtain this album as a totally free download or pay 11 euros to get a physical copy.

But if you want to discover anything about the band themselves then your work is going to be cut out for you. I think this is a debut album, and that the band hail from Germany, but it has taken quite a bit of work to get that far! The line-up is René Krov (vocals, guitar), Sascha Trojahn (lead guitar, vocals), Robin Steffens (bass), Chris Müller (keyboards) and Robert Braune (drums) and they play an interesting mix of prog metal that has obviously been heavily influenced by the likes of My Dying Bride. The eight songs are well crafted, with just a hint of darkness and feeling of sorrow that flavours each track. Opeth could probably be referenced a little as well, and the result is an album that is heavy both in terms of the metallic content and in the emotional. This is not music to lift the spirit, with Black Widow style keyboards and a general feeling of opression. Anyway, this is yours to obtain free from the band so what have you got to lose? Just go to the site above, and follow the instructions and you too could be playing what is to my mind certainly an interesting album although not indispensable.
May 2013

GUILL & JEM
TWO SIGNALS
This is the third album from Argentine Guillermo Guill Cazenave and American Jeremy Morris, following on from 'Two Seconds' and 'Two Suns', and in many ways is the most complete of the series. There has never been any doubting the musical integrity of the other releases but here they have taken it to a whole new level. At times this is classic space rock with a lighter take on Hawkwind while at others it is nothing more or less than the mighty Steve Hillage – with guitars combining with keyboards in a way that is solid Seventies. There are very few people these days who make instrumental albums as consistently exciting and interesting as this, and fans of Ozrics really ought to stand up and take notice as this will slot into their collection as well.

If I was going to fault this album, it is just that some of the backing music can seem a bit pedestrian at times, and this could probably had been taken to yet another level with a strong drummer, but that is just nit-picking on what is an album of gentle yet melodic guitar-led instrumentals that are a real delight to listen to. Music to drift away to as well as music to really enjoy in its' own right.
July 2011

GUILL & JEM
TWO SECONDS
This 2008 album was the second collaboration between Guillermo Cazenave and Jeremy Morris, and yet again they have concentrated on creating a soundscape that is beautiful and beguiling. Both of these guys have released many albums in their own right, as well as each collaborating with others such as Anthony Phillips, so it is of no surprise that the sound is polished and that the music is inspiring. In many ways this is a release that belongs in the Seventies, bringing together the prog of Floyd and Gong with the atmospheric ambience of Eno and the electronic cinemascapes of Tangerine Dream. They use acoustic and electric 12-string guitars that at times sound like Hackett, at others Hillage, and often like Gilmour. These combine with the more restrained keyboards to create music that the listener will immerse themselves in.

If you want an album to listen to with the lights turned low, and a good brandy in your hand, then it really doesn't get much better than this. As with all of Jeremy's recordings this is easily purchased through his website and 'Two Seconds' is a real delight.
Dec 2011

The Progressive Underground Vol 4

STEVE HACKETT
GENESIS REVISITED: LIVE AT HAMMERSMITH

Was there ever a band quite like Genesis? Through their ranks have been some of the most commercially acclaimed (Phil Collins, Mike & The Mechanics, Peter Gabriel) and critically acclaimed (Anthony Phillips, Tony Banks, Daryl Stuermer) artists of the last 40 years. But, to my ears there is one who stands head and shoulders above all these, Steve Hackett. Since leaving Genesis he has pursued many different styles, including classical, and has been in the odd 'supergroup' (GTR, Squackett) as well. His albums are always, without fail, finely crafted pieces of work and always immensely enjoyable. Back in 1996 he decided to revisit some of the Genesis songs he felt most close to, then repeated the exercise last year and toured with a show guaranteed to make any diehard Genesis fan drool at the mouth.

To put some things into context. Steve was with Genesis from 1971 to 1976, recording four studio albums with Peter and two with Phil. From those six (plus one solo song, which was co-written with Mike Rutherford so can justifiably be included) he has produced a live album of 150 minutes in length. Back in 2007 Genesis reformed and performed to massive audiences throughout Europe, but of the set they produced on their 'Live Over Europe' album only two complete songs are the same as here. Genesis moved on when Phil took over lead vocals, and again when they were reduced to just three in the studio, and many fans talk about the Gabriel period or the Collins period being their favourite. Me, I'll say that the Hackett period is the one that suits me best thanks very much. Of all Genesis albums recorded with Phil on vocals the first three are easily the best, and I'm not a massive fan of the albums pre-Steve (although "The Knife" is and always will be an absolute classic).

Listening to this album is at first a blast from the past, as I spent my formative years listening to these songs, but then it turns into something far much more. Musically Genesis has always been controlled by Tony Banks who is an incredible musician (and very under-rated), but although he is also a guitarist, he is first and foremost a keyboard player, so the arrangements have always put the guitars somewhat in the shade. Now we have classic songs (mostly forty years old remember) given new life by a guitarist in control of his own band, with the additional confidence of always being on the road and proving himself time and again. He has mostly stayed very true to the originals, but when he has the opportunity to crank his guitar out, he certainly does. "The Musical Box" may start gently, but it rips into a version that gives the song much more life and drama than one could ever imagine from the original. Also of particular note is the ending of "Shadow of the Hierophant" which is intense, powerful, moving, and compelling all at the same time.

This album is what I always refer to as a review killer as once it hits the player all I want to do is hit 'repeat' and it takes concerted effort to move on to something else. If I had to ask for one song that isn't on this set it would probably be "Squonk" but that is picking straws as we have everything else from "Supper's Ready" (all 27 minutes of it) to "Eleventh Earl of Mar" from the criminally overlooked 'Wind & Wuthering'. I could

play this album all day, every day, and just wished that I had been able to see this performed. But as I live on the wrong side of the world, I was unable to do so, so I will just have to keep playing this instead. Superb.
Dec 2013

HAKEN
THE MOUNTAIN
I was sat at my desk the other day when I was asked if I had yet played Haken's 'The Mountain'. When I responded by saying that it was on my list and hadn't got to it yet, I was told that I needed to. So, when I got home that night, I made the time to play it for the first time. It was a lot later when I was asked if I was going to go to bed, as I had just sat there in awe, taken away into a new musical world. To say that this is one of the finest albums to ever come out of the prog scene is something of an understatement, but accurate. I've just had a quick look on PA to see what others feel about this and note that there are two collaborator/expert reviews, both of whom give it 5*'s, and I am convinced that the only reason they have done that is because we're not able to give it anymore.

This is absolutely stunning stuff, arguably taking Spock's Beard to a whole new level. But, that argument would be flawed as they have instead looked to one of SB's influences, the incredible Gentle Giant (surely still one of the most under-rated British prog acts ever, and I know that they are rated highly, just not highly enough), and have moved on from there. Honestly, I have no idea where to start with writing about this. The vocals and harmonies are incredible, and they go from full on metallic monstrosity to a cappella in a way that should never be possible, but somehow with these guys it makes total sense. Metallic riffs combine with harmonies, strong bass with 'out there' keyboards, and the feeling that here is a band very much in control.

It is just not possible to fault this album, everything they do is accomplished and polished yet never loses that feeling of spontaneity and rawness that is so important. Unlike some progressive acts, there is nothing here that sounds contrived, the music just oozes honesty and passion. This is not something created by navel gazers in a sterile environment to prove how clever they are, but rather is the product of a band that are not going to conform to any pre-conceived ideas of what they should be producing but instead are out to do whatever they damn well please. I mean, what on earth is a prog band doing starting a song with a barbershop quartet? ("Because It's There"), but within the feel of the album it makes total sense with what they are doing.

My album of the year, of any genre, is Clive Nolan's 'Alchemy' (yes, I know it's only September, but given how often I am playing it I just can't imagine anything else getting even close). But, although that features many famed progressive performers, it is in fact a theatrical musical production as opposed to a prog epic. When it comes to prog, I am convinced that I have found my album of the year and am listening to it now, as this is one of the most exciting and vibrant pieces of work that I have ever come across. The way they can go from complex bombast to restrained and simple beauty, such as on "As Death Embraces" where the vocals and piano interplay is quite different to what has gone before, but still contains a compelling majesty.

Looking at reviews that have been posted in various places I note that not everyone shares my opinion, but life would certainly be boring if everyone had the same view on everything. However, if you have never heard Haken then the time to do it is now, and if you have, then you can rest assured that these guys have kept pushing the envelope to create something which is stunning, just stunning.
Sep 2013

HALF LIGHT
BLACK VELVET DRESS
Polish band Half Light were formed in May 2009 when vocalist Krzysztof Janiszewski and keyboard player Peter Skrzypczyk decided to join forces, the line-up being completed by the addition of guitarist Krzysztof Marciniak. They describe their musical purpose as wishing to carry the listener into an intimate, warm, yet sometimes turbulent half-light, where a man, lost in the contemporary, may find a hideout and discover himself. They do this by using electronic sounds and combining these with the natural vocals and subtle guitar so that the listener is moved between music that is very electronic and almost Kraftwerk/Pet Shop Boys in style and something that is far deeper with lots of jazz and prog tendencies.

This is their third album already, so the guys haven't been hanging around and it is extremely well polished indeed. Like many Polish bands they sing in English, and in many ways, it is accessible although probably at the end of the day just not quite to my style. For me the combination of electronic and pop (and of course an annoying drum machine) isn't what I like to listen to, but conversely, I can imagine this being very successful indeed in the current environment. It is all very good, but not for me.
Nov 2012

HAZE
THE LAST BATTLE
A long time coming, this is the first CD of new studio recordings from Haze for over 25 years ('Stoat & Bottle' was released in 1987). The classic line-up of Chris McMahon, Paul McMahon and Paul Chisnell have been joined by Cat & Ceri Ashton of The Outlandish Knights (which is the ceilidh band which features all five of them – so one could argue that this is an Outlandish Knights album with Haze influences, or possibly the other way around). One thing these guys have always managed to do is keep different bands going with different names and musical styles (I have seen Chris onstage at least three times, but never as part of Haze!). So here we have

a prog album with plenty of folk influences. While Haze have always swapped instruments and all taken lead vocals, the addition of the Ashton sisters who are both happy on woodwind and strings has given the music a further depth and a much stronger folk sound.

If you can imagine classic Seventies rock mixed with Red Jasper and later-period Fairport Convention, then may just get close to what this album sounds like. It is all over the place in terms of what is going on so a folk number may get blown away by an electric rocker while the drum kit may be replaced by congas or a yambu. This is all about quality melodic songs, not about being flash and over the top so consequently the listener soon finds themselves wrapped into their world. All three guys take on lead vocals, sometimes duetting or swapping lines, which again adds to the depth of the album.

I greatly regret never having seen Haze in concert but do have fond memories of World Turtle (the McMahon brothers with a drum machine) who not only released incredible albums but were amazing live, and I can only imagine that Haze was even better! I would love to have been at the Haze 30th Anniversary show where some of these numbers were showcased for the first time. They have also tried a couple of these out with some of their other bands before settling them into Haze.

There is no doubt in my mind that Haze is one of the most criminally overlooked bands from the UK, whatever genre. These guys are all about producing class music that is accessible and layered that can be enjoyed from the very first play. Chris is the happiest guy I have ever seen onstage, always with a huge smile on his face, and isn't music all about having fun? Sadly, this turned out to be Paul Chisnell's swansong as he had to retire due to suffering severe tinnitus. So, keeping it in the family the new drummer is Danny McMahon (Paul's son) while the band has permanently expanded to a four-piece with the full-time addition of Ceri Ashton. If you go to the website not only can you order the album (either physical or downloads) but you can also see the details for each song, who played what and the story behind it plus the lyrics. Of course, while you're there check out the gig list, what other items they have for sale and of course the rest of their bands. If you haven't a copy of their 20th Anniversary double CD set, then there is just no excuse and you need to pick that up at the same time.
Apr 2013

HAZE
STOAT & BOTTLE
And so, in 1996 Haze released what was going to be the first of a trilogy of CDs, making available the recordings they made in the Eighties. At this time, I seem to remember that the band were no more, although Paul and Chris McMahon were working as World Turtle and were also in Treebeard with Haze drummer Paul Chisnell but given that these guys have resurrected the Haze name more than once as well as playing in other bands nearly every night of the week I could be wrong! A mere four years later and the second CD appeared, and as quick as a flash (okay, it took

another eight years) the final part arrived, 'Stoat & Bottle'. When they attempted to remix these, it was discovered that the original tapes were not exactly up to the task so instead they concentrated on just digitally transferring them. So, what this means is what I am listening to sounds close to how it would have been played back in 1987 (vinyl and cassette no less). That means that at least for the first song I found I was concentrating more on the quality of the recording than of the quality of the music, but soon moved on to discover the delights that are contained within.

The original album contains some gems that the band still play in concert today, such as "The Vice" which has always been one of my personal favourites. It is the longest song on the album, and it always amazes me that somehow Chris manages to switch between keyboards and bass so effectively when playing this in concert, the only other musician I have ever witnessed managing to pull this off with aplomb is Geddy Lee! As with much of Haze's music, this is driving over the top neo-prog with crunching guitars, swathes of keyboards, pounding bass all being muscled along by powerful drums. "Autumn" starts off as a blues number, with some strident soloing from Paul and it is the combination of different styles that makes this work so well.

There are lots of additional tracks, and while the sound is undoubtedly the product of being an old recording originally made on a budget by an underground prog act, there is no doubting that any fan of the band or of neo-prog in general will need to discover this further. These guys knows that the word 'rock' is as important as the word 'progressive' and provide plenty of blast to go with the finesse and skill. For me I enjoyed going back to hear the original versions of some songs I already knew, plus plenty of new ones, but for a newcomer to the band I would get one of their Anniversary show concerts first and then come back to discover some great music from a prog band that started in the Seventies and keep coming back for more.
Jun 2013

HAZE
30TH ANNIVERSARY SHOWS

It is incredible to note that Haze was formed in 1978, and that this 30th Anniversary concert is already five years old yet they are still gigging, have just released a new studio album, and show no signs at all of slowing down. When I moved to NZ I lost touch with Chris McMahon, but recently we started swapping emails and he sent me 'The Last Battle', the reissued 'Stoat' and this one. Given that they had already released a 10th Anniversary album and a 20th Anniversary (where I was thanked in the credits, which was much appreciated), there was always going to be an issue with repeated content, but they got around this by playing some rarely aired numbers, a few by World Turtle and Treebeard, and some songs which would later appear on the new album as well as the old favourites. In addition, they also extended their sound by moving away from the set trio of Paul Chisnell (percussion, vocals), Paul McMahon (vocals, guitar, guitar synth) and Chris McMahon (keyboards, bass, vocals) by bringing in Ceri Ashton to provide flute on various songs, who has since joined as a full member of the band. There are also a couple of guests on the final song of the night, namely Rog Patterson and Greg Smith from Twice Bitten, another Eighties band who never gained the recognition their music fully deserves.

The plan was to record two nights in 2008, but there were sound issues at the first gig in Kingston so only one song has been included from that set, a version of "Seven Stones" which they didn't play the following night in Sheffield. The rest of the songs are all from Sheffield, in the order in which they were played so if you were lucky enough to be there that night this was what you would have heard. Haze are one of the prog bands that I have never managed to catch in concert (in my defence they were gigging hard in the Eighties but didn't know about them until the Nineties when they were not as frequent), but I did manage to see World Turtle which was the McMahon brothers plus a drum machine and they blew me away that night (plus I have managed to catch Chris a few times as well).

All the guys are incredible musicians, and they blast through a set which contains just about everything a fan would want with "The Vice" and "Another Country" being real standouts, while they also play "Let Go" which is my favourite World Turtle number and here it gains an additional presence. Chris is a master of switching between bass and keyboards, often in the same song, so this rarely sounds like a trio while Paul is a polished guitarist who points out that thirty years earlier, he only owned one guitar, which was the one he was playing then!

Haze is a band that have always been masters of the live environment, and here they have the space to shine in front of hardcore fans in their home base of Sheffield, and they certainly relished the experience. If you are new to this band then this is the album to start with as neo-prog doesn't get any better than this, and if you are aware of Haze what is your excuse for not having this already?
Jun 2013

HEADSPACE
I AM ANONYMOUS
This album was eagerly awaited by many progheads, and with good reason. The line-up alone is enough to get anyone interested, and I tend to have a standard rule of thumb that anything that involves Damian Wilson is worth investigating. The first time I saw Damian on stage was a solo artist with an acoustic guitar opening for Shadowland and Jadis at the Marquee on the Lurve Ambassadors tour a million years ago, and since then I have been lucky enough to catch him in concert with other groups and have most of his recorded output. To my poor abused ears one of Rick Wakeman's finest albums of his entire career is 'Out There', and who is the singer? Damian. But wait, there's more, who is the bassist? Lee Pomeroy. The Wakeman connection doesn't quite end there as drummer Richard Brooke has also played with Rick and is where he met the others. In fact you have to feel sorry for guitarist Pete Rinaldi as he is the only who hasn't played with Rick – but at least now he is playing with his son as the keyboard player is none other than Adam Wakeman, who has well as being known

for playing with his father has been with Ozzy for the last eight years and I can remember interviewing him years ago when he had the band Jeronimo Road. Now who could have been the singer with that band? Oh yes, that would have been Damian. It's all very incestuous in the prog scene.

So, given that we have world class musicians, songwriters, producers, and singer would one expect an ordinary album? Of course not. Perhaps somewhat surprising is that the album is more metal oriented than one might expect with Adam's presence but given than he plays with the Prince of darkness and Damian fronts Threshold maybe not quite as much after all. But it isn't all blasting guitars and riffs, one of the most effective songs is "Soldier" which is a poignant short number with Damian being accompanied mostly by gentle piano chords – the use of a tolling bell in the background is simple yet incredibly effective, taking the song to a whole new level of emotion and atmosphere.

"Daddy Fucking Loves You' is based on a conversation that Damian had with a soldier, where the soldier told him of the time, he was trying to describe to his young child why he had to go overseas and eventually he burst out with that statement in frustration. It is fifteen minutes long, and starts with gentle acoustic guitar and clear vocals, but it soon becomes a prog metal monster. The riffs sound as if they could have come from Fear Factory, not a prog act, and one can imagine a mosh pit going for this one – until Lee and Pete decide that they are going to lock horns and provide a load of complexity not normally associated with industrial metal. Discords and jagged edges as the song twists and turns means that this takes on a life of its' own as it cross musical boundaries and creates a huge statement.

It has taken these guys five years to produce their first album, something to do with them all being busy on other projects, let's hope that it isn't as long until the next one as this is the beginning of an incredible musical journey.
Nov 2012

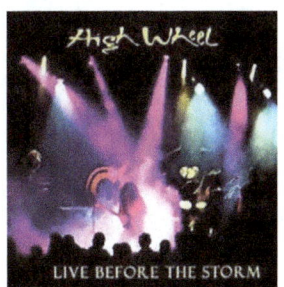

HIGH WHEEL
LIVE BEFORE THE STORM
Here is a German prog band that have been together since 1990 and have released four studio albums with this being their first live release. I am surprised that I have not come across these guys before, as this quartet have produced a double CD that is full of top-quality prog. In many ways this is a bit of a throwback, as there are no Flower Kings or Spock's Beard influences, but instead we have material that has been heavily influenced by Twelfth Night, IQ and Pendragon. No bad thing I hear you say, and you would be definitely right in that regard. Recorded in Germany it is of no surprise that they speak in their own language between songs, but the lyrics are all in English, and are clear with good harmonies. But even though three of the four guys provide vocals it is during the purely instrumental passages that they really shine. Complex complicated prog with a good mix of shorter numbers combined with some solid epics means that there is something here for everyone.

Something I particularly enjoyed was the very strong use of light and shade. This is a band not afraid to really slow it down and use minimal and delicate backing as well as being bombastic and over the top. The result is a well-paced set that is always of interest even to the casual listener. By now the four studio albums should have been re-released and this album is certainly strong enough for me to want to find out more.
Sep 2007

ALLAN HOLDSWORTH
HARD HAT AREA
Here we have Allan's 1993 album 'Hard Hat Area' lovingly reissued by Moonjune who remastered it, placed it in a digipak, and provided some wonderful sleeve notes by Barry Cleveland who puts everything into context. Allan has long been one of my favourite guitarists, and like John McLaughlin I can happily listen to him all day long, and when the guitar lines are as fluid as this that is especially true. Unlike many of Allan's solo albums this has very much a band feel about it and it is no surprise to discover that much of this was recorded by the guys playing together in the studio. Long-time collaborators Gary Husband (drums) and Steve Hunt (keyboards) were joined on bass by Skuli Sverrisson when Jimmy Johnson was unavailable due to touring commitments with James Taylor.

As well as regular guitar Allan also provides some SynthAxe and baritone guitar, not as much as on some of his other albums, but still enough to provide additional facets to the sound. There are times when Allan just lets the others fill the spaces and he sits back nary playing a note, allowing them the freedom to demonstrate their musicianship and feel, then he comes back in and provides some blistering runs that are breathtaking in their audacity. This is fusion in its' truest form as he mixes and melds jazz with prog, letting the music take him and us on an incredible journey. The title cut is a masterclass demonstration of how a guitarist can be centre stage while allowing complex fills and lines from the rest of the band to complete the soundscape. Skuli's fretless bass is wonderfully expressive and warm, providing a contrast to the cleaner and more clinical guitar.

If you ever wondered what fusion can sound like in the hands of an expert, then look no further as this is sheer class.
Jan 2013

ALLAN HOLDSWORTH
NONE TOO SOON
Prior to the recording of 'Hard Hat Area' Allan had been working with pianist Gordon Beck, and together with bassist Gary Willis and drummer Kirk Covington they had recorded a version of "Michelle" for a tribute album. After 'Hard Hat Area', Gordon was again with Allan and he suggested that they do something quite different – namely record an album of interpretations of jazz standards by the likes of John Coltrane, Django

Reinhardt etc. Allan was taken by the idea, and Gordon suggested which songs they should undertake, and they were mostly unfamiliar to Allan who became an avid pupil. They brought back the same rhythm section, and Allan provided all the guitar and synthesizer sounds on the SynthAxe. The basic tracks were recorded as a group, with the guitar overdubbed afterwards, but to these ears it sounds as if everyone was cooking in the studio at the same time.

This is a jazz album with no room to hide and all four musicians are obviously on the very top of their game, bouncing the ideas and melodies. Gary and Kirk obviously have a great understanding between each other and provide an extremely complex bedrock while Gordon's impact on this recording is immense. Gordon was house pianist at Ronnie Scott's and his knowledge of the genre was extremely wide and varied and it is no surprise that there are times when Allan defers such as on Joe Henderson's "Isotope" where Gordon leads the way (followed by some stunning bass it must be said).

While most songs are indeed jazz standards, one that isn't is "Norwegian Wood" which is given a very different arrangement and again Gordon has a huge impact on this, whether it is providing a melodic lead or simply repeating a chord sequence that allows Allan to spread his wings. I doubt if Lennon and McCartney ever imagined that the song could be treated in this way, but it has taken what is for me one of their lesser numbers and has moved it into a totally new direction. It is interesting to note that Gordon had originally recorded the song himself back in 1968 on his 'Experiments with Pops' album, but Allan provides a fluidity and note density that makes this his own.

All in all, a very different album from the one that preceded it, yet I would be hard pressed to pick between the two as they are both stunning pieces of work. This has been reissued by Moonjune in a digipak, the recordings have been remastered, and there are great sleeve notes from Barry Cleveland.
Jan 2013

ALLAN HOLDSWORTH
FLATTIRE
After suffering a difficult divorce, Allan had sold most of his gear and had no access to a studio. In addition, the house he was now renting wasn't suitable for recording live guitar or drums, so he decided to take the opportunity to make a record using only the SynthAxe. Of course, he had also sold most of his synthesisers so only had access to certain sounds. The subtitle of this album is "Music for a non-existent movie", as Allan decided to record music that would fit the scenes he could imagine in his head. The result is something that is certainly unusual, although it would take a braver man than me to say that it was 100% successful. The problem in many ways is due to the instrumentation being deployed, as it comes across as a synth album yet

without the depth that one would normally expect. It is a very stripped sound, yet this approach clashes with the sounds being heard so it doesn't really work as a synth album, nor as a guitar album (which in fairness it isn't – although it was recorded by Allan playing a guitar-type instrument, if that makes any sense). Most of the reviews I have read come to the same conclusion as me, in that Allan is one of the most incredible and versatile musicians you will ever come across, but that this is most definitely not the place to start. It's great that Moonjune have made it available again, especially with Barry Cleveland's insightful (as always) comments, but this is an album that I played repeatedly as I felt I needed to so that I could write a fair review as opposed to playing it because I loved it.
Aug 2013

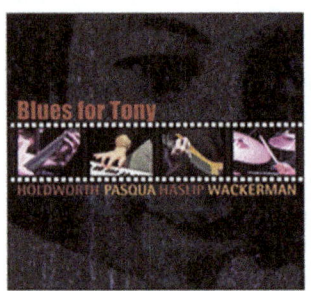

HOLDSWORTH PASQUA HASLIP WACKERMAN
BLUES FOR TONY

The Tony Williams Lifetime was founded in 1969 by drummer Tony Williams as a power trio with John McLaughlin on electric guitar, and Larry Young (aka Khalid Yasin) on organ. Their debut album 'Emergency!' is a classic and everyone interested in jazz or fusion should have a copy in their collection. The line-up changed over time (Jack Bruce was there for the second album) and in 1975 Tony formed a quartet he called The New Tony Williams Lifetime featuring bassist Tony Newton, pianist Alan Pasqua, and guitarist Allan Holdsworth. Some thirty odd years later Allan and Alan decided that the time was right to go on tour with a band to pay homage to those days, and recruited drummer Chad Wackerman (Zappa, Holdsworth) and bassist Jimmy Haslip (Yellowjackets) for the occasion.

This double CD set brings together the best versions from the whole tour, edited together so that the listener has a complete evening's entertainment with no overdubs whatsoever (the DVD that is available is just from one night). The concept may have started as a tribute, but by the time that these songs were recorded it was morphing into a fusion band with a life of its' own. This is jazz combined with prog as the guys bounce off each other and the note density and complexity of what is being performed is quite staggering. Allan has a fluidity that is rarely matched – just listen to the runs in "It Must Be Jazz" to see what I mean, but Alan does his best with some incredible electric piano/organ. The photo on the rear cover shows four guys with scores in front of them with simple lighting and no fancy gimmicks at all. This is all about the music, and the music is stunning. If you want music to be complex, played by guys at the very top of their game, then this is something to be savored.
Jan 2013

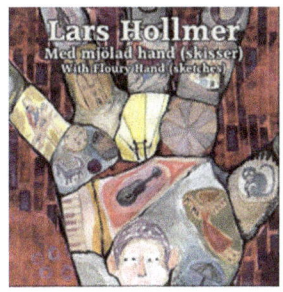

LARS HOLLMER
WITH FLOURY HAND (SKETCHES)

Lars Hollmer was a Swedish composer, accordionist and keyboardist who first came to prominence with his RIO band Samla Mammas Manna in the 70s and into the 80s. He also performed with other bands as well as having his own solo career, exploring what could be done with a piano accordion in modern music. Towards the end of working on the album 'Viandra' he started talking about releasing an album that would be full of weird ideas and strange songs, and he started looking back through his archives to see what he could use for that purpose. However, in May 2008 he was diagnosed with severe lung cancer, from which he succumbed at Christmas of the same year - he was just 60 years old.

In Autumn 2009 his son Gabriel started working through the hours of music that Lars had put aside for the project, and this is the result. As Gabriel says, "It is a mix of more or less unfinished songs and sketches that I love. It is full of wild and crazy ideas and antics, pieces of utter frivolity, but equally places full of delicate beauty. This is music straight from the heart. Just like how my father was." It is certainly a very strange ride, with beautiful numbers against some which are erratic and hard to listen to – it is certainly not easy listening but eventually the listener is rewarded by visiting places within a musical repertoire that are far from the beaten path. It certainly shows that the accordion should hold a much more important place in music than many would imagine.

I was provided with this CD as a download by the record label, but it is worth noting that the physical version comes with a 45-minute DVD of a 2005 performance at the Gouveia Art Rock Festival in Portugal which is the only professional video footage ever released of Lars.
Oct 2012

I AND THOU
SPEAK

This album is basically a solo project from Jason Hart (Renaissance) who has been joined by John Galgano (IZZ), Steve Hogarth (Marillion), Matt Johnson (Jeff Buckley, Rufus Wainwright) and Jack Petruzzelli (the Fab Faux, Patti Smith) among others. Even Annie Haslam makes an appearance, although to be honest this time it is not for her incredible vocals but as artist as she provided the cover! Just five songs, but still an hour of playing time, this is an incredibly reflective album and one that is full of class and power. There are obviously many prog influences, but if opener "Speak" doesn't sound as if it belongs firmly on 'Trick of a Tail' then nothing does. I've never heard a song that so epitomizes just what a group created on one album – the only dissent would be if you wanted to discuss if in fact it should have been on 'Wind and Wuthering'; he has really nailed a very short period of Genesis.

Then turn to the next song "...And I Awaken" and lo and behold if it doesn't start off like one of Neal Morse's early solo albums where he was reflective as opposed to bombastic. By this time, I was well and truly hooked and instead of trying to spot the reference I was instead just glorying in the sheer delight of what is an incredibly layered and polished progressive rock album. The album screams 'class' in capital letters ten feet high and this really is one masterpiece after another, always firmly anchored in the keyboards (often piano) of Jason who has a wonderfully delicate and emotive touch.

All progheads need to try and hear this as it is a delight from start to finish.
Nov 2012

GENNADY ILYIN
THE SUN OF THE SPIRIT
Little Tragedies were formed in 1994 around a graduate of St. Petersburg Conservatory, composer, and keyboard player Gennady Ilyin, in the city of Kursk. Their early music focused on the genres of instrumental suite, variations, different combinations of classical, contemporary, and rock music. According to Gennady Ilyin, it was more like improvisations without lyrics and vocals - he was just interested in working with 'pure' music. At the end of the Nineties, he recorded two solo albums, of which this is the first. Originally this was released as a Little Tragedies album by Boheme in 2000, but it was reissued by Mals in 2009 with a bonus track (and new artwork) and this time correctly under Gennady's own name.

Gennady was assisted on this album by Igor Mikhel (guitars) and Evgeny Shchukin (sound engineer); and he used his music with the poems of Russian poet Nikolai Gumilev. I swear if you listen to opening number "Parrot" you will believe that you are listening to a long-lost song from The Enid (okay, with Russian vocals and lyrics it must be said), but there is something about it that reminds me of Robert John Godfrey's finest works. It is bright, and very powerful and doesn't sound at all like a solo album so perhaps it isn't surprising that it was originally issued under a band name.

Gennady is an incredible keyboard player (not surprising given his background and training), but while there are some Russian classical influences in his playing there is also plenty of Wakeman and Emerson alongside some of the great prog bands such as After Crying and Solaris.

It is virtually impossible to split these two albums and given that they were recorded at virtually the same time perhaps that isn't overly surprising. So instead of working out which one is the better, why not just get both?
Nov 2011

GENNADY ILYIN
PORCELAIN PAVILION

This review starts with the same comments as that which I provided against his debut album, but just in case you didn't read that one here it is again. Little Tragedies were formed in 1994 around a graduate of St. Petersburg Conservatory, composer, and keyboard player Gennady Ilyin, in the city of Kursk. Their early music focused on the genres of instrumental suite, variations, different combinations of classical, contemporary, and rock music. According to Gennady Ilyin, it was more like improvisations without lyrics and vocals - he was just interested in working with 'pure' music. At the end of the Nineties, he recorded two solo albums, of which this is the second. Originally this was released as a Little Tragedies album by Boheme in 2000, but it was reissued by Mals in 2009 with a bonus track (and new artwork) and this time correctly under Gennady's own name.

Gennady was assisted on this album by Igor Mikhel (guitars) and Evgeny Shchukin (sound engineer); and as with his debut he put music to the poems of Russian poet Nikolai Gumilev. This is progressive music, with more than a hint of classical forms, and the piano is an extremely important focal point. Given that this is a keyboardist's album one of the questions is normally whether it is more like Wakeman or more like Emerson. Well, it's like neither for the most part, and like both at others – this is music that has more in common with Hungarian prog bands After Crying (particularly) and Solaris. Maybe it is because they have similar influences, but I know that I thoroughly enjoyed this from beginning to end. The lyrics are in Russian as one would expect, but I never find listening to vocals in a foreign language to be a problem – in fact it allows me to concentrate more on the sound, and as this moves from fairground to deep classical with wonderful prog bringing it all together there are some great sounds and arrangements to be heard. Well done on Mals for re-releasing these two gems.
Nov 2011

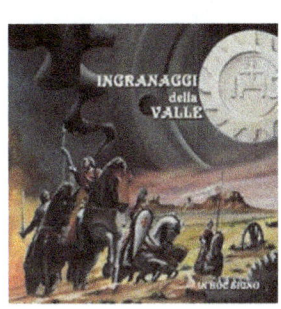

INGRANAGGI DELLA VALLE
IN HOC SIGNO

I can just imagine the conversation, can't you? It probably went something like "I know it's a debut, so let's base it on the First Crusade, okay? Let's approach the Italian progressive form from the fusion end, ensure we include plenty of KBB-style violin work, and we'll get in loads of guests to add dramatic bits and pieces including VDGG's David Jackson. They won't know what's hit them!" Albums and groups tend not to come out of left field like this very often these days, so it is always a very pleasant surprise when they do, as there is no way that a band recording their debut after only being together for a few years should sound as polished and convincing as this. Mattia Liberati (keyboards) and Flavio Gonnellini (guitar), were already members of the funk/jazz-rock trio The Big Chill when they decided to do something different, but they have brought their jazz influences with them (Mattia also brought loads of keyboards and

I think he used all of them somewhere, listing Hammond B3, Mellotron M400, Fender Rhodes Mk II, MiniMoog, MiniMoog Voyager, Korg MS20, Elka Synthex, Jen SX1000, Clavia Nord Stage Revision B).

I have always been a fan of Italian Progressive Rock, and these guys have certainly brought together influences such as PFM, with the incredible violin jazz prog of KBB to create something that has multiple layers and incredible depth. Igor Leone has a wonderful voice, and breaks through when he needs to, lifting above everything with clear diction and great control. But what really makes this album work so well is the blending together of some many different ideas and instruments into something that is incredibly complex yet is always extremely easy to listen to. This is not being clever just for its' own sake but is all about making music that is easy to understand and leaves the listener with a smile on their face. Prog doesn't get much better than this.
Aug 2013

IONA
TREASURES: THE VERY BEST
Iona must be one of the UK's best kept secrets. Over the years they have continued to produce albums of outstanding quality yet somehow have never managed to gain the recognition they so richly deserve. While praise and riches have been lavished on Celtic artists such as Enya, for some reason it has never been the same for Iona who in some ways have followed a similar musical path, bringing together Celtic and traditional music with the lighter forms of prog in a way that always delights. I first came across the band when I reviewed 'The Book Of Kells' back in 1992, one of the three albums that are used as the basis of this compilation. At this time, they had one Nick Beggs providing bass and chapman stick, who some people may recognize from his time with Kajagoogoo! But for me the mainstays of the band were Joanne Hogg on vocals, Dave Bainbridge on guitar/keyboards (who are both still there today) along with Troy Donockley on various traditional instruments (who departed in 2009).

So why am I looking at a compilation album that only covers a subset of their releases, which is more than 15 years old! Easy, Iona have made this available as a free download from their site. Yes, that is right, free. Gratis. No payment required. So, what excuse can you possibly have now for not discovering one of the finest bands around in their field? This is wonderfully atmospheric album from start to end, with a warmth provided by fretless bass and a cut through by drums and whistles, while the keyboards and guitars build a blanket of sound that allows Joanne to rise above it all. In some ways it is somewhat reminiscent of Renaissance and Annie Haslam, with complex layered music allowing a free vocal to really dominate the overall sound.

This album has reminded me just how wonderful their music really is and has inspired me to find out more about the albums I do not already have. This is a great compilation and given that it is free why not give them a try?
Dec 2012

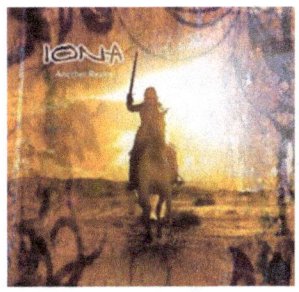

IONA
ANOTHER REALM

This is the latest album from Iona, coming out in 2011 and comes in a wonderful double CD digipak. Like their music, the artwork is immediately evocative and takes the observer to a different time and place. For those who are unaware, the band name is taken from a small island in the Inner Hebrides off the western coast of Scotland. It was a centre of Irish monasticism for four centuries and is today renowned for its tranquillity and natural beauty. Although I have never visited the island itself, it is an area that I know well as my grandfather was District Officer Coastguard for the Western Isles, and my father was brought up in (and has now retired to) a tiny village next to the Mull of Kintyre, called Southend. St Columba (one of the twelve apostles of Ireland) first landed at Southend (where his footsteps can still be seen) before moving to Iona and whenever I listen to their music, I find myself transported to a land where the weather and scenery are rugged, the people incredibly friendly, and while life is hard there is a real feeling of mysticism and a closeness to religion. This is also very true of the very Christian nature of the band's songs, yet even if you view yourself as a non-believer this is never in your face enough to cause offence.

Thanks to their musical style, combined with Joanne Hogg's vocals, these guys will always find themselves compared to Enya and Kate Bush but in many ways that is unfair as they don't really sound like the latter and there is way more complexity and layers than the former. The current line-up is Joanne Hogg (vocals, vocal loops, piano, keyboard, beer shaker), Dave Bainbridge (electric & acoustic guitars, bouzouki, piano, keyboards, autoharp, beer shakers), Frank van Essen (drums, percussion, violins, violas, electric violin, vocal, glockenspiel, keyboard), Phil Barker (bass guitar, electric upright bass) and Martin Nolan (uilleann pipes, low whistles, tin whistles, vocals). Together they produce music that is timeless, folk and prog coming together to wrap around the listener and create a world that in many ways is far away from the present day.

If ever there was music that should only be played on headphones this is it, as to get the full benefit one needs to play this without distraction, preferably at night with a glass of Springbank Malt in hand, just sitting looking at the stars and drift away into their world.
Dec 2012

IQ
TALES FROM THE LUSH ATTIC 30TH ANNIVERSARY

Can it really be 30 years since IQ released their debut vinyl album? I still regret not hearing them back then, and to be honest only came across this album when it was reissued by GEP in '94. By then I had seen them in concert and was wondering why on earth I hadn't been a regular at their gigs in the Eighties. Originally this was just 5 songs long, yet this reissue (excluding the DVD) contains 33! And I loved hearing every one of them! IQ have been at the top of the UK underground prog scene for many years, and the original songs contained here seem like old friends, whether it be the 20 minute plus opener "The Last Human Gateway", "Awake and Nervous", the 14 minute "The Enemy Smacks" or the much shorter "Through The Corridors" and even Martin's great piano piece "My Baby Treats Me Right 'Cos I'm A Hard Lovin' Man All Night Long" which makes me think of Spinal Tap every time I play it ("You know, just simple lines intertwining, you know, very much like - I'm really influenced by Mozart and Bach, and it's sort of in between those, really. It's like a Bach piece, really. It's sort of... this piece is called "Lick My Love Pump".)

It is important to put this album into context. According to www.progarchives.com this is the third most highly rated album of the year, and the one above it? 'Script for a Jester's Tear'. But while that was getting the full EMI publicity, this album slipped out with little or no publicity (before you ask, the top album is Bacamarte's 'Depois Do Fim' which is well worth hearing but I wouldn't place it above these two). The one thing that lets the album down was the production, so thirty years on the band have rectified that issue, and how. I have never heard these songs sound so clear and polished, yet the power and emotion is still there. This is a band that like Marillion, Pallas, Twelfth Night and others were looking back into the Seventies for their inspiration and in fact some of the music on this album was written and performed by the band's predecessor, The Lens, as long ago as '76. So, while some critics may say that some of this was influenced by Marillion they are way off base, and if you listen to Mike's guitarwork and Martin's keyboards it is obvious that they are coming from different places than Steve and Mark.

What this set brings together is remixes, bonus songs, the original mix of the album, the original mix of 'Seven Stories Into Eight' (which in fairness was also reissued when they revisited and re-recorded that album as 'Seven Stories Into 98'), plus unreleased songs, writing sessions, and an extremely interesting interview which brings that period of the band's history very much to life. Then to cap it all there is a live DVD recorded in 2011 where the band performs the album (minus Martin's piano piece as he is no longer involved) plus a photo gallery etc. If you are a proghead then you are probably already familiar with this album, but even if you already own it in multiple versions, you also need to invest in this as this is definitive. As an IQ fan, all I can say is bring on the same for 'The Wake'! You've got two years guys to match that up to this!!!!
Jan 2013

JACK DUPON
JÉSUS L'AVENTURER
When I was first approached by Jack Dupon and asked if I would like to review this album I made the incorrect assumption that Jack was a person, when in fact this is a quartet who have been around since 2004 and this is their fourth studio album. Their website is full of information (and thankfully is also available in English as I have forgotten pretty much all the French I learned at school), and it is interesting to see how they describe themselves:- "There's no need to search for JACK DUPON in the civil registration, because this legendary character doesn't exist! We're

talking of a French band here, made of four crazy people, phlegmatic adventurers of the imaginary. Improvisers and storytellers. Polite and rude. Full of oppositions, contradictions... In one Word : Alive. Their music is like their existences: out of styles and boundaries".

The gatefold digipak comes with a poster, and when it is opened up one of the things one can see are the details of all the people this album is about. That's because the album is about the great adventure. Special adventures like Ulysses, small stories like Mata Hari or Laïka, criminal stories like that of Raymond Callemin... One musical walk with the stories of many strange people. The first time I played this album I really didn't like it, and in fact I was relieved when it finally finished as this is RIO/avant-garde that makes Art Zoyd, Zappa, Beefheart, Can and Gong seem quite normal and mainstream in comparison. But, I am no quitter so went back and played it again, and again, and the weird thing was that each time I played it the less it became a chore, and the more I found that it was making some sort of strange musical sense.

This is not music for the faint-hearted, and the vast majority who come across this will run away screaming. But, if you are of an adventurous nature and are willing to put in the effort then I promise that there are hidden delights that only make themselves known when one has listened to this many times. When I first played this I thought that the fault had to be with my own preconceived ideas as opposed to the band, and I am truly glad that I persevered as this is quite some piece of work.
May 2013

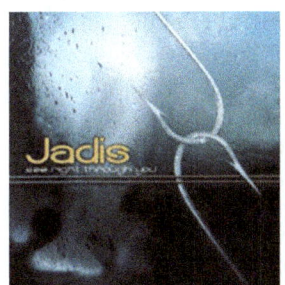

JADIS
SEE RIGHT THROUGH YOU
I just need to check the calendar before I write this review. Yep, it's 2012, it's just that at the moment it feels like the best part of twenty years ago. Over the last few months, I have written reviews of Galahad, Landmarq, Citizen Cain, Big Big Train and others that were active in the Nineties and now here are Jadis back with their first album in six years. I have to confess that 'More Than Meets The Eye' is one of my favourite albums of all-time of any genre, I am probably the only person in New Zealand with a Jadis ringtone (a snippet of "Wonderful World"), and still have very fond memories of the first time I saw Jadis in concert with some outfit called Shadowland on the 'Lurve Ambassadors' tour (and that was 20 years ago!).

So, let's be honest, the chances of me writing a bad Jadis review are slim. Since the last album, 'Photoplay', both Martin Orford (keyboards, flute, backing vocals) and John Jowitt (bass) left the band, and they were initially replaced by Giulio Risi and Andy Marlow respectively, but Giulio has also since left and on this album the keyboards are provided by Arman Vardanyan. But the stalwarts over the years have been the backbone of drummer Steve Christey and the heart and soul of guitarist/singer Gary Chandler. If they are there, then Jadis keep going.

I don't know what has been happening over the last six years, as there are very little details on the website, but let's hope that it isn't another six years until the next album as yet again this is superb. Jadis have a sound like no other, with the dual-tracked vocals and the focus on the guitar. Keyboards and bass have their role in all bands, but here it is to provide a backdrop to allow Gary to fly, something he does extremely well indeed. Yes, there are times when all the guys have their turn in the spotlight, but this is all about the guitar. If one must put in another band reference, then the nearest is probably Camel, but to me Jadis are Jadis: they steer their own path, with less layers and demonstration of virtuosity than many others, yet always very melodic with songs that stick in the mind and demand to be played time and again.

If you have yet to come across this great British band, then you owe it to your ears to do so.
Oct 2012

JANEL AND ANTHONY
WHERE IS HOME

In some ways Janel and Anthony are one of the most unusual bands I have ever come across yet are also one of the most enthralling. Based in Washington DC, this instrumental duo brings together so many styles and structures that it is difficult to know where to begin. Janel is Janel Leppin, a conservatory trained cellist steeped in North Indian and Persian classical music, free improvisation, and jazz while Anthony is Anthony Pirog, a guitarist who seems to be totally at home whatever music is being played. I think what has enthralled me with this album is how it can go from beautiful classically inspired call and response to Hindustani ragas, surf rock licks, to Appalachian laments and post-bop harmonies. Musically and sonically, this is all over the map, refusing to sit in any particular style so that the only true response is to call this "progressive" as it truly is; although most prog fans would not think of this in the same context as Yes, but there again possibly it could sit with King Crimson or Magma?

This is their second album, following on from a self-released debut in 2006. Apparently, they knew each other at high school but only started playing music together when they were at college. Both musicians have very broad musical backgrounds and have both studied very different musical forms extensively (both have music degrees). Somehow, they have managed to bring all of these strands together in one album that is invigorating and beautiful, simple yet hard to fathom, beguiling and entrancing yet also harsh and unforgiving. In many ways it is quite unlike anything I have ever heard, yet I am quite sure that I would very much like to hear more. Only for those with eclectic tastes, but if you are like me in that regard then rest assured the mainstream only music fans are missing out and this is essential.
Apr 2013

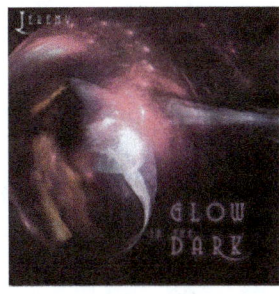

JEREMY
GLOW IN THE DARK

Over the years I have heard many of Jeremy's different recordings and styles; he is one of the few artists who genuinely seems to be at home in many different areas (and normally playing a multitude of instruments). But while I really do enjoy his forays into other areas it is his progressive music that I enjoy the most, and 'Glow In The Dark' is the latest example in a long line of stunning albums. Here he has deliberately moved into what can only be described as a more regressive stance on progressive, incorporating not only some powerful lead guitar work and lengthy instrumentals (opener "In The Beginning" is more than 12 minutes long) but also some classic keyboard sounds from Mellotrons, Mini-Moogs, and Arp Synthesizers. This gives the album a 'classic' feel, earlier psychedelic Floyd than the 'Dark Side' era, more Tangerine Dream than Genesis.

There is the feeling that this is serious music, to be enjoyed, but to be played to be listened to and for the message to be heard as opposed to some background noise. When the Mellotron starts proceedings with the acoustic guitar on the title track, then one is just waiting for Justin Hayward to bring in the Moody's, or for Jon to get Steve to blast away. This is solid music, music with real substance – both depth and breadth, and is something that 'traditional' progheads need to search out quickly.
July 2009

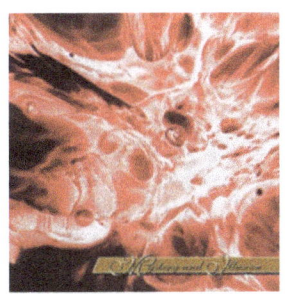

JEREMY
MYSTERY AND ILLUSION

As if it isn't enough for Jeremy to be releasing material on his own label, he sometimes goes off to others and here he is with another 2008 album on the Russian Mals label. This is another progressive album from Jeremy, but this one contains vocals on all songs and is even more psychedelic than 'Glow In The Dark', and there are some definite ELO influences going on here as well. As with all his work, the musicianship and songwriting is first rate, although I do have to wonder at times how someone who has released more than 50 full length albums manages to keep doing so time after time. Especially when one considers that as well as recording and gigging, he runs the record label and has other jobs as well – does this guy never sleep?

To get two prog albums from Jeremy in the same year is a real blessing, and interesting to compare as there is a feeling of lightness with 'Mystery' that is somehow darker and heavier on 'Glow'. There is more a of a pop feel, as Jeremy brings together the genres that he loves so well into a mix that is going to be appreciated by lovers of many different styles, let's just call this 'good music'.
July 2009

JEREMY
POP EXPLOSION
And so, we come to yet another 2008 album from the multi-faceted Jeremy, here back strongly in the realms of psychedelic power pop. Here we have an artist who wears his love of The Beatles strongly and proudly for all to see yet manages also to make this style very much his own. I really am starting to run out of superlatives for this guy – I just don't know how he does it. I haven't managed to hear all his albums (which I think is in the region of 40!) but have listened to most of them and I have yet to come across anything that could remotely be considered a dud. Again, this is very much a case in point with 14 songs that display all that is good about this type of music from strong melodies and harmonies to powerful hooks, always managing to stay on the right side of sugar overkill yet still being incredibly radio friendly (if you had a decent radio station that is). "I'm Still Waiting" should be on every AOR lover's playlist, with riffing guitars and hooks even some distorted guitar!

Now, if you weren't yet intrigued enough to look out this album already then how about the bonus CD that comes with it? Fully justified in being released in its' own right, 'Under Cover' contains more than twenty songs where Jeremy takes on numbers like "I'm Not In Love" and "A Little Bit Me, A Little Bit You" and moves them into his swirling late Sixties world. Jeremy continues to defy the popular belief that one can only be a master of one area, while managing somehow to maintain a phenomenal output in many different genres.
July 2009

JEREMY MORRIS
ALIVE
Here we are in the unusual position of having a Jeremy album which is credited to the whole person, instead of just the Christian name. The reason for that is this is an extended reissue of his debut some 25 years on. This is a mix of progressive with American melodic rock, with influences such as Genesis, ELO, The Beatles, and Tom Petty readily apparent. Even though this was a limited edition release when it first came out (5000 copies), it has gained some kudos within the scene as a 'must find' album as here Jeremy really concentrated his efforts in one area (these days he can actually be working on five albums at the same time!), and the mix of brass with a harder edged guitar than one often finds in his music these days really works. This isn't an album to be searched for as it was the starting point for what has been an extremely prolific career, but rather that here is an album full of songs that are extremely accessible and melodic on first hearing. Sure, some of the keyboard sounds are a little dated but they would have been dated when the tracks came out in 1983 so it is quite deliberate...

This is an example of all that was good about mid-Seventies albums, but without a lot of the pomposity and 'look at me' mentality. To the point, it is more AOR than progressive,

but should easily appeal to those who just want to enjoy their music without having to worry about which pigeonhole it should fit under. Yet another Jeremy album worth investigating (as if is there are any that aren't).
July 2009

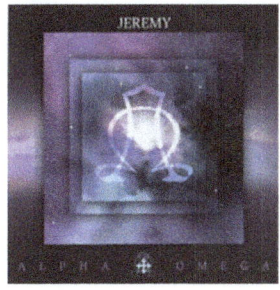

JEREMY
ALPHA & OMEGA
This is one of Jeremy's Christian praise and worship albums, and apart from assistance with the drums and percussion, he provides all the vocals and instrumentation. Stylistically it combines the two styles that Jeremy is most well-known for, namely power pop and progressive rock. "Let It Shine" is one of the longest songs on the album, and in some ways is an unusual opener as it is very reflective and certainly has nothing musically in common with the number that follows "His Burden Is Light" which is much more in your face and has a catchy chorus that I can see being sung in gusto when this is performed at church gatherings. "Do Justly, Love Mercy, Walk Humbly" is all jangly 12-string guitars and great melodies and pop hooks as Jeremy yet again shows that he is no stranger to The Byrds.

It also proves time and again that Christian music can still be enjoyable music. I remember getting very bored listening to praise music in the Seventies, and it wasn't until I came across acts like Larry Norman and (particularly) Stryper that I realized that there was truth in the words "Why should the devil have all the good music?". If you enjoy power pop, late Sixties pop, psychedelic and even some mild progressive music and are a Christian then this is an album that you will turn to repeatedly.
Jan 2012

JEREMY
GUITAR HEAVEN
From the album title, and artwork, there are no guesses that this is another in Jeremy's praise series but this time instead of keyboards we are given the opportunity to listen to his delicate touch on acoustic guitar. Each time I play a new album by Jeremy I am always blown away by how much at home he sounds in that particular genre. I mean, here is music that wouldn't sound out of place on an Anthony Phillips album but while I can imagine Anthony producing a stunning prog album (let me think, ah yes, 'Trespass') I can't think of him going off into realms of psychedelia or power pop. Yet Jeremy somehow is a master of different genres as well as different instruments.

If you enjoy acoustic guitar that at times does have a feel of Giltrap or Phillips and is also extremely well produced, then look no further then here
Aug 2012

JEREMY
FROM THE DUST TO THE STARS

It must be twenty years since Jeremy Morris and I were first in contact. Back then his albums were released on cassette (I still have all of them – just nothing to play them on), and often on his own label Jam Recordings, but his latest effort has been released by Mals and sees him move slightly more into the prog field. Of course, being Jeremy there are also huge slabs of psychedelia and power pop and to be honest it is the former that takes centre stage for much of this album. Also, given that there is a photo of three musicians on the rear of the case one could think that this is a group effort, but apart from two guys sharing drum duties, and recording colleague Guillermo Cazenave on one song, this is very much a solo effort. Jeremy lists his own instruments as vocals, guitars, Mellotron, bass, synthesizers, piano, dulcimer, drums before he puts 'etc.'. Yes, he is very much a one man band.

When Jeremy was telling me about this he did tell me that it was a prog album (Jeremy releases normally three or four albums a year, in many different styles) but I'm really not so sure. There are some proggy elements (anything with a Mellotron is almost automatically prog isn't it?) but it is much more a psychedelic piece, with some wonderful layering and atmospheric keyboards and vocals. At times it is quite dreamy, while at others it contains some of the most direct electric guitar solos I have ever heard Jeremy record. Lyrically this is very much a Christian album, with Jeremy using his words to get across some strong messages.

Overall, the result is yet another Jeremy album that it is possible to listen to with a smile on the face – it may not be what a lot of people think of as a prog album, but whatever tag you wish to put on this it is a damn fine listen.
Sep 2012

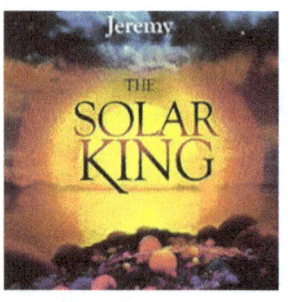

JEREMY
THE SOLAR KING

Jeremy Morris has released well more than 50 albums now, but this is the one that should have been the first but has only just been made available. Released on 12/12/12, this contains recordings that were made by Jeremy with his brother Mike on drums between 1980 and 1982. Originally destined to be his debut release, it was shelved after Mike lost interest in the project and some thirty years after the fact Jeremy has revisited the tapes and cleaned them off and made them available. Interestingly the comments are that they have been remastered, no comment at all about re-recording so it appears that these are as they were. Also, unless the original idea was to release a double album, instead of putting together the album as it would have been back then Jeremy has instead chosen the best of the recordings as the CD is over an hour long.

What immediately strikes the listener is that it doesn't sound as if it were some young guys just starting out. Remember, this wasn't a full band, as while Mike provided the drums Jeremy was singing, playing guitar, bass, and keyboards so there would have been a lot of multi-tracking going on. Also, this is very much Jeremy as we now know him as opposed to an amateurish project. In fact, when I played this the first time, I hadn't read the CD booklet and the only thing that really struck me as strange is that not only was there a very long song included, but also that there are times when Jeremy seems much more in love with his guitar than usual with some rock soloing and power chords. I had thought that he was moving in a different direction (again), not realizing that this was how it all started.

Very much a Christian album, this fits in more with his power pop/rock style than that of his prog ventures, but again this is an album that those who enjoy his music will want to discover, and if you enjoy The Byrds with plenty of psych and melodic harmonies then this is for you.
Feb 2013

JEREMY & PROGRESSOR
SEARCHING FOR THE SON

The last time that Jeremy Morris released an album with Progressor (Vitaly Menshikov) was back in 2005 when they joined forces for 'The Pearl of Great Price', so it has taken them a while to get back together but given Jeremy's recording output probably that isn't too surprising. They both provide different instrumentation, while Jeremy provides the vocals, but there are also a few other musicians involved, notably John 'Rabbit' Bundrick. I was playing his superb 'Moccasin Warrior II' album just the other day, so it was interesting to find him on here. I was asked to provide a much more detailed review on this album, something that I very rarely undertake due to the amount of music I listen to and the time I have available to write about it, but given that Jeremy and I have known each other for some twenty years why not? In fact, I finally got all my cassettes out the other day, and still have 'Green', 'Soul Saver' and 'Dreams Come True' from all those years ago! One never knows quite what to expect from Jeremy in terms of what style will be in place on each release, but this is mostly songs with vocals, Christian lyrics, and a musical style that is reminiscent of the last Sixties.

Searching for the Son (8:07) – Gentle bubbling keyboards lead way into a solid dose of psychedelic progressive pop, as the chords become more strident and the full band comes in. Dreamy, atmospheric, and evocative, the addition of saxophone onto this track gives it even more power and emphasis while the slightly strained guitar also brings back memories of a time gone by.

Future Flight (7:44) – Gently picked guitar, and delicate Mellotron combine with some 'spacey' sounds to lead us into another number that could have come straight from the end of the Sixties. Picked guitar and a driving bass leads us through a number which swirls, shifts, and changes throughout.

The Blind Man's Dream (6:53) – Layered keyboards and gentle 12-string slowly introduces us to some phased distorted guitar, as the guys gradually kick into one of the heaviest numbers on the album. There is a real edginess to this one, with plenty of guitar soloing, and although it is only seven minutes long it contains many distinct musical sections, with the repeated lyrics and themes returned to nearer the end. Throughout, the keyboards act as a bedrock for the guitars to do very much their own thing, with more than a hint of later-period Beatles.

Distant Light (10:28) – Lots of clarinet-style keyboards on this number gives it quite a different feel, as does the use of gently strummed acoustic guitar. But, as with others, this number has multiple sections, and when it starts to drive along there is a much greater impact due to the softness of what has gone before.

Wings of the Wind (11:16) – The longest song on the album, this also has multiple sections, and brings in loads of different musical elements trumpet combining with electric piano at one point, with distorted guitars all adding to a very jazzy feel. In fact, it seems quite chaotic at times, very different to the more structured and laid-back feel of much of the album. But what really makes this for me is the wonderfully delicate piano that comes in and out throughout the song and closes it out as a solo. There is wonderful touch and emotion contained within those notes.

Messiah Will Come (7:09) – This starts as a far more orchestral piece with layers of synth strings, and some real trumpet, before it moves into a more psychedelic number led by some jangly guitar. Bill Morris' trumpet is again an important factor in this song, before guitar and keyboards dominate with some wonderful interplay.

Had Enough (4:34) – This is one of three totally solo Jeremy songs on the album and is the most poppy/psych of everything. A repeated chorus line gets into the mind and stays there, and there is a distinct groove and underlying emotional current that makes this a real joy to play time and again.

Way to Zion (6:01) – A total contrast to what preceded it, here we have a number that again is very orchestral in style, and it takes quite a while for the vocals to kick in, so much so that the first time I played it I wondered if it was going to be an instrumental. In many ways this reminds me of Gryphon, with synth instrumentation taking the place of the real thing.

The Mirror (6:29) – The next Jeremy solo song is based much more on his vocals with gently picked guitar for accompaniment, with delicate keyboards providing some accents. This is quite an uplifting number, with less layering of the vocals and therefore more cut through.

On A Cherub (5:23) – The final Jeremy solo finds multi-layered vocals on top of picked guitar, with delicate Mellotron for support, before some phasing takes place that moves the music in and out. There is some fine jangly guitar soloing on this piece, as prog and psychedelia combine.

Sonic Dances (4:05) – Vitaly provides the final song, apparently recorded back in 1993. Multi-layered acoustic guitar picking gives us a closing number that is musically quite at odds with the rest of the album, but somehow is a fitting final piece as it rounds it off nicely.

There you have it, 78 minutes long, mixing lots of different influences together in a way that is enjoyable and fun to play. The final words must go to J&P, as on the booklet it states, "Repeated listens required: Don't even try to dig it upon the first spin!"
Nov 2013

KAMPEC DOLORES
EVALIYÉ

Kampec Dolores are one of my favourite Hungarian bands, so I was pleased to hear that they released a new album in 2011, the first one since 2006, and I have finally managed to hear it. They were founded back in 1984 by Csaba Hajnoczy and Gabi Kenderesi and soon found themselves supporting artists like Nico and Pere Ubu as they toured throughout Europe displaying their own unique style. These days the line-up is Gabi Kenderesi (vocals), Csaba Hajnóczy (guitar), Arpad Vajdovich (bass), Istvan Grencsó (sax, flute, wind instruments) and Csaba Nemeth (drums).

To say that they have their own unique style and sound is an understatement. In some ways it is world music mixed with jazz, but it is both more and less than that. Gabi has a very pure high clear voice which she uses to great effect, but as she sings in Hungarian, I really have no idea at all what she is saying! That leaves me to concentrate on her vocals as another instrument, as it mixes and melds with the rest of the guys. Istvan is apparently one of the top musicians in the Hungarian scene and is very much in demand, and here when he plays, he makes a real impression but he isn't always present as the band move the music around, and he is used at just the right moment. Some of the numbers are quite rocky with bass pedals and riffs but in others it is very light and folky with a fretless bass making its' presence felt. This isn't music for everyone but is well worth investigating.
Nov 2012

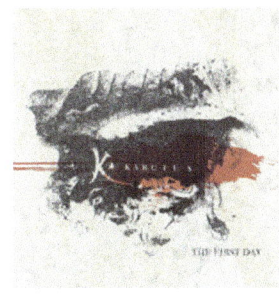

KARCIUS
THE FIRST DAY

Karcius is a Canadian group that was formed in spring 2001 with Simon L'Espérance on guitars, Thomas Brodeur on drums, Mingan Sauriol on keyboards and Sylvain Auclair, who joined the band in 2009, on bass and vocals. This is their fourth album to date, but the first with Sylvain as there has been a four-year gap since 'Episodes' which was released in 2008. Karcius refuse to sit within the 'normal' prog boundaries, as they are also heavily influenced by jazz, RIO and even African rhythms. The end result of the melding of these is an album that is always interesting, always pushing the boundaries, but not always necessarily easy to listen to. There are times when the music just feels angular with sharp edges as the staccato use of piano chords puts a menacing edge onto the proceedings.

There is no doubt that this is often challenging, yet for those who persevere you will find some great music contained within. "The Word" starts as if it is going to be a metal monster before changing into something that is quite different, with vocals that are quite laid back and feel almost throwaway/demo in atmosphere which puts a very different slant on the whole song. There is often a strong use of piano and fretless bass in combination, and this mix of cold and warmth is a very powerful dynamic.

Truly progressive, this album will alienate a lot of listeners but is definitely worth investigation.
Sep 2012

KARDA ESTRA
LAST OF THE LIBERTINES

I have been a fan of Richard Wileman's work since I first became aware of his previous band, Lives & Times, yet I was surprised to see that this 2007 release was his eleventh as Karda Estra. The concept this time is of a man who exchanged his soul for a life of indulgence and the inevitable sadness when it comes to an end. Richard has again brought together a strong line-up to assist him in bringing this story to musical life, and as always has delivered an instrumental album of incredible complexity and depth. In previous reviews I have often commented on the cinematic quality of his work, combined with a great breadth of almost orchestral stylings. This album contains those elements but is now very tightly focused with some almost jazz-stylings from the brass and woodwind. It is also interesting to hear Richard adopting some of the rockiest guitar playing I have heard from him on "Life Drawing" which is very much in direct contrast to "Atom Of Warmth".

I have been playing a lot of Antony Phillips in recent weeks and I can hear some of the same use of instrumentation and acoustic guitar here, especially when Richard produces some of his acoustic touches. Interestingly there are also sections that are quite reminiscent of Steve Hackett, but there is no way that his could be considered a homage to Genesis! Yet again Richard has produced a standout work that lovers of good music are encouraged to discover for themselves. It may not be rock, it may not be jazz, it may not be truly classical, but as an amalgam of all three plus much more, this is a delight from the first note to the last.
Mar 2010

KARDA ESTRA
WEIRD TALES

KE's 2009 album is possibly, to my humble ears, the finest work to come from Richard Wileman. I haven't heard quite all of his CDs, but I have been lucky enough to review most of them, and here is a work of such depth and power to make even the most hardened cynic stand up and take notice. Richard has moved to the dark side and made music that is full of the joy and delight of Hammer House of Horror, yet without the gore and more than enough light to counterbalance the shade. Every track is a delight, with "Skulls In The Stars" potentially my current personal favourite. The orchestration is spot on, the combinations of musicians and Ileesha's wordless vocals combine to bring together that is light and airy yet ominous and brooding all at the same time. This really is music that belongs on the soundtrack of a major film, and I am stunned that he has yet to find a wider audience.

Still, those who have been lucky enough to come across his work before should be searching this album out with urgency – and if you haven't then this couldn't be a better place to start. Richard has been creating some of the most wonderful symphonic/orchestral/cinematic music in the UK for some years, and if you haven't investigated his work until now then you owe it to your ears to start. This is a joy from start to finish – depth and simplicity combining with melody and sometimes discord to create harmony and balance.

I can't say too much about this – it is simply wonderful.
Mar 2010

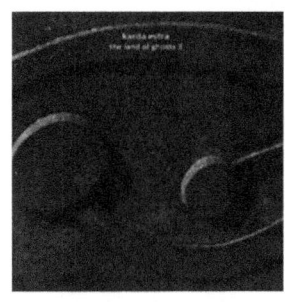

KARDA ESTRA
THE LAND OF GHOSTS 3

This four-track collection of rarities has been released as a download through Bandcamp where the purchaser can pay as little as £1. It includes two pieces that originally appeared on Cyclops samplers along with one from another compilation and a new live solo acoustic guitar number. Richard is a modern classical composer who knows exactly what he wants to achieve and brings together musicians that act much more as a mini orchestra than a band. Even through his Lives & Times days he has used the female voice as an additional instrument and Ileesha is the perfect accompaniment to the music with her wordless arias taking the music to a new level.

It is dreamy, it is atmospheric, as always it is incredible and when one is in the mood to be reflective there is little that hits the mark as perfectly as this.
Aug 2012

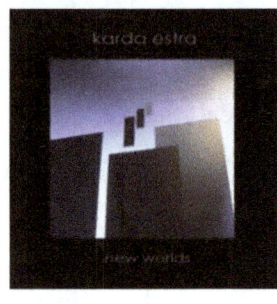

KARDA ESTRA
NEW WORLDS
There is no doubt in my mind that Richard Wileman is one of the finest composers working in his field, and it is criminal that his work isn't more widely known. The reason for that is he firmly straddles the two camps of progressive rock and modern classical probably more than anyone else I have had the pleasure of listening to. Sure, Steve Hackett and Anthony Phillips have made steps in this direction, but they have yet to go as fully down the classical path as Richard. As ever he has been joined on this project by Ileesha Bailey whose ethereal vocals add a haunting beauty to this work. Here he has created twelve futurist nostalgia instrumental tracks and has collaborated with some external sources such as Kavus Torabi (Cardiacs/Knifeworld), Don Falcone & Bridget Wishart (Spirits Burning/Hawkwind) and Stuart Rowe (Lighterthief/Andy Partridge).

This album hasn't been released on CD, but instead has been made available at Bandcamp where the purchaser can pay as little as £1 to download the album in whatever format they wish. Richard has also provided details there of who plays on what song, who assisted in the composition etc. It is the perfect accompaniment to a darkened room and a large glass of malt or do as I did, which was listen to this at night on the deck looking at the stars with the moreporks (our local owl) adding their own eerie voices to proceedings.
Aug 2012

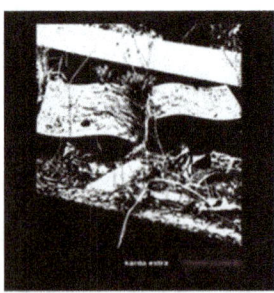

KARDA ESTRA
MONDO PROFONDO
So, Richard is back with his latest album, and as a bonus he has also included his 2011 album 'New Worlds' which was never actually released on CD but was available only as a download. Now, I gave that one 4 *'s when it came out so what about this one? Well, while the cover of 'New Worlds' was bright and colourful (and is shown as the rear cover of the booklet, a nice touch), this one is much darker and immediately makes one think of 'Voivode Dracula' from 2004. So, are we in for a dark gothic progressive classical soundscape? In some ways a definitely "yes", while in others not so much. There are times in this album when we are treated to an orchestral version of Goblin, capturing the dark cinematic essence that they are renowned for, while at others it is lighter and not nearly as oppressive and gothic (including what I can only think of as Star Trek meets 70's cinema adverts). What I have always enjoyed about Richard's work is his refusal to conform to what anyone thinks of his music and will not fit inside any musical form but instead does whatever he feels is right.

It could be argued that this isn't progressive music, as it has much more in common with modern orchestral, yet he is using many different musical themes, instruments, and mediums to create something that is layered, complex, and refuses to be pigeonholed. The two albums contained in this one CD work really well together as they show

different aspects of his work, and the fact that he brings in musicians to play all the separate parts, instead of just using a synth to artificially create them, definitely gives his music a layer of class and sophistication often missing. In the past I have compared his work to Steve Hackett and Anthony Phillips among others, but really, he is in a place of his own design as he melds and moulds his music to be far more visual and cinematic. This CD benefits from being played on headphones, and in the evening sat on the deck looking at the stars this is definitely the perfect accompaniment.
Aug 2013

KATATONIA
DEAD END KINGS

So, back with their 9th album are Swedish group Katatonia. I was really looking forward to this as they played NZ as part of a festival line-up a couple of years ago and to my mind were one of the best bands of the day. I have also enjoyed all of their other albums, and I am glad to say that yet again this didn't disappoint. Many people when they think of Katatonia, imagine them as a metal act. Now, that was true possibly twenty years ago, but these days they have morphed into something that has as many, if not more, links to prog than it does to the metal scene. True, they never move totally away from their roots, and they can still bang the riffs out when they want to, but there are times when they have much more in common with Porcupine Tree and Muse (and there are moments that could be Coldplay) than Candlemass.

It is hard to convey, but there is a bleakness, a despair, in much of their music as if they are tapping a vein of deep sorrow. Their music always makes me feel cold, there really is a physical reaction, and a darkness that is all-pervading. But this isn't a depressing doom album all about reflection and navel-gazing, it is just that they want to shine a little light into a very dark place. There is a great deal of space within this album, but at others it is almost a blanket of combined sound that threatens to overpower. The production is spot on, and the wall of sound is something they do very well indeed. Katatonia will never be to everyone's tastes, but if you enjoy your prog and/or metal to be a little different then you need to seek this out.
Sep 2012

KBB
PROOF OF CONCEPT

KBB are undoubtedly my favourite Japanese band, and not just because of the mastery of violinist Akihisa Tsuboy who leads the group, but the way that the quartet (Toshimitsu Takahashi (keyboards), Dani (bass) and Shirou Sugano (drums) are able to move seamlessly through different styles and seem at home in all of them. When I first came across Akihisa's album with Natsuki Kido, 'Era', I was blown away as he reminded me so much of Ric Sanders, and that is the same here. He has a wonderfully fluid sound, and can bring a deft touch, knowing exactly what needs to be produced to get the best out of the song. I was more than a little confused when "Rice Planting Song" came on, as that is gypsy folk at its' best and this is much more fiddle-playing than violin, but there are others when we are treated to progressive jazz rock at its finest. Opening number "Inner Flames" commences with some drum fills before becoming something quite down and dirty, reminiscent of Colosseum II (violin instead of electric guitar) and some great Hammond organ sounds.

The major downside for me is that this album was released in 2007, and it doesn't appear they have done anything since so I am not sure if they are still active or not. But given that it isn't unusual for them to have long breaks let's hope that there are still more albums to come.
Oct 2012

KEBU
TO JUPITER AND BACK
I first came across keyboard player Kebu when he was playing with Prime Mover, and now here we have his debut solo album which when released charted in the Top 30 in Finland. This is a fully instrumental album using vintage analogue synthesisers and was recorded using only sequencers, tape machines and analogue mixers. This in itself gives the album a very distinctive sound, and in many ways is also quite dated. Although Kebu lists a few musicians that he feels he has been influenced by, one stands head and shoulders above the rest, Jean Michel Jarre. Yes, here and there one may say that this is more Kraftwerk, or more Vangelis, but this is all about layers of simple repeated structures. One could never play this and think that this was an album by Tangerine Dream or Rick Wakeman.

It feels modern, yet also thirty years old, which is due to the sounds being deployed and the way he has approached the arrangements; and for a style of music that can be clinical in the wrong hands this is surprisingly warm and embracing. If you enjoy the style of JMJ then you will get a lot out of this, if not then look elsewhere.
Nov 2012

KINGBATHMAT
TRUTH BUTTON
It has been quite some time since I came across anything from these guys. In fact, when the only other album of theirs I have heard, 'Fantastic Freak Show Carnival', came out in 2005 the band was just one guy, multi-instrumentalist John Bassett, but these days it is a genuine four piece with John providing guitars and vocals, David Georgiou (keyboards), Rob Watts (bass) and Bernie Smirnoff (drums). They are particularly proud that reviewers find it almost impossible to properly describe their

music, and just listening to this the very first time, the one thing I was very sure of was that I really liked it. How to put those feelings into words for others to understand who hadn't heard the album was a little more problematic however. The album is basically the bringing together of hard rock and neo-prog, and with that as a basis there are plenty of art rock, alt rock and even psychedelic influences so that as the listener moves through the album one is never really sure of what is coming next, which in turn is one of its' great joys.

It is a timeless album, almost as much at home in the late Sixties as it is in the current day, refusing to sit in just one space but instead bringing together a cornucopia of sounds and ideas in a way that is somehow always accessible, and never hard work. True, it can go from keyboard led to fuzzed guitar and bass at a drop of a hat as they move happily from one genre and style to another within the same song, but it always maintains a sincerity and conviction that carries it through. Whereas some albums tend to drift, this has a focus and intensity that means that the listener feels compelled to keep coming back to it time and again.

The one annoyance I have with this album is that between the last one I heard and this one is that there have been two others, and thanks to this I now need to go back and see what they are like as well. If you have never come across these guys then you owe it to yourself to go and do so now. And if you ever wondered what Black Sabbath would sound like if they were crossed with 10CC then play "Book Of Faces" and wonder no more.
May 2013

KINGBATHMAT
OVERCOMING THE MONSTER
I was on Facebook one night, when I was interested to find someone telling everyone about this great German prog band that he had come across called KingBathMat. As I pointed out, the last time I looked they were very British (and according to their website are from Hastings), so I am somewhat intrigued to understand why someone thought they were from across the Channel? But it does go to show that after multiple albums and a discography going back to 1998 (when the band was just John Bassett) these guys have somehow stayed very much under the radar for most people. But, with some bands starting to get more recognition possibly this could be their time. If only I could work out how to describe their sound.

Here we have music that at times is heavily dosed in psychedelia, then at others it is Muse at full blast, then it is space rock, then art, then it is all mixed up so that I have no way at all of working out what to say but smiling while I'm typing it. If you want keyboards mixed with harmony vocals and lots of clapping then this is the album for you, at least on "Reality Mining". It is progressive in the truest sense of the word, bringing in multiple styles and types of music then mixing them all together in a way that is different and exciting, vibrant, and fresh, without ever losing sight of their musical roots.

"Kubrick Moon" has some wonderful guitar (and is that a theremin I hear in the background?) that is delicate and spacey, full of emotion and restraint that also contains a naivety that is quite late 70's indie alternative in many ways, while also containing some Twelfth Night moves to boot! That is one of the joys of this album for me, in that it refuses to conform to any genre or sub-genre, and instead the band take great delight in just doing whatever they like. This won't be to everyone's tastes, and certainly not to those who say that they enjoy 'progressive' music when they mean 'regressive', but to these ears this is easily the most ambitious album of theirs that I have heard to date and is well worth discovering.
Jul 2013

KNITTING BY TWILIGHT
AN EVENING OUT OF TOWN
Knitting By Twilight was first organized in sound and vision during the spring of 1994 by musicians/composers John Orsi and Michael Watson. Initially, the collective was percolated to be a springboard for compositional ideas unsuited in nature for either player's regular combo. 'An Evening Out Of Town' was released in 2008, and like much of their work brings together avant-garde with smatterings of jazz and film-score style music to create something that is extremely individual – imagine if you will Richard Wileman and Robin Taylor joining forces and this is approaching that sort of partnership. One of the most prevalent forces in their music is not the discord or unusual use of instruments, but the space between the notes. At times there is the feeling that this audio tapestry has gaps that you could drive a truck through, but it is the space that gives the music the structure it needs to twist and evolve.

It is melodic yet there is discord, it follows standard musical structure but has nothing in common with normal music and like everything which is worth listening to, it takes many repeated hours to get the full benefit from it. The pieces may not be interlinked, but they are very much related, and it is best to play the whole instrumental album in one sitting when one will not be disturbed and just let the music take you away a to better place. Yet again KBT have released an album that transcends most musical styles and is something that is very much their own.
Oct 2011

KNITTING BY TWILIGHT
RIDING THE WAY BACK
This 2009 EP contains music that for one reason or another didn't make it onto 'An Evening Out Of Town' (mostly for thematic reasons as opposed to quality control). There are also a couple of reworked versions of a couple of songs that have appeared previously, but to my ears this is mostly about continuing the good work of the previous album. All the trademarks of quality that one expects from KBT are there in

spades: complex atmospheric filmscape music that demands to have full attention always paid to it – it is yet another triumph. It is certainly not for those who like their music to come to them in easy-to-understand 4/4 bars with pretty harmonies and boy meets girls lyrics, but if you want a full meal as opposed to a snack then this is for the connoisseur.
Oct 2011

KOMPENDIUM
BENEATH THE WAVES
Many years ago, I was sent an album by Cyan, 'For King And Country' (can that really be 20 years ago?), and I was so impressed that it made it to the cover of Feedback #18. A short while later I was at a Steve Hackett gig that was taking place in a village hall (a warmup for his UK tour that year, it was stunning) and ended up chatting to Robert Reed who had arrived with some Welsh reprobates (good old Ezra, another great band). I am sure that neither of us ever expected for him to be masterminding an album on which Steve would contribute. Over the years Robert worked next with The Fyreworks and then of course with Magenta, but he always had a desire to release a concept album that he felt could be talked about in the same breath as 'War Of The Worlds' and while I don't think he has made it quite to those heights, he has indeed released an album of incredible beauty, majesty and breadth.

Of course, if you are going to set your aim that high you need a strong group of musicians to assist in achieving that and Rob has pulled together an incredible bunch of people. Rob of course provides all of the songs and plays keyboards, but he is joined by Steve Hackett, Francis Dunnery (It Bites), John Mitchell (Arena, It Bites), Nick Barrett (Pendragon), Nick Beggs (Steve Hackett Band, Iona, Kajagoogoo), Jakko Jakszyk (20th Century Schizoid Band), Gavin Harrison (Porcupine Tree), Mel Collins (King Crimson, Camel), Dave Stewart (Hatfield and the North, National Health, Bruford), Troy Donockley (who I always think of as Iona but I saw him play with Nightwish at the beginning of the year in Auckland). For vocals he has Steve Balsamo (Jesus Christ Superstar stage production), opera singers Shan Cothi and Rhys Mierion, plus assorted choirs, and orchestration.

Musically this is symphonic, orchestral, and Celtic all rolled up together with wonderful production and great performances throughout. At times I am reminded of Mostly Autumn, at others Kansas, then off into Magenta. I have a real regret that this was provided to me as a download to review, as it has been released with a 20-page book with the feeling that this is all about the complete experience, as it used to be when I was younger. Back in the Seventies the only way to listen to music was by putting the record on the player and studying the artwork/lyrics while the sounds took over the world: listening to music was an end to itself, something that was tactile and real as opposed to just a click of a mouse. There is a real feeling here of something special that has been accomplished, and I am sure that repeated plays will find this move from 4 *'s to 5. This really is an outstanding achievement and something that all progheads should investigate.
Mar 2013

GREG LAKE
SONGS OF A LIFETIME

What we have here is a one-man show, combining Greg performing some of his most well-known songs (with a backing track) along with stories of things that have happened in his life. So, we hear about the Beatles, and when he saw Elvis in concert and so forth. The one thing I did learn from this was that the artist behind 'Court of the Crimson King' died only three days after he presented the artwork to the band, at the age of 21. There is no doubting Greg's musical ability or his stunning voice, but is this really the best way to hear him? Rick Wakeman has been performing a similar show, on and off, for some ten years or more where he tells stories and plays the piano. The major difference there is that Rick is providing new interpretations of songs, with no backing music whatsoever, whereas here we have instances such as on "From The Beginning" where there is quite an extended keyboard solo yet at that point all Greg does is play chords as that was his part in that section of the song.

I have always enjoyed Greg's performances with ELP (and I loved it when he fronted Asia, I just wish that they had recorded a studio album together), but he hasn't done a great deal outside that and comes across better in the band environment. This has been billed as 'Songs of a Lifetime' but the most recent song here is the mighty "Touch and Go" from the Emerson Lake & Powell album in 1985, so what happened in the last 28 years? Greg also performs some covers that were important to him in his musical life, such as "Heartbreak Hotel" yet while it is interesting to hear Greg's version, I would much rather hear more ELP. The stories are lengthy, which means that the album doesn't benefit from repeated plays either.

All in all I would rather play the compilation of his that was issued a few years ago, 'From The Beginning', but although I can't see myself returning to it very often he still has a wonderful voice...
Jun 2013

LANDMARQ
ENTERTAINING ANGELS

It has been some 13 years since the last Landmarq album, due in no small part to Tracy's battle with cancer. This got me thinking, as the keyboard player is Mike Varty who is also in Credo – whose singer Mark Colton also suffered a life-threatening illness which long delayed an album. If I was in DeeExpus, Shadowland, or anything else Mike is involved with I might be concerned.... Anyway, I first came across Tracy's singing a million years ago when she was in Quasar with Dave Wagstaffe and Steve Leigh, and after they all left that band they formed Landmarq, although with Damian Wilson on vocals while Tracy worked with Clive Nolan and also followed a solo career. It was only towards the end of the Nineties that Tracy became the singer on a full-time basis (after Damian, then Moon, and then Damian again if my memory serves me right) and she appeared on their last studio album 'Science of Coincidence', but this is the first to feature Mike as he has only been there seven years. The rest of the guys are those who have been there since the beginning, namely Uwe D'Rose (guitars), Steve Gee (bass) and Dave Wagstaffe (drums). Although since the release of this album Dave has had to announce his sad departure as he is no longer able to commit to touring, as he also plays with Martin Turner's Wishbone Ash.

So, what about it then? Production is top class, as one would expect from Mike, and although Tracy has been through a lot in the last ten years it doesn't show in her voice at all. I have always felt that Tracy is one of the most under-rated singers from these shores (go and find her solo album if you don't believe me), and is easily on a par with Lana Lane, and here she sings with a passion and strength that totally belies what has been going on in her personal life. In many ways this is easy listening prog, in the sense that the music is here as an accompaniment to the vocals and although there is a lot of complexity in the arrangements it is all about the singing. There are Floydian moments ("Mountains of Anglia" features some great slide guitar as well as sax) and others that are more in your face, but always it is about mood.

My favourite Landmarq album is always probably going to be 'Solitary Witness', but in many ways this is a rebirth and to my ears is a totally different band who produced that album 20 years ago, not just in personnel but in approach. 2012 has been a wonderful year for bands that first came to prominence in the 90's to produce great albums, and Landmarq are no exception.
Nov 2012

LANTINOR
ENSIGN OF FAIRIES, BOOK 1
Lantinor originally started life as a hard rock group in Barnaul, the administrative centre of Altai Krai in Russia. After some changes in line-up the style also moved to something that was more British, containing folk elements. They managed to attract a following, but having released their debut album, the band seem to disappear from the scene. Band leader Alexander Kaminsky recorded four albums during this period under the guise of Lantinor, with the group 'proper' getting back together in 2005. Since then, they have released first 'Book of Rites and then 'Last Wonder of the World', and have now returned with 'Ensign of Fairies, Book 1'.

Apparently, this is a concept album, but given that the lyrics are in Russian it is meaningless to me so I have to use the voice as another instrument. But musically there is more than enough going on as they appear to have taken mid-Seventies Horslips and Jethro Tull as a base and have then brought in Jadis and Steve Hillage to create a sound that is very much of times past, classic retro prog if you were. The guitars are clean and clear, with some concise but dynamic solos, and the guys shift the style around. They have no problem from moving to power pop or punk-lite if that is what is needed as part of the musical progression, or to be more layered and harmonic if that is what is needed.

If, like me, you don't worry too much about the language then this is worth investigating further. It isn't indispensable but is worth hearing.
Jul 2013

SVEN LARSSON
BAD MAD MAN
Back in 1992 I was in contact with some young Swedes who had formed a band called Galleon and released the album 'Lynx' on their own label. I duly reviewed it, and for the next few years we were in constant contact (they even sent me a really nice long-sleeved t-shirt which my wife promptly stole), although we lost touch somewhere around the millennium. So, I was pleased to receive this album as Sven joined Galleon in time for 'Beyond Dreams' and among the many guests included on this there are Ulf Pettersson and Göran Fors. In addition, some of the tracks are again feature Sven's bandmates from Street Talk, Fredrik Bergh (keyboards), Björn Lodmark (bass) and Christian Johansson (drums) as well as singer Göran Edman. Other singers involved include Thomas Eriksson and Anders Åhlund.

The variety of musicians, as well as Sven's own different interests (AOR and prog among others) has resulted in a wonderfully grown-up extremely well-crafted album that is a sheer delight to listen to. At some points it is almost like Chris Rea with the simple guitar lines at the front, while at others it combines a myriad of styles in a laid-back almost lounge jazz-lite manner that is warm and embracing. The highlight for me is the penultimate song, "Castle of Mine", which is a soft prog number with fretless bass and simple piano that builds into a number that has an amazing hook – if ever something should be a radio hit it is this. This is Sven's second solo album, and if the other is anything like as good as this then I want to hear it. Awesome stuff.
Oct 2012

LEGEND
RITUAL ECHO
One of the best pieces of musical news that I heard last year was that Legend were coming back to life. They were a band way ahead of their times in many ways, and while bands such as Nightwish are now held in high regard there has been scant recognition for a group that was pursuing symphonic prog with delicate female vocals all those years ago. This compilation has been released to celebrate 21 years since the band first began – next year will be 20 years since their debut album! It is hard to think that the last of their three albums was released as long ago as 1996: I was lucky enough to catch the band live a few times, and rate them as some of the musical highlights of my concert going career.

Paul Thomson revelled in his role of guitar god, crunching out riffs, while Steve Paine provided loads of melodic runs – really taking the music to new heights while Debbie Chapman provided the vocals – haunting and melodic, delicate yet powerful. This compilation features songs from all three albums but the ones which represent the debut are here live versions previously unavailable on CD. John Macklin provides drums throughout with Martyn Rouski providing bass on some and Paul adding it on others.

Playing songs such as "Windsong" I am struck again at how relevant this music is in the current scene. This doesn't sound as if it is now nearly twenty years old but rather that this is a new band that are seeking to stamp their own take onto symphonic prog. From a fan's viewpoint I will always moan that a compilation doesn't feature this song or that, but here I think Steve has done a great job in pulling together something that is fully reflective of the band, with "The Wild Hunt" always a given with me for inclusion.

If this wasn't enough, the long unavailable video 'Playing With Fire' will soon be available on CD (and hopefully DVD) while the band are also working on new material with Dave Foster of Mr. So & So providing assistance on guitar, and they are planning for a new album by the end of 2010. Now could not be a better time for finding out about one of the UK prog scene's best bands.
Mar 2010

LEGEND
CARDINAL POINTS
I'm not sure how long I have known Steve Paine, but it must be about 20 years. During that time our discussions on music have changed into something far greater, and in many ways, I view him as a guide, and he has been very important to my whole family during stressful periods of our lives. That friendship had stayed strong even after Legend ceased to be, something that I viewed as a great musical loss. During their time together they produced three wonderful albums, which musically were quite different to anything else that was around at the time – symphonic prog rock with strong guitars that combined with soaring female vocals may not sound out of the ordinary now, but back then it really was. Let's put some things into perspective, the first Nightwish album was released in 1996, the first Within Temptation was 1997, the first Legend album was 1991!

Their final album, 'Triple Aspect', was a tour de force and when I heard that they were going to go their separate ways I was extremely disappointed as here was a band that had become firm friends, and they had introduced me to other music such as Incubus Succubus (who I first saw supporting Legend at Oxford Stocks – still one of my favourite all-time gigs), The Rattlers, Talis Kimberley and Mr. So & So (all of whom Steve and live engineer Jon Moreau had produced). They were incredible in concert, and when they thanked me from the stage of Croydon Fairfield Halls it was all over, way too soon.

Fast forward too many years and Steve contacted me to let me know that he was going to be reforming the band and was writing music again. He had had a number of conversations with drummer John Macklin and original singer Kerry Parker (at this point Kerry was not even being considered as vocalist – she is simply one of Steve's closest friends) and as John and Steve both really missed playing, they gradually worked out a way of possibly making it all happen. Work had commenced on 'Cardinal Points' before the band had called it a day, so now seemed the right time to start on it again even though they had no idea what was no going on in the prog scene

The personnel changes were really down to both Paul Lamb and Debbie Chapman being committed to their careers, and Steve had lost touch with Paul Thomson, so Dave Foster (of the So & So's) was the next logical choice. When Debbie was reluctant to get involved, Kerry Parker was again the obvious choice as she'd been the original vocalist of the band in the embryonic stages. However, Kerry's work commitments meant she couldn't step into the role, though she did start helping Steve to find a new vocalist and assisting him with the lyrics. Though once Kerry heard the demos and got into writing lyrics and a fortuitous change of employer she jumped at the chance. So even though the new version of the band has ended up without two significant members of the band, the new line up was also wonderful as it included people who had been a part of the Legend family over the years. Kerry in particular, as she was the first person to sing many of Steve's songs – such as 'Light in Extension', 'Windsong' and 'Evidence of Autumn'. The line-up was completed by bassist Dan Nelson, and they roped in a few friends to help on additional instruments such as Dave's wife Claire on flute.

So, four songs are what we get on the new album, ranging from just under 13 minutes to just over 17 minutes long. The sound is instantly identifiable as Legend, with keyboards often taking the lead role but also room for plenty of guitars as well. Dave has fitted in well with the role of power foil to Steve but given that they have been working together for so many years that isn't really surprising, and in Kerry they have a great singer – given that she was the original vocalist for the band it probably isn't surprising that she has a similar style to Debbie, but she has added an extra element to the proceedings.

If anyone wants to listen to just a few minutes that sum up the album easily then the place to go is track three and listen to the beginning of "Spark To A Flame" where there are wonderful harmony vocals, punchy music, power chords, drama and much, much more.

This is easily one of the most powerful and inspiring progressive rock albums to come out for years – one that those lucky enough to discover it are going to be playing time and time again. The band have been stunned by the reception to date and are planning the next album and hopefully some live dates as well – now if they could come to NZ, I would be a very happy man indeed.

Legend – Cardinal Points. You owe it to your ears to get this
July 2011

LEGEND
PLAYING WITH FIRE
After the release of 'Light In Extension' Legend found that they were popular in Japan,

but as they were a small band with no record label support they couldn't really tour there so instead released a live video for which they hired a great light system and had a blast. For some reason they never released a live album, but that has now been corrected by Steve going back to the tapes for the video and releasing 'Playing With Fire'. This is Legend in concert live in 1992, and as anyone who was lucky enough to see them back then knows, this was a prog band with a concentration on power rock, great interplay between keyboards and rock guitars (think a far more modern sounding Uriah Heep with the emphasis on the keyboards as opposed to the guitars). I was lucky enough to see them three times in concert, and I was always blown away by the sheer power and might of the band. Somehow singer Debbie Chapman managed to soar above it all: there may have been melodic chaos going on but her clear and powerful vocals shine above it all.

Someone coming across this now would say that there are strong elements of Nightwish in this album, but remember that Legend pre-date them, they were doing this first! This album contains many of my favourite songs, including "The Chase" – which is a perfect example of what prog rock instrumentals can be like, exciting and invigorating it is incredible and set the heart racing every time I play it.

Legend are back, with a compilation, this live album and the stunning 'Cardinal Points' – so if you were unlucky enough to miss them first time around, and many did as they didn't fit in with the normal prog scene, then you owe it to your ears to find out about them this time. Awesome!
July 2011

LEGEND
SPIRIT
I probably need to put some sort of disclaimer at the top of this review, as I have been involved with these guys one way or another for some twenty years now, and keyboard player/composer/band leader Steve Paine is one of my closest friends from the music scene. A few months ago, he sent me a mix of this album and asked me for my views and opinions before he undertook the final mix as he was looking for a fresh set of ears. Listening to the album for pure production as opposed to trying to formulate ideas on the music was an interesting challenge, but I played my part as best as I could, and in the fullness of time the final product arrived and this time I could listen to it as it was intended.

When the band reformed for 'Cardinal Points' it was quite a different line-up from the one that recorded 1996's 'Triple Aspect' (well it was fifteen years between the two). Steve Paine was there of course, as was drummer John Macklin who had been involved since 'Second Sight', but original singer Kerry Parker (who left the band before they recorded their debut 'Light In Extension' in 1991) had returned instead of Debbie

Chapman, and there was a new bassist in Dan Nelson and new guitarist in Dave Foster. Dave of course is guitarist with Mr. So & So, a band that was originally signed to Steve's Pagan Media label. Well, that was 2011, and now here we are in 2013 with more changes, which makes the band more like the original. Anyone who has ever seen Legend in concert or has seen the cover of 'Playing With Fire', will know that while Dave is one of the most incredible guitarists you will ever find (I have a memory of him holding a conversation with John Wetton's manager while playing an incredible solo at the same time) the one person who should be there is the original metal god himself, Paul Thomson. And he's back. His interplay with Steve and connection only comes about from many hours spent sharing the same stage, and many years sharing the same musical dream so it is great that he is onboard once again. Then, we also now have a new singer in Beck Sian (who apparently is Kate Bush's cousin). Apart from having an extremely positive impact of reducing the average age of the band, she has also brought with her a new depth and vitality as she not only has a powerful voice, but an incredible range. Although she often reaches into soprano, she also has a firm control of alto so while at times she comes across as a mix of Debbie, Talis Kimberley and Anna Ryder, she also belts it out in the lower registers. Macca is back again, while Steve provides bass as well as keyboards.

So, what of the album? I have seen a few reviews of this album that have stated that in many ways this is a logical progression from 'Cardinal Points', but I'm not sure that I agree with them. In many ways this feels to me that it has much more in common with the earlier period, especially 'LIE', but taken to a whole new level. It is more complex, more layered, with Paul relishing the opportunity to yet again provide crunching riffs that take the music further. Although they are definitely more progressive than symphonic, these guys use Paul's heaviness to move them more into that arena while multi-tracked vocals also provide additional edge. Macca shows no sign at all of the RSI that he has been suffering and is never content to sit on a 4/4 beat but instead really works the kit, providing a level of intensity that the rest of the band have to lift themselves to match. He can often be found matching the complex arrangements note for note, emphasising the melody. Steve is, well, Steve. His songs and arrangements are distinctive, they just couldn't be by anyone else. One of my favourite songs is "The Wild Hunt" from 'Second Sight', and there is quite a lot on this album that reminds me of that approach, and that can only be a great thing in my book.

After saying all that about the music, it would not be the same without a great singer at the front and in Beck they have a real find. She can be clear and fine, she can be powerful, she can throw her voice around as if it is another instrument, be contrary to the melody or absolutely bang on. She is an incredible talent, and the combination of her vocal style, wonderful songs, and great musicianship, has made this a more than worthy addition to Legend's canon. In fact, it may well be their finest hour. But I will have to live with it for a few more years yet before I can confirm that.

This is an album of incredible depth and passion, and the five songs (the album is just over an hour long) pass by far too quickly. A real triumph.
Nov 2013

LEPROUS
COAL
There is no doubt that when these guys released 'Bilateral' in 2011 that they created a lot of noise in the prog scene, literally. Here is a band that is happy, really happy, to be a metal outfit and tour with bands like Amorphis, Therion, Opeth, Pagan's Mind et al yet also have one foot firmly in the prog camp. And if you didn't know, these guys have acted as fellow Norwegian Ihsahn's backing band so they really have no qualm with producing music at the heaviest and most complex level. When I started playing this, two bands sprang to mind immediately, and the more I played it the more I was convinced that I was right. Here is a band that takes the melodic soundscape of Muse, and then mixes it up liberally with Devin Townsend to create something that at times is almost breathtakingly beautiful and yet at others is a wall of sound as they crank up the energy and the volume to 11.

There is no doubt to my mind that this is metallic prog metal of some class and power, yet I am sure that it will upset some listeners who feel that prog should be more sedate and not in your face quite so much. But if prog is about progressing and pushing the boundaries as opposed to regressing and attempting to be a clone of the great bands that have gone before then this is it. This is modern, with the odd nod back to King Crimson, and is very much modern metallic progressive music for the 21st century. The more I played this the more I enjoyed it and while I think 4*'s is the right mark for now, ask me again in a few months and it may have made it up 5. If you want a dynamic soundscape then this is it.
Jun 2013

LIGRO
DICTIONARY 2
I need to investigate how long it will take me to get to Indonesia from NZ, hopefully not that long, and while there I am going to go to Jakarta and make sure that I catch these guys at a gig. I know that Leo says that there is loads of untapped and unknown talent in that part of the world, but bloody hell! These guys are absolutely stunning! Agam Hamzah (guitars), Adi Darmawan (bass) and drummer Gusti Hendy formed the band in 2004 and this is their debut international release. Ligro when read backwards, means "crazy people" in the Bahasa (Indonesian national) language – but crazy signifying fearlessness and playful abandon.

Pick a song, any song, and prepare to be blown away by a trio that are so tight that it is impossible to separate them and just as you think that one person is the main player another comes along and makes you change your mind. Take "Stravinsky (with Bach intro)" for example. This commences as a solo exercise in bass dexterity and control before morphing into an arrangement of Igor Stravinsky's "An Easy Piece Using Five Notes: with Agam very much in control although he is pushed to the end by his

colleagues in time. This is an incredible album and proves that wonderful musicians can be found all over the world. This may not be a band that is known to many outside of their own country, but I sincerely believe that is going to change as here is a band that has the chops to rise to the top of their field.
Feb 2013

LODGIC
NOMADIC SANDS
Now, I hadn't come across this band before, but they had an interesting line-up, including Mike and Billy Sherwood on vocals and keyboards, and vocals and bass respectively, with Jimmy Haun on guitars and vocals. They were around for ten years, from 1977-1987, but this 1985 album is their only release. It was produced with David Paich, Tom Knox and Steve Porcaro, so perhaps it is not surprising given all involved, that this is an AOR album with some prog influences. The other thing that is apparent straightaway is that this was recorded in the mid-Eighties and brings together influences that in many ways are somewhat dated, but fun at the same time. Imagine '90125' era Yes getting involved with Go West and the Thompson Twins and you may get somewhere close to this. It is an album that brings a smile to the face, as it just needs to be accepted on face value and just don't expect any depth to this at all.

It is an appetiser as opposed to a main meal, something light that will keep you going until lunch, and at the end the feeling is that you have listened to something and it was okay, but you can't remember much about it apart from the fact that it is an 80's AOR/Pop/Prog album that is listenable, but nothing more. After Lodgic broke up, Billy of course formed World Trade and found fame and fortune, but if you are interested in his early career then this is pleasant without being essential.
Aug 2013

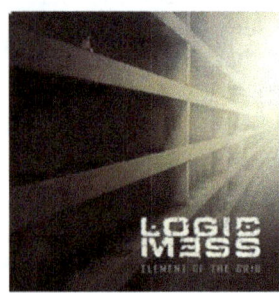

LOGIC MESS
ELEMENT OF THE GRID
Logic Mess originally operated as Crystal Lake under which name they released their debut album 'Safe' in 2009. However, a line-up change altered the sound of the band so much that they decided to start afresh, so here is their second 'debut' album (if that makes sense, and it probably doesn't to be fair). Marcin Gawelek (guitar), Łukasz Bienkowski (bass) and Piotr Wypych (keyboards) were joined by Krzysztof Owsiak (vocals) and Piotr Majka (drums) to come up with the new sound, with the band becoming heavier, while the way that they use synths has also brought in a new texture to what they are doing. This is definitely apparent on "The Guards of Integration" where in some of the sections they become Poisoned Electrick Head, no mean feat.

This is a concept album, but it is probably best not to take it too seriously as the scene

setting is a little clumsy to say the least, and saying the word "bucks" when referring to dollars just doesn't work in a Polish accent, honest. But, there is a lot of potential here and when they cut loose and go for it they really do hit the ground running. Obviously influenced by Dream Theater, the songs tend to be shorter with a good heavy edge and loads of melody. This is easily one of the best albums I have heard out of Poland in recent years, and while the concept may not be the most original and the voiceovers can be a little painful, this is something I really enjoyed. A solid effort indeed, and I look forward to the follow-up with interest.
Mar 2013

LOST WORLD BAND
SOLAR POWER
I first came across these guys somewhere around the time of the release of their official debut album, and it is quite hard to realise that 'Trajectories' came out some ten years ago while the original three members Vassili Soloviev, Andy Didorenko and Aleksander Akimov met more than 20 years ago at a music conservatory in Moscow. Over the years there have been a few line-up changes and since 2009's 'Sources' they have become a trio with Andy Didorenko taking on even more responsibility (violins, guitars, bass, keyboards, vocals as well as providing all the songs) while Vassili Soloviev is still there on flute with new member Konstantin Shtirlitz on drums. The biggest problem with this album is working out how best to describe it, as while I could list influences (King Crimson, Miles Davis, Kansas, After Crying, KBB plus many more) it just doesn't do justice to what is a wonderful collection of music.

There are times when the music is in perfect harmony, at others in imperfect discord, yet at all times making perfect musical sense and daring the listener to sit down and concentrate on something that is a perfect meld of prog rock and jazz while being beholden to neither, and instead creates something that is quite different. The classical training and influences also come through at times, with a resulting mix and morass that is multi-layered and complex yet is also easy to work through. If one sometimes feels that a song or album is just like a snack, over way too quickly and being okay but not really filling, then take it from me that this is a feast. If you are musically adventurous and want something to get your teeth into then this is it.
Apr 2013

LOST WORLD BAND
IN CONCERT
I was having a 'conversation' with Andy Didorenko one day, and I said that I had never heard their live album which was recorded in Moscow at the end of 2009. His response was that he was never entirely happy with it as it was hard for the four of them to reproduce the material on stage. There was a lot of instrument switching, arrangements had to be simplified and keyboards were utilised for bass. He finished by saying that he wished that they had an orchestra at their disposal like ELP had in '77, but if I really

wanted to hear it then he would send me a copy. Well, if he is disappointed in this I really want to hear something that he is entirely happy with! Lost World Band are Vassili Soloviev (vocal, flute, guitar, keyboards), Andrii Didorenko (acoustic and electric guitar, violin), Konstantin Yudin (keyboards) and Veniamin Rozov (drums), and they push the boundaries between prog, jazz and classical so much so that the lines are completely blurred as they trample all over any sort of musical restraints.

When Andrii is in full flight on violin then it is as if they are channeling KBB and turning them into something even more dramatic and powerful. "Samum" is a case in point, as while Andy often takes the lead, the reason that it works so well is due to the support with Vassili swapping between flute and guitar, Konstantin providing some incredibly deft pianowork and Veniamin driving it along ferociously from the back. But there are other songs when Vassili is very much the melodic lead and Andy provides support. The strength of these guys is their incredible musicality (remember these guys started off when Vassili and Andy met while undertaking classical studies at a conservatory), their knowledge of musical structure and arrangement, and their downright refusal to conform to any sort of preconceived ideas of what they should be doing.

This is what prog music should be about, musical dexterity and complexity while at the same time capturing the listener so that they have to stay right to the very end. Andy may not be completely happy with this album, but I am. If this doesn't deserve five stars then nothing does.
May 2013

JOHANNES LULEY
TALES FROM SHEEPFATHER'S GROVE
In December I heard from Moth Vellum founder and guitarist Johannes Luley who asked if I would be interested in hearing his new solo album. A short while later and I was staring at the incredible artwork from Harout Demirchyan and I felt that I had been transported back to the Seventies – but would the music pass the test? Well, I had nothing to worry about on that score. Johannes provides all the instruments himself (apart from a concert harp played by Stephanie Bennett) and uses three singers, Robin Hathaway, Kristina Sattler and Sianna Lyons, and the result is nothing short of stunning.

It is as if Jon Anderson has again joined with Vangelis, but without the wall of keyboards, and instead it feels much more 'real', containing lots of space and depth. In many ways it is extremely complex yet comes across in a simple manner. It is not music that can be played in the background as it may just disappear, but greatly rewards those who have the time to spare just to listen to the music as an end in itself. Electric guitar is used for emphasis as opposed to always being a central pillar, with plenty of room for mandolin and acoustic instruments. Instead of programmed drums or even a normal drumkit, Johannes has instead opted for handheld percussion which gives a very different feel to the norm and this builds to a climax in "Give and Take".

This is one of the most beautiful prog albums I have ever had the pleasure to listen to, and I am sure that when 2013 comes to a close that this will be on many people's Top 10's. I know it will be on mine.
Jan 2013

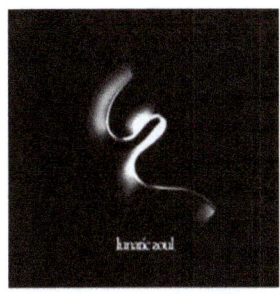

LUNATIC SOUL
LUNATIC SOUL
Lunatic Soul are a studio project that has been put together by Riverside frontman Mariusz Duda, and they released their debut album at the end of 2008. This is the first part of a diptych with two albums looking the same with just a logo and band name, no album title, just with the debut having a black cover and the second with white. The black album is a passage to the side of death, and the white one is a passage to the side of life. This is an album that is full of layers – one that is both immediate yet full of depth and passion. Strangely it is an album that doesn't have an electric guitar on it anywhere yet doesn't sound as if it is smothered in keyboards. It is melodic and thoughtful, bringing together many different styles in a way that the listener feels transported into another realm.

This isn't music that can just be left and played as background, it is far deeper and way more fulfilling than that. At times it is symphonic and orchestral while at others it is delicate, and one dares not even breathe in case the spell is broken. The use of guest musicians works really well with additional instruments being brought into the mix just for a few bars here and there where their impact is required. Just play "Near Life Experience" and you will understand exactly what I mean. Thankfully the Lunatic Soul website is in English as well as Polish and the second album should be out before the end of the year so now is the time to investigate the debut and marvel at its progtastic beauty.
Mar 2010

MACHINE MASS TRIO
AS REAL AS THINKING
Originally MMT were a side-project of douBt, which contains both Tony Bianco (on drums and loops) and Michel Delville (on guitar, bouzouki, and live effects – he also plays guitar in The Wrong Object), and here they have joined with Jordi Grognard who provides saxophones, bass clarinet and flute. 'As Real as Thinking' was recorded in just one day towards the end of 2010 in a small studio in Belgium, and the band is clear to make the statement that there are no overdubs at all. This album is all about expert musicians feeding off each other, going where the

music drives them, which isn't always as clear to the listener as it is to those who are undertaking the journey. The closeness with which Michel and Tony interact is just astounding, and Jordi takes little or no part on "Falling Up" which is by the far the longest song on the album as the guys just go for it – providing an intensity and note density which is incredibly powerful. It is pushing through the limits of avant garde into prog and even into areas that are almost outside of music itself – just an incredible experience. It is difficult to comprehend the relationship these two musicians have as they keep feeding each other with ideas and energy. In other pieces it isn't unusual for both Michel and Jordi to be changing instruments as well as styles so that it often feels that there are way more than three guys involved, performing all of this totally live. As the label describes it so well, this was a "session of bold, risk-taking improvisation". A final moving statement from Tony, "This record was recorded as my beloved wife, Mary, was fighting for her life. She has thus passed away and my playing is a tribute to her beautiful soul." If you want music that is challenging then this is it, but if you want simple clean repeated pop melodies then probably not.
Jan 2013

MAELSTROM
MAELSTROM
This American band were formed in the early Seventies and were led by guitarist/keyboardist/sax player Robert Williams, while the rest of the line-up was multi-instrumentalist James Larner, keyboard player Mark Knox, drummer Jim Miller, bassist Paul Klotzbier and Jeff McMullen on lead vocals/guitars. This album is a reissue of their debut, which came out in 1973 with the title 'On The Gulf', along with two additional songs recorded in concert in 1980 (although the line-up had changed dramatically by then). If this album had come out just a few years earlier I am sure that these guys would be household names by now, but the tide was already shifting by 1973 and this album would have be seen to be a little dated even then.

This is something that really belongs at the end of the Sixties, with psychedelia having a huge impact on the overall sound. The use of saxophone combined with the guitar does give the music a somewhat fusion sound but for the most part doesn't really belong in that genre (the problem with trying to pigeonhole music is that music isn't a pigeon, so often doesn't fit where people think it might – cue long discussion on what is progressive music anyway). But whatever genre it may or may not belong to, the important question is it any good? Well, it is dated not only musically but also in the arrangements and production but is something that I really enjoyed playing. The guys obviously spent a lot of time together and this comes off with the interaction, and the use of different ideas such as vibraphone on "Law and Crime" which gives the song a very different feel with the (dated) drums driving it along while Jeff provides good strong vocals. It is an effective album, definitely belonging to a bygone era, but is still something that while not essential is certainly worth hearing.
Aug 2013

MAGIC PIE
CIRCUS OF LIFE

There has always been a vibrant and fruitful prog scene in Norway, and the second album from Magic Pie shows no sign at all of letting up. Unusually for a prog band this sextet includes not one but two lead vocalists – and then relies very heavily on instrumental passages as well! The title cut is a true epic broken into five parts – one of which is 22 minutes long, and it really showcases a band that wants to move forward with the sound but at the same time is rooted in the Seventies with wonderfully dated Moog and Hammond sounds. They have been likened to Spock's Beard by some but in sheer attitude and guitar sound they are far closer to The Flower Kings in my opinion, with generous doses of Gentle Giant thrown in for good measure.

The one, tiny, thing that did grate just a little was that during the last part of the epic there is some fairground music in the background. I am convinced that it is the same piece that forms the introduction to Queen's "Brighton Rock" – and consequently found it very annoying indeed! I could of course well be wrong but would be grateful if anyone else thinks the same! That is just a niggle on what is a very good prog album indeed. If you have yet to listen to Magic Pie, then this is a great place to start.
Sep 2007

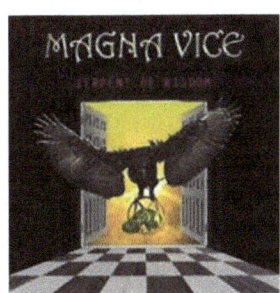

MAGNA VICE
SERPENT OF WISDOM

'Serpent of Wisdom' is the debut album of Turku, Finland-based Magna Vice. The label describes it as an ambitious 70-minute progressive heavy metal concept album. It tells the story of war veteran Ed Diamond who suffers from hallucinations. He realizes a helping hand is closer than he expected – but first he must free himself from the shackles of yesterday. The story is carried by numerous clues and soundscapes in between songs.

When they say ambitious, they possibly should have said slightly over-ambitious as what we have here is a band that is trying extremely hard, sometimes too hard, to get it right and be over the top. There are elements of this album that work very well, with some very strong guitar and some good songs, but what lets them down is the production and some of the execution.

The drums are just too high in the mix, and after a while the snare drum becomes annoying, but what really lets this album down are the vocals. The vocalist is very nearly a great singer, but not quite. So, there are times when he sings just too high, or just slightly off, or often with a strident edge that really does cut through everything, but not in a good way. These guys do show some real promise, and there is no doubting that they have loads of ideas, but they need to work with a strong producer who can keep everything under control, and then we might get the album that is undoubtedly there, but this isn't it.
Nov 2013

MAHOGANY FROG
SENNA

More and more I seem to be coming across albums that appear to have more sonic connection with my teenage years than the current day, but as that isn't an issue all I can say is "bring it on!" This is Mahogany Frog's sixth album, but somehow is a band that I have managed to miss altogether but I see that I am going to have to rectify the omission. The four-piece comprise Graham Epp (electric guitars, MicroMoog, Farfisa Organ, Farf Muff, ARP String Ensemble, Korg MS2000, electric & acoustic pianos), Jesse Warkentin (electric guitars, MicroMoog, Farfisa Organ, Farf Muff, ARP String Ensemble, Korg MS2000, electric & acoustic pianos), Scott Ellenberger (electric & acoustic bass, Briscoe organ, percussion) and Andy Rudolph (drums, percussion & electronics) yet are a far more in your face rock band than you may imagine from the impressive list of keyboards.

This is progressive rock mixed with krautrock mixed with post rock mixed with jazz, all thrown into a melting pot and allowed to brew and take on a life all its own. Imagine Can playing with Tortoise with Soft Machine on the sidelines while someone decides to throw in some filthy guitar riffs to tie it all together. This is early Seventies sweat and long hair combined with certain drugs and the music being played at incredibly high volumes. They provide tight melodies and controlled chaos while at others there seems to be no control at all and they ride the thick basslines a la Chris Squire until it all starts to make sense again. This is not music to be gently listened to on headphones, but to be played at parties where alcohol is in abundance, and everyone is having the time of their lives. I mean, there are times it sounds as if Dik Mik is playing with his audio generator.

Filthy, rough, and raw, this is great
Feb 2013

MANNING
NUMBER TEN

To my mind, Guy remains one of the UK's most under-rated prog musicians, who consistently provides great pieces of work that often get overlooked. I first came across Guy when he was a member of PO90, and of course he was also later in The Tangent (both of which also involved Andy Tillison who provides some keyboards and drums to this album). Years ago, we sat together in his studio and discussed his music, and our mutual love of Jethro Tull. True, there are times when that influence comes shining through his music, but it is unfair to concentrate on that element although some reviewers seem unable to look past it. Guy does at times sound like Ian Anderson, in a similar fashion to Mark Colton (Credo) sounding somewhat like Fish – it's the way they sing, not mimicry.

This was his tenth album in ten years, released in 2009, and is full of the things I expect

from Guy – great musicianship, a large variety of music and orchestration, well-constructed and thought-out lyrics, and layers upon layers of instruments that make an album that is immediate yet with great depth that rewards the listener the more time they devote to it. In another time and space Guy would be a prog superstar, but as it is we just must be grateful that he is so prolific and keeps delivering the goods.
Sep 2012

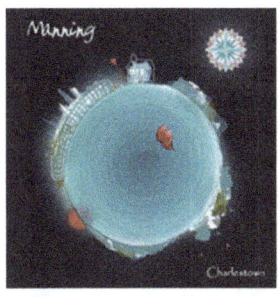

MANNING
CHARLESTOWN
Sticking to his normal routine, just a year after 'Number Ten' we get number eleven from Guy, 'Charlestown'. Interestingly, although this has been recorded in yet another short time from the previous album, here only one person (Kev Currie) has been retained. But of course, with a multi-instrumentalist at the helm there isn't a major change in musical direction. This time Guy kicks off with an epic, a 35-minute piece about a sailor lost at sea. The guitar and flute interplay within this song is masterful, really breathing life and vitality into it, but the drumming seems somewhat flat and instead of driving the song along is instead dragging it down so that it isn't nearly as effective as one would expect it to be. The sax is used sparingly, so when it appears it has great impact, and there is a warmth coming from the bass, but there are times when it just feels that there is something missing and that is probably the impact (or lack thereof) of the percussion.

After the power of the opening number, we are treated to something far more delicate in "Caliban and Ariel" where Guy has just gentle piano and cello as the song develops. One of my personal favourites is "Man In The Mirror", which is more upbeat with some great sax, while there is no doubt that closer "Finale" is one of the most intricate and powerful instrumentals he has undertaken. Overall, this is a very solid album, just not with the power of 'Number Ten'.
Sep 2012

MANNING
MARGARET'S CHILDREN
This is the follow-up to 2006's 'Anser's Tree' (yes there have been other albums in between, so consider this a part two), and just to ensure that this is apparent the artwork and lettering is in the same fashion as the release from five years earlier. All the concerns I had from the previous album have been mitigated and this is a much more polished affair. There are elements of this album that could have been released forty years ago, and again the musical arrangements are wonderful. Here Guy has exemplified that not only is he skilled in the art of songwriting and lyrics but also in understanding what it required to take a song to the next level when it comes to additional instruments and their role within that. Take the beginning of "Amy Quartermaine..", this

seventeen minute piece starts with acoustic guitars, bouzouki and mandolin, yet it is the violins that really makes this – that and the lack of drums, bass or electric guitar. So when they all make an entrance, with the percussion providing a very funky beat, the song is transformed.

Although 'Charlestown' is a very good album, and one that I enjoyed immensely, it isn't really in the same league as this one. I think I have probably heard most of Guy's albums over the years – both solo and with other bands – and this is one of the finest to date. This is an album that any proghead can investigate with confidence, knowing that it is something that they will want to play time and again.
Sep 2012

MANNING
AKOUSTIK
Now, I have never had the opportunity to see Guy in concert with his band, but six or so years ago I went to his studio to interview him and while we were chatting away, he picked up an acoustic guitar and sang a few lines so even back then I knew that if he ever decided to record a back to basics album that it would be quite special. Some years down the line and he has done just that, although he has done so with the full group instead of a pure solo piece. He of course provides guitar and vocals, and he has been joined by Chris Catling (guitar), Kev Currie (guitar and backing vocals), Steve Dundon (flute), Rick Henry (drums), Kris Hudson-Lee (bass), Julie King (vocals), David Million (guitar) and Martin Thiselton (keyboards).

Guy doesn't hide the fact that he has been very influenced by Jethro Tull, just as well given that his singing voice is not too dissimilar to a certain Mr Anderson, and one could imagine Ian going back over his back catalogue and producing acoustic versions of old numbers that previously had been treated very differently. This shows a very different side of Guy's music, and one that I enjoyed a great deal. I have been known to visit the odd folk club in my time (just for the beer you understand) and am partial to acoustic music (still one of my favourite gigs would have to be Roy Harper), so for me this album ticks lots of boxes. When music is slowed down and played like this there is no place to hide, it must stand on its' own merits, and this does that incredibly well. There is a warmth and depth to this music that makes it incredibly special indeed. Even if you have never heard Guy before but enjoy standout songwriting played with care and emotion then this is an essential purchase.
Nov 2012

MARBIN
BREAKING THE CYCLE
Guitarist Dani Rabin and saxophonist Danny Markovitch started playing together in their native Israel in 2007, then after relocating to Chicago released their debut album in 2009. This gained them a lot of critical attention and they were asked to collaborate with 7-time

Grammy winner and former Pat Metheny Group drummer, Paul Wertico on his album 'Impressions of a City'. The trio decided they had a special chemistry together and that they wanted to keep playing and Paul brought in his former bandmate and current Pat Metheny Group bassist, Steve Rodby, to complete the line-up. What I like so much about this album is the sheer diversity of styles, and at times it is hard to comprehend that not only is it the same band but all from the same album as musically they are all over the place, which makes it fun not only for them but also to those listening to the album. Take "Mom's Song" for example, this contains some scat vocals and is gentle and restrained but is followed by "Bar Stomp" which is a "Minnie The Moocher" with dirty guitars and plenty of emotion. The first time I played it I had to check what I was listening to as it is just so different to what is before and what follows. There is some wonderfully distorted and fuzzed guitar and slide guitar and a laid-back feel that just brings a smile to the face. But for all the times when they swap leads, moving through lots of different styles and antics, it is the very last song on the album that I have found myself returning to. In many ways it is the simplest, and is the only other song to feature vocals, but Daniel White has a commanding presence and the arrangement provided for "Winds of Grace" is perfect. In a perfect world this acoustic ballad would be top of the charts worldwide, and the sax would be seen as providing additional class with its' simple presence. But I guess this will just be our secret. A wonderful album from start to the end.
Feb 2013

MARBIN
LAST CHAPTER OF DREAMING
A short while ago I was raving about Marbin's 2012 album 'Breaking The Cycle', and I now have in the player their third album 'Last Chapter of Dreaming'. There have been a few line-up changes, with Danny Markovitch (saxophone) and Dani Rabin (guitar) now joined by Justyn Lawrence (drums) and Jae Gentile (bass) who replaced Paul Wertico and Steve Rodby (who both make appearances on the album on certain songs). There are also plenty of guests, but the focus of this album is the interplay between Danny and Dani which has been honed by touring anywhere and everywhere and playing live as much as possible.

The music moves from hard rock fusion, swirling through jazz and into gentler climates with acoustic guitar, glockenspiel, and vocals in "Café de Nuit". I won't say what I was listening to before and after I heard this album for the first time, but it really put them into the shade as to my poor abused ears this is faultless. The sound is spot on (congrats Rich Breen), the interplay between all involved is perfection itself while the musicianship is second to none. All of this would be meaningless if the music had no soul and groove but that is there in abundance. If this isn't a five-star album, then I don't know what is.
Mar 2013

MARILLION
SOUNDS THAT CAN'T BE MADE

There are certain bands where fans say that they prefer this era of the band or that, and while I can honestly say that I enjoy all periods of Genesis the same cannot be said for Spock's Beard or as in this case, Marillion. I still have the single "Market Square Heroes" (and the next four or five releases) on 12" and lapped up everything the band was doing, and when 'Misplaced Childhood' came out I played it again, and again, and again. But then Fish left. I eagerly made my way to Wembley Arena to see them in concert on their first tour with 'H', but after Little Angels had proved themselves to be the better live band I was devastated. What had happened to the group I loved so much?

Over the years I have seen them in concert again, and have also purchased all their studio albums, hoping that one day I would be able to yet again feel how I did about this band back in the Eighties. The line-up has stayed the same all those years, Pete Trewavas has done some great stuff with Transatlantic, and I have always rated Kelly and Rothery, so where are we in 2012? Well, they kick things off with the longest song on the album, "Gaza" which is more than seventeen minutes in length and is one of three that are more than ten. Lyrically this is a challenging area as well, so it seemed like were off to a good start. There is some good guitar, and symphonic keyboards, but my attention soon drifted and before I knew it the album was over, and I couldn't remember anything about it.

So, I put it on again and found that when I really listened there is a lot going on, but again I was easily distracted and realised that the biggest problem was that I was getting bored. But if you read the comments on the web many people are saying this is their best album for years, but to my ears how much is that really saying? They are very good at what they do, but it's not what I really want to listen to. So, three stars because it isn't poor enough to get two, but I doubt if I will be coming back to it in a hurry.
Nov 2012

MARS HOLLOW
LIVE

I hate it when I seem to be the last to know what is going on within the prog world. Back when I was running Feedback, I seemed to know what was happening most of the time, but that was certainly easier in the early days when everything was by letter or phone. Of course, now we have the world of the internet which allows me in NZ to download an album from America: the only issue I have with all of that is that this is Mars Hollow's third release and it is the first time I have come across them! Normally I will play an album for quite a while before I write about it, but I only got this yesterday and here I am writing just because if I don't it will stay on the player for the next month and I won't get anything else reviewed!

Back in 2005 drummer Jerry Beller and bassist Kerry Chicoine worked on a project with Ryo Okumoto (Spock's Beard) and after that ended, they decided to form their own band with Steve Mauk (keyboards) and John Baker (lead vocals/guitars). They released their debut in 2010 and followed it up a year later, which is also when they were asked to appear at RosFest where this album was recorded. The band have a different approach to many within the prog scene, imagine Rush with Spock's Beard combining with 'Discipline' era King Crimson and then dropping in some Yes (particularly with the bass sound) plus Kansas references here and there. Every musician is a virtuoso, which allows for intricate interplay along with almost Gentle Giant-style harmonies.

I have read one review where it was stated that the reviewer hadn't been this excited about a new prog band since he first heard Spock's Beard, and while I may not go quite that far I certainly can understand the statement. The band had a dramatic line-up change at the beginning of this year with both Beller and Chicoine leaving, but they have been replaced by bassist Joe August and new drummer Bob Craft and these four recorded the bonus studio song "So Far Away". Based on this I can't wait to hear the next album. If like me, you hadn't come across this band then you need to go to their website to discover more. The new song is being released as a single, so why not give them a try?
Oct 2012

PETER MATUCHNIAK
UNCOVER ME

Back in the 1980's Peter Matuchniak was part of the neo-progressive rock movement with Janysium and Mach One, before taking a break from the scene. He recently started making music again and has released albums with Gekko Projekt and Evolve IV while this is his debut solo album. One of the names I recognized from the band list was that of drummer Jimmy Keegan who replaced Nick D'Virgilio in Spock's Beard (as well as playing with Santana etc.). This is an album of countless styles, yet they are all brought together by Peter's strong guitar work. There is a liberal use of sax which adds greatly to overall proceedings, and singers Natalie Azerad and Ted Zahn do a great job. While playing this I was trying to think what it reminded me of and it took a long time before I realized that in many ways this encompasses much of what Jeremy Morris delivers, except while Jeremy usually has just one style an album, Peter goes from acoustic to psychedelic to 'classic' to prog to jazz to whatever he likes all in the one place. But, far from feeling disjointed this is very much a complete piece of work.

On the rear of the digipak Peter classifies this as "Adult Contemporary Rock (Progressive/Jazz/ Folk)" and who am I to disagree? This is an album that can be enjoyed on first hearing, but the more it is played the more the listener gets from it as there is something here that draws you in, whether it is the calm and warm brass or the soaring Floyd-esque vocals. This is a mature album that fans of good music, whatever the genre, will find indispensable.
Aug 2012

MAYFAIR
SCHLAGE MEIN HERZ, SCHLAGE...

The album title translates to "Suggest my Heart, Suggest", and is the first new album in 15 years for this German outfit. Some of the songs are in English, and some in German, hence the German title. It has been interesting to read some of the reviews of this album, as there are plenty of people out there who are calling this one of the finest albums of the year, and extremely happy that Mayfair are back on the scene again. But there is a huge part of me who wonders if that emotional attachment has clouded their judgement as while this is an okay album it is never really anything more than that. There is a lot going on in terms of influences, with Rammstein, early Floyd, Radiohead and Porcupine Tree being just some of the more obvious. There are times when the music is direct, but for the most part it is dreamy and drifting, which is one of the issues I have with this, as there just isn't enough impact here. It is something that I have both listened to intently and have played in the background while doing other things and take it from me in the latter it just disappears with no real impact.

At times it is extremely atmospheric, and is often dark, and there are even some riffs here and there, but for some reason this doesn't come together and gel as it should.
Dec 2013

ROB MAZUREK OCTET
SKULL SESSIONS

Cornetist, composer, and conceptualist Rob Mazurek first learned the foundations of improvised music while studying jazz theory and practice with David Bloom at the Bloom School of Jazz in Chicago, and first came to prominence when he formed the Chicago Underground Collective (which ranges in size from duo, trio and quartet to full orchestra depending on what is required and has been going for well over 15 years). He has also worked with more mainstream acts such as Sterolab and Tortoise and has worked on more than 40 albums. This is the first album by the octet and is a combination of some composition and a great deal of improvisation in an incredibly charged atmosphere. While often in jazz there is one soloist at the time, with the rest providing the support, that is not really the case here as what we have is everyone soloing at the same time, but somehow keeping together providing a direction.

The personnel for this album, along with Rob, was drummer John Herndon, vibraphonist Jason Adasiewicz, flutist Nicole Mitchell, Guilherme Granado on keyboards and electronics, Carlos Issa on guitar and electronics, Mauricio Takara on percussion and cavaquinho (Brazilian ukulele), and Thomas Rohrer on C melody saxophone and rabeca (a rustic Brazilian viola associated with the northeast). It sounds as if Zappa at his most eclectic is having a battle with Miles which results in the sonic equivalent of a massive thunderstorm. This music is incredibly charged, and one can visualise the lightning passing between players as new ideas spark yet another onslaught of notes and a different direction.

Mazruek describes the approach as "personalities blending sound ideas that have the potential to expand or contract at any given moment in order to find the hidden spaces that must exist for the elevation and understanding of the origin of where we possibly come from and where we might be going." Complex and complicated, hard to listen to, this is music that is driving exploration into new areas of jazz that leave the listener drained by the end.
Mar 2013

MERMAID KISS
ANOTHER COUNTRY

Mermaid Kiss started back in 2000 when Evelyn Downing (vocals, harmony vocals, flute) and Jamie Field (acoustic guitar) met in a studio and decided to form a songwriting partnership. Over the years they have used different musicians, and even a different singer while Evelyn completed her degree, but this is their last album together as Evelyn is moving on while Jamie is going to be continuing with the band. This album is the culmination of their 'American Images' project and is full of Americana and in some ways is very English in feel and in others not at all. They were joined here by Wendy Marks (flute, cor anglais, oboe, recorder, harmony vocals), Pete West (acoustic, electric, and bass guitars, harmony vocals), Colin Henney (keyboards) and Steve White (drums), and the result is a very special album indeed.

I have managed to play this in the car with both my 15-year-old daughter and my wife present at different times to no complaints, which is high praise indeed given what they normally think of the music I write about. That is down to the match of Evelyn's vocals, which come across as a mix of Talis Kimberley, Cath Mundy and Judie Tzuke, with wonderful instrumentation. It is very layered and complex yet is also simple in its' approach, with the vocals very much at the front. I can play "Rhonda and the Paper Crane" all day as the combination of the story that is told with the music and vocals just seems 'right'. No more, and no less than that. There are a few short interludes where piano and cor anglais combine in a harmony that is reflective and full of emotion, and again they work extremely well indeed.

I can honestly say that I have played this album far more than I usually do before writing about it, and it is certainly worth investigation if you enjoy wonderful female vocals with powerful songs.
Dec 2012

METAMORPHOSIS
DARK
Metamorphosis is the brainchild of Swiss multi-instrumentalist Jean-Pierre Schenk who on this album provides vocals, keyboards, drums, and bass and is joined by two guitarists,

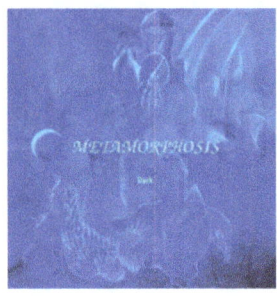
Olivier Guenat and Roger Burri. This is his fourth album and was released in 2009. His other albums saw him being inspired very heavily by Pink Floyd, but this album sees him stretch a little further and move away from the late Seventies feel that he previously favoured. 'Dark' is an interesting title, as it is the movement between dark and light that makes this album so interesting to listen to as there is just one contrast after another. There may be gentle vocals and repeated almost single finger keyboard motifs, but in the background, there can be frenetic riffing that would be more in keeping with Malmsteen than Gilmour. There are a great many layers in the music, and it is this that is still most in keeping with Floyd, but it can be argued that this has more in common with Porcupine Tree (especially), IQ and even Galahad at times. There is a real depth and purpose to the music, and although at times some of the melodies can be a little simplistic the overall impression is that this is an enjoyable album. It certainly benefits from repeated plays and is a step forward from his previous albums. Well worth investigating.
May 2012

METHEXIS
THE FALL OF BLISS
When I was approached by Nikitas Kissonas to review this album, I wasn't sure what to expect. I mean, firstly he is from Greece which is not a country normally associated with progressive rock music (with Vangelis and Aphrodite's Child being obvious exceptions) and secondly this is a solo album in the truest sense of the word with only one other musician, Nikos Miras who provides drums, with Nikitas doing everything else. He told me that he decided to release it himself as either the labels weren't interested in him, or eventually he wasn't interested in them as he wanted to have complete control himself, so I was intrigued to hear the result.

Then one day an envelope arrived, and I certainly wasn't expecting to open it and find a digipak and booklet filled with great artwork (care of Dmitra Papadimitriou who deserves a namecheck), with all the lyrics etc. It certainly doesn't seem like a one-man effort, and the music reinforces that. Nikitas used to be a member of Verbal Delirium and is currently a member of the Greek conceptual avant garde performance band Yianneis and it was following the release of their debut album that he locked himself in the studio to start work on this which he describes as symphonic-progressive.

It is an album of great depth and complexity, with lots going on. At times it is over the top and in your face while at others there is a real feeling of space with just gentle instrumentation. The use of 'real' drums enhances the feel, and there is a controlled dark emotion that pervades the music as a separate layer, and the vocals are sometimes delicate and almost whispered and at others they are passionate and fraught. The combination of fragile vocals and delicate piano at the beginning of "Lines on a Bust" are Hogarth-era Marillion at its' best, but for the most part the one band that appears to have influenced Nikitas more than any other is probably Discipline, and any fan of their music will appreciate this album.

It is an incredible piece of work, even more so as it is just one person creating this world, and I believe that the next album will be more of a band piece, but in the meantime, this is highly recommended for all progheads.
Dec 2012

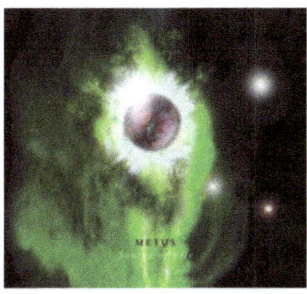

METUS
SOURCE OF LIFE
Metus is the project name of multi-instrumentalist Marek Juza who hails from Kraków in Poland, and this is his (I think) seventh album to date. This was sent to me to review by Artur Chachlowski of www.mlwz.pl who is based in the same city and I am going to have words with him as I can only wonder why it is 2012 when I have first come across him when he has been releasing material since 2007. Although this does fit within the prog genre it could also be described as atmospheric, dark, ethereal, and possibly almost ambient. My understanding is that Marek provides all of the instrumentation himself, although it wouldn't surprise me if there is a guest here and there as the strings that are employed certainly sound real to me.

What makes this album stand out so much from the norm are the vocals, which are just incredible: Marek states he has never had any formal vocal training and if that is the case then these are even more remarkable. Imagine a singer that brings together Pete Steele, Geoff Mann, and David Bowie (depending on what style of singing he is using) and you may just come close to what I am hearing. The music is important, but it is all about providing a vehicle for the vocals. Sometimes it is upbeat with Marek singing higher and with more directness, while at others it is far more laid back as the gentle baritone conveys such a depth of emotion and power that the listener feels that he can walk away on the notes. All in all, this is an album of incredible depth and passion, and if you enjoy music that isn't always in your face and is more thoughtful than most then this is highly recommended.
Nov 2012

MILLENIUM
THREE BROTHERS' EPILOGUE
This 2008 EP brings to a close the story that had been developed through earlier albums and then coming to a climax on 'Numbers and the Big Dream of Mr. Sunders'. There are two reworkings (with vocals) of songs from that album, but the highlight is definitely the fifteen minute "Epilogue", where we learn that the three Sunders' brothers, Daniel, Adrian and Johnny, all end up together in the same asylum. As with all of

their more recent works, the vocals are in unaccented English, while the lyrics are provided within the booklet in both English and their native Polish, a nice touch. I have never been able to understand why Millenium haven't managed to achieve quite the acclaim within prog circles as Riverside, as everything I have heard of them is extremely polished and enjoyable and here is another case in point. Although not an album, we have 28 minutes of music that has not appeared in this form elsewhere which needs to be sought out by fans of the band as it really does provide a major link between their previous works and what was yet to come.

As always, the music and concept is by keyboard player Ryszard Kramarski, who then worked with singer Łukasz Gall on the lyrics, and complexity can often be replaced by a simplicity that is breathtaking. Listen to the introduction of "Dream About Aliens" to see what I mean, with Piotr Płonka's guitar taking the lead and being supported by keyboards before switching roles. Elements of Collage, IQ and possibly Pendragon combine to provide prog that is symphonic and elegant and so very easy to appreciate.
May 2013

MILLENIUM
EXIST
What one notices immediately about this 2008 album, is the artwork where on the front cover a boy is crawling towards the sea through open doors, while on the beach next to him is the band name and album title written in the sand. On the rear of the booklet is a hand poking out of the sand. Are we witnessing a birth in a similar fashion to that of a baby turtle, or is it the last frantic movement of someone who has been buried and is dying? That may all seems a bit dark and deep, but take it from me here is a band that want you to think about the lyrics – which is why they are printed in both English and Polish (although sung in English). Musically they also want you to take a breath and dive into their world with opener "Embryo" having more than a hint of Pink Floyd about it. This is more symphonic, with plenty of 'trad prog' elements, although they do also riff to remind us that they are generally neo-prog.

Only four songs, but the shortest is just under twelve minutes long and the extended length allows them to really explore. They mix up Mellotrons with more modern sounds, with the guitar often being allowed to take the lead while bassist Krzysztof Wyrwa and drummer Tomasz Paśko are such a complete rhythm section that it is possible to overlook their contribution: if they are just to provide simplicity then they are there, but if complex runs and fills are required then they can deliver it with ease.

This is again an album of great maturity and musical dexterity while also being immediate and totally accessible.
May 2013

MILLENIUM
EGO
The latest release from Polish band Millenium is probably their most complete to date, with a great deal of work having taken place on the arrangements. The five guys have also brought in some guests on backing vocals, sax and trumpet but these have been used sparingly and consequently to great effect. There are times when I find myself reminded of the way that IQ also uses a sax, bringing it in just to add a further touch of class to music that is often quite Floydian and symphonic in nature. This is in direct contrast to "Dark Secrets" which is a bouncy romp with plenty of in your face guitars and keyboards. But, that in turn leads to "When I Fall" which starts off just with piano and voice. Music doesn't need great complexity to be enthralling, and that is definitely the case here.

Millenium are not only one of the top prog bands to come out of Poland, but are one of the top prog bands around, period. They continue to produce high quality work album after album, and this is probably their finest achievement to date. I have been lucky enough to hear most of their releases, and hopefully this will be the one which finally breaks them through to a wider audience. If you think that Riverside are the only prog band worth knowing about from Poland then your musical education is sadly lacking, and this is an album that should be high on everyone's lists to discover. Symphonic, complex, immediate, accessible, beguiling and bewitching, who could wish for more?
May 2013

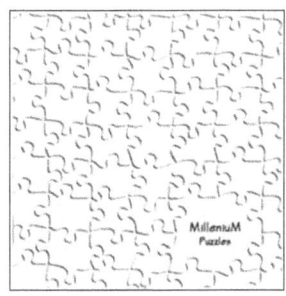

MILLENIUM
PUZZLES
Over the years, I have been fortunate to review pretty much all Millenium's albums, but it was only when I was writing about 2013's 'Ego' that I realised that I hadn't heard 2011's 'Puzzles'. I soon rectified that, and as with all of their recent releases I was impressed even before I put the first CD into the player. This is a double CD digipak, with both CDs looking as if they are old fashioned vinyl, and there is a booklet containing all the lyrics (in both English and Polish, although they are sung in English) as well as some artwork. Keyboard player Ryszard Kramarski again wrote all the music and recorded the album, while he co-wrote the lyrics with singer Łukasz Gall. So, after looking at the packaging, it was time to listen to the actual music, and settle back for 90 minutes (14 songs) of some of the best neo-prog around.

To be honest, I have never been disappointed by the output of these guys, who have been incredibly consistent since I heard their debut some fifteen years ago. Although all the music is written by the keyboard player, one would never imagine that to be the case as this is very much a band album with loads of guitar parts and times when Piotr Płonka is very much in control with Ryszard playing a supporting role. This is neo-prog that has much in common with Nineties IQ and will definitely appeal to those who are fans of bands such as Credo and Galahad although in reality they are quite different to all three and follow their own path. The production is superb, with a real clarity and space for everyone to shine while Łukasz is simply a star throughout. A concept album, each song adds an additional piece to the story, just like the jigsaw that is pictured on the cover and is about relationships, using the names of Adam and Eve to make the point.

Yet again this is a wonderful album, and if you have yet to hear the joys of Millenium (and there are plenty of albums to choose by now) then this is a great place to start.
Nov 2013

RICK MILLER
IMMORTAL REMAINS
This is my first experience of Canadian composer and multi-instrumentalist Rick Miller, but he made his debut with 'Starsong' as long ago as 1983, at which time he managed to sell 30,000 units. He followed it up with 'Windhaven' in 1987, but then there was quite a gap until 'Interstellar Passage' in 1998. But, in 2003 he really hit the ground running, and this is his eighth album since then. I am at a loss to explain how he managed to stay off my radar for so long, as this album is a sheer delight, and if the others are of this quality, then I definitely want to hear more. This is real crossover prog, with a refusal to stay within any one genre as he brings in psych, Floydian prog, crunching guitars, plenty of space, bongos and so much more.

Rick describes the album himself as "The music is soft, dark and melancholy because that's the way I like it. This particular album is rather angry and even darker than my previous ones, so if you're looking for a pick me up, you'd best look elsewhere." For me it works just fine, with some beautiful Gilmour style guitars offset by delicate acoustic guitar and piano. There is a great deal of space in the music, with Rick's vocals quite laid back, and there is no hurry, no pace. It is music for a sunny afternoon when it is possible just to lay back and let it all soak in. He has used guest musicians here and there, and it is a wonderfully arranged album where he uses additional instrumentation and orchestration incredibly well. But "My Atom Heart" is basically Rick's voice and some reverb and it is simply stunning.

This album is a sheer delight and has been a joy to listen to, now how often do I say that about prog?
Jul 2013

DAVID MINASIAN
RANDOM ACTS OF BEAUTY
David Minasian is a well-known composer and video director who released his debut solo album as long ago as 1984, but it is this 2010 album that has made many progheads stand up and take notice. Of course, many Camel fans know of David as he directed their 'Coming of Age' DVD and here Andy Latimer has repaid the favour by providing guitars

(and vocals on one number) on his first outing since 2002. David's son Justin also provided guitars, with Guy Pettet on drums and David everything else. This is classic prog, steeped in the early Seventies and the sounds of The Moody Blues, Al Stewart, Camel, BJH and Renaissance. In many ways it is a very English sounding album, and with the liberal use of Mellotrons it does sound as if it comes from that time as opposed to the present day.

This is music that makes me smile; it may not be earth shatteringly original, but it is a real delight. There is just enough use of acoustic instruments and even a harpsichord to take away from the saccharine that at times almost envelops the listener, with some great guitar cut throughs. Latimer was having fun no doubt, while there are enough Hackett stylings and orchestration to please even the most hardened cynic. If you enjoy prog music then you will love this album, it is as simple as that. It isn't challenging music, but rather something that the listener can put on and relax into like a well-worn armchair. Layered and delicate, full of harmonies and melody, who could ask for more?
May 2012

MR SO & SO
SUGARSTEALER
So, there I am working my way through a load of files and I came across a press release for this album. "That can't be right" I thought, "I reviewed this years ago". A quick check later and it appears that this one fell through the cracks, for which I am both very annoyed and embarrassed. The only thing to do is to right the wrong and get on with it now.

Well, who exactly are Mr. So & So? To answer that you must go back to 1991 when they released the cassette 'Thoughts of Fear & Principle' (yep, still got my copy), which was recorded at Pagan Media. Steve Paine saw promise in this group of young lads and offered them a deal, and a year later they released their first CD 'Paraphernalia'. What made these guys so very different to the rest of the prog bands around was that not only were they all extremely talented at a young age, but also that their sound was based around bass/guitar interplay as opposed to keyboards. Drummer Leon Parr and keyboard player Kieran Twist were great musicians, but it was guitarist Dave Foster and bassist/singer Shaun 'Magoo' McGowan that gave them the edge.

The next album was 'Compendium' where the band became a five-piece with the addition of another singer in Charlotte Evans. It was about this time that I saw the band play live for the first time, supporting John Wetton, and they had their slot cut short as they were going down so well! Steve Rothery entered the story at this point, and he signed the band to his own label for their next album 'The Overlap' and they found themselves as the support act for Marillion on their 'This Strange Engine' tour (I caught them at Shepherd's Bush Empire, and they were just stunning). But the album wasn't ready in time for the tour and in 2000 the decision was taken to fold the band. Dave, Charlotte and Leon formed Sleeping Giant (whose album 'Primates' is well worth grabbing if you can find it) and played some gigs (I managed to catch them support Karnataka, and there is no doubt in my mind who should have been supporting who). But, in 2005 Dave and Shaun met, and after some discussions started playing music together again. Charlotte became involved and the decision was taken to resurrect Mr. So & So. Kieran and Leon weren't available, but they managed to find replacements in Anthony Hindley (keyboards/vocals) and Stuart Browne (drums).

And so, in 2009 they released 'Sugarstealer'. To say I was nervous when playing this for the first time was something of an understatement. Back in the Nineties Dave and I often spoke to each other, I had travelled many miles to see them in gigs, I had even given a flexi of theirs away in 'Feedback', and these days we were friends on Facebook! What would I do if I didn't like it?

Luckily that was never an issue. From the first note it was just like old times, yet way more polished and mature. I did sometimes used to have a concern with how Charlotte would be able to make room for herself in a band so tightly musically dominated by Magoo and Dave, but here the balance is just right. There are passages where Charlotte is absent, or just providing backing vocals, and others where she is centre stage – it is all about balance. I remember Bill Bruford once received a songwriting credit in King Crimson for a song where he didn't play – his decision to be absent made the song what it was, and that is the same here. The guys have grown up and there is no need for anyone to be wrestling to be above anyone else, it is all about the result.

There really is no prog band that sounds like these guys, they have taken the normal prog influences, added Tool, FNM, The Police, Zappa and a while load of others to create a sound that is truly and uniquely their own. They are touring again now and will be supporting Marillion again in Europe (you lucky, lucky people) with plans to have a new album available at the beginning of 2013.

I should have reviewed this three years ago (and thought I had, honest) – but here it is now. This is a five-star album from a five star band. Welcome back guys.
May 2012

MOEBIUS CAT
END OF TIME

Moebius Cat is the project of composer and multi-instrumentalist Roman Bershadsky, and this is their second album. Originally released in 2010 it has now been made available through Mals. Roman provides a whole host of instruments himself, but also uses a lot of other personnel which really gives the album a lot of depth and class. The female vocals are clear and delicate in a way not too dissimilar to Mermaid Kiss or Iona, and while the emotive atmosphere is probably what really makes this stand out in so many ways it is a very

different form to the latter. The use of string instruments, wind and an accordion among others pushes this into a quite different area to what many people would think of as 'progressive', but to my mind this is Renaissance being stretched and moved into a new area. Progressive/classical/folk maybe? Roman himself says that it is a mix of dark wave, progressive rock, experimental, world fusion, gothic ethereal, electronic, and neoclassical styles. I may not be sure what to call it but I know that I like it, and given that you can download it for free why not give it a try? Roman only asks that if you like it and decide to keep it then pay what you feel it is worth. It is also possible to obtain their debut 2003 album 'Arrivals <> Departures' in the same way. This is a very class act.
Oct 2012

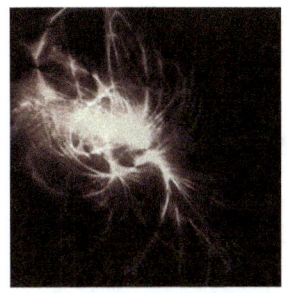

MONDRIAN OAK
AEON
There are some types of music that are almost impossible to describe, and when you put it into words and then look back at what is on the page can only think that it really doesn't sound like that at all. I mean, what can you say about music that is a combination of improvised jazz, trance, doom, New Age, sludge, and the kitchen sink? To say that this contains a brooding atmosphere is like saying a hurricane is a bit windy. It is oppressive yet inviting, hard to understand yet simplistic, dark and heavy, yet light and meaningful. It is music to play late at night and get quietly drunk to while sat looking at the stars. It is all about self-inspection and study as opposed to be the life soul of the party. In many ways it is quite depressing and should carry a health warning. I can't imagine that anyone can say that they enjoy playing this, I'm sure I can't, but I do know that I personally gained a great deal from doing just that. Here finally is an album for those who think that Tolstoy is quick read. These layers take a lot of work to fathom out, but it is worth the effort.
Apr 2013

MOON SAFARI
[BLOMLJUD]
I was playing this wonderful album yet again the other day when I realised to my horror that for some reason, I had never got around to reviewing it, which is why I am now in 2010 writing about an album that was released in 2008. When Sweden's Moon Safari released 'A Doorway To Summer' in 2005 they made an immediate impact on the prog scene, with their highly layered and complex vocals which reminded me, at least, of The Carpenters. Combine that with strong songs and great musicianship and it was a marriage made in heaven – wonderfully melodic and easy to listen to but with many layers and complexity. The question was would they ever be able to follow it up? Well, they are back with a double CD that in many ways surpasses the debut! Anthon Johansson has left to be replaced by Pontus Åkesson (guitar, vocals), and the rest of the guys are still Simon Åkesson (keyboards, vocals), Petter Sandström

(acoustic guitar, vocals), Johan Westerlund (bass, vocals) and Tobias Lundgren (drums, vocals). Yep, vocals are important to these guys.

The music is so harmonious that there is always the risk of falling into a cloying saccharine parody of the genre, but these guys are so adept at what they are doing that instead they take the music into pastures new. There are elements of many bands in what they are doing, with The Carpenters and The Beach Boys being major parts, while progheads may be thinking of laid-back Genesis or The Moody Blues as a point of reference. This isn't an album where you are going to find discord and punishing riffs or massive changes in direction, but rather somewhere the music is very much thought out and every note has its place without wanting to cause friction with another.

This is very much an album where the song I am playing is my favourite. There are more than 100 minutes of music spread over the two discs, and even then, it is way too short. Whereas some bands just drag the music out and you wish that you could edit it for them, here it is just passes far too soon. This is music to play on a summer's night, looking at the stars and hearing the moreporks (our only remaining native owl here in NZ - in Māori tradition, the morepork or ruru was often seen as a watchful guardian. As a bird of the night, it was associated with the spirit world. Its occasional high, piercing call signified bad news, such as a death, but the more common 'ruru' call heralded good news).

While this album is filed with the sounds of joy and beauty, it belongs in a place where there isn't too much light so that the listener can lose themselves in a most wonderful world. This will be appreciated by fans of any of the bands mentioned, but also by so many more. You owe it to yourselves to hear this.
Apr 2010

MORAINE
MANIFEST DENSITY
Playing this album now, some four years after it was originally released, it is somewhat hard to realize that this is a debut. Here is a band that somehow fuses the strange, weird anarchy of Art Zoyd with traditional Chinese influences, avant-garde jazz, hard rock and everything in between. The name of the band is a clue to the music to be found inside the covers, as it is often defined as "An accumulation of boulders, stones, or other debris carried and deposited by a glacier". What we have here are various talents who have somehow ended up in the same place and have formed a band, and sometimes they even sound as if they are on the same planet. I don't want it to seem that there is no structure to what they are doing – rather it is the opposite, the only way musicians can play so diversely yet make total musical sense, is by always having an innate agreement and strong understanding of the direction.

The line-up on the debut is Dennis Rea (electric guitar), Ruth Davidson (cello), Alicia Allen (violin), Kevin Millard (bass, baliset) and Jay Jaskot (drums) and while the rhythm section provides the foundation the three melody players vie for centre stage. I have lost

count of how much I have been playing this, as it is one of those albums that has somehow refused to be reviewed, as every time I have tried to write the words I have instead sat back and let this incredible album flood over me. Personal favourite (today) is the title song, which starts with a repeated guitar line which is then joined by the others. Amazingly, this album was recorded in just three days yet is highly complex with purpose and direction. There is a real sense of togetherness and understanding of the journey to be followed which is often missing from this style of music where those involved are creating the path as they go along. Here the path is known, if only to them, and they follow it to new heights as if they know the route to the top, which may seem either impassable or invisible to others. An absolutely stunning album from the first note to the last.
Feb 2013

MORAINE
METAMORPHIC ROCK
One year after their stunning debut Moraine found themselves at NearFest, by which time the line-up had changed. Stephen Cavitt was now sat in the drum seat, but the most interesting change was the departure of cellist Ruth Davidson and the introduction of James DeJoie (baritone saxophone, flute, and percussion). This has changed the dynamic of the band for the better, as they have even more depth and width than previously. The album itself contains interpretations from Dennis's solo album 'Views From Chicheng Precipice', which although not released until 2010 had been recorded prior to Moraine's debut and featured all of those who had been involved with 'Manifest Density' as well as James, plus of course songs from the debut plus some that have yet to be made available elsewhere.

This is fusion combined with avant-garde combined with prog combined with whatever on earth they feel like playing at the time. Although there is more improvisation with this album than with the debut, as would be expected in front of a live audience, there is still the complex control that made the debut so impressive. The use of baritone sax gives the band a bottom end that previously was unavailable, and the loss of the cello is not noticed. There are times in some of the longer numbers when the guys suddenly take off and it is if they are as one, a multi-armed multi-headed being that is in total control although it may seem that anarchy is going to prevail. They can go from chaos to structure at will, and the change is so dramatic that it catches the listener off guard.
Feb 2013

PATRICK MORAZ
THE STORY OF I
After the release and ensuing tour of 'Relayer', the members of Yes decided that it would be a good time for them all to work on solo projects. In keeping with the times, Patrick decided to record a concept album based on a story that he had written (which is included in the booklet of this remastered issue). But what makes this album so very different to

many of the others that were released in the mid Seventies is the high Latin and percussive elements involved. Certainly, one couldn't imagine Patrick's predecessor and successor in Yes releasing an album quite like this – even though Rick himself has recorded in a multitude of styles. This is very much a truly progressive album, bringing in different styles and ideas and attempting to explore the boundaries of what was then available with electronic keyboards.

The result is that while in many ways it is an album of its' time, it is also light and refreshing and something that can still be enjoyed very much today for its' musical content and not just for the fact that it was recorded by a member of Yes. In fact, listening to this makes one wonder just what the next Yes album would have been like if Patrick had stayed with the band, but there again this sounds nothing like what Patrick worked on with The Moody Blues either.

It evokes a feeling of summer, and the long complex instrumental passages are a delight. Within the booklet not only is there the story and all the lyrics but also a handwritten plan showing what is happening at what point within the music. If you haven't come across the solo music of Moraz before, then this is the place to start.
May 2010

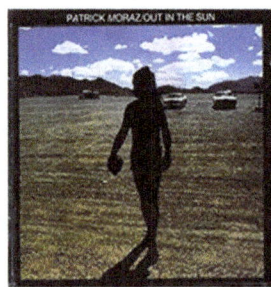

PATRICK MORAZ
OUT IN THE SUN
Patrick followed 'The Story Of I' just a year later with 'Out In The Sun', using many of the same musicians who had featured on his debut. Here Patrick moved more into the funk sound, yet all the time experimenting with the sounds that he could get from his keyboards – some of which are commonplace now but back then took a great deal of programming. But Patrick is also very much at home on a plain piano and on 'Rana Batucada' leads the band through a great percussive dance. Overall, the album has even more of a Seventies feel to it than the debut, and in some ways is a little dated, but it is still fun to listen to and has a real summer freshness to it. This is not the album to purchase if you are looking for bombastic progressive rock, but it is still progressive in its' own way as the electronic sounds interact with the percussion. Some of the numbers are quite poppy in nature, and as I say it does feel dated, but overall is still worth investigating.
May 2010

PATRICK MORAZ
RESONANCE
'Resonance' was originally released in 2000 and shows a totally different side to Patrick from his 70's solo albums. This is an hour of Patrick on piano playing classical music of his own composition, nothing more and nothing less. Is it any good? Well, to be honest I

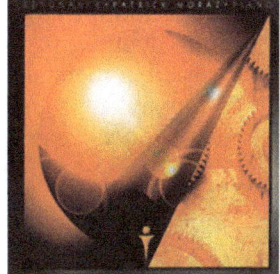

don't listen to much classical piano these days and all I can say is that it is very well played with a lot of finesse and feeling. It isn't something that is going to necessarily appeal to progheads unless they also enjoy listening to the classical form, so in many ways Patrick has probably moved away from his prime audience – which seems strange in that on the cover there is a smaller version of the symbol from 'The Story Of I' as if he is reminding people of what else he has achieved in the past.

I played the album a few times so that I would be able to comment on it but having done so I doubt if it is something to which I will often be returning – not through any faults in production (which is superb) or musical ability (which is also superb), but rather that this isn't a type of music that I generally listen to. Aimed at the classical market as opposed to the one with which he is more readily associated.
May 2010

MORAZ
ESP

In 2003 Patrick released the follow-up to 'Resonance', and again it is an album of classical music performed solely by Patrick on piano, and again the symbol from 'The Story Of I' makes an appearance on the cover. For some reason Patrick has dropped his first name from this release, which at the time of writing in 2010 is still his most recent. Even to my rather jaded ears I find this a more harmonious and interesting release to its' predecessor, possibly because it has been broken into sonatas, preludes, and etudes and from my days playing the piano (a very long time ago) I recognise these styles. These days if I listen to classical music it tends to be from people such as Steve Hackett, but there is something about this album that has led to me to return to it more often that I would have imagined.

It is gentle, harmonious, and pleasant, so will probably be of interest to many listeners but if you are a proghead looking for bombast then this not the place to find it.
May 2010

NEAL MORSE
LIVE MOMENTUM

One of the disadvantages of living at the end of the world is that these days I get most of my promos as downloads, which generally isn't too much of a pain but here I find myself reviewing a DVD set where I haven't seen the DVDs! Okay, so this has been released as a double DVD (more than 4 hours), along with a triple CD set and it is the latter that I am reviewing. This recording took place on October 11th, 2012, at The High Line Ballroom, New York, and captures the band in incredible form. I have no idea how many live recordings of Neal there are in my collection, from duetting with NDV through Spock's Beard and Transatlantic and of course his solo work, but there are one or two. I have seen him in concert with SB as well as on the 'Testimony' tour and have had the privilege of interviewing him a few times as well, so I guess you can say I am a fan.

I greatly respect the way he decided to stand up for what he believes in (even though I don't share those beliefs), although I still regret that SB never had the chance to tour 'Snow' which is easily their finest work. I have never given anything that he has been involved with a bad review, and there is no reason at all to start now as this triple CD set (2 hours 45 minutes) is as close to perfection as one could hope to hear. When it came to choosing the musicians to form the band, he brought in close friends Mike Portnoy and Randy George and then used YouTube for the audition process! He ought to do that more often, as during "Sing It High" he gets it right when he says that the guys are "Sick". Adson Sodré (guitar, vocals), Eric Gillette (guitar, keyboards, percussion, vocals) and Bill Hubauer (keyboards, violin, sax, vocals) do a stunning job. Mind you, it's handy when you have three multi-instrumentalists in a band as it does mean that you can spread the wings. Vocally they are all in fine voice as well, just listen to "Author Of Confusion" to see what I mean.

Both Adson and Eric really riff and shred as the need requires, and this is probably the heaviest that Neal has ever sounded as he works his way through material from throughout his career: this is much more than just a live rendition of the latest album. The suites from 'Testimony' and '?' work incredibly well and it is the longer sections that really allow Neal and the guys to shine. There are four songs more than twenty minutes long and one more than thirty!

But, for me one of the major highlights sees Neal taking a back seat, literally. One of my favourite live albums that feature Neal is 'One Night in New York City' by Yellow Matter Custard. This was a band put together by Mike Portnoy to play Beatles' numbers, and the line-up was completed by Neal, Paul Gilbert and Matt Bissonette. The whole purpose of that band was to provide a new take on classic numbers and have fun at the same time. Well, on "Crazy Horses" Neal takes over on drums while Mike becomes the frontman, and everyone has an absolute blast. Mike says he first heard the song when he was five years old and it was the heaviest song that he had ever heard, and the band certainly do it justice. I defy you to listen to this and not smile throughout. There are some people who don't enjoy what Neal does and feel that he hasn't dramatically changed since he left SB, but I sincerely hope he keeps going in this vein for the rest of his very long career as I love it.

So, there you have it, a five-star review for a DVD set that I haven't even seen. But to me they are just a bonus as this triple CD set is just mindblowing.
Mar 2013

The Progressive Underground Vol 4

TIM MORSE
FAITHSCIENCE
This is the second album from Tim, following on from 'Transformation' which came out in 2005. Originally this project started out as a concept album based on the life of Charles Lindbergh, but eventually strayed from that original vision to be more all-encompassing. Tim provides all keyboards, many of the guitars and most of the vocals while Mark Dean has also had a massive input into this album as he did with the last. David Ragsdale also makes a return appearance, providing violin where required. Overall, this is a very interesting album, with some great musicianship throughout – comment also needs to be passed regarding the production which is superb and really makes the listener feel that they are in the middle of the band.

The booklet is very basic, but to make up for it the listener can go to the website and uncover information regarding every song from Tim himself which makes it all very personal (and if you haven't purchased the CD yet then it is possible to also play tracks at this page as well). This is a solid album with lots going for it, but I do feel that there are times when it loses its' way a little, and that is probably because this isn't a group album – but rather a multi-instrumentalist with additional hired hands. To me this is at its' finest when Tim allows himself to remove all restraints and provide some blistering keyboard runs and interplay. He has great confidence in his touch and ability, and this really comes through with the delicate piano on album closer "The Corners" which moves through swathes of orchestration to something that is both powerful and poignant.

It is an album that I enjoyed playing, and I am sure that while it is not totally essential many progheads will feel the same and I urge you to check out the website and give it a try.
Aug 2012

MOTH VELLUM
MOTH VELLUM
This is another album that I was sent quite some time ago, but for some reason it wasn't reviewed when it should have been. I have been searching the web but can't find any indication that this band is still going, which is a real shame as this is a bloody good listen. It brings together the sound of classic groups like Yes and The Moody Blues and mixes it up with more recent acts like Porcupine Tree and especially Mr. So & So to bring together a sound that is accessible and inviting. Sure, there will be some critics who feel that there isn't anything dramatically new and that this is another prog band that is looking backwards instead of forwards but there is nothing wrong with that to my ears. This is genuinely an album that progheads will listen to with a smile on their faces and isn't that what music is all about?

This Californian quartet, Tom Lynham (keyboards, drums), Johannes Luley (guitars,

producer), Ryan Downe (bass player/vocalist) and Matt Swindells (drummer/vocalist), have produced a prog album that sounds great and while they have the opportunity to show off their skills and vocal talents this is all about a great set of six songs, with half of them breaking the ten-minute barrier yet never being too long. Overall this is a fun album that is well worth hearing.
Sep 2012

MUSE
THE 2ND LAW

These days when I am reviewing albums, I often search the web to see what others are saying before I commit words to the page. I never change my opinion on the music, but sometimes I find some facts that may have been missing from the press release (if indeed there was one). So before starting on this one I of course went straight to www.progarchives.com and started to read the first review by AtomicCrimsonRush, where he stated that Bellamy's vocals on this album is just incredible, especially the way he moves to falsetto. "That's exactly what I thought" I said to myself. Then he commented that opening song "Supremacy" would have worked very well with the new James Bond movie. Well, that answered one question for me, as I had again thought the same and was going to check to see if it did indeed make an appearance. Then he goes on to say that they come across as Queen and at that point I decided to stop reading any further so that I could write my review without feeling that I had copied someone else's in totality!!

Bellamy is at his absolute best here, of that there is no doubt, and the more I have played the album the more convinced I have become that Muse in 2012 are what Queen would sound like if they had started in the Nineties instead of the end of the Sixties. I haven't heard any of their albums since 'Absolution', which incredibly is 9 years ago now, so the change in their style over time is probably more obvious to me than those who have followed their career more closely. Although they do retain their harder roots, they are obviously a much more polished and refined band than they used to be and they aren't afraid to play whatever style they want, often switching inside the same song.

This is an album that screams 'class' from the highest rooftops, and all I can say is that the local boys have done good. There isn't exactly a plethora of bands from Devon, although Kirk Brandon attended the same school as me, and Wishbone Ash have always been seen as the local heroes (although they actually came together in London and only two of the four were from Torquay), but these Teignmouth lads have done the old county proud. There may not be as many crunching guitars as there used to be, although there is a nifty powerful digression in "Survival" (which is highly influenced by Brian May).
Dec 2012

MY SOLILOQUY
THE INTERPRETER
Originally just called Soliloquy, this band was formed by Pete Morten as long ago as 2002, but they have only recently released this their debut album. Some of the reason for it taking so long is that Pete has been playing guitar with Threshold since 2007, but also apart from Damon Roots on drums this ended up being a solo album as Pete provides everything else. However, the band is now back to being a full unit, as they have been joined by Chris Sharp (bass), Andy Berry (keyboards) and Mike Gilpin (guitars, backing vocals). This doesn't sound as if it was a solo project though, as Pete is a very skilled musician as well as a great singer. True, the keyboards may not be as in your face and dynamic as some prog metal outfits, but the guitars more than make up for that.

Although covering a similar genre to Threshold this is quite a different form as there is a lot of space within the arrangements, and not nearly as much intensity. That's not to say that this album doesn't belt it out as it does, but there are bits and pieces contained within that almost don't feel like they belong to the same band as they take the music in a quite different direction. Renowned prog producer Rob Aubrey has taken control of this, and that must have been a deliberate approach to take a step away from Threshold and give the music a more prog sound as opposed the more metallic that would have come across if he had used Karl.

Overall, this is an enjoyable romp, and I certainly didn't realise that he is such a strong singer. Obviously, fans of Threshold are going to be intrigued with this, but if you enjoy any prog metal, especially those that can be lighter in places then this is for you
Jun 2013

MYSTERY
BENEATH THE VEIL OF WINTER'S FACE
It was many years ago that I first came across Canadian prog act Mystery, led by guitarist and songwriter Michel St-Père. Back then nearly all communication was by letter, but Michel was the first person in the world that I ever had an email conversation with - so this is a band with whom I have always felt a strong connection. On top of that they were releasing some great music and I fell in love with 1996's 'Theatre Of The Mind' the very first time I heard it. But in 1999 Gary Savoie, who had been the frontman for 7 years decided to leave. Michel knew who he wanted to be the new singer, but at the same time he was signing other bands to his fledgling label and that became the priority.

And so, it wasn't until 2007, nine years after their third album 'Destiny?' that Mystery released the follow-up – this time with an unknown singer who Michel had seen with a Yes tribute band, one Benoît David. Of course, Benoît is now more widely known as the singer with Yes on their best studio album of recent years, but back then this was still in the future. Of course, that connection will mean that people will often try to compare the two bands, but that is unfair on so many levels. While Benoît obviously connects the bands, and they both play progressive rock, it is there that the similarity ends. While never a metal act, the band leader of Mystery is primarily a guitarist and consequently the music is approached from that area and crunching guitars and power chords show that here is group that remember there is 'rock' in prog. The group at this time comprised Steve Gagné on drums (who had joined the band in time for 'Destiny?'), Patrick Bourque (who had been with Mystery since 'Theatre') on bass and Michel St-Père on guitars, bass, and keyboards and of course Benoît on vocals.

Looking back at this album some five years after it was released is like visiting an old friend – it is full of life and vigour and any proghead cannot fail to fall in love with it. There is real melody and control, and while there is plenty of note density, they are all there for a reason. This is not prog for someone to nod their head to and sagely comment that the musicians are stellar – yes, they are, but this is music to be played and enjoyed, bringing a smile to the face. As I write this in 2012 the guys are just releasing their third album with Benoit, 'The World Is A Game', which I am eagerly awaiting, but if you haven't investigated their back catalogue you owe it to your ears to do so. Superb.
Aug 2012

MYSTERY
THE WORLD IS A GAME
Mystery is back with a new album, and pretty much a new line-up to boot. Michel St-Père of course is still here on guitars and keyboards, while Benoît David seems suitably rested after his sojourn with Yes. Joining them this time is the extremely talented Antoine Fafard (Spaced Out) on bass and additional acoustic guitars and drummer Nick D'Virgilio (Spock's Beard, Tears for Fear, Genesis, Big Big Train).

I have been eagerly awaiting this album, as I was intrigued to see what these guys would pull off and I wasn't disappointed. This is a soaring prog album that allows everyone to play their part without ever losing focus on the music. While Nick can be providing a bombastic backdrop, driving the music on with quick and complex fills, he is also absent from proceedings altogether in other areas, allowing space to play its' part. It is an incredibly complex album, with multi-layerings of music and vocals in places, whereas in others it is just Benoît and Michel, just vocal and acoustic guitar. Antoine's fretless bass also provides a real warmth to the overall sound, while his ability to play just behind the beat or to drive it on, or indeed take the lead melodic role is a huge bonus.

Michel has brought together a band that I sincerely hope will be around for a few years as if this is what they do when they play for the first time, what on earth are they going to produce in the future? Soaring symphonic prog, with plenty of guitar, complex melodies, and great vocals, this should be in everybody's collection.
Oct 2012

BADER NANA
WORMWOOD

Thanks to the internet the world is a much smaller place these days, but even I was taken a little aback when this turned up in the post recently. I live in NZ, the label that sent me the CD is Russian, and Bader Nana is from Lebanon who lives, works and has his own studio in Kuwait! This is pretty much a completely solo album, although he does have a couple of guests here and there, so it is somewhat surprising to hear an album that is extremely complex and sounds as if it was recorded by a full band. He is obviously influenced by Neal Morse (which is never a bad thing in my book) as well as Dream Theater and some Threshold, although he often doesn't crunch out as much as the latter bands are prone to do.

It is an incredibly polished album, with loads of hooks and plenty going on to keep the listener both intrigued and interested. From the very first track to the last, one is amazed that this is just one guy, and who would release as a debut an album loosely based on the European bubonic plague in the Dark Ages?!? This is definitely something that warrants further investigation and I for one will be looking for the next album when it comes out. There is nothing on the Mals site about this one yet, but I'm sure it will be there soon.
Nov 2012

NEMO
SI 1 & 2

There is no doubt in my mind that Nemo are one of the most interesting bands ever to come out of France, and in 2006 they released arguably their finest album 'SI Partie I' and followed it up a year later with 'SI Partie II'. Now here we are in 2012 and Quadrifonic have released the two as a double digipak for the price of a single album. Obviously having the two albums together as a set for such a good price is worth the investment if you are missing either, but this is one of the most tactile and well-thought-out releases for a while so even if you already own both you ought to consider getting it just to enjoy it like this. The two discs are in the middle two sections, either side are the booklets for each album, then remove the booklets and you are faced with the original artwork for the covers but reversed. The new front cover (and reverse) folds out into artwork that is related to the two original albums. It just cries professionalism, thought and care, even before either album is put into the player!

It is always hard to review albums that one feels are like old friends, and I'm not sure where to start, so let's put these into some context. According to www.progarchives.com, 'SI Partie I' is still the top-rated album from 2006, while the follow-up is 24th for 2007, so not bad. Although all their albums are always sung in French, I have never found this an issue, as it allows me to view the voice as yet another instrument. Musically they have links with symphonic bands such as Pink Floyd while also containing elements of jazz, yet as well as musical mastery they also have a great control of space and dynamics. Songs can move from sweeping keyboards to acoustic guitar, harmony vocals, tight rock riffs, in fact whatever they want. They can feel loose and relaxed or intense and over the top, often within the same song, and length doesn't hold any fears for them as they can be twenty-minute epics or two minute wonders such as "Décadence" which in itself shows what the band are all about as they move and sweep through different emotions and styles.

If you have ever wondered if you should investigate the band or these albums, then the answer to that is a resounding "yes' and the time to do that is now.
Oct 2012

NEMO
LA VERS DANS LE FRUIT
It is always a pleasure to be sent an album by one of my favourite bands, so when I heard that Nemo were releasing a double CD I knew I was going to be in for a treat, and I wasn't wrong. These guys always put a lot of effort into how their release looks, and here we have a double digipak with a booklet, and great artwork. Interestingly, the painter is depicting a tree in full leaf in a field, but if one looks at the rear of the pack one can see that in fact the tree is dying, surrounded by empty oil drums and rubbish, while the ghost of a wolf and a person can be seen, as well as a goat and ravens. What does it all mean? One of the joys of Nemo for me is that I don't speak French, so the lyrics and melodies become just another instrument and I listen to the album as a whole, instead of concentrating on the words.

Yet again, the guys have produced what I have come to expect of them, namely a structured, layered, complex progressive rock which contains numerous elements and influences yet somehow is constructed in such a manner that is immediate and inviting. There are times when the Mellotrons almost overpower the sound, then others when they are much more into a heavy prog area, with wonderfully emotive vocals throughout. There is power, there is passion, and if you ever want to hear a prog band put the hammer down then listen to "Un Pied Dans la Tombe" where they somehow keep the guitars in check just enough.

The music ebbs and flows, taking the listener on a musical journey, always with a clear direction and intent. Is that a hint of Muse I hear there, or Porcupine Tree here? Nemo have brought together many influences, as always, and created something that is all-encompassing and while highly structured always manages to contain a sense of freedom. I have heard that long-time bassist Lionel B. Guichard has just left the band, so it will be interesting to see how Nemo replace him as this quartet have yet again combined to bring some wonderful music to the world.
Nov 2013

NEVER WASN'T
NEVER WASN'T
From what I can see, this 2008 album was the only release from this American outfit, and the website doesn't appear to have been updated for some time so I'm not sure if they are still active or not. Anyway, what we have here is an album that could easily have been released some thirty years earlier as this is late Seventies 'prog' for Americans who feel that bands like Styx and Angel are the pinnacle of that genre. When I first heard this, I had to check the release date, as even the artwork could be from that period, but I don't want to give the impression that this is a bad album because of that; it's average not due to the feeling of being in the past, but because there are times when it just isn't as good as it could be.

Ronny Lapine mostly has a strong vocal style, but there are times when he goes a little off-key or doesn't seem able to hold the long notes, which does somewhat detract to the overall feel. But incredibly there are times when he hits loud and clear which makes me wonder if the recording sessions weren't as long as they might have wished and that they weren't able to capture all the best takes. There are hints here and there of Yes, and at times of Saga, but mostly this is an American rock album that has will find some fans. I'm just not one of them.
Nov 2012

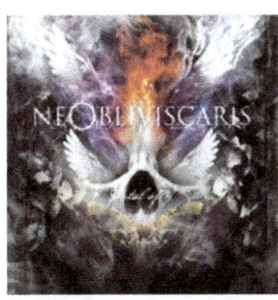

NE OBLIVISCARIS
PORTAL OF I
Although I am just over the ditch as it were, I must confess to not knowing a great deal about Australian bands (apart from the more well-known ones such as The Angels, Cold Chisel etc.). But one of my favourite prog albums of all-time hails from there (Aragon's 'Don't Bring The Rain') so when I saw this described as "Intense Progressive Extreme Metal like you never heard before" I was intrigued. I then noticed that it had been mixed and mastered by Jens Bogren (Opeth, Ihsahn, Katatonia, Devin Townsend), which also got me interested. I mean, why would someone of this stature be involved with an unknown band from Australia? What is going on?

It didn't take long to find out the answer – all I had to do was put it on the player. This is an incredibly intense album, and in many ways indescribable (which isn't exactly helpful to anyone who hasn't heard it). These guys are operating at an incredibly high musical level with a line-up that includes violin, two guitars, bass, drums (which is intense – I mean, they can all play but the speed of these double kick drum hits are stunning), clean and extreme vocals. Their influences are at times classical and progressive while at others they go through the extreme genres of black, thrash and death metal while also not being afraid to be extremely melodic at some times and insanely over the top at others, and of course you can also add jazz and acoustic noodlings to the mix as well.

But what makes this work so incredibly well is that it doesn't feel like a hotchpotch when one is listening to it, it just makes total musical sense. There is a clarity and single purpose of vision that is outstanding, and I won't be surprised to see this make 'album of the year' in many quarters – not bad for such a complicated and complex musical offering. All power to Aural Music for digging these guys out and giving them the opportunity to impress on a larger stage. Of course, now I know about them I'll have to see if they're heading this way for some gigs – you never know
Oct 2012

NINE STONES CLOSE
TRACES
When first looking at this CD, even before it makes it to the player, it is obvious that the music is going to have a lot to live up to as the artwork from Ed Unitsky (The Flower Kings, The Tangent, Unitopia etc.) is stunning. This album deserved to be released in the good old days of vinyl so that listeners could have studied the sleeve in depth while playing the music (just as I used to when I was younger...). This is the second album from the band, but the first was a solo project by Adrian Jones (guitar, bass, keyboards) and it was only a series of coincidences that led to a full band being formed who then worked together on building the songs for this CD, which was released in 2010.

This must be one of the most layered albums I have had the opportunity to listen to for quite a while. It brings together a feeling of melancholy with the textures of early Porcupine Tree, the restraint of Pink Floyd, Hogarth-era Marillion and even Japan. This certainly isn't music to play when you are feeling a little down, and really isn't music to be played on a bright sunny day, but rather this is for reflecting in the dark of the evening when the world is at peace and the required time to be taken to immerse into the world.

I rarely quote from the press release, but I couldn't put this better myself as it states that it "is a journey through loss, growing up and getting older. Letting things go and learning how to move on. Asking questions that don't have immutable answers, telling stories that don't necessarily have happy endings. Coming to terms with things you can't change or control. Mood music not for elevators. Understanding that being alive sometimes means hurting, but somehow uplifting rather than morose." This is not fly by night manufactured music that will only last for 30 seconds; there is a depth and majesty that progheads will truly love.
May 2012

NINE STONES CLOSE
ONE EYE ON THE SUNRISE
When one has raved over an album by a band, there is always a small concern when the next one arrives that it may not be in the same league, so it was a little hesitantly that I

started playing this one when it arrived. Happily, I can report that I had absolutely nothing to worry about! The follow-up from 'Traces' is in a similar vein, but perhaps with just a little more polish and finesse. Adrian Jones (Numb, Lie Big) Brendan Eyre (Riversea) and Marc Atkinson (Mandalaband, Riversea) have been joined now by Peter Vink (Q65, Ayreon, Star One, Finch) and Pieter van Hoorn (Knight Area) and the result is yet another extremely layered and complex album with elements of Porcupine Tree, Pink Floyd, Marillion and Flower Kings.

If you want to hear just how majestic symphonic prog can be then look no further than "Janus" where every member has a chance to shine, and even simple repeated piano arpeggios can have a major impact on the overall sound. The acoustic guitar on this brings a whole new facet to proceedings and the only complaint is that at six minutes long it is just way too short! I could happily play it all day. This is a very easy album to listen to, as opposed to easy listening, with music and melodies combining to take the listener on a musical journey. There is no stress or strain, just a whole new world. I am writing this review in a McDonald's whilst listening to this on headphones, and what I can see away from my screen is a world far removed from the one in my ears and therefore in my mind. The world of Nine Stones Close is a place of harmony and serenity, one where it all makes sense, and this album takes you there.
Nov 2012

CLIVE NOLAN
ALCHEMY
It has been more than twenty years since I first contacted Clive, and since then I have followed his musical adventures with great interest. I spent one summer holiday playing Shadowland's 'Ring of Roses' almost constantly as one of my daughters (who was all of five years old at the time) declared that it was the most amazing thing she had ever heard. Fast forward to 2004 and another of my daughters had me play 'The Hound of the Baskervilles' constantly as she was of the same view with this particular album (and she was older at eleven). Me, I have enjoyed everything Clive has been involved with, from Strangers on a Train and Pendragon through Shadowland and others and have always enjoyed our chats in various pubs and venues. But, having seen photos of the Polish show of this album, would it live up to expectations?

I initially received this as a digital download to review, but it wasn't long before I bought the CD and the t-shirt (literally) as I just had to have the complete package in my hands. To say that this is by far Clive's greatest achievement may be quite a statement to make but playing this through just once will ensure that you agree with me. Clive has brought together some great musicians to assist him in providing the wonderful backdrop, but it is the singers that steal the show. This is much more than 'just' a concept album, it is a full-blown musical, and even though there is further explanation in the detailed booklet that comes with the double CD set, the lyrics and narration ensure that the listener knows exactly what is happening. It is a quest, a fight of good against evil, with Professor King (played by Clive) and his colleagues attempting to foil the dastardly plot of Lord Henry Jagman (Andy Sears).

In all there are eleven characters, with most of the singers well-known to the prog crowd, but it may surprise some to discover that vocalists such as Tracy Hitchings (Landmarq), Damian Wilson (Threshold etc.) and Paul Manzi (Arena) have small roles. The other main male role is taken by David Clifford (Red Jasper) who is William Gardelle, while the two main female roles are Agnieszka Swita who plays Amelia, and Victoria Bolley who plays the part of Eva. As I said, it is the singers who steal the show, with all of those involved putting in stunning performances.

I honestly believe that Andy Sears has channeled all the anger and angst that he used to make "Creepshow" into a full-blown performance that has him singing better than he did 20 years ago. Clive is a revelation, as surely this can't be the same person who supports Nick in Pendragon, while DC was Red Jasper's drummer, not their lead singer (although he has now taken that role), yet comes across as a polished performer of real class. Add to that the incredible sopranos of Agnieszka, Victoria and Noel Calcaterra who plays Jessamine, and it is an incredibly powerful mix.

But there is much that makes this a compelling album. For me one of the major elements is the complexity of the vocals, which sometimes means that three or four singers can all be singing different melodies and lyrics against the same musical backdrop, mixing, and melding together in a way that is hard to comprehend yet is in such clarity that every word and nuance is fully heard and understood. There are songs such as "Quaternary Plan" or "Tide of Wealth" that brings together elements of 'Fiddler On The Roof' with 'Mary Poppins' as the listener wants to join in the chorus, while others are far darker and harder. There are showstopping ballads, with room for everyone to shine.

To me this is the logical progression on from 'Journey To The Centre of the Earth' and the aforementioned 'Hound of the Baskervilles' with 'Les Mis' and 'Fiddler' also making important contributions.

I was dropping my youngest daughter at the bus stop the other day (she is 16, I am blessed with four daughters, and I've tried to train them all in the joys of music, with differing levels of success), and she asked me what I was playing. I told her, and she said, "it's really good, and the singers are incredible aren't they?"

'Nuff said. I can't imagine hearing a finer piece of work for a very long time indeed
May 2013

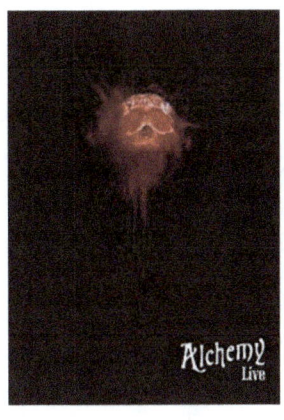

CLIVE NOLAN
ALCHEMY LIVE

Earlier this year I was provided with some downloads to review, and although I noted that one was a new album by Clive Nolan, I didn't pay it any more attention than any of the others, as although we have known each other for many years, I wasn't aware what it was. When I eventually listened to it for the first time I was blown away, and since then, I have played at least part of the album once a week, every week. It has become the 'go to' album in the car when my youngest daughter is with me (her favourites are "Ambush" and "Burial At Sea" while I always go to "The Unwelcome Guest", "The Warning" and "The End Justifies The Means"). It is rare for me to play music for pleasure (get out the violins and handkerchiefs) as I am normally listening to the next set of albums I need to review, but there is something incredibly compelling about this piece of work that brings me back time and again. The last time I can remember an album having this much impact on me was 'Snow', and I know I didn't play that as much as I have this. But this isn't a review of the double CD of 'Alchemy', but rather of the five-disc set which is 'Alchemy Live'. Two CDs of the performance, an additional CD of bonus numbers, a DVD of the live show, and then a further DVD containing loads of bonus material which gives a real insight into how this all came together.

For those who haven't heard 'Alchemy', it is a musical that brings together prog rock with many other styles, and while the musicians are all top class, it is the singers and arrangements that steal the show. It is a story of good over evil, with Clive being the good Professor Samuel King while Andy Sears is the evil Lord Henry Jagman. For the original album Clive brought in a good number of people he had worked with previously, and then it was decided that a full-blown live performance would take place at Wyspianski Theatre, Katowice, Poland. Although this has been written as a full musical, time and money dictated that this performance would see the singers standing in front of microphones, with the band onstage throughout. Mark Westwood (guitars - Caamora), Scott Higham (drums - Pendragon), Claudio Momberg (keyboards - Subterra) and Kylan Amos (bass) do a wonderful job, with backing tracks provided by Penny Gee (violin) and Ian Stott (horn).

Virtually all the singers who were on the album are here with three exceptions. So, as well as Clive and Andy we have Agniescszka Swita (Amelia Darvas), David Clifford (William Gardelle), Victoria Bolley (Eva Bonaduce), Tracy Hitchings (Jane Muncey), Damian Wilson (Captain Joseph Farrell) and Paul Manzi (Milosh). In Andy, Clive, DC, Tracy, Damian and Paul we have singers all used to fronting bands. The 'new' singers are Sohelia Clifford (Jessamine), Christopher Longman (Ben Greaves) and Chris Lewis (Thomas Anzeray). So, just four musicians but 11 singers, and what an incredible night this was.

One thing that I noticed when playing this is that there are a few times when a voice goes slightly sharp, which is great as it proves that if you were there that night then this is what you would have heard. Now, I can't believe that anyone is going to buy a five-disc set unless they already know the material, so instead of a full track by track review, here are just a few highlights.

First off, Andy is the consummate villain. He was born to play this, and of all those involved is the most theatrical of the main roles, and at the same time he is singing better than ever. When he hit the high notes in "Deception", which is only the second song, I knew we were on for a good night. Agniescszka is a star throughout, with incredible range and pitch, and her duet on "The Warning" with Victoria is a joy to hear. But I have to confess that the song I was waiting for was "The Unwelcome Guest" which starts as a duet between Tracy and Christopher before Victoria and DC join in on one of the most complex vocal arrangements of the whole performance, as they all sing different lyrics and melodies. Although it is still a standout song with a stunning performance from Tracy, I felt that Christopher's voice is just too smooth for this, and lacked the edge provided by Paul Menel in the studio. Also, it must be a nightmare to count in and Claudio was trying to help by providing some additional notes, but it doesn't really come off.

Sohelia is DC's young teenage daughter, and her voice belies her age as she owned the role of Jessamine and her major solo, "Desperate Days" is a triumph. But her dad is no slouch either and "Amelia" among others shows what a wonderfully clear voice he has. Paul plays the part of a pirate to perfection in "Ambush" and relishes the role he was given, while Damian could never be anything but the consummate professional. With his hair tied back, and beard in place, can this sailor captain really be the same singer that has fronted so many bands?

Then of course there is Clive. This was his night, the culmination of years of work, and the result is just staggering. He more than stands his ground with the rest of the singers and given that he is normally a keyboard player in the background that is no mean feat. But, if I was to point to just one song, one line, in fact one word, that makes this indispensable to those who already have the studio album then that would be Victoria in "Treachery", where when confronted with Jessamina who she believes has betrayed them, she calls her "bitch". That one word, is sung with such power and passion that the hatred is palpable and makes this all feel so very real indeed.

Metal Mind have brought together an incredible package, with a five-disc fold-out digipak, each side showing a photo of one of the singers, and a 40+ page booklet with all of the lyrics plus more photos, details of where all of the songs from the bonus CD come from. Some of these are original demos, while others are songs that never made it to the final album or morphed into something else.

Of course, as well as the music there are two DVDs containing the complete show plus loads of additional material including interviews, fundraiser footage, 'Making Of' etc. The result is something that is worth far more than the lousy 5/5 I can give it. Looking at the Top 2013 in PA, I can see that 'Alchemy' is currently at position 22 (a travesty) so there are obviously many people who have purchased the studio album, and if they love that half as much as I do then this is an essential purchase. I wasn't able to get to the

Cheltenham shows in September (something to do with living on the other side of the world), but until I do manage to catch up with this wonderful cast then this is something to which I will often be returning.
Nov 2013

OCEANS 5
ROAD TO MINGULAY
Now, I am a proghead and a metalhead, but to be honest my tastes are way more diverse and complex than that, so while the only framed record on my study wall is a 60-year-old jazz album, I also listen to and enjoy folk music. Not just folk rock you understand, but good old-fashioned folk, and have been known to attend folk clubs (and not just for the real ale). So, when I was presented with this album I was somewhat intrigued as the two main protagonists are from quite different areas as while Andy John Bradford (vocals, 12 string) is a folkie, guitarist Colin Tench is a proghead with a tendency to pull off wonderful runs and plenty of riffs. So, what are they doing together?

Apparently, Andy wanted to record a version of the 200 years old "Road To Mingulay", and had so much fun with Colin that they decided to make it a project and bring in some others to join in the hilarity. But, in fact this is no laughing matter, as what we have here is an album that in many ways defies normal description, but that's not going to stop me from trying.

At the heart of this album is Andy, and if you just listen to his guitar and vocals and block out everything else you will find music and vocals that could have come straight from the mighty Show of Hands, minus the fiddle. In fact, that one band kept coming to mind as I listened to this, and I kept thinking of the lyrics to "Roots" from 'Witness', "A minister said his vision of hell, is three folk singers in a pub near Wells". Well, I wonder what he would have thought of this as this is folk Jim, but not as we know it. So, firstly they brought together a band to give this a much fuller sound, and then decided to let Colin have his way. There are times when he is hardly playing, just the odd touch here and there, and others where he is right in your face and the combination of folk, prog and classic rock come crashing together into something that very special indeed.

If I had to pick just one prog band as a reference then it would be Floyd, especially with some of the Gilmour style noodlings, and they convinced Lorelei McBroom to add some of her very special vocals to "6000 Friends". But that is just one standout track among many, and if like me you have eclectic tastes, or if you just enjoy great music whatever the style then take it from me this is immediate, accessible, and above all an incredible piece of work.
Dec 2013

ODIN'S COURT
DEATHANITY

I have had some real struggles to try and write this review, and have scrapped it a few times, but it's time to give it another shot. There is some incredible music on this 2008 prog metal album, with the guys showing that they can lock horns and provide shredding complex melodies as good as anything you may find on Poverty's No Crime or Presto Ballet for example. There are some spoken word passages in places, the music darts and drives into different stylistic areas with complex changing time signatures, counter melodies etc....But... (it was obvious that there was a "but" coming) it just isn't all that it could be which is a great shame. It's just that it doesn't all work all the time. Take Matt Brookins' vocals for example, there are many times when the vocal style and delivery is perfect for the accompaniment, but there are other times when it jars.

Overall, this is not as much a killer album, but one that promises what could be if there was a producer strong enough to keep everyone focused and to cut out the elements that detract. That being said, it is still worth investigating if you like your prog good and heavy, but you may just come way disappointed.
May 2012

ODIN'S COURT
HUMAN LIFE IN MOTION

In 2011 Odin's Court released their fifth album and to say that they had moved on from the previous release is something of an understatement. This is a band that is highly driven, focused on the job in hand, and know what just needs to be done to produce a great prog metal album. Rick Pierpoint is a stunning guitarist, but he can be matched note for note by bassist Craig Jackson and they both mix and change their styles while at the same time providing incredible shred. Drummer John Abella is no slouch behind the kit, providing a dynamic backbone that allows the rest of the guys to keep moving on, while singer Matt Brookins is now in perfect harmony with what is going on musically.

I originally thought that it would take an external influence to pull this band in the right direction, but Matt stood up to the task and engineered, mixed, and produced it himself. This is powerful prog metal that at times has more than the latter than the former, but never losing the melody and complexity. Whereas those into prog metal may be disappointed with the previous release, this is a killer and needs to be played loud. Very loud.
May 2012

The Progressive Underground Vol 4

ØRESUND SPACE COLLECTIVE
ORGANIC EARTHLY FLOTATION
Back in 2006 I was sent a copy of the debut release by Øresund Space Collective, and I was amazed at the spaced-out improvisation that I was presented with. Now, just seven years later and the 'band' is back with their 16th release. This is a band in the loosest concept, as only synthesizer players Mogens and Dr. Space have been on all the releases and here they are again joined by all the members of the Danish band Papir (Kristoffer - drums, Nicklas - guitar, Christian - bass (only on 'Neptune Rising')). In addition, Pär from the bands Sgt. Sunshine, Carpet Knights, and Hoofoot played bass. The line-up for this album was completed by American guitar player Daniel Lars for whom this was his first trip ever to Denmark and playing with the Øresund Space Collective.

The opening track, "Walking on Clouds" (composed by Daniel, which the rest of the band jammed on) was the only one that was pre-written, with the other three being totally improvised. There are only four songs, but it still has a total playing time of 48 minutes. If you have never come across these guys, then they are well worth investigating. There is something incredibly entrancing and inviting about this style of space rock which has as much in common with jazz as it does with Hawkwind as the guys all take their cues from each other and goes wherever the music takes them. It is inventive, compelling, and somewhat incredible all at the same time. This album had as much of an impact on me as their debut did, and now I see that I am going to have to spend some time investing in some of the others that have passed me by. This is a band that very much follow their own path, bringing together elements from many, to create something singularly and definitively theirs. All the band combine to make this all work, building a sonic soundscape that allows the guitars to bring together the best of Hillage and Allen, in a truly wonderful way.
Nov 2013

ORPHANED LAND
ALL IS ONE
There is no doubt that Orphaned Land are one of the most important bands in the world today, in the way they are working hard at bringing together different people and religions who are often at war with each other. "I could never imagine in my wildest imagination that one day an Israeli band would be followed by thousands of Muslims from all over the world," says frontman Kobi Farhi, noting that Orphaned Land are the proud recipients of four Peace Awards issued by their Turkish brethren. "If we do a show in Istanbul, Turkey - which is the only Muslim country where we're allowed to play - people come all the way from Iran, Egypt, Lebanon and Jordan just to see us. These are enemies that are fighting each other coming to see us as one group of people. I'd say that historically the Jews and Arabs are brothers because we are all descendants of Abraham, but the conflict and the differences are so big that we've

forgotten that. Discovering the fact that our music is the instrument to remind people that we are all one is shocking to me. I never imagined that blood enemies would open their eyes because of it. That's why the title of the album is 'All Is One'." The album was mixed by Jens Bogren (Kreator, Amon Amarth, James LaBrie, Devin Townsend Project, Opeth) and was recorded in three different countries: Israel, Turkey, and Sweden. Ironically, these are countries that are Jewish, Muslim, and Christian respectively, which strengthens the Orphaned Land message of unity through music. Over 40 musicians were used to flesh out the sound, including 25 choir singers and eight classical violin, viola, and cello players from Turkey. When one studies the artwork, one sees that it is comprised of the symbols of Islam, Judaism and Christianity. But all of their work would be of no use if the music wasn't worth hearing, so what is it like?

First off it is virtually impossible to describe, although they often remind me of System of a Down for some reason, as they mix metal with folk, then add in elements from symphonic and power, plus death and plenty of traditional sounds from Israel. I don't know much about Jewish music but can hear elements that I recognise immediately. It is this flux and change of styles that make this band musically so interesting. I first became interested in Orphaned Land when I read about 'The Never Ending Way Of ORWarriOR' (which was produced by Steven Wilson), and knew that I had to grab a copy for myself and when I heard it I was just blown away. But this new album is a step change, as they have moved far beyond what they have produced previously. This is progressive metal in the truest sense, as it is creating something that is mixing and blending from so many different styles and cultures to create something that is new and exciting yet is always accessible and dynamic.

I fell in love with this album the very first time I played it, and repeated listens have only reinforced my view that this is truly essential.
Jul 2013

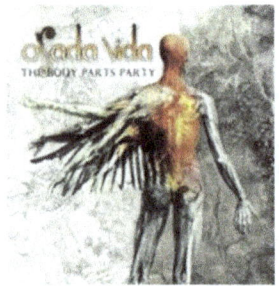

OSADA VIDA
THE BODY PARTS PARTY
This 2008 release was the fourth album by Polish act Osada Vida, but is viewed by many as their second as the first two were locally released affairs that weren't heard internationally. What we have here is a prog act that often moves into much heavier and darker waters, but although it could be called 'prog metal' it is a long way from the class and diversity of bands such as Dream Theater or Threshold. There are times when the album is quite laboured and also the sound is often muddied and not nearly as clear as it should be. For a band that had been releasing music for eight years at this point, I was somewhat surprised as it sounded much more like the outpouring of a band that had yet to find their feet and were throwing lots of different things into the mix in the hope that it would somehow come to fruition.

There are some interesting ideas and constructs, but they somehow fail to be pulled together in a way to make them appealing. The end result is the idea that this is a work in

progress and that the band had yet to decide what they really wanted to do and how they were going to achieve it.
May 2013

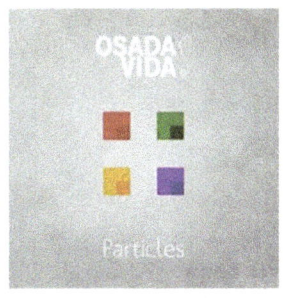

OSADA VIDA
PARTICLES

I haven't heard 2011's 'Uninvited Dreams', although I know that it has had some very strong reviews, so all I had to go on before playing this album was the 2008 'The Body Parts Party' which I wasn't exactly a huge fan of. So when I put this on and "Hard-Boiled Wonderland" literally blasted out of the speakers before moving into a driven neo-prog number I was somewhat taken aback. To say that the band has moved on in the last five years is quite an understatement. Whereas previously there was confusion and lack of clarity, now we have a band that is full of confidence and know exactly where the music is going to take them. It is polished, heavy without being too metallic, and there is even a sense of humour in the some of interplay and nuances. Great vocals with a real feeling for accessibility and immediacy makes this album an absolute delight from start to finish. Now a confirmed five-piece, this is yet another band that is flying the flag to show just how much great music is coming out of Poland.

Bartek Bereska's guitar sound is superb, and his control and fluidity of solos really lifts Osada Vida to new heights. As much as I felt disappointed by the last album of theirs that I heard, this time I am excited and looking forward to the future. I also realise that I am going to have to go back and get 'Uninivited Dreams' after all as if that is in the same vein as this then I am in for a real treat. If you want commercial Dream Theater with some great It Bites hooks then this is for you.
May 2013

PAATOS
V

Paatos came together in Sweden in 2000 and was originally formed by two guys from Landberk (Reine and Stefan) and two from Agg (Ricard and Johan) to act as a backing band for the folk singer Turid. From there they decided to create their own band and brought in Ricard's partner Petronella as lead singer. A year later they recorded their first single, "Tea", which had been written for them by Turid. Now all these years later they have released their fifth studio album which has four new songs and four that have either been revisited or remixed, and "Tea" is one of those.

Although I haven't heard their last studio album, I do have the other three and I have always been impressed with the way that Petronella's clear vocals work so well with the often complex and sometimes dissonant music that is underneath. She soars high above whatever is going on, allowing the guitar to play chords, pick a few notes, or even be

absent altogether. These are songs that don't look back in the way that some prog music does, but instead is all jagged edges and being very much of the present. In a perfect world this would be chart music or at the very least get radio play as it brings the listener into their world yet manages to maintain a certain commercial feel throughout. There are some who will question if this album even fits into the genre at all, as it is right on the edge, but to be honest who cares? This is a strong album, with powerful yet ethereal female vocals and is one I could play all night.
Nov 2012

PADRE
FROM FARAWAY ISLAND
This turned up one day from Artur, and I know nothing at all about the band as there seems to be very little written about them on the web, and their own site isn't exactly overflowing with information. But I do know that this is their debut album and that the band was put together by Krzystof Lepiarczyk (keyboards) who is active with different bands such as Loonypark and Metus, and he was joined by Maciej Tomczyk (guitars, bass), Gregory Fieber (drums), Mark Smelkowski (vocals) and Julia Stolpe (vocals). This is a class album, nothing more, nothing less. Musically much of this is based on wonderful piano with some additional keyboards tied in with some great vocals. It feels like 'Trick of a Tail' era Genesis but in reality, sounds nothing like it at all.

This is music that I know I can play in the car and even my wife would enjoy it – it is certainly quite different to what I normally expect from Lynx Music who have been making a name for themselves as one of the top Polish prog labels. But while I compare them to Genesis, someone else may say Train, or Coldplay, or none of these. The one good thing about their website is that it is possible to go there and listen to some of the songs and that I highly recommend. This is music that may not fix into a fashionable musical box, but who cares? This is an album that will enrich all those who care to search it out.
Mar 2013

PANIC ROOM
SKIN
It's strange to think that Panic Room are on their third album – they of course formed out of Karnataka, a band I caught in concert years ago. To be honest I had gone to see support act Sleeping Giant who were themselves an offshoot of Mr. So & So and having such a great band as support plus having Steve Rothery stand up to play with SG as well probably didn't help any and I wasn't overly impressed with what I saw in the main act. But I have always loved Anne Marie Helder's vocals, so I was really looking forward to this album, and straight away I knew I wasn't going to be

disappointed. The effective, atmospheric, artwork demands that the listener plays close attention, so I did. The music is effective, complex, and layered, and is obviously just there as a vehicle as all focus are on the vocals. There is a good use of strings and plain old piano as opposed to complex keyboards, and the drums are sometimes incredibly effective. Ah, there is the word "Sometimes". Yep, many are going to see this as a truly great album and not for the first time, people are going to disagree with me, but I feel that while there are some truly great songs and wonderful performances this isn't a great album.

Why? Because vocal delivery on many of the songs are similar throughout and there isn't enough variety in the music either. I found that if I just played one song (and I honestly do love the opener "Song For Tomorrow") then I enjoyed it much more than if I played the whole thing. There are times when the drums can be intrusive, and while the bass is warm and inviting the strings and production do make me feel that I am being smothered in a blanket. "Screens" stands out like an oasis with it's harder more rocking style which I thought was great, although the vocals weren't as rough and ready as they could have been, and I just wish that there had been more of this.

So for me this is a missed opportunity and while I am sure that I will be returning to this often, it will only be for one or two songs at a time as opposed to working through the album in its' entirety.
Dec 2012

PENDRAGON
PURE
Pendragon have been around for nigh on thirty years now, and while there used to be the odd change in membership, they have remained the same since 'Kowtow' which was released in 1988. However, 'Pure' some twenty years later finds the band with a new drummer (in Scott Higham), and almost a new Nick as Pendragon become much heavier and powerful than ever before. To be honest it did take me a while to really get into this album – there was never a doubt that it was a great piece of work, but was it really Pendragon? I have all their albums, I have seen them live, and have even interviewed Nick a few times, but it was the 1991 album 'The World' that really set things alight for me and that was the album that I marked all others by. When 'The Masquerade Overture' came out in 1996 I waited for the band to become as well-known as Genesis and Pink Floyd, and for years proudly had a poster of the cover hanging in my stairwell. They may not have hit the heights they have so richly deserved for so many years, but I always knew where I was with Pendragon.

But where now? There are definitely sections within the 14-minute opener "Indigo" where it is the band I have loved for so many years, but at others they are something else altogether with a much harder hitting drum sound and a guitar edge that has no place in a prog outfit. But the more I played it, the more I realised that the only problem with this album is that I had preconceived ideas in my mind as to what they should sound like, and

this band has moved on, they have truly progressed. Once I got past my own shortcomings, I was able to hear what in many ways is a truly incredible album, as it is such a dramatic change of the Pendragon of old in that it is almost a totally different band – but there is still enough of the old to ensure that fans can recognise where they are coming from as well as understanding where the band is going to. Nick Barrett, Peter Gee, Clive Nolan, Scott Higham – Pendragon. This album is immense.
Oct 2011

PENDRAGON
KOWTOW
I was only a little confused when I saw this album, as the sleeve wasn't how I remembered it, but a quick check at the collection proved I wasn't going insane, it is just that this reissue has a black cover instead of the white. This was Pendragon's third album, but the first with what became their most stable line-up of Nick Barrett (vocals, guitar), Peter Gee (bass/vocals). Clive Nolan (keyboards, vocals) and Fudge Smith (drums). To be honest it was only after I was sent 'The World' that I tracked back to their earlier material and investigated this and fell in love with it. Years later I was over at Clive's with my good friend Artur Chachlowski (www.mlwz.pl and Radio Alfa) and Clive presented us both with vinyl editions, which sit proudly with the 'Fly High Fall Far' mini-album and the "Saved By You" single that I managed to find.

Pendragon's sound has changed over the years as the band has matured, but it is to 'Kowtow', 'The World', 'The Window Of Life' and 'The Masquerade Overture' that I turn to time and again of all their releases. The use of sax by guest Julian Siegel on a couple of numbers adds a depth and Dire Straits feel, while opening number "Saved By You" is a bouncy singalong. "Solid Heart" was often used as a set closer, with the band walking off one by one until just Fudge is left, and to me it typifies Pendragon in concert. It is an album that always makes me smile, it is fun from start to finish, and is simply put one of the best UK prog albums from the Eighties.

This reissue comes in a slip sleeve with a nice booklet, and three additional songs that were recorded as demoes by Peter and Nick. Both "The Mask" and "I Walk The Rope" were re-recorded for the album proper so it is interesting to see how these compare. Great to see this album available again, and a nice reissue from Madfish.
Oct 2012

PERHAPS
VOLUME ONE
Even after reviewing music for more than twenty years, I am still pleased when I am contacted by a band I have never heard of and am asked if I would mind reviewing their album. So, after hearing from bassist Jim Haney, I went off to Bandcamp where I had a couple of surprises. The first is that there is only one song on the album, but it is 38 minutes long to be fair, and that it is also possible to buy this on cassette! I mean, when

was the last time you bought anything on tape! Perhaps are a Boston trio of Jim, guitarist Sean McDermott and drummer Don Taylor, and this was recorded live in the studio with assorted guest musicians who come and go during the piece, providing sax, trumpet, cello, viola, and violins.

The one word that really sums this up is "intense" as in many ways it is quite draining and almost too much to take in one go. I know that this is a mixture of composition and improvisation but there are some obvious break points and personally I would have preferred if this had been cut into smaller chunks. But as it hasn't, it's a case of dive in and keep going right to the end. I am not surprised that this album has been reviewed so much and every reviewer seems to pick on a different element (although Yes and Krautrock are consistent themes). These guys mix Art Zoyd with Protest The Hero, Miles Davis with Steve Vai; it really is all over the shop as it brings together free form jazz with mathrock and progressive to create something that is both intriguing and quite hard to listen to at times.

All of the guys are brilliant musicians, and they obviously have a deep understanding of each other, and they can lock in tightly when they need to, providing great complex runs and hooks, while there are other times when they all go off on tangents and one wonders if they are even in the same room. There is a false finish to the album at about 28 minutes, and I did wonder if we were going to be 'treated' to the longest outro of all time, but they break free of constraints and the climax is superb. This is something that can only be appreciated by those who want their music not only to break down boundaries, but to stamp all over them and bury them under a morass of minor chords so that they never darken their ears again.
Dec 2012

PERIHELLIUM
THE NEW BEGINNING
At the beginning of 2004, Gerard Wróbel (guitars, songwriting) formed Perihellium and the band quickly found success in their native Poland by winning various competitions. This brought them to the attention of Insanity Records who signed them and released their debut 'The New Beginning' in March 2008. From looking at their website the band have been busy, playing gigs and winning more competitions, but what about the CD itself?
Well, what we have here is another superb example of prog metal by a band confident in their abilities to provide melodic counterpoint both aggressively and passively as the need dictates. I note that on the CD vocalist Marcin Sułek is designated as a guest (although looking at the website, thankfully available in two languages, it appears that he is now a full member), which may explain why the band seems often to concentrate on long musical passages as opposed to many with vocals. Marcin sings without accent and actually this is a very Western sounding album, and even though there is one longer song (eighteen minutes plus) this is an album that is very

immediate and impressive.

To be honest, I knew within the 30 first seconds that I was going to enjoy this album as opener "Chrome" kicks off with some Tan Dream style noodlings which gradually intensifies before the whole band comes crashing through. It is intense, dramatic, and great fun! This band may be becoming well known in Poland but music of this quality demands to be heard far more widely. If you enjoy prog metal, then this is essential.
Oct 2009

THE PINEAPPLE THIEF
ALL THE WARS
It has been a long time Vulgar Unicorn's guitarist Bruce Soord decided to stretch his wings and create another vehicle for his music, but I hadn't realised that it was 1999 when 'Abducting The Unicorn' came out; it all seems so very long ago now. Over the years Bruce has kept developing the sound of the band, and in many ways is still very 'progressive', but to be honest that label may not be used much by many reviewers these days. To me it is truly progressive in that the band has kept changing and are bringing in loads of influences, most notably lots of Muse with some Porcupine Tree and Radiohead and aren't afraid to mix up the instrumentation. But while I think that "Believe A World" is a great example of progressive music, i.e., music that is trying to break down barriers and cross genres (some great strings, simple staccato piano chords, combined with a pop mentality and a great distorted guitar break) there will be many that do not and instead will call this alternative rock.

Yes, that is indeed one way of looking at it, but frankly who cares about labels anyway? It is just a way of describing music so that someone reading a comment might get an idea of what the music is about and then may decide based on that. In this case, if you enjoy the bands mentioned above then this is an extremely polished rock album that you will gain a great deal from and you ought to investigate further.
Nov 2012

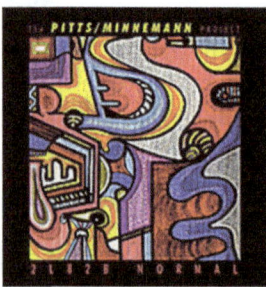

THE PITTS/MINNEMANN PROJECT
2L82B NORMAL
What we have here are 27 songs by Jimmy Pitt (keyboards) and Marco Minnemann (drums) with assorted virtuoso musicians including Bill Bruce, Fountainhead, Joe McCroskey, Pete Pachio and Jeremy Barnes (all guitar) and Eddie Kohen, Cheikh Ndoye, Ray Riendeau, Jerry Twyford and Jeff Williams (all bass). This is progressive rock combining with jazz and fusion in a determined effort not to fit into any particular box and instead challenges pre-conceived perceptions of any particular genre. There is always the age-old argument that there are in fact only two types of music, good and bad, and it doesn't matter what the type of music it is, it can always be

described by one of these two words.

This falls into the former camp – the note density alone on this is just staggering and there are times when I can't believe what I am hearing as the interplay between the different musicians is phenomenal. I wonder just how many times they had to capture the runs on "Envy Becomes A Motherfunker" to get them matched so well (yes, these guys have adopted the Zappa form of song titles – and some of these songs are only a minute long..). For any person interested in virtuoso musicianship and music that not only stretches boundaries but stamps all over them in hob-nailed boots then this is essential listening. Incredible.
Nov 2012

POOR GENETIC MATERIAL
ISLAND NOISES
Poor Genetic Material was founded by Stefan Glomb (guitar) and Philipp Jaehne (keyboards) as an experimental project mainly working on soundtrack material. Singer Philip Griffiths (son of the legendary Beggars Opera singer Martin Griffiths) joined the original duo to work and record together and line-up changes brought in bass player Dennis Sturm and drummer Dominik Steinbacher along with flautist Pia Darmstaedter. The different personnel also saw a movement in musical direction, and they became more prog and songs oriented. 'Island Noises' is their seventh release and is a double concept album that is based on Shakespeare's 'The Tempest'. I can just imagine the gnashing of teeth in certain quarters who felt that musical elitism was blown away by the 'fresh air' of punk music.

It is not a retelling of the play itself, but rather a story based on elements and themes that can be found within it (so Caliban gets a whole song to himself). Of course, a decent epic prog concept album like this needs a narrator so Philip convinced his dad to step up to the mike once more (somewhat like Rick Wakeman narrating 'Jabberwocky' for Oliver). Not surprisingly that gained a lot of attention by some, but to be honest it is exactly what it is – a linking performance to assist in bringing the whole thing together. Although this does have songs, it is much more about being a single piece of music with movements. In places it is dreamy and at others quite Hackett-ish, all the time with a certain ethereal other worldly quality which is in keeping with the subject matter. It is music that those into early Seventies prog will get a lot from, as opposed to those who prefer their prog to be more neo and rocky. Philip has a great voice, much like a young Michael Sadler at times, but although there are many layers of keyboards this is much more trad prog than Saga.

Overall, a very enjoyable album but be warned that at 1 hour 37 minutes it is a lot to listen to in one sitting, but rewards those who have the time to do so. It is not something that is easy to dip in and out of.
Aug 2012

PRIMITIVE INSTINCT
ONE MAN'S REFUGE

When I wrote a Jadis review recently, I said that I had to check the calendar to confirm that I was in 2012 and not in 1992, so when I heard that Primitive Instinct were releasing a new album as well, I did a serious doubletake. PI were one of the very first bands signed to Cyclops Records when Malcolm started the label ('Floating Tangibility' being the third on the label) yet by the time that album was released in 1994 the band had already been around for seven years. They were active on the London circuit but for some reason I never actually caught one of their gigs, although I regularly bumped into guitarist/vocalist Nick Sheridan as he was often attending the same concerts as me. I had put them into the bucket of 'bands I should I have seen but are now long gone', yet here we have a new album and a 25th anniversary gig to launch the album!

So after all this time, what would the album be like? In many ways this is mature yet also with a naïveté that makes it truly appealing. There are elements of It Bites, some of Hogarth-era Marillion, some BJH, some Howard Jones, but essentially lots of PI. The songs are built around Nick's vocals, with a very loose structure so that there is loads of space and room for the music to live and breathe. There are many more pop sensibilities than many other prog acts, and these guys could easily work with a well-known Prog band but could also cut into musical areas dominated by bands as diverse as Mumford & Sons or Coldplay.

It is an album that makes me smile while I listen to it, for no particular reason (any reference to too much alcohol will obviously be ignored). The band have grown older (well we all have), yet to my abused ears we could be back in the early Nineties when British prog was truly underground and everyone in the scene felt that were involved in something special together. It's been 12 years since the last album, let's hope we don't have to wait so long for the next one.
Oct 2012

PROFUSION
REWOTOWER

This Italian group originally started life as a trio called Mardi Gras Experience, but they changed to Profusion, a combination of 'Progressive' and 'Fusion', in 2002 and at that time also expanded into a five-piece. This is the follow-up to 'One Piece Puzzle', which was released in 2006, and there have been a few line-up changes since then which may have impacted the time it has taken to deliver the follow-up. I can only hope that it isn't another six years until we hear the next one as this is quite an achievement. 'Rewotower' moves through loads of styles and emotions, combining neo-prog and metal with heavy AOR and art-rock in a way that is instantly accessible and appealing.

This album may shift through different styles, but Luca Latini's clear and powerful vocals are always to the fore and this is never short on melody. In fact, there are so many hooks that some will argue (with some justification) that this isn't prog at all, but a melodic metal hybrid. Every person who listens to this will pick up on one influence or another as there is just so much going on; for me it is Porcupine Tree mixing with Dream Theater and possibly Sylvan, but the way that this is melded together is a delight and does it really matter who may have impacted their sound? The short version is this: if you enjoy music that is full of melody, extremely well played by guys who aren't averse to complexity and note density who like stretching perceived boundaries, then this is something you simply must have. Four solid stars in anyone's book.
Sep 2012

PRYMARY
THE ENEMY INSIDE

Prymary are a Progressive Rock/Metal band from Southern California that came together in 2000 and decided from the beginning that they were going to play exactly what they wanted without necessarily fitting within any musical genre. This has allowed them in turn to bring together lots of different styles and they have delivered their own version of prog rock/metal with the emphasis on musicianship, melody, and complex rhythms. Their debut self-titled and independently financed album was released in 2003 by the band and to promote it they performed with bands such as Fates Warning, King's X, Spock's Beard, and Enchant. After the success of their second album 'The Tragedy Of Innocence' the band turned their attention to this their third, which was released in 2009.

What makes this album stand out so much for me is the way that the band are at home whatever they are doing, so if it is gentle keyboards and vocals then it is a masterclass, but it feels the same way if the band are upping the ante and getting much more in your face and it is somewhat surprising that these guys don't have a higher profile as they are superb musicians. I hesitate to pick on just one stand out, but there are passages within the five-section opening number where guitarist Sean Entrikin shreds in a way that wouldn't sound out of place with Dragonforce.

This is album packed with light and shade, piano over the top of blasting guitars being just one of the highlights, and the feeling throughout is that of a band at the very top of their game – begging the question just why aren't these guys more well-known? A bill of these guys supporting Dream Theater would be a match made in heaven and I strongly urge those who like their metal melodic, or their prog to have balls, to search this out at once if not sooner.
Aug 2012

PSEUDO/SENTAI
NATURE'S IMAGINATION (CHAPTER ONE)
This ten-minute four track EP captures the band as a duo, with Greg Murphy and Scott Baker sharing all instruments and vocals. As with their other material there is a real refusal to conform to any perceived norm and instead are creating whatever they wish, mixing and melding loads of different styles. It's a shame that they had to use a drum machine, but according to Bandcamp they are later going to release versions of these songs with Kyle Boggs playing on them, so I'll forgive them for now.

There is quite a lot of acoustic guitars within these four songs, and plenty of vocal harmonies, with a definite edge to everything that they do. There is real angst here, which comes over very strongly in "A Battling Brook" where the line is repeated "They'll never take us alive". As with the other release by these guys there will be plenty of progheads who won't feel that this should be called prog as it is way more indie than many would like, but it's all good to me!! As with most of their material, it is available for free download from Bandcamp so why not give them a try?
Jul 2013

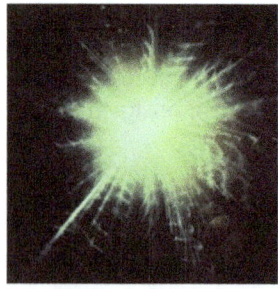

PSEUDO/SENTAI
NATURE'S IMAGINATION (CHAPTER TWO)
This fifteen-minute-long five-track EP captures Pseudo/Sentai as a quartet and is very different indeed from Greg's solo project. This is experimental alt rock that is all over the place, bringing in elements from punk and electronic as well as prog, and with some songs under two minutes in length they certainly don't fit the normal view of many as to what prog is and what should be. It is a fresh sound, and feels very much like a young sound, with an attitude of "this is who we are and if you don't like it, tough!" about it. The vocals can be gentle and harmonious and at other times are very much in your face and aggressive. There are acoustic guitars and electric, piano and eighties synths, it really is a total mix of sounds and styles in a very short period of time.

It can be quite hard to understand what they are trying to achieve, but what you hear is what you get; this isn't music that you have to concentrate on to get inside, it is there in your face. The longest song, "Keeper of the Stars", is also their best as it gives them enough room to stretch out and somehow bring in Indian style noodlings with The Offspring and gentle harmonies and fuzzed distorted guitars with indie pop sensibilities. Intriguing. Available from Bandcamp
Jul 2013

The Progressive Underground Vol 4

PSEUDO/SENTAI
BLUE SOLO MISSION:
The full title of this EP is 'Blue Solo Mission: Making a Hole in the Center of the First Outside Planet', the reason being that although it is indicated as a group effort it is a solo project from Greg Murphy (Blue) who here just plays keyboards. It's always hard making a judgement call on the worth of a recording when there is only one song which is less than four minutes long. But there is definitely something going on here, as the electronic keyboards drive into the brain and there are some subtleties that make it stand out. It is these additional layers that make it stand out more than many solo keyboard pieces I have come across, although in some ways it has more in common with art rock than prog. It is quite different to the rest of the band's material, and again is available as a free download from Bandcamp.
Jul 2013

PSEUDO/SENTAI
THERE'S ALWAYS A FUCKING PROBLEM
22 songs, total length less than 45 minutes, and an album title that is strong to say the least, this sounds far more like an extreme metal outfit than something that is deemed 'Crossover Prog'. But that is what we have here, and the Americans have come up with a collection of songs that are diverse, sometimes commercial, sometimes challenging, instrumental, poppy and so on. I have been racking my brains to come up with an accurate comparison and the closest I can come up with is the mighty Cardiacs, but even that isn't quite right. Some progressive bands take a whole load of ideas and then find a linking theme to combine them into epics, whereas these guys take a far more direct approach and if they want to have a song that is under a minute in length then that is fine by them.

Some of the songs are very staccato in nature, very abrupt and 'pronk' (hence the Cardiacs reference), but others are far dreamier, so much so that at times it feels that there could well be different bands involved. There is always a real alternative lo-fi feel to what is going on, so much so that one could imagine this being delivered out of a bedroom in the early Eighties and then being devoured by fans on one of the many independent labels that were around at the time. This would never have been mainstream prog, but it may well have found friends in that underground subculture when the music scene was just exploding with new ideas and styles. Fast forward to 2013 and although the independent label is now Bandcamp, in many ways this is very true to that period, even down to some of the keyboard sounds being used (just play "AP4: Ghostman (Boss Battle)" to see what I mean). There are times when the vocals are almost throwaway, when at others we have harmonies, always with passion and angst.

This album is always going to appeal more to those who enjoy their music to be a little less refined and want to be constantly challenged and this one does all of that. This is a

band that keeps coming up with new ideas, and the result is an album that in many ways is all over the place which means that if you don't like the particular style or song don't worry about it as another will be along in a minute, literally. Easily the best of their work I have heard so far.
Sep 2013

PSYCHIC FOR RADIO
STANDING WAVE

As well as being head honcho at Progrock Records, Shawn Gordon also runs an internet radio station at progrock.com. There are more than 20,000 songs loaded and they are played randomly. One day Shawn went out for a walk and as one does, started listening to a song inside his head – "Cities", by Henning Pauly's band Chain. When he returned to the office, not only was that song playing, out of a random list of 20,000 songs, it was at the same point as the playback inside his head. He called Henning to tell him the strange occurrence, and declared that he was 'Psychic for Radio', and thinking about it, wasn't that a great idea for a band name?

One thing led to another, and Shawn decided to get a band together to record his songs, some of which went back 30 years, but with lack of commitment he eventually hired Henning and together they brought in a load of musicians to work on the project and after only five years this is the result.

It probably isn't a surprise that given the timeframe and the number of guests that this is more of a collection of songs than that of a distinct group identity, but for me this really isn't an issue when the songs are as good as this. The first time I played this I picked up on "She Knows", with delicate acoustic guitar, wonderful piano and flute (care of Martin Orford – time for another solo album Widge) that brings just right the feeling to the song. Todd Plant (Cryptic Vision) is the singer on this, and he just nails it. In some ways this is reminiscent of "Entangled" or "Mad Man Moon", but it is more the atmosphere than the overall sound. Like all the songs on the album this is extremely well produced (I would expect nothing else when Henning is involved), and the arrangement is both simple and complex. Peter Matuchniak nails a Hackett-style guitar solo which adds to the ambience. I could play this one song all day, there is just something about it, but what about the rest of the album?

Henning is an incredible guitarist, as anyone who has heard any of his albums will know, so it is of no surprise that there are great riffs on some songs (along with some driving fretless bass from Miles Gordon), and that in places this becomes much more of a rocker's album than some progheads will appreciate. Sure, there's Genesis in the odd place, and OSI in others, but this is all about producing great music as opposed to fitting within any particular genre. Even so, the choice of the cover version is a little surprising.

My personal view of cover versions is that if all the artist is going to do is exactly replicate the original then it is a waste of time for everyone. However, if they are going to try to do something a bit different then I am all ears. But "School's Out"? Shawn's idea was to have Nine Inch Nails meets Alice Cooper, heavy, industrialized, and over produced. Bill Berends of Mastermind (years ago I was lucky enough to see them in concert, and they blew me away) asked Shawn if he needed any guitar and the results more than speak for themselves. This is "School's Out" brought kicking and screaming into the current day, as if Hawkwind and Poisoned Electric Head conspired together to have a bastard child, and this was the result.

So, this is a proggy, industrial, commercial album loaded with great songs, numerous hooks and stunning performances from different musicians and singers who all add to the whole. I can guarantee that the more you play it the more you will get from it. Now does this mean we have to wait five years for the next one Shawn?
Oct 2012

PSYCHEMA
THE ENTRY POINT
Psychema appeared on the Finnish metal scene in 2007 and within two years their demos were attracting attention, which led to the deal with Inverse Records to release their debut album. The label says that the band could be called semi-progressive metal, and that the album presents even more variations in musical styles with elements of aggression and atmosphere, "with progressive nuances of course". I probably agree with the latter statement as there is no doubt that prog has had some impact on what they are trying to achieve, but these guys are approaching it from the metal end as opposed to most prog metal bands that do it the other way around. The vocal style is also far harsher than one would normally expect from this genre, and the result is much more Opeth than Dream Theater.

Solid as opposed to ground-breaking, this is an album with large blocks of dark from the twin guitars riffing hard but with enough light from the breaks in style and integral use of keyboards to make it interesting for those who want to play their music loud. Very loud.
Nov 2012

PSYCHO PRAXIS
ECHOES FROM THE DEEP
One thing I really enjoy about listening to so much music is that there are times when I come across gems that I know would have passed me by if I didn't spend so much time in the scene, and this is very much a case in point. Apparently, this is a 2012 album from a young Italian band, but one wouldn't guess that from just playing it. While I think that I would have worked out the country, there is no way that I would have thought this was a new album as instead it sounds as if it is yet another record I have only come to some forty years after it was originally released. There is nothing false

about this album; it doesn't sound at all as if it is trying to recreate the progressive sounds of times gone by but rather that this is indeed from that era.

Classic Italian progressive music, with swathes of Hammonds and Mellotrons, mixed in with flute and quirky time signatures and shifts in moods and we have here a bringing together of PFM, Jethro Tull, King Crimson and VDGG in a way that is inviting and somehow familiar while also being fresh and new. It may not be breaking any new ground and in many ways is totally regressive, but it is approached in such a manner that progheads will welcome this as fresh and inventive and totally genuine. Superb.
Jul 2013

PUZZLE KING
ANNA'S REVOLUTION
Puzzle King is a project by François Puzenat who for his debut concept album wrote the script and lyrics, composed the music, programmed the drums, recorded the guitars, keyboards and vocals (in French and English) and added sound effects. The bass was recorded by Nathalie Prost while Guillaume Ninon from Studiolaf (Nemo, Wolfspring ...) was responsible for the mixing and mastering. It tells the story of two lovers during the Russian Revolution, Anna and Anatoli, who are struggling to preserve their love in spite of the war, in spite of the revolution. So, quite a concept, and one that is very personal to François whose grandparents were inspired by the Russian revolution when they were growing up in France.

My views of the album have changed quite a bit the more I have played it, and although there are some high points this is more points for the idea than the execution. The vocals don't always work, and it really does have the feeling of a solo project as opposed to band effort. For me this just doesn't cut it in terms of musical ideas and execution, and I found that I was only playing it repeatedly as I had to review it as opposed to playing it because I enjoyed it. It is not an awful album, far from it, but it just doesn't work for me.
Nov 2012

QUASAR
FIRE IN THE SKY
After a gap that is probably the best part of 20 years, Keith Turner and I recently got back in touch again. To celebrate he sent me Quasar's two studio albums, and a live set capturing the band in 2011. So, starting with the very first, I have been playing 'Fire In The Sky' which came out in 1981 so it is now more than 30 years old! The prog scene in the UK really needs to be put into context here, as basically it didn't exist at the time. With the advent of punk, 'prog' was seen as a bad thing by the music press who then decided that it didn't exist. Of course, that didn't stop bands from forming and playing, it just meant that it was virtually impossible to get any publicity.

Quasar were formed in 1979 by Keith Turner and Mike Kenwright, but soon the line-up changed quite dramatically so by the time of the release of their debut album only two years later just Keith was left. Cyrus Khajavi came in on guitar and keyboards, Paul Vigrass was vocalist, Peter Ware on keyboards, Peter Shade on vibes and keyboards, Steen Doosing on drums while Keith Turner handled the bass, Moog Taurus and twelve string guitar and provided all the songs.

One wonders what would have happened if these guys had stayed together long enough to properly tour this album as even now it is a joy to listen to. Yes, it does sound dated, but not as much as one might imagine. If I were to take one single album as a starting point then it would probably be 'And Then There Were Three', particularly with some of the keyboard sounds, but in many ways, this is an important piece of work as it is one of a small number that was coming out of the underground in those days that would influence those yet to come. Twelfth Night had released a few tapes, and Pallas came out with 'Arrive Alive' in 1981 but IQ, Pendragon, Marillion et al had yet to release an album.

One of the real joys of 'Fire In The Sky' is the confidence of singer Paul Vigrass who really shines throughout. The production is a little thin in places, but I found that it actually works really well and adds to the 'other worldy' aspect of the album as a whole. Coming to this album 'fresh', as I hadn't previously heard it, I found it quite surprising as I hadn't realized that the band had a male lead singer in the early days. But the dynamics in the band work incredibly well and given that this was an independent release more than 30 years ago that is something that should be recognized.
Mar 2013

QUASAR
THE LORELI
After the release of their debut album in 1985 the band changed approach bringing in female singer Susan Robinson (Solstice) on lead vocals and hitting the road. They definitely suffered with line-up changes, but in 1985 provided a track for the EMI compilation 'Fire In Harmony'. Dave Wagstaffe had joined on drums by then, and not long afterwards there was yet another major change with Tracy Hitchings joining on vocals, Steve Leigh on keyboards and Uwe D'Rose on guitar (Keith Turner was of course still there at the helm, providing bass). So, it wasn't until 1989 that the band started on this their second album, but during recording both Steve and Uwe left so Toshi Tsuchiya came in on guitar and midi guitar.

I still remember the first time I played this album, something over 20 years ago, as I fell in love with it immediately. It was the first time I had come across Tracy, and this felt like a perfect combination of soaring prog with vocals to match. Unlike the debut, where Keith had provided all of the material, this is much more of a band album although only the title song was co-written by two current members of the band. The keyboards do sound a little uncomplicated but given that they were being played on a midi as opposed to 'proper' keyboards that probably isn't surprising. The star of the show is Tracy, and the music is designed to show her off in the best light. Here she is full of confidence and the production is spot on, allowing her to be a little 'dry' in places to really show off her quality as opposed to coating everything in reverb.

Although some of the keyboard sounds do appear little dated, since it is the best part of 25 years since it was released that really is a little picky as here is an album that neo-prog fans should investigate. Not long after it was released and this line-up, like so many others, had disappeared. Dave joined forces with Uwe and Steve to form Landmarq with Steve Gee (Artemis), and Tracy departed to work with Clive Nolan on his Strangers On A Train projects and others, before finally joining Landmarq herself. So, Quasar were never really able to maximize the potential of a wonderful piece of work, and as I write this (at the beginning of 2013) they have yet to release another studio album. That is nothing short of criminal as this is something that belongs in all prog lovers' collections. As with the debut, if you go to the band's website you can play all of the songs, so why not go and discover some prog history?
Mar 2013

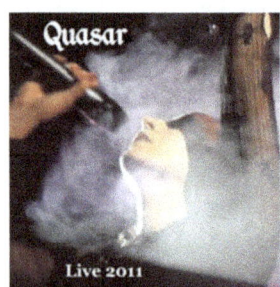

QUASAR
LIVE 2011

After literally hundreds of gigs, and nearly as many line-up changes, Keith decided to call it a day. But then in 2006 he reformed the band with new members Paul Johnson (drums), Robert Robinson (keyboards/vocals), Keren Gaiser (vocals/keyboards) and Clancy Ferrill (guitars). So, from the band not having a 'real' keyboard player they now have two, but the real change to these ears is that they also now have two singers. This means that on numbers such as "Seeing Stars (I & II)" they can utilize the strength of both, and they happily take turns at the front of the stage, while Keren takes the main role. Of the three albums to date, this is easily the best. The band are relaxed and happy onstage and know exactly what they want to achieve with symphonic neo-prog that is inviting and easy to listen to without ever falling into the trap of being easy listening.

This is reminiscent of late Seventies Genesis, yet somehow in a more symphonic style, with stunning vocals throughout. Indeed, the only real question that has to be asked is why has this band never gained the acclaim they so richly deserve? Now based in the States, surely there are enough progheads over there to take this band to heart and provide the impetus for them to get out there, record a new studio album, and show everyone exactly what they are made of. Songs like "As You Fall Asleep" are way more powerful on this album than on the studio version, imbued with new life and strength.

Based on what I can hear, Quasar are a much stronger band now than they were in the Eighties and deserve to be a name known by far more than just a few.
Mar 2013

QUIDAM
POD NIEBAM CZAS
When this was originally released back in 2002, I was absolutely blown away and to this day it is still one of my favourite Polish albums. This reissue is a double disc set, with the original album and a DVD – more of the latter in a minute. My lack of understanding of the Polish language in no way detracts from the album as a whole, as for me the vocals become another instrument. Emila Derkowska had a wonderfully clear voice and the whole band gels and shines together in a similar fashion to the way that Pink Floyd once did. With a flautist within the band (Jacek Zasada) it gave them the opportunity to move away from the (reasonably) standard five-person prog set up, and they also used guests to fill out the sound even more (oboe, flugelhorn (!), mandolin, accordion).

This is a progressive album that really is, one that brings together different instruments and players in a way that makes it feel as if they belong together. There is a cover version on the album, a brilliant take on "No Quarter" that nearly breaks the twelve-minute mark, and the second half of the album is taken up with a complex piece which is thirty minutes long (although it can be subdivided into five songs). I still believe that this is the best of all Quidam's albums, showing the majesty and grace that only a band at the height of their powers could achieve.

At the beginning of 2003 after Quidam had come back to Poland from shows in Belgium and Holland, they started preparations for a special show in the band's hometown, Inowroclaw. As it turned out later, this performance was the last one of the band's line-ups of that time as singer Emilia Derkowska decided to quit the band. On 16th February 2003 Emilia bade farewell during the sold-out show in Teatr Miejski in Inowroclaw. Soon afterwards, the rhythm section, Radek Sikorski and Rafal Jermakow also left, and the band had to regroup. Luckily, that final show was captured by three digital non-professional cameras, and this is the DVD. If you have never been fortunate enough to see this line-up of Quidam in concert (and most of us haven't) then this is the only opportunity we will have. Also, this was one of the times that Colin Bass (Camel) made a guest appearance with the band, so it is definitely worth catching. A great reissue of a great album,
Sep 2012

RACHEL'S BIRTHDAY
AN INVITATION TO
Back in 1996 Rachel's Birthday released their only album on the German label Music Is Intelligence, yet although it had critical success both it and the record company had gone within a few years. There were some great prog acts released through WMMS/M.I.I. yet with the folding of the label many of them just simply disappeared. Keyboard player and main songwriter Alfred Mueller started a new one-man project called Soniq

Theater, releasing his first album under that name in 2000, and producing one a year since then. All of these have been made available just on CD-R as they are a hobby, and as part of this Alfred has also released this one on CD-R.

I was lucky enough to review this back in the day, but it has been years since I have played it so when Alfred sent me every album he had released but I had yet to write about, it was an opportunity to revisit it. Soniq Theater is very much a one-man keyboard outfit, but Rachel's Birthday was a full band with Alfred joined by Michael Six (bass), Jürgen Hägele (drums), Bernd Mueller (guitars) and Ralf Glasbrenner (vocals). I had forgotten just how good this was, with these guys coming across as a melodic Twelfth Night mixing it up with classic Marillion and Citizen Cain. With one song nearly 25 minutes long, and another at more than 15, these guys have given themselves enough time to explore their music yet incredibly the longest "Waves" contains some passages that would fit in a melodic rock album, while at others it has hints of "The Collector". I'm not aware of any other releases by Ralf Glasbrenner which is a crying shame as he had a great vocal presence, not too dissimilar to Geoff Mann or Peter Nicholls.

Classic prog, symphonic prog, neo-prog, they all make an appearance on this album, which still stands up today. This is a band that managed to make little impact on the prog scene in the 90's yet have left behind an album that is well worth investigation.
Nov 2012

RED JASPER
STING IN THE TALE
Towards the end of 2011 I was perusing through the internet and started thinking about bands that I used to deal with in the early Nineties and this led me to conduct a search for Red Jasper. I was surprised but extremely pleased to see that they were again active, and that they had an interesting website. The person I always used to talk to had been singer Davey Dodds, but he is no longer involved, so I thought that I would contact them and see how they were doing. Drummer/singer DC and I were soon swapping emails and I offered to send him copies of every review I had ever written on the band, and eventually managed to be organized enough to be able to do so. DC told me that he was hoping to find a record label that may be interested in releasing all their old albums on CD, and I asked if he had thought of Angel Air and would he like an introduction to the person in charge? And so it was that a few weeks later the band had agreed with the label to reissue five albums, with 'Sting In The Tale' to be the first (which also includes as a bonus the songs from the "Pull That Thumb… (off the top of your head)" EP), and that yours truly was going to be writing all the booklets.

As I write this only 'Sting' has been reissued to date, but 'A Midsummer Night's Dream'/ 'The Winter's Tale' will soon be available as a double pack, with 'Action Replay' following soon afterwards. Of course, some people may now say that isn't possible for me to be completely objective when writing a review, so perhaps it might be best to go back to what I said all those years ago: "you cannot fail to fall in love with this. Red

Jasper's strength is not only their musical and song-writing ability but the fact that within each song they combine instruments and moods in a constructive, challenging yet interesting manner." I still stand by that: this is an album of music where the guys are challenging each other throughout – a real refusal to fit into any one particular style and heavily political to boot. What I find interesting is that this album was originally recorded and released in 1990 yet here in 2012 it is still a damn fine listen and hasn't dated at all.

If you enjoy folk rock with more than just a hint of edge and power (described by Davey himself as "Motörhead meets Jethro Tull"), then this is for you. Mention must be made of the fine remastering that Lloyd George has undertaken, and come to think of it the text in the booklet is particularly interesting as well….
May 2012

RED JASPER
ACTION REPLAY

On 26th January 1992 Red Jasper took to the stage at the Fleece & Firkin in Bristol with the intention of recording the gig for posterity. This was the second time of asking as the equipment had failed during the originally planned recording at the end of 1991, so this was the 'action replay'. At this time the band didn't have a recording contract, although their previous release 'Sting In The Tale' had been well received, so they felt that a quick way to get more product out was to release a live set. The line-up had also changed, with Davey Dodds (vocals, mandolin etc.), Robin Harrison (guitars) and DC (drums) being joined by bassist Jon Thornton. But they felt that they ought to expand the sound again (previously having sax and keyboards etc.), so roped in keyboard player Lloyd George (of Just) to guest for this night only.

The result is an album that has really stood the test of time and is still as lively and vibrant 20 years down the line as it was on that night. There was/is a very Englishness about this band that was matched by very few in the prog scene, and probably their only real contemporaries in the underground was Grace, but these guys really knew how to put the 'rock' into prog rock. The band have been compared to many others, but really, they had no comparison. Of course, people who haven't heard them do need a peg on which to hang their musical hat so to speak, so let's say that they had the folk and balls of Horslips, as well as the whistle and keyboards (and even perform 'The King Of The Fairies') yet at times come across as a metallic Jethro Tull. There is a venom in Davey's vocals that provide a harsh edge to proceedings; the folk/punk ethic combining strongly.

It is great that this album has now been made available on CD at long last. No bonus songs, but there is an incredibly well-written booklet……
Jul 2012

RED JASPER
A MIDSUMMER NIGHT'S DREAM/THE WINTER'S TALE
After the release of 'Action Replay' the band hit the road again and managed to secure a distribution deal with the Dutch label SI Records. The record sold so well that label boss Willebrord Elsing offered the band a three-album deal. This was the first time that they had been given the luxury of being able to spend time writing something that would hopefully appeal to a wider audience, and as they were seen as an English band why not Shakespeare? Both albums were released in 1994, and they are often viewed as part of the same piece, so it makes perfect sense for Angel Air to reissue these together as a double set. The band were by now working well together, having again been gigging hard, with 'guest' keyboard player Lloyd George now very much a full member of the band.

These two albums were extremely complex, both lyrically and musically, but never lost the punch and power that RJ had built their reputation upon. Yes, there were crunching guitars, but there was also delicate mandolin, and keyboards rising majestically above proceedings while the bass and drum interplay kept everyone nailed to the floor. I was lucky enough to hear (and indeed review) these albums all those years ago and now, as I did back then, can only wonder why these didn't lift the band into the heights that they undoubtedly deserved to be. They are a delight from start to finish and Lloyd's remastering has provided an additional crispness that allows the listener to just sit back and savour everything that is going on.

Two very English albums from a very English band (even the sonnets are true to the original concept with four quatrains followed by two rhyming couplets). Here they have been presented with some additional live songs taken from RJ's successful European tour and are a worthy addition to any music lover's collection. Oh, can I just also mention that the booklet text is particularly fine??
Jul 2012

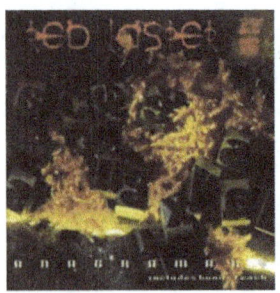

RED JASPER
ANAGRAMARY
And so, we come to the end of the first phase of Red Jasper. Following on from the two albums recorded for SI Music and the promotional touring that followed it the band took a break, and by the time that they came back together to record what was to be their final album the band had moved in different directions. In fact, singer Davey Dodds wasn't involved a great deal in the writing process, which was spread out much more evenly over the remaining four guys. The album was recorded at the same studio as the previous two, but this time Davey was only there when it was time for him to record his vocals and it was little surprise that the band broke up not long afterwards. As Davey had been involved with many publications as the main contact, it also wasn't surprising that few even knew that it had been released as he bowed out of proceedings.

Although I had been a fan of the other albums I didn't hear 'Anagramary' until 2011, some fourteen years after it was originally released, so in many ways this is a 'new' album for me and looking back it is possible to see that here was a band in transition. Davey no longer took lead vocals on all songs, with drummer DC stepping to the fore and giving the band a different sound with "In Her Eyes" being both a departure and yet also familiar. There are times when Lloyd is content with piano, but there are others when swathes of Hammonds are what is required while the rest of the guys show why the band were mentioned as being "Motörhead meets Jethro Tull".

It is hard to fathom that this album basically sank without trace, being known to only a select few, and that it has taken 15 years for it to be made widely available again, but here it is with a bonus live number (and again a great booklet) and if you enjoy prog that is very English in its' style then this is essential. Red Jasper are recording again in 2012, with DC as the lead singer and new drummer Nick Harradence (Shadowland) filling his drum seat and are playing the Fleece in December so get your tickets now!!

If, like me, you will be unable to attend (I live the other side of the world, what's your excuse?) then you will just have to satisfy your musical cravings by picking up all the Angel Air reissues.
Aug 2012

ALEC K. REDFEARN AND THE EYESORES
SISTER DEATH
This is the seventh album from Alec and his band, who have been purveying their rather unique style of alternative music for more than ten years now. The music is complex and very different, grounded in his own accordion work, but somehow it is also easy to listen to with its' melodic nod back to the era of psychedelia when anything was possible. To say that there is an eclectic mix of instrumentation is something of an understatement as the band deploy stand-up bass, accordion, French horn, percussion, doumbek, organ, and electronics, among others. This really is music that refuses to be pigeonholed, with The Velvet Underground, Tom Waits and Frank Zappa just some of the obvious influences. The songs are all very different to each other, so while krautrock may influence one song the next could well be from French café culture

There is no doubt that the discovery of Orion Rigel Dommisse has had a major effect on the band as her high clear vocals provide another facet to the experience, sometimes taking lead or harmonising with Alec her voice is a delight. Sadly, an album that contains this much depth and musical ability will be ignored by much of the mainstream and is unlikely to get the recognition it so richly deserves, especially as it refuses to sit in any particular category. But if you enjoy 'good music' without worrying about what the label says on the packaging then you need to investigate this further.
Oct 2012

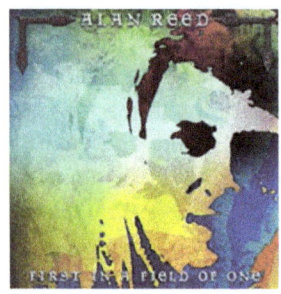

ALAN REED
FIRST IN A FIELD OF ONE

Alan first came to my attention when he started singing with Pallas, and then on the Strangers on a Train projects so I then worked backwards to discover his work with Abel Ganz and have always been impressed with his skills as a vocalist. Now, I'm not nearly as in touch with the UK prog scene these days as I used to be (I live on the other side of the world; that's my excuse and I'm sticking to it) but I was somewhat surprised to hear that he was no longer with Pallas, as his work with them was always of the highest quality. However, that is all in the past and now we have his first full-length solo album which see him reunited with keyboard player Mike Stobbie. Others taking part are Scott Higham (drums, percussion), Jeff Green (guitars), Kalle Wallner (guitars) and Christina Booth from Magenta on additional vocals.

It did take me quite a while to get into this album, not because it wasn't any good but rather because I wasn't quite sure what to expect but I was pretty sure this wasn't it. In many ways this is a very laid back album with quite a folky element, almost as if Clannad have gained a male lead singer who has some prog influences combined with some Mike Oldfield. Alan is singing as well as ever, and this album is all about his vocals and being at the fore. It isn't nearly as complex or symphonic as I would have liked and possibly that is why it feels more of an opportunity missed than one taken.

"Teardrops In The Rain" is a great song that captures all that is good about the album, but is spoiled somewhat by an annoying drum pattern that I could have done without. Alan is one of the finest singers around, but while this is an enjoyable album I would much rather hear him belting out with a full prog rock band behind him.
May 2013

RESERVE DE MARCHE
THE LAST TWENTY YEARS

Reserve de Marche are not a French band, although that is implied by the name (which translates to 'Power Reserve') but are in fact an instrumental trio from Moscow. The band was formed by Alexander Alekseev (guitar) along with Dmitry Pomogaev (drums) and Andrey Bagdasarov (bass), and only two years after their formation their debut CD is out and I can see from their site that they are gigging a fair bit as well. There is very little information around on this band, but luckily their site is in English and there they state that their music is "*Classic rock elements, heavy riffs, sound experiments and sensuous melodies merge in music that feels like thrill and adventure. RdM combines a mix of multiple styles, including progressive, post-rock, shoegaze and atmospheric sludge to celebrate the unique moment or here and now.*" So now you know.

What I found with this album is that there is a real presence, a forceful nature to the

music, with an intensity and dynamic that is unusual in a band that is so young. I certainly didn't miss the vocals, yet this is an album that is much more about songs instead of long passages with no meaning. The music ebbs, it flows, with very much a hard rock feel yet there is also a space within the music as the individual lines and melodies make themselves heard. The production is very strong as well, with the result that this is an album that definitely needs to be heard by a much wider audience.
Sep 2012

RETROSPECTIVE
LOST IN PERCEPTION
I don't know why it has taken these Polish proggers four years since 'Stolen Thoughts', but at last they are back with their new album. What we have here is a solid combination of prog rock, prog metal, classic rock, and a host of other influences. Jakub Roszak has a very strong voice and can either drive a song along or be more reflective as on "Lunch" where he duets with Beata Łagoda. They mix Muse with Porcupine Tree in a way that is immediate and inviting to the proghead, while never losing any of the power and thrust of a hard rock band. They can slow it down or speed it up, yet always with the vocals at the heart of what they are doing.

In many ways this is a very mature piece of work, layered and thoughtful with strong production. This is yet another album that proves that prog music is very much alive and well in Poland, and luckily their website can be read by those who prefer English. Sheer class from beginning to end.
Dec 2012

RIVERSIDE
REALITY DREAM
Many years ago, my good friend Artur Chachlowski was over in the UK, and he handed me the debut album by a new Polish band and he told me they were going to be huge. Now, I have been lucky enough to hear a lot of Polish prog over the years (SBB and Collage being particular favourites) so I knew that this was high praise and paid some serious attention to the music and agreed totally with the sentiment. This double live CD from 2008 brings together songs from the first three albums, and the four guys really know how to kick up a storm on stage. Mariusz Duda (vocals, bass guitar, acoustic guitar), Piotr Grudziński (guitars) and Piotr Kozieradzki (drums) had been there since the beginning and Michał Łapaj (keyboards) had been there since the second album so there is no surprise that they could bounce off each other.

There has been quite a lot of debate regarding the songs chosen for this recording, but if this is how they were touring at the time what's the issue? Comment must be made on the production which is stunning for a live recording, with a crispness and clarity often missing. Mariusz's vocals are spot on with plenty of emotion and edge when required, and his basswork is very Squire-like at times with a real punch. An early Seventies feel is provided by Michał when he uses the Hammond, but for large parts of the concert he is happy to provide a support role while Piotr K nails it from the back. It is Piotr G who really makes this for me, with some superb guitarwork which can be straight ahead rock when required, or at times a mixture of Gary Chandler and David Gilmour. I had to smile when I heard the strains of "Shine On" during "Back To The River" as I had already been thinking just how Floyd-like they were at times, and it fitted in perfectly.

They are just so good at what they do, that one often forgets that this is a live album which is both a strength and a weakness. They may not vary too much from the studio versions, but as an introduction to the first three albums one can't really ask for more.
Jan 2013

RIVERSIDE
SHRINE OF NEW GENERATION SLAVES
Somehow Riverside just seem to keep on getting better and better, with the new album being a case in point. As I write this it has had 73 ratings on ProgArchives and is rated as the second-best album of 2013 so far. Now, I know it's only January, but it won't be far from that mark at the end of the year, I'm sure. The four musicians have now been together for a long time, and it shows. Production is yet again just wonderful, and not only has the band really come of age but they mix up bouncy hard rock from the Seventies with a much more laid-back Floydian feel. For some reason I keep thinking of Opeth, although they are nothing alike, so it must just be due to approach as opposed to sound.

"Celebrity Touch" is a fun bounce along rock number with great Hammond that apart from the vocals could be classic Spock's Beard. This is a prog album that is guaranteed to make the listener smile from the first note to the very last and there is only one thing to do when it ends, and that is to play the whole thing again. The louder I played it the more I enjoyed it, as the guys really know how to hit that perfect vibe. Highly recommended. It doesn't get much better than this.
Jan 2013

ROSWELL SIX
TERRA INCOGNITA: BEYOND THE HORIZON
This is an interesting album in many ways, and not all of them musical. Well-known author Kevin J.Anderson has long had an interest in progressive rock music and in 2007 he was working on the first Terra Incognito novel when he was contacted by Shawn Gordon of Progrock Records. Shawn introduced him to some of the bands on the label and the idea came up of Kevin being involved with an album that would be based on the new

book. Keyboard player and composer Erik Norlander became involved to write the music while all the lyrics were written by Kevin and his wife Rebecca Moesta. Of course, this is a concept album, but on a rather grander scale than most. To do justice to the vision Erik brought together a great group of musicians including four vocalists, so while he provided keyboards and his wife Lana Lane was one of the singers the rest were James LaBrie (Dream Theater, Fates Warning etc.), Michael Sadler (ex-Saga) and John Payne (ex-Asia) and they were joined by Kurt Barabas (Under The Sun, Amaran's Plight) on bass, Chris Quirarte (Prymary) drums, Gary Wehrkamp (Shadow Gallery) electric guitars, Chris Brown (Ghost Circus) acoustic and additional electric guitars, David Ragsdale (Kansas etc.) violin, Mike Alvarez on cello and Martin Orford (ex-IQ, ex-Jadis, John Wetton) on flute.

I'm not going to talk to the story of the album, as you can buy the book to get the full details, but to put each song in context there is a passage before the lyrics for each one in the booklet so that the listener knows where the story is going. To be honest though, this album stands up very well indeed on its own. The first time I played this was when I was working on the land, and I think I smiled throughout the whole thing – it is immediately incredibly impressive. I have long been a fan of Erik's work, and love Lana's vocals so to have it all brought together with this wonderful group of musicians with great songs was just amazing.

Subsequent plays found me studying the booklet and lyrics, getting the most out of the storyline, enjoying the artwork etc. This is symphonic prog with many of the elements of Erik's past music that has made him so popular, combined with elements of Ayreon that definitely allow the guitarists to shine without fully moving into the realms of prog metal – although there are times when they come close!!

Many progheads enjoy reading fantasy, it seems to fit in well with our mindsets, and I am sure that Roger Dean and Rodney Matthews have a lot to answer for in this regard as well. In fact, I am currently reading Terry Brooks but for some strange reason have never read any of Kevin J. Anderson's books. I am going to remedy that by buying 'The Edge of the World' to see how these guys have brought that to life. Let's hope that there are more in the pipeline as it would be criminal if this is the only release. A wonderful album from the first note to the very last.
Apr 2010

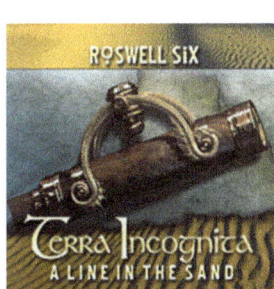

ROSWELL SIX
TERRA INCOGNITA: A LINE IN THE SAND
This is the follow-up album to the debut "Terra Incognita: Beyond the Horizon" but whereas that album was put together by Erik Norlander, this time that duty falls to Henning Pauly who has surrounded himself with musicians he knows well - vocals are by rock legends Steve Walsh (Kansas), Michael Sadler (Saga), Sass Jordan, Alexander Froese (Frameshift) and Nick Storr (The Third Ending) and guest appearances by Charlie Dominici (solo, original Dream Theater vocalist), Juan Roos

(Shadow's Mignon) and Arjen Lucassen (Ayreon and many others). For those who are unaware of the concept behind Roswell Six, it is worth repeating. Acclaimed author Anderson developed the universe and story of "Terra Incognita," a tale of sailing ships, sea monsters, and the crusades. He then expanded on some of the storylines and with his wife Rebecca Moesta, wrote all the lyrics to the songs. The first novel in the series, 'The Edge of the World', was released in June 2010 and this ties in with debut album, while the second CD ties in with 'The Map of All Things'.

So, overall, a very ambitious project and Anderson and Moesta penned the lyrics/story again for this album and even co-wrote two songs with multi-Grammy winner Janis Ian. When a project has such importance and is really under the microscope, it can be extremely hard to produce music that stands up to all the attention – but this really does. Henning is no stranger to producing complex music, and while he has brought in 7 singers – he does everything else himself! But, as with all of Henning's albums this sounds very much like a band – not one guy in a studio laying down track after track. He has stamped his own authority all over this while continuing from what Erik started as opposed to creating a totally brand-new identity.

This is progressive melodic rock as its finest. Yes, there will be some decriers who say that the music itself is nothing new, and there is nothing here that is contentious or challenging – but when it comes sheer listening pleasure, it rarely gets any better than this.
Nov 2011

ANDREW ROUSSAK
NO TRESPASSING
Andrew Roussak is keyboard player with Dorian Opera, but this is a solo album where he has composed all of the material (apart from two classical pieces by Bach) and has been joined by some guests so that at times this does sound like a band project. Normally progheads are the most forgiving music fans when it comes to different styles, but I am not sure that many would be expecting lounge in the middle of what is predominantly a prog album, witness "Do Without Me". But you know what? I think it works to a large extent, just not within the context of the album. But this is a solo album and part of the reason for recording outside of the band context is that the musician is free to do whatever he/she likes and obviously Andrew feels that it belongs.

However, overall, this is an enjoyable album with some very strong passages. The vocals aren't always as powerful as they might be, but they work well with the music. This is melodic neo-prog that is firmly middle of the road in that it isn't challenging any musical boundaries, but it is extremely accessible and enjoyable even on first hearing and at the end of the day isn't music there to be enjoyed? I feel it could have done with more push and power but for a debut solo this is a worthwhile effort, and it will be interesting to see where Andrew goes from here.
Oct 2009

The Progressive Underground Vol 4

ROZ VITALIS
PATIENCE OF HOPE
This is the first time I have come across Roz Vitalis, although the band was conceived by St. Petersburg composer and multi-instrumentalist Ivan Rozmainsky more than ten years ago. Since the inception of his keyboard-dominated studio project, he has produced recordings which combine elements of solo instrumental, sacred music, experimental, and modern folk with art-rock and avant-prog. The more I played this the more I felt we were listening to music that had a great depth not only in the styles that were being portrayed but also in the amount of atmosphere that was being created. Sometimes I felt it was reminiscent of Gentle Giant, Gryphon, Anekdoten and even Cardiacs or Mike Oldfield!

Musically it is all over the shop, both in the instrumentation being deployed (come on, how many times have you heard a flugelhorn?) and in the types of music. Some of this is in keeping with the work of Richard Wileman (Karda Estra) with a heavy cinematic focus and complex classical interplay. It is a stunning album in so many ways, and for the more adventurous this is indispensable
Nov 2012

ROZ VITALIS
LIVE AT ST. PETER PROG FEST #5
I received an email telling me that this album had been made available through Bandcamp, but what intrigued me was the line "Like any Roz Vitalis stuff, the style is the "Unclassifiable Branch of Prog Rock", and music is about The Ineffable and The Unfathomable, in particular, about human aspiration for The Unapproachable Light." I mean, with a comment like that how on earth can you go wrong? I only have one of their previous albums, 2012's 'Patience of Hope', but I gave that 4 *'s, so I was looking forward to this, and I wasn't disappointed. Just eight songs, and a smidgin under 40 minutes in length, here we have instrumental progressive rock that has much in common with orchestral sounds of Karda Estra as well as bringing in elements of Gryphon, Jethro Tull, and a little pronk here and there. Five of the songs were recorded on one night, and three the next with a line-up comprising band leader Ivan Rozmainsky (keyboards), Vladimir Efimov (electric guitar), Vladimir 'Energoslon' Semenov-Tyan-Shansky (electric guitar) (although the band doesn't sound nearly as heavy as one might expect from two guitarists, Vladislav Korotkikh (flute and low whistle), Ruslan Kirillov (bass guitar), Philip 'Phill' Semenov (drums and percussion) and Yury Khomonenko (percussion on the first five songs).

This is complex music, highly arranged and layered, with just no room for a singer as the different musicians take their turn at lead or combine to provide the perfect support. At times laid back, and at others very much in your face with some power chords, this is modern progressive classical music that works incredibly well with a fresh and inviting sound. I find this is an album that I can become immersed in, and certainly doesn't sound like a live recording as there is so much structure within the sound. Ivan provides a lot of piano on this album, and the clarity of that instrument provides a great deal of cut through against the picked guitar and the dirty bass, while the percussion also plays a huge part.

All in all, this is an exciting invigorating album that is over far too quickly, and somehow doesn't feel over-engineered or over-played, with everyone understating their part and that this is a group of musicians combining as opposed to all having egos that need to be fed.
Nov 2013

THE SAFETY FIRE
MOUTH OF SWORDS
It is always refreshing to come across bands that refuse to conform to any particular musical genre and create their own path. Such is the case with British outfit The Safety Fire, for whom the term progressive metal is really the only one that fits, not because they sound like what many people may view of as a prog metal act, but rather that they obviously have never read the rulebook, let alone ignored it. There are huge elements of djent and mathcore in what they are doing, and I already had Protest The Hero down as an obvious influence long before I realised that they had actually toured together. The Safety Fire draw from a large pool of influences, from bands they've always listened to such as Deftones, Tool and Alice In Chains to former tour mates such as Between The Buried And Me and Gojira among others.

This is brutal staccato music that is always twisting and moving in new directions, but always with incredible intensity. It is this over-the-top passion that almost knocks the listener back, such is the anger and directness of the music. It is as if they have decided to capture the emotion of the most over the top hardcore band they could find and have then created complex and bewildering time signatures and riffs. Loud and raw, the note density is immense, and the tour with PTH must have been just incredible (please can both these bands come to New Zealand? Pretty please??).

This is never music that can be played in the background as it is too much in your face and your ears. This is music that refuses to be ignored and will crunch into your brain even as you are trying to follow the musical structure. Sean McWeeney manages to keep his vocal melodies far simpler than what is going on beneath him, and this combined with the intensity provides a compelling musical statement. Songwriter Dez says "Being called a progressive band encapsulates the fact that we don't do one thing. We think about prog in the experimental sense. We connect more with bands like Mastodon than Dream Theater, so that's how we relate to the word 'progressive' with our music." Progressive, metallic, intense.
Sep 2013

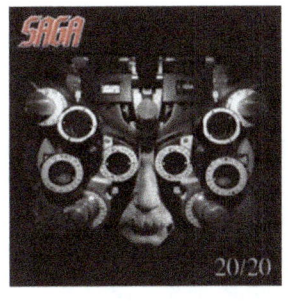

SAGA
20/20

It must be more than 30 years since I first became aware of Saga, and after purchasing a cut-price single, invested in my first vinyl album of theirs, the wonderful 'Images of Twilight'. From then on, I picked up the occasional release, and finally caught them in concert about ten years ago (where they won the award for being the quietest rock band I have ever seen). By then they had, at least to me, settled into a sound that was always very much Saga and they could always be relied upon to release a solid album, but normally not a spectacular one. The last album I heard of theirs was 2006's 'Trust', and in the intervening period they have released two other studio albums and singer Michael Sadler has left and returned, so have I been missing anything?

Well, if this is anything to go by then probably not much. While opener "Six Feet Under" is very much a typical Saga song, with driving keyboards and guitars and over the top vocals it is let down by much that follows, especially "Ellery" which highlights a more reflective side of the band that just doesn't work at all. For every song that raises the hopes there is another that dashes it, and the overall effect is that while die-hard fans will acclaim Michael's return as a masterpiece the rest of us won't feel the same way. If only there were more like "Show and Tell", which is classic Saga in so many ways, then it would be possible rate this more highly but it's not worth it.
Dec 2012

SÃO PAULO UNDERGROUND
TRÊS CABEÇAS LOUCURAS

There are times when I come across a jazz album that breaks through traditional boundaries and creates something that is quite different to anything I have heard before, and that is definitely true of this SPU's third album. The press release that accompanies this states "you'll reach for such sonic signifiers as "jazz," "Brazilian music," "avant-garde," and "electro-acoustic" in an attempt to tag 'Três Cabeças Loucuras'. When American cornetist Rob Mazurek gets together with his Brazilian buddies Guilherme Granado (keyboards, electronics), Mauricio Takara (drums, percussion, cavaquinho (a small string instrument of the guitar family with four wire or gut strings), electronics) and "fourth member" Richard Ribeiro (drums), all of the aforementioned flavours are on the musical menu, but ultimately, it's best to just term the end result a kind of joyful "chef's surprise" that gleefully upends expectations."

It is definitely jazz, and often avant-garde, but it is the way that the guys approach this and the instrumentation they use that makes it so inspired. There are pieces that are very dreamy, with keyboards and electronic sounds being quite reminiscent of Can, while at others this is full-on. Mazurek has studied with Art Farmer, and it shows, while of course Miles Davis is also an obvious influence although Mazurek himself states that Bill Dixon is his biggest inspiration.

I know I don't listen to nearly as much jazz as I should, something I am working on, but this is an inspired album that fans of jazz or avant-garde music in general will get a great deal from.
Sep 2012

ANDY SEARS
SOUVENIR
This CD is a special limited-edition release, which was put out to combine with Andy's solo European tour. It is not a fully-fledged album but is more a collection of demos and is a work in progress in readiness for his planned solo album which will be called 'The Dragon Inside'. Some of these songs may end up on that album in a very much reworked form, and others will not. Andy played all the music, which will not be the case in the 'proper' album with just some assistance from TN bandmate Dean Baker who assisted with some keyboard programming. But, to my hearing Andy is really selling himself short as this is a fun album that would happily form part of any proghead's collection.

Yes of course the main purchasers of this album will be Twelfth Night fans, and they will be pleased to see reworkings of three TN numbers – but this is an album that does stand very much on its' own merits as opposed to something that is for fans only. Andy has lost none of his vocal range or power over the years, and this collection shows that his instinct for melody and passion have also not faded away. It starts with a delicate piano-led piece, "Satellite" which in all makes three appearances on this set (as the opener, as an extended version and as an instrumental video) – in many ways this reminds me of Phil Collins, and I can't think why for the life of me. But the highlight is a solo rendition of "First New Day" which has been considerably reworked – it has a depth and passion that is somehow more than the original, although instrumentally it is much less!

Within the booklet Andy explains each song and overall, this is a set that many people will enjoy. It certainly fulfils the original purpose of having something available for those who saw him tour, and if I was there I would definitely have purchased this, but for TN fans who can't wait or just for those who want good melodic songs with great vocals then this is worth getting.
Oct 2011

SH.TG.N
SH.TG.N
It is of no surprise to me at all to discover that the debut album by this Belgian six-piece was recorded live in the studio in one day. The brainchild of Antoine Guenet (keyboards, vocals – also in The Wrong Object), he brought together Fulco Ottervanger (vocals), Wim Segers (vibraphones), Yannick De Pauw (guitars), Dries Geusens (bass) and Simon Segers (drums) to bring his vision to life. And what a strange and anarchic vision it is too. Here we have Zappa and Beefheart going at it hammer and tongs, with Art Zoyd and Can

also weighing in for all they are worth. This is not easy music to listen to, and certainly isn't easy listening! But, as I have found with all music of this style, if you are willing to persevere and get inside the heads of the musicians then the effort is more than repaid.

Fulco may not have the gruffness of the Captain, but he shares a similar approach to both him and Damo Suzuki. He may not believe too much in melody etc., but what he is doing does make sense amid the mayhem. Wim shows that a vibraphone can really rock when it needs to, and when he duels with the others it is something indeed. You will either be highly impressed with this album or think it is one of the worse things ever released. There is no middle ground.
Feb 2013

SHADOW'S MIGNON
MIDNIGHT SKY MASQUERADE

Henning Pauly is one of the most well-known multi-instrumentalists in the current scene, and one that seems to take great delight producing powerful guitar-based albums that are all very different from each other (he is also a huge fan of Douglas Adams – and I still can't believe that I was playing one of his albums for the first time on my 42nd birthday and realised that the song I was listening to was about HHGTTG, way too freaky!). He released two albums as Frameshift (the first with singer James LaBrie (Dream Theater) and the second with Sebastian Bach (ex-Skid Row)). He has released albums with Chain, solo, rock opera (Babysteps) and for this album he decided that maybe Eighties classic style metal would be an interesting way to go, and why not? He invited Juan Roos to provide the rock vocals, Stephan Kernbach to assist on keyboards and he provided everything else (of course).

He states that the influences are Dio, Whitesnake, Iron Maiden, Manowar, Rainbow, Foreigner, Ratt, Quiet Riot, Uriah Heep, Yngwie Malmsteen, Europe, Ozzy Osbourne, Gary Moore, Cinderella, Alice Cooper, Judas Priest, Accept and Halloween (but not many of those bands use a banjo to introduce a song...). But you could also easily add Poison, Great White, Bonfire, and a host of others. Henning likes to say that it sounds like "Awesome Metal from the 80s, the 90s and the best of today", and you know what? He's right!

It is quite possible that this album may be overlooked by the target audience, just because it is on a label that is usually associated with progressive rock music (well, it is in the name), and this is not progressive rock but incredibly well executed and catchy melodic hard rock that could have been come out of the LA scene twenty years ago. Label boss Shawn Gordon has long been a friend and supporter of Henning, so there really was never any doubt where this would come out, but if you don't normally listen to prog don't let the name of the record company put you off – this is a hard rock lover's delight! The

album closes with a very different acoustic take of the title song (which also appears as a rocker earlier) and brings the album to a fitting close. This is an essential purchase for any fans of melodic classic rock.
Nov 2011

SHINEBACK
RISE UP FORGOTTEN, RETURN DESTROYED
This is a new project by Simon Godfrey of Tinyfish fame, and he has brought in some guests to work on a concept album which is interesting, compelling, dynamic, and very layered. There are times when it is very dark indeed, which is not surprising given the subject matter. It is possible to read the complete story that goes with the album by visiting the website, but it starts with "My name is Dora. I am, and have been for many years, a permanent guest at the Wychwood Centre for the criminally insane, for killing my father. Which I both did and did not do." Intrigued? There are parts of this album that blow me away with the sheer audacity of what is being done, and yet others where I shake my head and ask why?

I think that part of this is down to more of my own musical tastes than it is any fault with the album itself. I enjoy music that is primarily made by musicians, whether that be prog, metal, jazz etc., but have some real issues when it comes to any of the dance genres, or most pop in general, which I believe to be artificially created, often by those who have little or no musical talent or skill. So, when I come across an album which does feature some of these styles, I naturally have some issues. When Fear Factory first hit the scene, it took some serious listening on my part to be able to work out if I felt that they were doing something exciting and new or whether it was just an aberration (I decided on the former and was extremely vociferous in my support). But there we had genres hitting headlong to create something new, and here there are passages where if it was taken out of context of the album it could be played in the clubs in Ibiza. "Crush Culture" is very much like this, and I know this is just part of the story but isn't the sort of thing that I listen to, given the choice.

I have read a lengthy review of this album where this is compared to "The Wall", and the statement is made that if that album was written now it would sound like this. While I do feel this is boundary pushing in many ways, somehow, I don't think that this is in the same level of importance. When these guys were offered to the Crossover Prog team for consideration it was an easy vote regarding the sub-genre, but I am still getting to grips with the album. It is an audacious piece of work, and I think that only many listenings will allow anyone to fully get to grips with it. 4*'s for now, but part of me feels that this just may be a 5* album that I have yet to come to terms with.
Sep 2013

SILENT VOICES
REVEAL THE CHANGE

Silent Voices was founded in 1995 by guitarist Timo Kauppinen, bassist Pasi Kauppinen, drummer Jukka-Pekka Koivisto and keyboardist Henrik Klingenberg. At the time their main influences were Dream Theater and Rush. A couple of years later the line-up was completed when Michael Henneken joined in on vocals. They may have had a break for a little while (six years since the last album) but they are now back with their fourth full-length release. Henrik and Pasi are also members of Sonata Arctica, and instead of replacing Michael (who left after the last album) they have instead brought in some guests to help them out, so vocals on this album are provided by Mats Levén (Therion, Yngwie Malmsteen), Tony Kakko (Sonata Arctica), Mike Vescera) Loudness, Yngwie Malmsteen, Obsession) and Mike DiMeo (Masterplan, Riot). To ensure that they got the sound right, it was mastered by Ted Jensen (Bon Jovi, Dream Theater, Megadeth).

The result is something that is progressive metal through and through, and will appeal to fans of both that genre and of those who want their metal to be melodic and hard hitting and may not normally think of prog as being their thing. The musical quartet behind this album have been playing together for years and it shows, as they trade runs and are tighter than a Mayan wall. The drum fills are wonderful, with real inventiveness that add to the overall sound without detracting from it, while Timo can surely shred with the best of them. Henrik has a very fluid style, moving between different sounds to get the best from each section of a song while Pasi can also take the lead when he wants to, but is often to be found at the back providing wonderful counterpoint to the main metallic proceedings.

With singers of this standard the overall result is nothing short of superb, and here we have a prog metal album that is probably more of the latter than the former, but that isn't necessarily a bad thing and here we have something that is hard hitting and fun throughout. If you haven't come across this band before, and it has been a while since their last album to be fair, then you owe it to your ears to get this now.
Dec 2013

SILHOUTTE
ACROSS THE RUBICON

This is my first experience of Dutch band Silhouette, although it is their third album, and I am now starting to wonder just what I have missed by not coming across them before. Although in many ways they are reminiscent of IQ, it is patently obvious that Barclay James Harvest has also played a large part in their musical upbringing. Dual vocals are often prominent, combined with swathes of symphonic keyboards and a cutting guitar. It is prog as a warm blanket, reassuring and comfortable and although others may snigger at the attire there is no way that you are going to let it go.

The production and arrangements are very strong, and this is class from start to finish with a place and time for everyone. "When Snow's Falling Down" sounds as if it could have come from the pen of Nick Barrett twenty years ago, while at other times there are hints of Marillion as we are taken on a mature ride through a landscape of immaculately written songs. At times the keyboards are just simple piano, at others it is an over-driven organ, while the drums sometimes are incredibly effective by not being there at all. It is an album which is full of space and layers, and while it does lose some of the passion and drive because of that, it more than makes up with sheer professionalism. It may not be anything dramatically new, but if you are looking for a very solid neo-prog album then this is good from start to finish.
Dec 2012

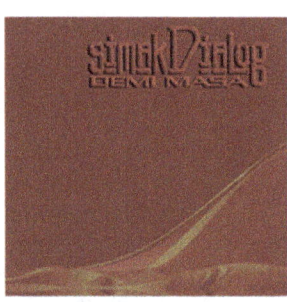

SIMAK DIALOG
DEMI MASA
To be honest, I'm not as au fait with Indonesian music as maybe I should be based on the evidence of this. It is worth listing the musicians and their instruments as it may just give an idea of what they are doing. The band was formed in Jakarta in 1993 by Riza Arshad (electric piano, acoustic grand piano, synths), and he is joined by Tohpati (electric and acoustic guitar), Adhithya Pratama (bass), Endang Ramdan (lead Sundanese kendang percussion, tambourine, claps, toys, vocals) and Erlan Suwardana (Sundanese kendang percussion, claps, toys, vocals) with a few guests. I have been listening much more to jazz in recent years and the breadth and passion of this album is just breathtaking. At times it is very melodic, with either the keyboards or guitar being the lead, yet at others it is much more 'free'.

This could never be considered background music as it demands close attention to what is going on. Of course, a major part of this music is the percussion which provides a very different flavour to that from many jazz albums. Tohpati provides some stunning guitar, but it is the way that he combines with Riza that is the highlight. Take "Tak Jauh Pertama" for example where Riza provides most of the melodic lead with simple chords, but what makes the song work is the note density and sheer bravado playing of Tohpati. At times his guitarwork reminds me of John McLaughlin, and if I was to pick just one act to compare Simak Dialog with it would be when McLaughlin and Carlos Santana combined together for a few albums, but it would be justifiable to mention Pat Metheny or Return To Forever, yet none of these tags do this justice.

If you enjoy jazz and fusion, then this is an essential purchase.
Aug 2012

SIMON SAYS
TARDIGRADE

Back in 1995 I was sent two albums to review that had been released on a small Swedish label called Bishop Garden Records – the first of these was 'Every Pixie Tells a Story' by The Moor, and the second 'Ceinwein' by Simon Says. Stefan Renström was the link between the two bands as he was the bassist for the former and was the leader of the second providing all the music (originally Simon Says were going to be primarily a duo of Stefan and singer Daniel Fäldt). I gave the album a rave review, loving the mix of Seventies and Eighties prog and the way that it moved – in fact I said, "In my opinion 'Ceinwein' is one of the top albums to come out of Scandinavia this year".

So of course, in the parallel universe the band sold millions and became household names, but in this rather more boring reality they split up. Stefan stayed with The Moor, touring Europe, and then in 2001 he contacted Daniel saying that he wanted to get Simon Says going again. They quickly got a band together and recorded 'Paradise Square', which was released on Galileo Records in 2002 (which I haven't heard) but again the band was shelved. It is hard to find out information on the band and what has been going as neither of their websites have been updated in a few years and that is a crying shame as this new album is nothing short of brilliant.

This is music that belongs in the Seventies, but it is very much of the present as well. Keyboards can be dominant, or just piano, guitars can be overpowering or non-existent. It has swathes of Mellotron and Hackett/Howe guitars with wonderful vocals. Imagine Genesis and Yes moved in a time machine from thirty years ago to now, and then were allowed just enough time to hear what was going on and to get used to modern equipment and then thrown into a studio with Derek Shulman to record an album, and this is what you get. This is a prog lover's dream – and every home should have this CD. What concerns me is that this band appear to have dropped off the radar again since this release and that is nothing short of criminal – this is the sort of music that got me involved with the genre in the first place. Modern progheads need bands like these.
Jan 2012

CARSTEN SINDVALD
THE KING'S CHAMBER

Carsten is a Danish multi-instrumentalist and composer who I first came across playing saxophone with Robin Taylor, although he is also adept at clarinet, piano/keyboards and church organ. He graduated as a classical saxophonist from The Royal Danish Academy of Music and has been involved in quite a few jazz ventures, including with his own quartet and with Jon Hemmersam, although I believe that this is his first solo offering. He has gathered together guest musicians who have strengths in different areas, which has allowed him to create an album that in so many ways sound like multiple bands yet at the same time there is a real identity throughout. This is jazz that has been carefully thought out, music that has been deftly arranged so that everybody can shine but never at the expense of the overall direction.

More than a few people will mention Chick Corea when reviewing this album (and percussionist Martin Spans who has been in Chick's band is a guest), but there are many different styles at play. One interesting element are the "Hippopotamus" songs. There are ten of these – the longest at 1:48 and the shortest at just 33 seconds, and these solo piano pieces act as palate cleansers. It's like the sorbet just as you get ready for the next delicious offering, so that it isn't tainted by what has gone before.

This really is a delight, a very different style of jazz to what he pursues with Robin Taylor, and one I enjoyed immensely.
Nov 2011

SKY ARCHITECT
EXCAVATION OF THE MIND
On playing this there are a few things that spring immediately to mind, such as wondering how on earth can this be a debut which is quickly followed by what on earth is this music doing in the 21st century? The reason for the latter question is that this is prog that has been heavily influenced in all the right ways by the Seventies and the only way I can describe it is by calling it "open". This is music that just begs the listener to come in, sit down and relax in the comfy armchair while being blown away by incredible multi-layered music that is somehow immediate and compelling. Apparently, these are five young guys from Rotterdam, and it has been a while since I heard anything from Holland that is as exciting as this. It takes me back to the days when a parcel from Holland meant the next set of promos from the much-missed SI Music and knowing that there would be CDs within to surprise and delight.

These guys obviously know their prog, and there are a whole host of influences (although the madcap section within "Russian Wisdom" owes more to a polka band than it does a prog act!), with Gentle Giant probably being the biggest (and in my book that can never be a bad thing). It is no wonder that no expense has been spared on the artwork, and Mark Wilkinson has again produced a masterpiece that is matched by the music inside.

One of the most exciting debuts I have come across in recent years, and I can only hope that these guys stick with it as the prog scene is surely richer by having them in it.
Aug 2012

THE SKYS
COLOURS OF THE DESERT
It never ceases to amaze me how music can make the world such a small place. I first heard from Jonas Ciurlionis back in 2006, when I was still in the UK, and I reviewed

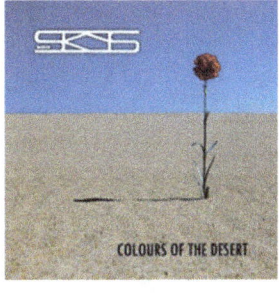
'Postmodern Game'. Now in 2012 I am reviewing the follow-up 'Colours Of The Desert' which has just been released on CD (it was available as a download last year) and I live in NZ, but Jonas, Bozena, Alexandr and Justines still live in Lithuania where they are recognized as one of that country's top bands. What is also interesting about this release is the quality of the guests who have been involved: Dave Kilminster (I think I have seen Dave in concert on at least three occasions, Roger Waters earlier this year, plus John Wetton and The Nice), John Young (ex-Scorpions, Bonnie Tyler, Greenslade) who also produced the album, Snake Davis (Eurythmics, P. McCartney, Ray Charles, James Brown, etc.), Martin Beedle (Cutting Crew, Sarah Brightman, etc.), Tony Spada (Holding Pattern) and Anne Marie Helder (Mostly Autumn, Panic Room). Not bad for a band that have yet to make a huge impact on the wider prog scene.

I do say "yet" as it surely can only be a matter of time. This is a stonking album, with great musicianship and songs throughout. The most obvious comparison is probably with Pink Floyd, but there are also elements of Renaissance, Marillion and others. This is a group that is happy to play complex intricate prog at speed or weave a soundscape that beguiles and brings the listener in to its' embrace. The use of female and male lead vocal interplay is particularly effective and overall, this is an uplifting piece of work that surely must get them more recognized on the global prog scene. If you enjoy progressive music, then you can't afford to miss this as it hits all of the right buttons – solid from start to finish and a delight to listen to.
Sep 2012

SLIVOVITZ
HUBRIS
The thing that strikes me most about Slivovitz is just how tight the musicians are, and how they easily move between taking lead, providing harmony or contrast and then back again. This is fusion in a constant state of flux and motion. 'Hubris' was the band's second album, originally released in 2009 (but also containing some tracks that were recorded as far back as 2004) and although a singer is credited, he is certainly conspicuous more by his absence than for his contribution to the sound. There just isn't room for him here. Interestingly there also isn't room in the band for a keyboard player, but with sax, violin and harmonica all fighting with the guitar and rhythm section for centre stage perhaps that isn't surprising.

What I really enjoyed with this is the way that the guys bring in so many different influences from South American Latin and bossa nova into Canterbury Scene, then Zappa and throw in all together with some European. This is all over the place, truly progressive as they refuse to acknowledge any particular musical form – why settle for one when there are so many available and somehow you can bring them all into one piece of music? They can be gentle and relaxing, thoughtful in approach, or they can bring together a

whirlwind of sound and dynamics. "Sig. M Rapito Dal Vento" is the final number on the album, and the restraint and control are evident here as drummer Stefano Costanzo works tirelessly to drive the band along while the rest of the guys are far more laid back and refuse to go faster than is required. Well worth investigation.
Feb 2013

SLIVOVITZ
BANI AHEAD
In 2011 Slivovitz returned with their third album, and there had been a few line-up changes in that singer Ludovica Manzo was no longer involved and they had a new drummer in Stefano Costanzo. It was no surprise to see that the guys were now a completely instrumental act as there is just no room in their music for vocals. The band were obviously not content to rest on what they had achieved with the previous album either as here they are taking a more aggressive stance with stronger guitar presence and a real edge from the brass. On top of this they move more into the avant-garde area, challenging the listener but never moving too far away from their fusion roots. Take opener "Egiziaca" for example, it may start with some hard rock riffs but moves through avant-garde and chaos only to turn into a highly complex jazz fusion that could be John McLaughlin and Santana at their finest when working with a big band.

It is an album that is hard to take off the player once it makes its' way on as it is just so good. They run with freedom when they wish, swapping the lead roles between every one of them, yet at other times they knuckle down to complex harmonic jazz that has purpose and delivery. This is much more than just moving an electric rock guitar into the jazz area, using the odd violin, and then calling it fusion. This is the real deal.
Feb 2013

SOFT MACHINE LEGACY
LIVE ADVENTURES
Soft Machine were formed in 1966 and have long been seen as one of the most influential of the 'Canterbury Scene'. Over the years they had quite a few musicians through their ranks, but by the early Eighties it appeared that it was finally over with everyone going their separate ways. However, in 2002, four former Soft Machine members - Hugh Hopper, Elton Dean, John Marshall, and Allan Holdsworth - toured and recorded under the name Soft Works. From late 2004 onwards, with John Etheridge replacing Holdsworth, they have toured and recorded as Soft Machine Legacy. Elton Dean passed away in February 2006, and the band continued with British saxophonist and flautist Theo Travis (formerly of Gong and The Tangent). In 2008 Hopper was sidelined by leukemia and the band continued live performances with Fred Baker, although following Hopper's death in 2009, the band announced that it would continue with Roy Babbington once again stepping into the role formerly held by

Hopper, as he had done previously in 1973 after the release of 'Six'.

It is this line-up that was recorded at two dates in October 2009 that makes up this album. Apart from Theo, all of those involved had played and recorded with the Softs in the Seventies so what we have here is not some hackneyed tribute band, but one that is truly valid and able to bring the incredible jazz and fusion of the band's history back to life. These guys know the songs intimately, as well as each other, and the result is a seamless electric performance that will delight fans of any era of the band. They certainly progressed and changed over the years, yet they have refused to rest on the history and instead many of the songs are from 'Steam' with just a few such as "Facelift" and "Song of Aeolus" from the distant past.

My personal favourite is probably "The Nodder" which contains a delicacy and control that is sublime, with John getting some wonderful notes out of his guitar. If you enjoy your fusion, then this is very much for you.
Feb 2013

SOFT MACHINE LEGACY
BURDEN OF PROOF
The Softs are back with their first studio album since the passing of Hugh Hopper in 2008, as incredibly it is six years since the release of 'Steam'. The line-up is John Etheridge (electric guitar), Roy Babbington (bass), John Marshall (drums and percussion) and Theo Travis (tenor sax, flute, piano), which must make it one of the longest serving line-ups in the extremely long history of the band (either as The Soft Machine, Soft Machine, The Softs, or Soft Machine Legacy). They may have been going down this furrow of jazz-fusion for more than thirty years, but they still don't show any sign at all of slowing down or running out of ideas. A special mention must go to Andrew Tulloch who mixed and mastered this album as the sound is incredible, allowing every touch and nuance to shine through.

The album is a combination of pre-agreed structures and melodies with improvisation and the result is a delight from the beginning to end. The interaction between all the musicians is of the type that only comes with years of playing in this sort of environment, where there is trust between everyone and a firm understanding of what they are all working towards. "Kings & Queens" is a masterpiece of understatement with Roy's simple repeated bassline allowing the others to expand the theme. While on "Fallout" Roy and John Etheridge start the piece linked as one, in perfect harmony and control before they move on.

Everyone interested in fusion and jazz will have come across Soft Machine sometime in their musical education and take it from me that 'Burden of Proof' is a more than worthy addition to their body of work.
Apr 2013

SONIQ THEATER
VISION QUEST

Alfred Mueller has been in different bands from the age of 18, but since 1999 he has devoted his musical attentions solely to Soniq Theater, which he describes as a "one-man project, presenting a blend of progressive styles, mainly symphonic progressive rock with elements of metal, ambient, electronic music, classical music and fusion. His 2009 album 'Vision Quest' is the 9th album he has released under this name, and is available solely through his website, and as with his other albums this is very much a low-key operation with the 'cover' being just paper, no proper booklet as such. But this really does bring back those days of tape trading that were so rife in the early Eighties – a one man operation producing music and then doing his best to get it heard by the world.

So, what about the album itself? Everything here appears to be played on synths and keyboards of various types, with Alfred layering the sounds so that it does appear much like a band with 'drums' and 'bass' making appearances as well. In many ways I find his style to be much more in common with Jean Michel Jarre than Keith Emerson, as there is less focus on the bombastic and more on the ambient. Often themes are repeated, but when he gives himself the opportunity to expand and push his boundaries a little more, that is when he really shines. The obvious standout track here is "Jonathan Seagull" (which I presume is a reference to the Richard Bach book as opposed to the Neil Diamond film soundtrack) where Alfred plays with far more dominance and presence, and the song benefits from that. Overall, it contains many ambient as well as some prog elements and is an enjoyable album that is a good introduction to Alfred's work.
Jan 2012

SONIQ THEATER
UNKNOWN REALITIES

In 2010 Alfred Mueller released his 10th album under the Soniq Theater name, 'Unknown Realities'. As with all his other releases, this is very much a one-man show with everything being played by Alfred on keyboards and synths, so if you don't like that sort of music then stay away. But if you do, then this is one of his finest works. The first two songs, "Longing For Freedom" and "Revealing A Dream" contain far more diversity and passion than I have heard in his music before – and the way the music shifts and changes works extremely well. The dynamics are powerful, and the interest is contained throughout. The latter is multi-layered and contains some elements that wouldn't sound out of place on a Wakeman album (last count I think I have more than 100 of his, and still more to get!). It is passionate, it moves, it swirls and changes with repeated motifs and new directions – superb.

In contrast some of the keyboard sounds used on the next number, "Revolution Hymn" just don't sound or feel right. The problem isn't so much with the song itself, or the

playing of it, just that this is showing the limitations of a one-man operation – I would really like to hear this song performed by a proper band, as it would take on a whole new life and being. When going through the album there are times when it is very good indeed, and others when there is the impression that it could be so much more if other guys were involved. But, if you enjoy keyboard albums then this is something that should be searched out, as Alfred has yet again shown that he is a fine songwriter and musician with some great ideas.
Jan 2012

SONIQ THEATER
SONIQ THEATER
After the demise of Rachel's Birthday in 1997 keyboard player Alfred Mueller decided not to be in a band again, but instead would create a studio only project where he could play all the instruments. Now, Alfred is not a true multi-instrumentalist but instead is a keyboard player who then uses samples and patches of other instruments. Now, some of the sounds deployed are not as bad as you might think, although to my ears it will never be possible to replicate the feel and textures provided by a band using 'proper' instruments, and although it will always detract away from the sound this is more than listenable.

Although this album came out in 2000, I am hearing it for the first time some twelve years later after Alfred sent me his back catalogue, and my immediate impression is how similar this is to some of Wakeman's rock ensemble recordings. There is a real feel of melody and intertwining of instruments. Alfred has also done the best he can to make the drums sound acoustic and 'real' instead of just providing a basic back beat. The overall feel is that this is an album worth investigating.
Nov 2012

SONIQ THEATER
A SECOND OF ACTION
The artwork shown here is the new version that has been created by a fan that Alfred is now using, but the original from 2002 had some of the letters highlighted so that it was possible to also read the title as 'Second Act', which of course it was. In many ways this is a direct continuation from the debut, although to my ears it doesn't work quite as well. I think one of the reasons for that is that there appears to be more use of sampled instruments in this album and the feeling is that this would have worked much better as a full band piece instead of doing it all through keyboards. I would really like to hear "Elephant Race" played by a group as it allows everyone to shine and really drive it along, but here with just keyboards and samples it does lose some of the effect. This is a rock number and I want riffing guitars!

Overall, there are some great songs and arrangements on this album, but it doesn't quite stand up against the debut although some of the shorter numbers are also quite interesting. However, if you have already searched out some of Alfred's work then this is worth having.
Nov 2012

SONIQ THEATER
THE THIRD EYE
Alfred's third solo album was released in 2003 and as with his previous album he not only inferred which number album it was in the title, he also played all the instruments. There are a lot of good things on here, especially "Bilbo Is Back" which is Wakeman to a tee as it gently bounces along with a poptastic refrain. The only thing wrong with this song is that it is less than three minutes long! But then it gets spoiled by the track that follows it "Vamos A Ver". This is one of the few times when vocals are utilised, where Alfred has sampled a singer called Suzann and has used her during the chorus and I really wished that he hadn't as the second scat line is massively out of tune with the music, and every time I hear it, I feel as if someone has dragged fingernails across a blackboard. And as it is sampled the same thing is repeated each time it is used. Either change the melody or don't use it!

To me this puts a dampener on what is one of Alfred's most accessible and enjoyable albums as he mixes Wakeman with Emerson and even throws in some JMJ for good measure. This is well worth hearing, but I bet you only play the third song just the once to see if I'm right. (I am)
Nov 2012

SONIQ THEATER
FORCE MAJEURE
This is one of Alfred Mueller's more recent releases, coming out in 2011. As with all his other releases this is a 100% solo effort with Alfred providing multiple layers of keyboards as well as some samples. Actually there is a higher concentration on 'pure' keyboard sounds on this album than on some others and it definitely benefits from it (although I do wish he would find a live drummer as well). This album combines the styles of a reflective Rick Wakeman with Jean Michel Jarre, while at others it is more direct and more in the vein of Keith Emerson. While Alfred doesn't finesse in the way that these players do, the result is yet again a very solid piece of work.

Although the style is fairly restrictive, once again he has produced an album that is easy to listen to and has enough complexity and depth of sound to maintain interest through to the end. If you have to discover Soniq Theater then this is a fine place to start.
Nov 2012

SONIQ THEATER
ENCHANTED
This was Alfred's sixth solo album, released in 2006, where yet again he provides all the instrumentation. In many ways this is one of my favourite Soniq Theater albums as there are some great numbers on here that any lover of keyboard-based symphonic prog would get a great deal from. I can even forgive him for using programmed drums as here they are not too overpowering. One thing I cannot forgive is that yet again he has used Suzann to provide scat vocals on a number, this time "Morgana". I have a real problem with someone singing out of tune with the music. I know that Alfred has probably just sampled this, but if he is going to use vocals, they need to fit in what he is doing musically. The first time I played this was when I was up the woods walking my dogs and I just could not believe my ears – it totally spoiled my enjoyment of the album. But the rest is so good that it still deserves hearing.
Nov 2012

SONIQ THEATER
LIFE SEEKER
This 2008 release was Alfred's eighth album, and as with most of his releases he was the only person involved in its making. I presume that means that he provided the vocals on the opening title cut as well, and I really wish that he hadn't, as for me it really detracts from what follows. While Alfred is a great keyboard player, composer, and arranger: he isn't a singer, and I just couldn't see the point. But, moving away from that, this is yet again a very solid album and again I found myself wishing that Alfred would get a proper band around him so that we could hear these compositions with the correct instruments instead of synthesized versions. Having played a great many of his albums recently, his unique style has become more apparent to me. Although there are obvious elements of Jean Michel Jarre, Emerson and (to a lesser extent) Wakeman, he has a certain turn of phasing and style that is very much his own. The songs are solid, and don't fall into meandering meaningless entities that some solo artists are guilty of. Yet again, this is a very solid album from Alfred Mueller.
Oct 2012

SONIQ THEATER
STARDUST MEMORIES
And so Alfred returns with his thirteenth solo album, which is interesting on more than just the pure musical level. Included on this album are two numbers that pre-date Rachels' Birthday, and one with guitarist Jens Klenk which was recorded after the demise of that band but a few years before Alfred started to record as Soniq Theater. Given that there is more than 25 years between the recording of some of these songs they have cleaned

up well and don't sound at all out of place. In many ways this is Alfred's most complete album to date, with everything coming together. While I have never been a fan of vocals on his albums, here they work, and the use of guitar (and the placement of that number towards the middle of the album) is highly effective. It makes one wonder what would have happened if the Alfred and Lens had continued playing together. While JMJ is still a large influence, there has been a definite shift more towards Rick Wakeman with "Stardust Memories" and if you like keyboards then there is much on here to enjoy. As always this is available directly from Alfred and can also be downloaded from his site so why not go there and listen to what he has been producing.
Mar 2013

SONIQ THEATER
THIS MORTAL COIL

This was Alfred's fourth solo album, released in 2004, and after 'A Second of Action' and 'The Third Eye" I half expected to find 'Fourth' somewhere in the title, but that idea only came back in for his seventh ('Seventh Heaven'). Unusually for Alfred there is an actual 'song' on here, normally when vocals are deployed within Soniq Theater they are used only for the odd line to enhance the music, but "Break The Frame" features a proper verse/chorus structure with Alfred taking on the role himself. All the music is played by Alfred, but here there are obvious attempts to move away from the pure synth sound normally associated with him, with the use of sampled guitars and a more obvious guitar-based approach. Of course, it is no substitute for the real thing, but it shows another interesting facet and, in some ways, does hearken back to Rachel's Birthday. Of course, producing a more 'guitar' based album means that the drums must be higher in the mix and that is undoubtedly a bad thing for anyone who doesn't like drum machines. Oh, that would be me then. I can't help it, but the artificial sound just permeates through the album, and I find myself almost wincing away from it. That is a real shame as there are some very strong pieces on here, especially "Minas Tirith" which combines symphonic and orchestral elements into something that moves from bombast to structure and back again. The album contains more Vangelis than JMJ elements and will appeal to all synth lovers out there.
Apr 2013

SONIQ THEATER
PANDROMANIA

This was Alfred's fifth solo album, released in 2005. As with most of his work this is a totally solo effort with Alfred providing all instruments plus the small amount of vocals on "Wheel of Fortune", so it is just the small sampling of Suzann on "Miles Beyond" and the title cut which is the only thing he doesn't do himself. I have been rather disparaging of her vocals on some of his other albums, but here there is a much better effect, and it makes more musical sense. As I worked through the album, I felt that this was what I have come to expect from Alfred, lots of Jean Michel Jarre and Vangelis influences, although there does seem to more piano than usual which is nice to hear, but the storm effects that start the title cut really grabbed my attention. Halfway through the album and here was something that had Wakeman written all over it with loads of bombast and power. If ever Alfred really rocked without a guitar or drummer in sight, then this is it. This is such a powerful song that it really wipes away everything that has gone before it on the album as the listener gets taken into a totally different world and mindset than previously.

But to my surprise that isn't the best number on the album, that honour goes to one of the longest songs performed by Alfred, "Wheel of Fortune" which is nearly ten minutes long. Loads of different styles and effects throughout really keep the listener involved. But it is also an example of why Alfred should really consider getting back into a band situation as while this is good it would be so much better if there were real drums, real bass, real guitar and a proper singer such as Ashley Holt who would be extremely well suited to this. So overall, another very consistent album from Alfred and if you enjoy pure solo synth albums then this may be of interest.
Apr 2013

SONIQ THEATER
SEVENTH HEAVEN
It isn't too surprising to discover that this was Alfred's seventh solo album, fittingly released in 2007. As with most of his work the music was composed, performed, produced, recorded, mixed, and mastered by Alfred who also provided all the instruments. This is really an album of opposites as while it contains some of Alfred's best work, it also includes some that just aren't to my taste at all. The album starts off positively with a sprightly rocker that is very much in the style of Wakeman but cries out for real guitar and drums. In fact, there are a few of the songs on this album like that, as if Alfred wanted to move more into the melodic rock and away from the symphonic keyboard sounds yet was restricted by being 100% solo. There are some wonderful light touches on "Welcome Home" which for some reason reminded me of some of Anthony Phillips' work and is probably the highlight of the album.

But while there are plenty of Vangelis and JMJ stylings here and there and "New Year's Eve" is wonderfully upbeat, the album is let down by the ubiquitous drum machine. It is an invention that I loathe for the most part, and just tolerate on occasion, but while it is just an annoyance on the aforementioned number it totally dominates the next song "But Seriously" and for me totally ruins it. But I know that I am probably in a minority and overall, this is another solid album from Alfred.
Apr 2013

SONIQ THEATER
OVERNIGHT SENSATION

'Overnight Sensation' was the 12th album by Alfred Mueller under the Soniq Theater name, and as with most of his solo albums is one where he provided all the instrumentation himself. Again, here is an album where the influences of Jean Michel Jarre and Vangelis are readily apparent although Alfred is much more than a mere copyist. He has an incredible work rate, usually releasing an album each year, and there is no doubt that this is one of the highlights of his career. I do feel that if he could bring in some additional musicians (such as a live drummer in particular) then there would be an additional facet to his work, but even as it is there is a great deal here to enjoy. The music is layered and complex yet with a simplistic almost naïve approach which allows the listener to really get into the album very quickly indeed. It is approachable and welcoming, drawing the listener into Alfred's world. While the recordings are only available on CD-R these do not reflect the quality of what is contained within and yet again this is an album of his that is worth much more investigation.
Mar 2013

SPOCK'S BEARD
BRIEF NOCTURNES AND DREAMLESS SLEEP

Many years ago, I was at a Marillion concert, and after the gig had finished the usual suspects got together and there was only one subject that we all wanted to talk about – had everyone heard 'The Light'? For me there was a band taking prog to a brand new level, and I then took every opportunity to see them in concert, rave about their latest releases and was lucky to meet the guys and interview them a few times. Then came the bombshell, Neal had left, even though the band had just recorded what was easily their finest ever album and an absolute prog classic, 'Snow'. But it was okay, they were going to do a Genesis and let the drummer have a go and NDV had a great voice didn't he? Well, 'Octane' wasn't too bad although I did think that they were trying too hard, and then they came to the UK again on tour. First up was CGT who were great, and then it was Enchant who I was really looking forward to as I had been a fan of their music right since the very beginning, and to top it all there was Spock's Beard. I left halfway through SB's set, totally demoralised and to be honest quite upset as well. I had witnessed what to me was a Spock's Beard cover band who just weren't as good as the original. I kept saying to myself that this must have been what it was like when Peter Gabriel left Genesis, but as I didn't start listening to them until 1978 or thereabouts, I hadn't been through it myself. I kept trying to like the 'new' SB, but instead found myself much preferring Neal's solo material. Maybe they'll get back together one day I thought…

Then another shock, NDV was leaving SB so tour drummer Jimmy Keegan would get his shot, but what about the singer? Step forward Ted Leonard from Enchant, and I immediately started to take notice. Enchant were a very different band to both Neal-era SB and NDV-era, so what would the new album be like? I found myself excited to hear an SB release for the first time since I had played 'Octane'. Now, the album arrived at the same time as the new Neal Morse live album and I couldn't help myself and played that one first, which was a mistake as once it got on the player it was hard to get it off. Then came the time to put on 'Brief Nocturnes...' and I sat back and waited to be impressed.

And boy, was I?! Forget everything you have ever heard by Spock's Beard, here is a brand-new band and while I understand why they kept the name after so much history I don't think that there would be much surprise if they had started afresh. This is simply stunning; it is as if bringing in Ted has given everyone a new lease of life and they have just relaxed and let the music flow. Ryo is playing with an incredible sense of freedom, and I have never heard him link with Alan the way he does here. Jimmy and Dave just lock in and get down to business with far less in the way of frills than previously, which provides a far firmer foundation for everyone. There has never been any doubt that Ted is a great singer, but here he is also demonstrating more styles and passion than previously.

I never thought that I would be able to say this again, but Spock's Beard have released a five-star album: just don't expect it to be the sequel to anything they have done before as they move into a more melodic rock/prog area, with "Submerged" surely destined to be an AOR radio classic! Ted gets a solo credit on one song, while Alan's brother also makes a return on "Waiting For Me". Welcome back guys.
Apr 2013

STANDING OVATION
THE ANTIKYTHERA MECHANISM

When I received the email containing the download for this album my initial reaction was that I had already reviewed it, but a quick check proved me wrong. The reason for my confusion is that Centric Jones have released 'The Antikythera Method', and this is 'The Antikythera Mechanism'. That led me to Wikipedia, where I discovered that the Antikythera mechanism is an ancient analog computer designed to calculate astronomical positions. It was recovered in 1900–1901 from the Antikythera wreck, but its significance and complexity were not understood until a century later. So there. Musically they are quite different as well, as while this is undoubtedly progressive these mad Finns also bring in plenty of metal as well as some pop. Imagine Opeth mixed with Muse with a large dose of Poisoned Electrick Head along with some lush harmonies and plenty of growls then you may get close. Only "may" though, as you really must hear this to understand what is going on. I've played it quite a few times now and the only thing I'm convinced of is that I like it, just not sure quite how to describe it. Given that I have been reviewing music for more than twenty years I'm not often stuck for words, but there you go.

This is the debut album from the band, following on from their 'Scars Suit Me' EP in 2010, which was awarded third place in best self-released record in the Finnish Metal

Awards, and was selected the band of the month by Finnish metal magazine Inferno. The album deals with the ancient, highly sophisticated machine and adds historical and science fiction elements. "Standing Ovation" mix genres skillfully, gluing everything together with a heavy, metallic touch and their own style which at times is raw and others very polished indeed with loads of hooks. Definitely worth investigating further.
Oct 2012

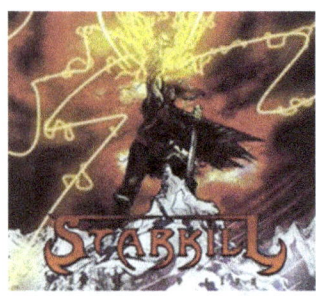

STARKILL
FIRES OF LIFE
Chicago-based Starkill was formed at the tail end of 2008 by Parker Jameson (lead guitar, vocals, keyboards, and orchestral programming), Spencer Weidner (drums) and Charlie Federici (guitar), later being joined by bassist Mike Buetsch. They state that their main influences are Children of Bodom, Nightwish, Amon Amarth, Dimmu Borgir and Dragonforce, and even if I hadn't seen the press release, I would have been mentioning most of those bands in the review, as these guys aren't making any secret at all of what drives them. "Whispers of Heresy" opens the album with some gentle Savatage-style piano and a single tolled bell before moving into Dimmu-Borgir/Nightwish symphonic keyboards and I was entranced already, long before the guitars come in, being driven along by some incredibly frenetic drumming and double kick drum work that makes most bands sound as if they just play at it. I mean, Spencer could find a job with any grindcore band if he ever gets fed up with this.

Here is an album that cries class from first to last, as the band mix and meld from many different metal spectrums. It is hard to comprehend that this is just a debut and renowned producer James Murphy has done a great job in capturing these guys. They have brought in elements of symphonic prog, death metal, prog metal, speed metal, grindcore and death to create something that at its' heart is probably melodic death but in reality, is all over the place and is very much the better for it.

I am convinced that these guys are going to become major players in the scene, yes, it is that good.
Jun 2013

STATE URGE
WHITE ROCK EXPERIENCE
State Urge is a young band who hail from Gdynia in Poland, formed by Marcin Bochenski (drums), Marcin Cieslik (electric guitar, vocals), Krystian Papiernik (bass) and Michal Tarkowski (keyboards). Although most people would call these guys neo-prog/prog, they have quite a different idea on how their music should be described: "We hate being classified, though, as we aspire to create an immersive atmosphere in our works,

especially in the spectrum of sound. Our compositions usually start out as instrumental improvisations, with elements of rock, blues and even classical music occasionally shining through. Despite all of this the original sound of our band becomes dominant in our creations and thusly we like to call our genre in our own way, White Rock".

Following on from two self-released EP's, and gaining a following in Poland with lots of radio airplay as well as performing with acts such as Votum, the band signed a deal with Lynx Music to record their debut album. They took the opportunity to record a mixture of both brand new songs and some that had been played for a while, but definitely wanted to be seen as being something different, hence the use of the words 'White Rock'. Of course, when I first saw the name of the band I thought that they were referencing Rick Wakeman's 1977 classic, which was the soundtrack to the Innsbruck winter Olympics, but while that is not the case they do make me think of fresh snow, as there is a crispness, clarity and clean feel to the sound and production that is rare for a debut. I then looked to see who had been involved on that side and found that Ryszard Kramarski from Millenium engineered some of the songs. At times they use sounds that are more often featured in dance, with electronic drums and beats, but one of the real joys is the way that they don't feel restricted or pigeonholed and they do exactly what they feel is right overall. Consequently, they are quite different to most of the other bands in the scene, and this is an album that feels like a breath of fresh air as it blows through, and consequently is one that I have been playing a great deal. Well worth investigation.
May 2013

STORMY ATMOSPHERE
COLORBLIND
Apparently, this album was originally released in 2009, but I have only just been sent a copy by Mals and I note that release is copyrighted 2012 so I guess that this is a reissue. In which case all power to Mike Lanin for grabbing this as it is a joy to listen to from start to finish. One for fans of bands like Kamelot, this is symphonic progressive metal with plenty of twists and changes. One of the sheer delights is the two lead singers, Dina Shulman and Teddy Shivets – while there is nothing that unusual in having two singers, it is definitely different to have two that both sound as if they have been professionally trained. There are times when their voices soar and mingle in a way that I just haven't come across too often in popular music. They both take lead as well, and there are times when that is against a gentle acoustic backdrop as on "Bridge" but there are others where they are against a musical maelstrom.

This is an album that I fell in love with the very first time I played it, and the more I have listened to it the more I have got from it. The use of additional musicians (flute, violin etc) has allowed the core band to spread their wings and the result is an album that at times is very different to anything else that is around yet is always accessible and melodic. This is one of the few bands I have heard from Israel, and I can only hope that the scene is vibrant enough for them to be able to cut another album as this is superb.
Sep 2012

SUPERNAL ENDGAME
TOUCH THE SKY

This band is a project formed by multi-instrumentalist John Eargle, singer/drummer Rob Price and guitarist Dan Pomeroy. There are plenty of guests, including Roine Stolt and Randy George – and given that these two are playing it is something of a surprise not to see Neal Morse's name as well, as these guys from Texas are working in the subgenre of Christian Prog. It shows how strong these guys beliefs are as prog in itself isn't the most financially rewarding genre out there, and if you aren't a Christian then you may find the lyrics a bit hard to take. But and it is a large "but", this is an album that is great to listen to and one that I really enjoyed even though my personal view on religion has changed considerably over the years. There are three different guest violinists, and this is an album that musically sits with Seventies Kansas but with a stronger emphasis on the AOR side.

This album is awash with hooks and melodies, and even a non-believer such as me found myself singing along to "Still Believe" – it's infectious stuff. The press release says something that I don't think I've ever seen in the thousands I've read, "this music just makes you feel good". Do you know what? They're right – for some reason I can't play this album without having a smile on my face, and sometimes that is what you need.
Aug 2012

SYZYGY
REALMS OF ETERNITY

The roots of Syzygy can be found in Eighties cover band Abraxas which featured guitarist/lead vocalist Carl Baldassarre, keyboardist Sam Giunta and bassist Al Rolik. After the group disbanded, Carl and Sam kept working together and with the addition of drummer Paul Mihacevich they recorded their debut 'Cosmos And Chaos' in 1993 under the name of Witsend. A period of writing and raising families resulted in a hiatus but they returned as Syzygy with the critically acclaimed 'The Allegory Of Light' which featured Al as a guest musician, released in 2003. All of the vocals had been handled by the band themselves up to this point, but for the new album they felt that they needed someone else to take them to the next level and after a long search brought in Mark Boals (Ted Nugent, Yngwie Malmsteen, Uli Jon Roth, Erik Norlander etc.).

Bringing in a heavyweight singer such as Mark means that many reviewers (myself included) would expect great things of this album even before it made it to the player. I was possibly expecting even more things as I have been lucky enough to hear their earlier works, so I was extremely keen to know what they had been doing in the intervening years.

Well, to say that I wasn't disappointed was something of an understatement. Musically

the band aren't afraid to go back to some classic prog bands such as Gentle Giant, Yes and UK while also bringing in the AOR style of Styx and Journey, throwing in some more recent references such as Spock's Beard and letting the pot just swirl and mix as it feels. This is an album that is incredibly complex, but the sheer musicality and melody means that the listener doesn't get overwhelmed by everything. Note density? Check. Keyboard/guitar interplay? Check. Abrupt changes of musical direction? Check. Strong complex palette of keyboard sounds? Check. Great vocals and harmonies? Check. Incredible album that I want to play repeatedly? Check and triple check. This is an awesome album, every time I play it I hear something new that just takes my breath away. Play the 10 minutes plus "Dreams" and you will see what I mean – just brilliant.
Oct 2011

SYZYGY
A GLORIOUS DISTURBANCE
There are times, not often it has to be said, that I open a package and can't wait to get the music onto the player as I am so excited just by the content that I already know that this is going to be something special. The first thing out of the envelope was an A4 loose leaf folder which is packed full of biographies, photos, and stacks of information. There is one page just dedicated to the comments from a certain Mr. Steve Hackett who contacted the band regarding their album 'Realms of Eternity' saying "It's beautifully written and recorded and easily the best I've ever been given to listen to" and "I usually hope for a masterpiece every time I play an unknown quantity (to me) but this is the only time the dream has been fully delivered" among other comments. Now, unlike Steve I am aware of Syzygy and Witsend but even I wasn't prepared for what was next out of the envelope, a double digipak of their new album. When I looked more closely, I discovered that was I had in my hands was a triple disc live set, with two DVDs and a CD plus a small fold-out booklet with loads of pics. I mean, for heaven's sake, this is a band that does it all on their own with no record label support yet have produced one of the finest live releases I have ever come across. And at this point I had yet to put in on the player!!!!!

So, being the contrary person I am, I went for the third disc first which is the CD. Now, rock vocalist Mark Boals sings for these guys, but they are primarily an instrumental act although he does appear with them both live and in the studio, so there are always long instrumental passages which gives them the chance to stretch their wings, and they take the opportunity. Classic symphonic prog, through neo-prog, fusion as they toy with jazz styles, melodic rock, great harmony vocals, keyboard/guitar interplay, it's all here as the guys demonstrate what incredible musicians, they all are. To be honest, I would have raved about this album if there was only just the one CD, let alone having two other concerts to watch, interviews and discussions etc. There are 3½ hours of DVD and well over an hour on the CD, and if you have yet to come across this incredible band then you need to right that wrong now. The only reason that I give this five out of five is that I'm not allowed to give it more.
Mar 2013

t
ANTI-MATTER POETRY
This 2010 album from Thomas Thielen is the third under the 't' moniker, while some may also remember him as the leader of Scythe. It took four years to write, perform and record this album and it isn't surprising as this is a 100% solo effort with Thomas providing all the vocals and instrumentation. What makes this such an outstanding effort is that this just doesn't sound like a solo album at all. There are none of the issues that can often appear with being in the studio with no sounding board or outside interaction, instead what we have is a polished and extremely dynamic album that engages the listener from the first note to the very last. I can remember hearing his previous album (the 2006 'Voices') and while I enjoyed playing it, I didn't come away with the same feeling that I do for this one.

This may not be Genesis-style retro prog but brings together Porcupine Tree and Radiohead in a style that is truly progressive. At times challenging, always compelling, this is quite an album. This isn't prog that fits within a safe preconceived idea but instead is pushing boundaries so the listener never knows what to expect next. The vocals are also very strong and melodic, with the focus being on proper songs – just stretched and moving in different directions as opposed to meandering meaninglessly with loads of instrumental overplay just for the sake of it. Overall, this is an album that those with open minds will enjoy a great deal.
Sep 2012

t
PSYCHOANOREXIA
Both in the press release and on his website, Thomas Thielen has a mission statement about this album which is well worth reproducing here. "This is the time when ringtone applicability equals musical quality. This is the place where the greed of being a popstar has replaced the sublime experience of creativity. This is the era in which democracy means mass phenomena, not choices. When we have become too lazy even for subterfuges. And too busy to feel the loss. This is the age when equality means mediocrity, fame defames excellence, education encourages despondency. We excel in conformity; we celebrate our empty hands. We may not burn books, but we skim them. We may not slaughter heretics, but we overshout them. We strive, long, hunger for nothing, thus nobody strives, longs, hungers. Fascistic, yet aimless aposiopetic selves. Timetabled freedom. Death in Bologna. Psychoanorexia."

Yes, this is an album that wants, in fact demands, that we think. Thomas wrote, performed, recorded, engineered, and produced the album but it doesn't come across like a one-man band, as it is so carefully constructed and layered. The piano may well be the bedrock of all that he does, but this is more than just a pianist attempting to bring in some other instrumentation to pad it out, but instead this is all about the right instrument for the right emotional feel and approach. When he brings in electric guitar it fairly blasts out of the speakers, with "Kryptonite Monologues" managing to have more than just a hint of Rammstein about it. There are times when this is crunching stadium-filling anthem rock with blistering guitar solos, while at others it is Muse on steroids, Floyd for the masses, Porcupine Tree for the many.

It is not an album that will make its' full presence felt on just one or two plays, this does need some work but rewards the listener for their patience. Apparently, Thomas states that he is a "strictly under-average musician on quite a few instruments, none of which he is capable of playing properly". Somehow, I think he is a master of understatement, as certainly that doesn't come across on the album. Complex, complicated, majestic and soaring, this is quite a piece of work. There are only four songs, but it is still well over an hour long, and well worth investigating.
Nov 2013

THE TANGENT
LE SACRE DU TRAVAIL
The Tangent have certainly come a long way since Andy Tillison decided that he needed another project outside of PO90 and formed this band with Guy Manning and Roine Stolt. Neither are there these days, but he does have Jakko M. Jakszyk (Level 42) on guitar, Theo Travis (Robert Fripp, Gong, Porcupine Tree, Bill Nelson, No-Man, Steven Wilson etc.) on sax, flutes and clarinets, Jonas Reingold (The Flower Kings) on bass, Gavin Harrison (King Crimson, Porcupine Tree) on drums and singer David Longdon (Big Big Train) so none of these are slouches. This is a concept album, based on 'The Rite of Work'. There is a narration where it is explained that on this island 50 million people wake up, and an hour later they must be more than 30 miles away doing something that they don't want to do, so that for a short period of time they can say that they own a building!

This is a very English prog album, both in music and lyrics. I wonder how many people who have never heard 'Steve Wright in the Afternoon' will understand the reference to factoids, but for someone like me who remembers when Steve was on Radio One (as opposed to Radio Two), all of this just made me smile. Musically it is very diverse—one obvious reference is 'Days of Future Passed' which starts with the beginning of the day and ending with the night, while here we start with the beginning of the day and ending up with "Evening TV" having survived the trip home through the rush hour. There is a lot going on as Andy brings in influences and textures from all forms of music. Some of the music is designed to make you think, while at other times it is almost pure pop. It doesn't always hit the mark, but when it does it is both enthralling and exciting.

Many years ago, Andy eked out a living as a sound engineer and was responsible for recording many independent bands at the end of the Seventies, and it is back to this era we go with the punk power pop version of "Hat", which may or may not be from 1979 as stated in the title.

It may not be perfect, but again Andy has produced something that is definitely worthy of investigation. If you haven't come across this band before then you owe it to yourself to do so now.
Jul 2013

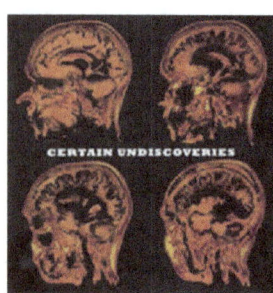

TAYLOR'S UNIVERSE
CERTAIN UNDISCOVERIES
Robin Taylor was born in Copenhagen in 1956 and started playing guitar at the age of 12. Although he experimented with recording in the Seventies, it wasn't until a chance meeting with keyboard player Jan Marsfeldt in 1988 that led him to record an album which he released in 1991. Since then, he has been making up for lost time and this 2006 album is his 22nd in one form or another. Here Robin shows his skill not only on guitar but also on keyboards and percussion, while he is joined by Karsten Vogel (from famed Danish act Secret Oyster) on saxophones and bass clarinet and Rasmus Grosell on drums. It is hard to categorise the music being played, and from looking through the web I can see that many others have had a similar problem. Robin is sometimes categorised as RIO (which I can understand but don't necessarily agree with), jazz or progressive, or any combination thereof, but the one thing that everyone concurs with is that here is music that is worthy of investigation.

Although the album is enjoyable on first play, it is only from repeated listenings that one really understands where Robin is coming from. While the music can at times be bombastic and almost undisciplined as the jazz traits shine through, it is the use of space and restraint that really makes this stand out. There is a lightness and deftness of touch that draws the listener in – some progressive bands literally blast out their skills and expect the listener to be stunned into submission by their skill and musical dexterity, here it is far more delicately done. There are times when the music is quiet, with just one or two instruments, and I found myself drawing closer to the speakers – not wanting to turn it up as I was afraid of losing the moment.

This is music that needs to be listened to – if you try and do something else whilst playing it (the first time I played this CD was in the car which is most definitely the wrong idea) then you will not get the most out of it. This needs to be savoured in a peaceful environment, and I found that playing this while looking out over the dark hills with a sky full of stars made it work just fine…Mind you, when he lets rip as he does towards the end of closing number "A Beautiful Garden With A Lot Of Depressed Animals Including Norse Sculpture" then it does give a very different feel to the whole piece. Search on the web, and you will find that many reviewers rate Robin highly, something I agree with.
July 2009

TAYLOR'S UNIVERSE
TERRA NOVA
Terra Nova was Robin's 23rd release and came out in 2007. Here Robin was again joined by Karsten and Rasmus and also by trumpet player Hugh Steinmetz on one song, and singers Louise Napper and Jytte Lindberg. In some ways this is more immediate than the previous album, with personal favourite "Amhage West" incorporating elements not only of jazz but also the feel of some of the great Seventies progressive bands such as Alan Parsons and even Kansas. In fact, it is interesting to compare some of the stylings here to the original Kansas (now known as Proto-Kaw) who also used woodwind (as opposed to the later violin). But while Kerry Livgren is renowned for leading his compositions into extremely complex areas, this album again has a lightness and almost fragility that is both entrancing and compelling. Again, this is music that takes time to really understand and grow with, although there are some numbers such as "Meccano" which are far more immediate (although Karsten does get let loose near the end), yet the end result is more than worth the effort.

Progheads are used to complex time signatures and musical brilliance, it tends to come with the genre, and jazz freaks are the same and while there is more than enough of both on this CD to attract them it is the restraint and space that will keep them returning time and again. Space is probably the most unused element within modern popular music – extreme bands want to have everything louder than everything else without realising that it is contrast that truly makes music vibrant and exciting. Here again the listener is invited into a world, to sit down and rest awhile and look around and see what is on offer instead of being blasted off with yet another complex riff and shred. When Robin moves the pace, such as on "They Usually Come At Night" where there is a shade more urgency and more attack from all the players it really does come alive.

Yet again another very powerful release from Robin Taylor that fans of good music, whatever label you wish to ascribe to it, really should be investigating further.
July 2009

TAYLOR'S UNIVERSE WITH DENNER
SOUNDWALL
Taylor's second album of 2007 saw him again with Karsten, Rasmus and Louise yet as may be guessed from the name of the band this time, there is also an additional musician. Michael Denner needs probably no introduction, having played with Mercyful Fate and King Diamond as well as Force Of Evil (my personal favourite of the three). His guitarwork is renowned and when I saw he was involved with this release I braced myself for a load of heavy metal histrionics with Robin et al taking a back seat. But Michael has sat here with an aim of taking on board what Taylor's Universe has to offer and has provided another facet to the polished gem of the music. While there are times when Michael does take an obvious lead, it is far more restrained

and in keeping with the feel of the band than one might imagine.

Initially I expected some Steve Vai-style shredding over a jazz background, but here we have a musician being very much a team player and not losing sight of the musical goal. "Step Aside" has a repeated motif which allow all musicians to show off some chops but at no point does it become too much of a 'see what I can do better than you' competition but instead stays true to the theme. One can almost imagine the musicians sat in a circle in the studio just bouncing ideas. I don't know how much was recorded 'live' or layered, but there is a feeling of spontaneity and Michael feels part of the band instead of a guest musician brought in to play a role.

Musically I expected this to be the one album of the three that I would enjoy the most, given that I have been known to listen to HM/HR far more than jazz stylings, but I have to say that while Michael adds a great deal in some respects, I found that in others I missed some of the space that has now been filled by his presence. It is still a great album that is very much worth hearing, but of the three TU albums I have been able to hear it is to 'Certain Undiscoveries' to which I will be returning most.
July 2009

ROBIN TAYLOR
CLOZE TEST TERROR
'Cloze Test Terror' was Robin's second album and was originally released in 1992. He provided guitars, keyboards, bass, percussion etc. and was joined by Jan Marsfeldt (keyboards), Jakob Mygind (saxophone), Jacob Christensen (bass) and Anders Schumann on drums. Only Jan remained from the musicians who had contributed to Robin's debut album the year before, but as I haven't heard that release, I can't comment on what musical changes may have taken place. I do know that I find it hard to believe that this album is now some eighteen years old. The production is spot on and again there is the use of space that I have found in so many of Robin's releases. This is an extremely melodic album, mixing jazz almost with loungecore before also treading into areas more usually associated with RIO.

The drums aren't as impressive as they could have been, and in fact if a musician hadn't been listed, I would have assumed they were programmed, but that is only a minor niggle as Robin puts together a tapestry of music that is always enjoyable and thoughtful. This is music to drift into and to allow it to wrap you in layers of complexity and warmth. Jakob may not always be allowed to vent forth but the times that he does it is in perfect harmony with what is happening around him. Interesting to hear music from so early in Robin's journey which already shows the trademark sounds of what I expect today.
Feb 2010

TAYLOR'S UNIVERSE
TAYLOR'S UNIVERSE
Robin's third release, in 1994, saw him at the forefront of a jazz trio with some additional musicians. Jan was still there on keyboards while the drummer was now Mads Hansen. Additional musicians could be found in the welcome return (to my ears at least) of Jakob Mygind on saxophone, along with Hugh Steinmetz (trumpet), Henning Plannthin (guitar) and Henrik Andersen (guitar). Although I really enjoyed the previous album there are far more elements and clarity of vision with this release. The drums are far more involved, driving the music along while the strong brass section gives some extra power in the top end – and of course there are now three guitarists. Strangely that doesn't mean huge passages of complex interplay or frantic workouts, but just some differing styles and moods that are brought together to take the music to the next level.

Strong pianowork combines with the keyboards and some glissando style guitar to hearken back to the powerful days of bands like National Health while also looking forward. Sometimes the guitars are acoustic, while in others there are some strong rock type riffing going on. It really is a case of if you don't enjoy what the band are playing then hang on a minute as it is all about to change. If you love experimental music and/or jazz, then this is an album that is truly essential on so many different levels.
Feb 2010

TAYLOR'S UNIVERSE
PORK
Robin's fourth album again appeared under the Taylor's Universe banner, although it was now down to a duo of Robin and Jan. Mads and Hugh were there as guests, along with Jytte Lindberg (voice). Yet again Robin takes the music wherever he wishes – feeling no need to conform to anyone's idea of what boundaries he should stay within. While maintaining the use of space and even silence that one expects from him, there is even more experimentation and use of discord. But it always gives way to melody and there is the feeling of direction and purpose that can be missing from some forms of jazz. This is rarely music that will be appreciated by those who follow the herd, but if you wish to listen to music of substance and depth that requires some effort on the part of the listener then of his early works it is this album that I feel needs to be discovered first.

Just because Robin has been releasing a lot of material it is never down to poor quality control, rather that he has many musical ideas inside him that luckily for us he wishes to share. Again, this is more of a buffet served on a long table with many dishes for the listener to delight in as opposed to the snacks often served up as 'popular music'.
Feb 2010

TAYLOR'S UNIVERSE WITH KARSTEN VOGEL
EXPERIMENTAL HEALTH

Robin's fifth album was released as Taylor's Universe with Karsten Vogel, who is probably one of the most well-known saxophonists in the world and is highly regarded for his work in the Seventies with Secret Oyster. TU was this time just Robin, joined by Rasmus Grosell on drums, with Jan now a guest, as was Kim Menzer (flute, trombone, saxophone), Henning Plannthin (guitar) and Jytte Lindberg again providing some vocals. This CD has all that anyone could wish for from avant-garde music with melody interspersed with experimentation, gentle ambience mixed with rock riffs, controlled chaos mixed with lounge core. Songs such as "Elephant Kiss" really show what this band is about with powerful playing throughout and interactive complexity that is quite Zappa-esque.

Sounds effects (as usual) are brought into play but in a manner that definitely add to as opposed to detract from the music as a whole. I would guess that quite a few jazz lovers would have started listening to Robin's work at this point due to the connection with Karsten but it is the guitar at the beginning of songs such as "Inner Space" that really drive home the clarity and vision. While Karsten is a key player and component to the overall sound, this is very much Robin's music. Worth discovering for discerning fans of music.
Feb 2010

ROBIN TAYLOR
HEART DISC

Robin's sixth album was released as a solo CD but contained many of the musicians from previous TU albums. Hugh Steinmetz returned on trumpets, Karsten Vogel (saxophones), Rasmus Grosell (drums), while additional musicians were Peter Friis Nielsen (bass), Louise Nipper (voice), Al Taylor (voice) and Steen Grøntved on guitar. Interestingly this was the first release where Jan Marsfeldt did not make an appearance – here all keyboards were handled by Robin (along with other instruments of course). Play the second track of this to many people and you are almost guaranteed to hear howls of derision as the free form jazz of "Cello & Hammer" takes music to the limits. The brass instruments dare each other to produce something even more strange and potentially at odds with each other while an incredible piece of bass playing struggles to make itself heard. This is sonically challenging stuff, music that can wear the listener out, but it is compelling and driving something that is incredibly compelling. It is almost as if sanity is being driven out of the brain – but who cares? To the insane this makes perfect sense.

In many ways this is the 'hardest' album to listen to, yet is also fulfilling and rewarding. This is not music for those who like their jazz and music in general to be packaged into a neat box but for those who wish to challenge accepted norms of what is good and bad. It

may be hard work but is extremely rewarding.
Feb 2010

ROBIN TAYLOR
SAMPLICITY
I have yet to hear Robin's seventh or eighth releases, both of which were released just as 'Robin Taylor' or his ninth which was a group effort with Communio Musica, so I have no real way of knowing what the background was leading into his tenth album, but I do know that while there are links to his earlier works this is in many ways something completely different. Robin provided many more instruments than normal, including many different types of samples, and he was just joined on this release by Karsten Vogel (saxophones), with Jan Fischer and Louise Nipper providing some voices. This is an album that is very much experimental, but here Robin is going more into ambient and New Age and mixing that with the jazz forms he is more normally associated with.

Yes, there are times when Karsten is at the forefront, but often this is just one man mixing sounds to create a trance-like world of his own creation, one where there are no real rules. This is music to get lost inside – it seems multi-layered and constructed, yet at the same time those constructs are like gossamer, ready to fly away in the gentlest breeze. I cannot see how anyone playing "BTI" can fail to be moved by the sheer innocence beauty of it all.

This is a truly superb album and while it may not be indicative of his canon, as a piece of art this stands on its' own merits.
Mar 2010

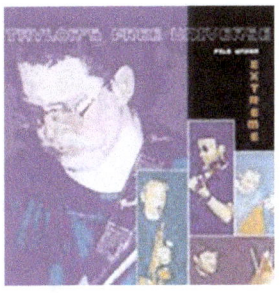

TAYLOR'S FREE UNIVERSE
FILE UNDER EXTREME
So, from his previous album which had been carefully constructed by one man we move to an album that was recorded on 28th January 2002 (although there were some subsequent overdubs) with a group. Here Robin was joined again by Karsten, and also by Pierre Tassone (violin, electronics), Johan Segerberg (double bass, electronics) and Kalle Mathiesen (drums, samples). When it states 'File Under Extreme' it really does mean that. What we have here is Present-style RIO melding and moving with free jazz – anything goes, and it does. This isn't music that is meant to be gentle and laid back – this is music that is defiant and full of discord, music that is challenging – almost daring the listener to turn it off.

But, if this style of music is what you enjoy listening to, then these guys show how it should be done. The interplay and complexity are breathtaking and the feeling very much

is of a band that is really cooking. Robin is well known for the use of space and minimalist approaches, but there isn't room or time for that here as each musician is out to make a point while at the same time contributing to and not detracting from the whole. Karsten has been given full rein to go berserk and the note density he generates at times is incredible, but all the guys here more than hold their own – each taking turns to be the front man. This is music at the very edge, only just together, and at times is nothing short of genius.
Mar 2010

TAYLOR'S UNIVERSE WITH KARSTEN VOGEL
ONCE AGAIN
'Once Again' was Robin's 15th album, released in 2004, and again is credited to Taylor's Universe with Karsten Vogel. Alongside Robin and Karsten, this time we saw Kim Menzer (didgeridoo), Pierre Tassone (violin), Louise Nipper (voice), Mads Hansen (drums), Rasmus Grosell (drums) and Kalle Mathiesen (drums). This was the first time that Mads had recorded with Robin since 1996's 'Pork', and he was of course also involved with the very first Taylor's Universe album ten years prior to 'Once Again'. The album starts with some didgeridoo before again working on expanding the listener's musical boundaries. This is quite different music to that from Taylor's Free Universe, not nearly so challenging, yet mixing jazz and prog in a way that is always guaranteed to ensure that one has to actually think and pay attention.

There are a few minimalist pieces here that are just superb, with sections of "Way Back in '85" reminding of me of some of Roger Eno's best works with simple repeated piano lines, but this piece in particular moves and melds with sax and fuzzed guitars to give it new life. Overall, this is a very enjoyable album, and while not as essential as some of Robin's other albums is certainly worthy of further investigation.
Mar 2010

ROBIN TAYLOR
X POSITION VOL. 1
The 16th album from Robin came about when he decided to revisit material that had been recorded over several years (going back as far as 1991) but had not been released for whatever reason. Robin then completed the songs ready for this album. Originally these would have been recorded as Robin Taylor, others as Taylor's Universe and there is also a live song by Taylor's Free Universe. While possibly not as focused as other albums (this is a compilation of unreleased material from a long period of time after all), yet again the listener is taken into the heady world of the Dane. "Don't Drink and Drive" is less than two minutes long yet is a powerful rock song showing how repeated melodic ideas can build to a climax.

Others such as "Baroque Ideas" are far more electronic in approach, while the final song "Lass Mich Los" is by far the most challenging – given that it is more than 12 minutes of free form jazz and RIO. For fans of Taylor then this album is of course essential as previously unreleased material is now available, but this may be too much for the casual listener, particularly the song by TFU.
Mar 2010

TAYLOR'S UNIVERSE WITH KARSTEN VOGEL
OYSTER'S APPRENTICE
Well, there can be no doubt who Taylor's 18th album was a tribute for, namely Secret Oyster whose leader Karsten Vogel is again credited. This album sees Robin stating when the songs were originally written and just the first and last are from 2005, while the others go back as far as three numbers from 1976. But strangely enough it is probably one of the most forward sounding albums of his canon. Here Robin is striking a strong balance between jazz and symphonic progressive rock, adding to both styles without diluting from either so that fans of both genres can fully take this album on board. It is incredibly open and inviting, melodic and layered while also containing the space and casual structure so often the important aspects of his work.

It is instrumental music that is never boring, always intriguing, yet not as challenging as some. It could never be considered middle of the road but here Robin has produced an album that will get far more attention just because it is so easy to listen to, packed full of enjoyable melodic stories and interludes. It is polished yet still contains the spontaneity of his more experimental albums. Overall if one is looking for a place to start investigating the vast amount of work Robin has produced then this could well be the place to start.
Mar 2010

ROBIN TAYLOR
X POSITION VOL. 2
Even before putting this CD into the player, the first thing that one notices is that all the song titles are in Danish – unusual as Robin's titles are normally in English. The reason for this is that this CD is what should have been Robin's recording debut back in 1985 when he was assisted by Jan Fischer. For whatever reason the songs never saw the light of day and it was only 20 years later that Robin revisited the tapes, cleaned them up with new technology and finally made the music available. This is quite an unusual album in many ways, as Robin appears to be seeking a style and isn't yet sure with this on what he wants to do. The result is an album that while interesting is fairly disjointed and somehow comes across as being less for that. This is a real shame as there are some really good songs here, showcasing just too many styles.

My favourite is probably the most unusual, "Finanslovforslag" which features Robin and

Jan on vocals, using them as an instrument and then treating them almost as musical drones. I have returned to this song several times and have decided that it is one of my favourites from Robin's many, just not sure why!! This is an album only for the completist, yet it has been released primarily for those fans who wish to have everything that Robin has been involved with and to see where he came from, and for those this is indispensable. But if you have yet to hear albums by Robin then I suggest you start elsewhere.
Mar 2010

ROBIN TAYLOR
DEUTSCHE SCHULE!
This album was inspired by Krautrock of the Seventies, especially bands like Can and Faust, and here Robin has been joined only by Karsten and drummer Rasmus Grosell. All the song titles are in German to add to the fun, and the result is an album that manages to definitely bring in the Krautrock feel yet for the most part doesn't recreate the carnage of a live Can performance (for example) – something which does somewhat surprise me given the way that Taylor's Free Universe approaches music. In fact, "Eisenbahn mit Sauerkraut" is quite pedestrian with only Karsten providing some levity. However, I am quite aware that I haven't played a great deal of the genre (in fact I am only recently being educated in this regard), and I think that my general lack of enjoyment of this CD is down more to my own personal likes and dislikes as opposed to any issues with the music on offer.

Looking through the net this release generally gains high praise so all I can suggest is that if the bands mentioned interest you, then listen to some samples to make up your own mind.
Mar 2010

TAYLOR'S UNIVERSE
RETURN TO WHATEVER
Robin's first release of 2009 saw a new version of Taylor's Universe, with no sign of Karsten Vogel and the use of many of the participants of his Art Cinema project including the return of Michael Denner (King Diamond/Mercyful Fate). The other musicians on this project are Flemming Muus Tranberg (basses), Carsten Sindvald (saxophones), Klaus Thrane (drums), Louise Nipper (voice), Pierre Tassone (violin) and Tine Lilholt (flute, harp) Also, this CD has been released on the Russian Mals label instead of Robin's own and is a superb digipak. But what of the music? This is easily one of Robin's finest moments, directing the musicians around him to bring together controlled chaos, melody and discord, note density and space – often in the same few bars of a song.

This is music for the music lover, whether it be jazz or progressive, with elements of Metal and avant-garde so that the whole is a discovery, a journey if you will. There are times when the brass just soars, at others it is more restrained, while at the heart of it all Robin provides simple yet poignant keyboards. Essential.
Mar 2010

TAYLOR'S UNIVERSE
ARTIFICIAL JOY
'Artificial Joy' was the second album from Taylor's Universe in 2009, and while the line-up is similar to the one that appeared on 'Return To Whatever' of course there are some changes. Although the comment appears in the booklet 'For maximum effect, play it loud!', and Michael Denner is again on hand this isn't nearly as rocky as one may imagine from that comment. There are elements, especially in Michael's tortured solo in "Atmosfear", where progressive elements stand out but for each of these there are also the more restrained layerings I have come to expect. Robin's keyboards are at the heart and in many ways, this is the perfect follow-on to the previous album although with not quite as much edge and excitement.

It is an extremely cohesive album, with some wonderful clarinet solos and great interaction with the sax. One of the huge strengths of Taylor is that he brings together musicians and instruments in a way that totally makes sense. The previous album to this one featured violin as a foil against the sax, here it is a clarinet. Denner played on six out of seven tracks on the previous album yet here has a much smaller role allowing Taylor the opportunity to play some guitar of his own. Robin is very much a composer, a bandleader and arranger, who has a vision for each album and yet again this is one that is well worth discovering.
Mar 2010

ROBIN TAYLOR
EDGE OF DARKNESS
There is always a problem with labelling music, in that labelling it can mean that the artist is pigeon-holed which can then mean that people who may enjoy the music don't get to hear it, as they don't think that they will like it. Take Burzum for example, I defy anyone to categorise Varg with just one style of music but those who have never played it will say that Burzum are Black Metal – without actually hearing the many different styles he has produced. And so we come to Robin Taylor – this was his eighth album and was released originally in 2000 (he has now released nearly 30!). While Robin will always be viewed as a jazz artist, often working within the avant-garde, there is something else going on with this album as well. Those who know me would say that my musical tastes are eclectic (if they are polite – my daughters often just state that I listen to some very weird stuff), and that I have been

known to often play atmospheric black metal along the lines of Agalloch or Negură Bunget etc. I was surprised how many times I kept thinking of that type of band while I was playing this – there is a lot going on, with the brass instruments particularly winding up and down the scales in a frenetic and frightening fashion. But the sound I heard most was one of coldness – this album chills me to the bone, and in that manner it has more in common with atmospheric black metal than anything else.

I can imagine some reviewers and listeners being quite frightened when they heard this for the first time as there is a menace present throughout which makes it unsettling and unnerving to say the least. There will be many that will feel that this album is to be avoided, but to my ears it is one that is to be welcomed and explored for what it is – a masterpiece. Maybe Robin ought to reissue it with a darker cover, changed the band to something exotic such as Norbilyator and see what the extreme mags think of this – I think they would have a blast.
July 2011

ROBIN TAYLOR
ISLE OF BLACK
This was Robin's 26th album, following on from the Art Cinema project and the Taylor's Universe release "Soundwall". In fact, this has the same musicians as that, apart from Michael Denner who wasn't involved with this one. It never ceases to amaze me that it is possible to play a Taylor album and find it so very different to any of his other releases. One would imagine that when an artist is extremely prolific that there would be a tendency to go back over the same old ground, but just like Jeremy Morris (who has released more than 50 albums now) it is more a case of just having so much music inside his head he just must get it out. The album starts with electronically treated vocals and simplistic chords that immediately makes one feel that this is going to have far more in common with classic Tangerine Dream than with the jazz that Robin is normally known for, but soon the vocals and chords have a small amount of dissonance that gives it a more threatening and frightening edge. There is a depth here that is way more than the simple chords and vocals imply.

One of my favourites on the album is the third track "Swinger" which after a quirky introduction melds into a sax and piano led jazz number that belongs in a small smoky jazz club. That these guys have played together for a while is more than evident, with a feeling they are playing off each other and having fun – no mean feat given that this is not a truly live affair as Robin is playing various instruments on this track. It moves away into chaos and freeform before coming back to the previous melody which now feels warm and even more welcoming than before due to the short diversion it took earlier. This is a song that is only four minutes long, but one that I feel I could put on repeat all day. This isn't the longest album in the world, even with the 11 minutes bonus of "Izmit" it is only just over 40 minutes long, but again it is sheer class. Definitely worth investigating.
Sep 2011

TAYLOR'S FREE UNIVERSE
9 ELEVEN
This album was recorded 9 years ago today (as I write this), on 11th September 2002 at the Copenhagen Jazzhouse. The line-up was Robin Taylor (guitar, electronics), Pierre Tassone (violin, electronics), Karsten Vogel (saxophones), Johan Segerberg (basses, electronics) and Kalle Mathiesen (drums, electronics). The result of these guys combining and building off each other is hugely powerful, with Robin taking the lead at times with incredible Gilmore/Hillage driving over the top guitars while at others it is Karsten with his incredible saxwork or Pierre flying through. There is a real togetherness and understanding which allows the five of them to blast off into extreme tangents knowing the others will follow, and that if they do end up taking a path into the wilderness together, somehow they will get back to some sort of civilisation. This is not music that the majority will enjoy, but who wants to be part of the majority? According to LastFM my tastes are eclectic – possibly because I will listen to jazz, folk, and death metal all in the same sitting – and I would much rather be eclectic than following the herd. That is the same with these guys – they are making music for themselves, knowing they will never make a fortune - but it is better to be true to yourself than doing something that is against the grain. If you feel intrigued enough by this review to find out more then I urge you to do so and listen to their music with an open mind. This is an awesome avant-garde outing that I truly wish I had been at.
Sep 2011

TAYLOR'S FREE UNIVERSE
FAMILY SHOT
So, Robin's 17th album is another under the label TFU, but this is with a different line-up to that which appeared elsewhere and the only one not to feature Karsten Vogel (here replaced by Kim Menzer). As one would expect from TFU – this is improvisational music at the cutting edge of avant-garde. I was intrigued to see that the prog bible dprp.net gave this just 1/10, which says way more about the person writing that review than it does about the music itself. Yes, this is not easy listening and yes, it is challenging – but that is exactly what it is supposed to be! This is not music that is aimed for large audiences and radio programmes, but music that is on the edge. Dissonance and the use of free form has its' place in modern music, as much as it did in classical.

There are some incredibly complex passages within this, and the short "Nice 'n' Easy" interplays are just superb, and there are times when the musicians all go their own way, possibly never to return but maybe, they just might. There is a lot of space in this album, and the use of the lack of sound and gaps where there could be notes, is just as important as the ones they actually play. Again, if you enjoy avant-garde jazz and music that is out there then try this – if you want simple repeated harmonies then don't!
Sep 2011

PETER FRIIS NIELSEN/TAYLOR'S FREE UNIVERSE
ON-PLUGGED IN ELSINORE

This is the 12th Taylor's Free Universe album, where they joined bassist Peter Friis Nielsen for a concert of improvised and eclectic jazz. As with all other TFU releases, this is either a masterpiece or something that you would play just a few seconds of before using the disc as a gun target. There really is no middle ground with these guys, you either love them or hate them and I fall into the former camp. The musicianship, as always, is incredible and the interplay between the five musicians is awesome. Peter is a great bassist, but what really makes this album work is the way that all the guys can (and do) take the lead, driving the band along before it is time for someone else to define the path. There are times when they all seem to be at the front, all vying to be heard, but it still works. "Picnic At Moon" features some great violin, both bowed and plucked, but within the background is a maelstrom of sound from the rest – all of which works to make this an incredible tour de force to my ears, although it may not seem the same to everyone.

I don't think Robin knows how to release a bad album, this is yet another killer and when released in 2004 was nominated for a Danish Jazz Award. But, if you want your jazz to be mild and meek and behave itself then be warned, this is not like that!
Sep 2011

ROBIN TAYLOR
THE BANDBIX TAPES

This was Robin's seventh actual CD release but is a collection of music that he recorded between 1980 and 1985. The opening song "En Nat Pa Vaerket" is the oldest as well as the longest and is more a collection of pieces than one pure long song with small breaks. It is only as the piece progresses that the dissonance and conflict that I expect from Robin begins to come through. This is very much an album where he is starting to stretch his musical ideas, which means that there is quite a lot more melody and proggy feel to the jazz – certainly quite different in many ways to what he started producing regularly in the Nineties and up to the present day. There is a larger concentration on keyboards within this number, but that isn't the case throughout the album, with some songs having no rhythm section at all and plenty of guitars, with a Gong/Hillage glissando style present at times.

Exciting and innovating, this album shows no sign at all of aging and even more than 30 years after the first song was recorded this is still invigorating and exciting and a major part of Taylor's canon. Well worth investigating.
Sep 2011

TFU
MANIPULATED BY TAYLOR
This is an unusual concept, in that Taylor's Free Universe are renowned for their avant-garde improvised pieces, yet the entire material on this CD was selected, mixed, edited and manipulated by Robin Taylor from live recordings made at Copenhagen JazzHouse on September 15th, 2005. It is a live album, but it has been mixed and changed in the studio. One may think that this would lead to a more melodic and restrained version of the band, but that is certainly not the case. Robin has taken this concept and has treated some of the instruments and combined them so that they stay true to the avant-garde sensibilities but have taken on a totally new flavour. The line-up is slightly different to normal, in that although he is joined by long-time compatriots Karsten Vogel (saxophones), Pierre Tassone (Grand piano, processed violin) and Lars Juul (drums, electronics), this is the only time that Klavs Hovman (acoustic bass, loops) has made an appearance – and a very fine fretless bassist he is too.

This may be a manipulated album, cut and lovingly spliced back together by Robin, but first and foremost this is a live recording that contains stunning interplay and runs from guys that live and breathe jazz. As always, this may contain too much dissonance, chaos and invention from those who would much rather have their music served up in radio-friendly 3-minute segments. But, if you want music that is on the very edge of being described as such, and who feel that Art Zoyd has a place in their own personal music collection, then this is an album for you. With this his 20th release, yet again Taylor proves to be a master of his craft.
Sep 2011

ROBIN TAYLOR
NOVEMBER
Robin's 13th album is very much a solo effort, where he provides all the instrumentation (piano and Crumar Stringman, electric and acoustic guitars, bass, percussion, drum samples, processing, etc.). Apparently, he was inspired by the November of his native Denmark, and the result is something that at times is eerie and certainly very dark. This is an album that has its' roots in the avant-garde, and then moves to polar opposites so that while there is some that could be described as prog with strong guitars there are others that are RIO to the extreme, music that is pure experimentation that Eno would be proud of.

Yes, there are elements almost of ambient, short pieces combined with longer more atmospheric, resulting in an album that is challenging yet consoling, jagged yet comforting, antagonistic yet welcoming. Confused? You should be. Listening to "Waiting For Something To Happen", it is hard to believe that this drone and gentle piano/acoustic intro is from the same hands that crafted the song before, "Lowest". But it's okay, before Robin gets too far down the Mike Oldfield track (and he is damn close, take it from me)

he throws in enough piano discord to shake the boat about. Having now listened to virtually all of Robin's albums I find it hard to understand how he managed to keep the quality so very high – it won't be to everyone's musical tastes but if you enjoy music outside the norm then you need this.
Sep 2011

ROBIN TAYLOR
TWO-PACK

The reason that this release is called 'Two-Pack' is because it literally is that, two mini CDs with the same cover (although the first is tinted brown and the second green). It is an interesting concept, and a neat way of showing the music as well, as here we have one CD with Taylor's Free Universe from 2006 and the other being the most recent recordings of Taylor's Universe in 2010. It is a brand new release, but half of it stretches back five years. The first CD is by TU, and this contains some great sax which links in with the dynamic drumming, while Taylor provides the rest of the instrumentation (guitars, keyboards, bass). There is a freedom in the music, but there is also a real structure and the combination of the two shows just how powerful jazz can be. There is light, there is shade, and there is real harmony and "The Gost Of Göran" is now one of my favourite TU numbers.

The second disc shows TFU in flight, and here Robin only provides guitar and is surrounded by consummate musicians. The first few times I played this I concentrated on a different instrument, whether it be the bass lines of Assi Roar, the staccato drumming of Rasmus Grosell or the (mostly) lead instruments of Karsten Vogel (sax) and Pierre Tassone (electric violin). It never ceases to amaze me that music which is so complex, and so different, somehow managed to move together and create something that was more than the sum of the parts. Robin Taylor's music will always be an acquired taste, and many people will listen to parts of this and ask what is going on (such as when my family come into the room), but for those with an open mind this is yet another strong offering from the prolific Dane.
Nov 2011

TAYLOR'S UNIVERSE
KIND OF RED

On August 17th, 1959, Miles Davis released probably the most important jazz record of all-time, 'A Kind Of Blue'. In November 1974 King Crimson released their final album before being disbanded, 'Red'. So is this album a mixture of the two? Or am I being somewhat simplistic or reading something into the title that isn't there? Having played this album numerous times I have come to the decision that maybe I am right after all. Take the second song, "Jakriborg"; there are some strong guitar lines that Fripp would be proud of – possibly some of the most direct from Robin himself on any of his albums – yet there is some wonderfully fluid trumpet and a real feeling that this is a 'progression' for Robin.

I have been lucky enough to hear most Robin's albums, whether solo, his free jazz group Taylor's Free Universe, as well as Taylor's Universe but for his thirtieth album he has brought together a group that musically has as much in common with VDGG, King Crimson and even Faust as they do with Miles. There are some incredibly simple yet poignant sections such as the syncopated rhythms in "Firestone", melodies that are repeated and are extremely effective, leading to gentle keyboards (is that a Hammond I hear?) that brings to mind memories of Procul Harum before the trumpet takes a more centre stage.

The more I listened the more progressive influences I could spot, with Colosseum being particularly noticeable, but this is way more than just a cobbling together of different styles in the vain hope that it will produce something listenable: there is a real structure and layering of the instruments that shows that a master arranger has been at work to produce music that is complex yet incredibly melodic and easy to listen to at the same time.

When artists are prolific it is sometimes hard to know where to start – I avoided Zappa for years as I felt that I needed a guide (in the end I just plunged in and am so glad that I did) – and Taylor is a case in point. But take it from me this is an incredible album – if you have ever enjoyed Robin's work in the past then this is something you will need to have, and if you have yet to start investigating then the time to do so is now. This is five stars in anyone's language – incredible.
Apr 2012

TAYLOR'S UNIVERSE
WORN OUT
One of the real joys of listening to Robin Taylor's work is that one is never quite sure what is going to come out of the speakers when the CD is put on. This was quite a lengthy recording process, with the sessions taking six months to complete, but the result is yet again another wonderful album from the mad Dane. What is particularly interesting on this album is the way that the music moves between progressive rock, soft jazz, fusion, RIO, avant-garde jazz etc. It is seamless, something which is enhanced by having three different brass players involved, with Karsten Vogel making an appearance back with Robin for the first time since 'Soundwall'. Robin also brought in renowned Danish guitarist Jon Hemmersam to assist with the solos. As well as playing jazz, Jon has recorded with Evelyn Glennie and has a real understanding of different types of music.

That is useful here, as in some ways this is one of Robin's most accessible albums while at others it is incredibly complex. There may be simple keyboard chords, while the drums drive along before a very dirty blues sax breaks through or we could be sweeping along

in pure fusion with great guitar. The jazz can be reflective at times while at others it can be almost impossible to comprehend. In lots of ways this is a good introduction to Robin's vast collection of work as it can be enjoyed on so many different levels. Yet again this is something that fans of adventurous music need to seek out.
Jan 2013

THIEVES' KITCHEN
ONE FOR SORROW, TWO FOR JOY
I was on www.progarchives.com the other night posting up some old reviews, and one of these was for TK's 'Shibboleth'. It was only then that I noticed they had a new album out, so I went over to their website and after swapping some emails with guitarist Phil Mercy I ended up with a copy of 'One For Sorrow'. I originally got involved with TK when they formed in the late Nineties as I knew drummer Mark Robotham who had previously been with Grey Lady Down, but he is no longer with the band. 'Shibboleth' was their third album, and to my ears easily their best, although I did question at the time as to whether the band should consider becoming an instrumental group as I felt that their complexity didn't always leave enough room for vocalist Amy Darby. Apparently, there has been an album between this and the last one I heard, and there have also been some line-up changes, in that while Thomas Johnson (keyboards, ex-Änglagård) is there with Amy and Phil, the rest of the band are currently guests with Paul Mallyon (drums), Brad Waissman (bass) and Anna Holmgren (flute, also from Änglagård).

But this doesn't come across as a project in any way as this is a band that know exactly what they are about. The music is incredibly complex, and at times has a hard rocking neo-prog guitar edge while at others it is much more symphonic. However, the big difference for me is that there appears to be a far greater understanding of the nuances of atmosphere and delicacy, combined with loads of control. This means that Phil and Thomas are quite happy to take the lead on instrumental passages yet also know when to rein it in and provide just the right amount of space for Amy. She has an incredible voice, particularly in regard to her breath and note control so that long drawn-out sections are not an issue for her. At these times her voice is very much to the forefront, lifted over the maelstrom that is going on behind her. Thomas uses a great deal of different keyboard sounds and textures and that adds to the picture they paint.

As always, Rob Aubrey has done a sterling job with the production, so it doesn't matter if it is a quiet passage or bombastic, everything can be clearly heard and give the right emphasis. If I had to pick just one band for comparison then the obvious would be Renaissance, but with Amy singing more contralto than Annie's soprano. I am extremely reticent to provide more than one album with a 5 * rating in a sitting, and I have just done that with the new Comedy of Errors CD, but in all conscience, I can't give it any less. I love it.
Apr 2013

THIEVES' KITCHEN
THE WATER ROAD

An interesting thing about the album when checking out the reviews on PA, is that among the Collaborators alone, this has been ranked at everything from 1* to all 5. This was their fourth album, released in 2008, but I have only just come across it. Having enjoyed their most recent album so much, I knew that this one had to be worth investigating and since receiving it have played it a great deal. I fully understand why there has been such a variance in the marks awarded as musically it is incredibly diverse, with the music sometimes in perfect harmony with Amy, and at others she is almost at odds, while for many passages she is absent as both Phil (guitars) and Thomas (keyboards) are more than happy being right at the forefront of proceedings, driving the music onwards.

Ah, the music. Both Thomas and guest Anna Holmgren are from Änglagård, and there is plenty of angular Swedish sounding prog on this album, with solid keyboards and lifting flute. But there are also times when these guys remind you that they are very much a rock band with driving guitars and pacy runs. This was Mark Robotham's final album with the band, and when I think back to the time when he played me a pre-release tape of GLD's debut album, his drumming has changed beyond all recognition as he is fully aware of the need for space and what he doesn't play is as important within the overall sound and context as what he does.

Opening song "The Long Fiachetto" clocks in at more than 21 minutes and is a real statement of intent, but for me the highlight is the fourth song, "Om Tare". It commences with a multi-tracked chant, but after the initial six seconds the guys burst forth with a complex burst of jazz rock that took me back to my teenage years. Somehow, towards the end of the Seventies I ended up with a copy of Colosseum II's 1977 album 'War Dance' in my collection. It was an album that I often listened to, wondering in the interplay between rhythm section of Jon Hiseman and John Mole, with keyboard player Don Airey and guitarist Gary Moore blasting over the top. There was no need for a singer, as there was no room for one, and if I had just heard the passage from TK with no knowledge of who it was, I would have bet my life that it was from CII.

But that is the only song like it on the album, and therein lies what for me is a strength but others may find confusing, in that this is an album where the band quite definitely refuse to sit within one musical style and instead want to expand their wings, developing and progressing as they go.

I awarded 'Shibboleth', the album immediately prior to this one, 4*'s and 'One For Sorrow', the one after it, 5 *'s and this is yet another fine example of an album worthy of top marks. It is definitely worth seeking out.
Jul 2013

THINKING PLAGUE
DECLINE AND FALL

I normally pride myself on knowing quite a bit about music, but when I come across a band that has been going since 1978 and recording since 1984 yet are new to me, I hang my head in shame. Although to be honest the form of music these guys provide is not likely to feature much in the mainstream press. This is experimental RIO free form that pushes the boundaries of what many would consider music at all, yet at the same time is strangely compelling. Singer Elaine Di Falco sings in a strange monotone that combines with the otherworldly music that is taking place around her to really take the listener to a discordant future. This is music that has so much space you could drive a truck through it, yet at the same time is incredibly layered and complex. It is modern classical music being taken to an extreme: the scores for this must be incredible.

It is emotional, hard to listen to, complicated and doesn't belong in any sensible music collection. But being fair, who on earth wants to be sensible? Most people will listen to a few seconds of this and turn away in horror to the latest pop creation, but if you want your music to be challenging and with substance then this may just be for you.
Dec 2012

3RDEGREE
THE LONG DIVISION

When I heard from band leader Robert James Pashman asking me if I would be willing to review their new album, I just thought that here was another new band just starting out. What I hadn't realized was they are an outfit with a history stretching back for more than twenty years, and while this may have been their first album for more than three years it was their fourth. So, I downloaded the album and put into 'The List' (yes there is such a thing, it is the way that I try and keep track of what I should be listening to so that I know just how far behind I am on the reviewing front). Somehow, I am never really ahead of the game...

In due course I put on the album and then proceeded to sit there with my mouth open, and my ears more so. Where on earth have these guys been hiding and why didn't I know about them before? To me this is the first band I have come across who understand what City Boy were about in the late Seventies (sometime around 'The Day The Earth Caught Fire') and have then added in huge influences from 10CC and Alan Parsons Project to produce an album that in many ways is sheer perfection. If you want your music to be complex yet simple, to be able to wash over you like a warm blanket yet still have soul and vigour then this is it. This album became a review blocker in the sense that when I had played it enough times to be able to write about it and move to the next one that just didn't happen as I was enjoying it too much.

I know this album would have been in my top 10 for 2012 if I had been aware of it, but here I am in 2013 so that can't happen. Bugger. Melody, passion, hooks to die for, this prog/melodic rock album is essential. 'Nuff said.
Apr 2013

3RDEGREE
NARROW-CASTER
After raving about 2012's 'The Long Division', it only seems right that I ought to go backwards and listen to something else by these guys. The band broke up not long after releasing 'Human Interest Story' in 1996, only getting back together in 2007 so perhaps it isn't surprising that this 2008 album is a collection of ideas from the Nineties together with some new ones. This was their third studio album altogether, and having now only heard it some five years after it came out, I am still at a loss to explain why these guys aren't far more widely known. This is radio friendly commercially acceptable classic rock/art rock/prog rock, so how come they aren't being spoken about as the next big thing? I'm sure it can't have anything to do with their age, how they look, or that they write their own material and can play their own instruments can it? Surely not, where would the music industry be if everything was just created crap for the masses (etc., etc.)?

As with the later album, this has many musical connections with City Boy and Alan Parsons Project, along with 10CC and Steely Dan: it is well-crafted melodic music with stacks of hooks and vocals to die for. There is something about the album that makes me smile as I play it, with the additional benefit that this is an album that brings summer to the coldest day. It's winter here in NZ as I write this, but there is a warm glow coming from my speakers that brightens the mood.

There is a feeling that these guys can really rock when they want to but keep a lid on it so the vocals and melodies stay at the forefront, even though there are times when there are some fairly brutal riffs coming out. Listen to "The Proverbial Banana Peel" to get a taste of just how controlled these guys are; at times there are gentle keyboards and a great bassline in the background with loads of space while at others there is some wonderful fuzzed distorted guitar that gives it a totally different feel.

This is an album that just begs to be played on repeat, and surely that is all anyone wants? For fans of good music, whatever the genre.
Jun 2013

THIS MISERY GARDEN
ANOTHER GREAT DAY ON EARTH
Originally formed in Geneva in 2005, TMG recorded some demo tracks in 2006 that gained them some attention in the local music scene and led to them recording this their debut album in 2007. Fast forward to the end of 2009 and the album was reissued through

Prog Rock, SPV and Galileo. Now in 2013 they have just released the follow-up, 'Cornerstone', so it seems like a good time to go back and see what the debut gave us. Straight from the off it is obvious that Katatonia have been a major influence on the guys, with a cold bleakness permeating through their riffing guitars. There is plenty of emotion and atmosphere on display, and I initially I was somewhat surprised that it has taken them so long to build on this.

A Perfect Circle is another reference point, as is The Cure, but it is the bleakness of Katatonia which has had a major impact on the band and given my liking of that group it can't be a bad thing. But I did find my interest wandering during the fourteen songs and was somewhat surprised to notice that it had finished playing in the background and I hadn't noticed. I went back through it again and found that while playing just a few songs was interesting, playing the whole album wasn't so much. Although the style and application is positive, more work is required on the songs. But this was a debut, and it has taken them six years to deliver the follow-up so maybe that new one is better, but while this is okay it is never more than that.
Nov 2013

THRESHOLD
MARCH OF PROGRESS
Many years ago I often used to catch up with Karl Groom in the early Shadowland/Strangers On A Train days, and we would stop and have a chat. Some time in 1993 we were both at the same gig and he told me that his own band Threshold were just about to release their debut album and he had just received his first CD. I said that I would love to hear it (meaning when all the stock had arrived) but he gave me his own copy and asked me to give it a fair play. That night I was blown away as I drove the 100 miles home and listened to what to me was the epitome of prog metal. I already knew Damian Wilson from Landmarq, and here he was blasting over the top of riffing guitars and intense keyboards from Richard West. To this day 'Wounded Land' contains two of my all-time favourite songs in "Paradox" and "Sanity's End". Over the years I managed to catch the band in concert a few times, and always enjoyed their output. Damian (and others, particularly drummers for some reason until Johanne settled in the seat) left for pastures new, but Karl and Richard kept the band going. Damian returned in 2007 and this is the first album since he rejoined the fold, so it was with great expectations that I put this on the player. Would the band be as good as I remembered? I hadn't heard their last album 'Dead Reckoning' but I highly rated 'Subsurface' from 2004 and had all the others, so would this be any good?

To be honest, it as if the band has never been away. All power to the other musicians who have been involved over the years, but the current lineup has a strength and presence that lifts this album to a whole new level. Damian's voice seems to be stronger than ever, and he hits the notes with ease and adds a class and presence that most singers would give their right arm for. Since leaving Threshold the first time he has performed at the highest level with Rick Wakeman, Ayreon, Star One and many others, and I still wonder what Maiden would have sounded like if they had picked Damian instead of Blaze after Bruce (Damian was shortlisted for the gig). This is prog metal at its' finest, yet is quite different to Dream Theater. This is much more riff based and far more metallic in nature so in truth this is metal prog as opposed to the normal billing. Given that Nuclear Blast aren't generally known for their progressive stance maybe that's not that surprising.

From first song to the last I played this with a smile on my face, just reaching over to the controls every so often to turn it up just that little bit louder. Johanne and Steve provide the bottom end, Karl and Pete lock the guitars in tight, Richard provides the finesse and Damian rises over it all. Who could wish for anything more than this? Whatever you want from a prog metal/melodic metal album then take it from me it is here. Threshold are back with a bang, just don't leave it so long for the next album guys.
Dec 2012

THRESHOLD
CRITICAL MASS

Some nine years after their debut Threshold released this their sixth studio album in 2002 (and was the first time that they had released two studio albums with the same line-up, following on from 2001's 'Hypothetical'). While they had had some line-up moves since 1991, the quartet of Karl Groom (guitar), Nick Midson (guitar), Jon Jeary (bass) and Richard West (keyboards) were ever present. Add to that the vocal talents of Andrew 'Mac' McDermott and drummer Johanne James and you have the band that was taking the banner of prog metal firmly to the forefront. This has just been reissued as a 'Definitive Edition' by Nuclear Blast and includes two 'new' songs plus a live version of "Echoes Of Life".

By the time this was released Threshold had built a reputation as the UK's, and possibly Europe's, finest exponents of this intricate style of hard rock. This is a band that is driven from the back, with Johanne hitting the drums very hard indeed, then add in the crunching riffs and bass lines that only come from playing together for so long, and the rock keyboards of Richard who is willing to provide walls of sound or lead roles as the song demands. With this album Mac firmly came out of the shadow of Damian Wilson to stand firmly in the spotlight of his own making – while the band had moved on musically to produce by far their finest work, he was more than ready to meet the task at hand.

It is melodic, it is gentle, it is heavy, it is hard, this is an album for all those who want music to be contemplative and thoughtful, intricate, and clever, yet also with plenty of balls and aggression to match. Songs such as opener "Phenomenon" are now viewed as classics, and ten years on from its' original release it still puts many other bands to shame. As relevant and hard hitting as it ever was, this is an essential addition to everybody's collection.
Jan 2013

THRESHOLD
HYPOTHETICAL

In 2001 Threshold released this their fifth full studio album, which has now been reissued by Nuclear Blast as a 'Definitive Edition' with three additional live songs (previously on the 'Concert In Paris' release). Yet again the band suffered with the revolving line-up issue with a seeming inability to record more than one album with the same guys, although this was the first time they had recorded consecutive albums with the same singer. Drummer Mark Heaney was the casualty this time; he had been there for the previous two albums but was replaced by Johanne James who is still there some 12 years after this was released.

It had been three years since the 1998 release of their previous album, 'Clone', and that had gained a great deal of attention and had led to the band touring in Europe with the likes of Dream Theater so after such a gap they were going to be under a lot of scrutiny, but there was no need for anyone to worry. Songs such as "Turn On Tune In" show just why they are held in such high regard, with riffs, hooks and great vocals, while in "The Ravages Of Time" Johanne showed why he was the new incumbent driving the band along from the back. While they may have suffered with drummers and singers over the years, the other four guys (guitarists Karl Groom and Nick Midson, bassist Jon Jeary and keyboard player Richard West) had been playing together since 1989 and the way they lock in shows the experience of playing so much together.

In my original review (#62 of Feedback) I said "The last time I saw these guys I got serious neck ache – if ever you thought that melodic rock couldn't stand up against 'normal' hard rock for power and passion then think again. Threshold are back in town." Playing this again is like revisiting an old friend, and with a couple of songs longer than ten minutes there is plenty of room for the band to spread their melodic rock. Yet again a masterpiece of the genre.
Jan 2013

THRESHOLD
SUBSURFACE

Given that the band had only recently released their wonderful live CD and DVD 'Critical Energy', I hadn't realised that a new studio album was going to follow so quickly in 2004. Again, this has now been reissued as a 'Definitive Edition' by Nuclear Blast and contains one new song plus two live versions. By this time one of the original quartet had departed, with bassist Jon Jeary being replaced by Steve Anderson who is still there in the current line-up in 2013, still linking in with powerful drummer Johanne James. Nick Midson and Karl Groom provide the metal riffs, while Richard West again either supports or rides melodic roughshod over the top of the maelstrom with some great keyboard lines. Add to that the great vocals of Mac and you have one of the finest metal bands from the UK scene. At the time you wouldn't have read as much about them in the 'normal' press as others because they pursue a lone furrow in prog metal: music that can be brutally heavy yet maintain strange time signatures and melodic twists.

"Mission Profile" opens proceedings – one of the more up-tempo numbers on the album, and one thing that really kicks home from the opening note is the quality of the production: this is an album that can be played extremely loudly, which sounds polished but not sanitised. For me the second song, "Ground Control", must be one of the best for defining Threshold. It is riff-laden, yet also contains some strong keyboards, loads of harmony vocals, gentle and quiet sections that are then offset with passion and Mac shouting, "How can you face the future?" At times there is almost a syncopated rhythm and always there is a definite feel that this is like nothing else around yet is also wonderfully powerful and melodic.

This is music that may not be fashionable but sure as hell is strong stuff. Yes, they can bring in acoustic guitars when they want to, yes they can bring in loads of influences but these guys really don't sound like anyone else. Simple ideas are used as well as the complex. At the end of "Stop Dead" Mac again sings the line "Well if you stop, dead" and the song does, totally. The first time it happened I actually stared at the player because it was so dramatic, not a good idea when you are bombing around the M25.... I ought to also mention the cover. The word on the TV says 'REFLECT' but look at the reflection and that states 'CONCEAL'. Again, this is a simple idea, but is extremely effective. This is an indispensable album.
Jan 2013

THRESHOLD
CLONE
And so to Threshold's fourth studio album, and consequently the fourth with a different line-up. Damian sang on the debut, then left only to return to sing on the third, but by this time had departed again. None of us expected to see him fronting the band ever again but he did return in 2007 and has been there ever since. But, with this album we are back in 1998 and Threshold had a new frontman in Andrew 'Mac' McDermott. Now, I am a Damian fan through and through, but I would be the first to stand up and say that Mac more than filled the shoes and dominates on this album. It was during this period that I saw the band in concert more than any other and playing this album after a break of a few years is like coming back to old friends. The songs are familiar, but only because I played this album to death when I first heard it, so it is hard to be objective about it all.

Here is the perfect mix of guitars, keyboards, and drums in a melodic metallic progtastic environment with a singer who knows exactly what he is about and then the whole package is wrapped up by the engineering and production skills of Karl Groom. Who on earth could wish for anymore? This is not going to be suited to everyone's taste, as metalheads may argue that there is too much prog going on while the progheads will state that it is too metallic and there isn't enough noodling and self-contemplation to make it worthwhile.

Me? I love it, from "Freaks" through to "Sunrise On Mars". Listen to "Change" to see what I mean. Here is a song that is controlled and slow in pace, yet there is passion in abundance and the guitar break is stunning, but what makes it such an epic is the way that everyone plays their part, and it all fits together so very well indeed. No-one could imagine that this was Mac's first album with the rest of the guys as he seems very much at home indeed. Yet again this is an essential release from the guys, now available again as a 'definitive edition' from Nuclear Blast with bonus songs.
Jan 2013

THRESHOLD
EXTINCT INSTINCT
When their third album was released in 1997, some three years after 'Psychedelicatessen', not only did the band have a new drummer but also a 'new' singer. Glynn Morgan had replaced Damian Wilson after the debut, only for him to in turn be replaced by Damian Wilson. Damian would only hang around long enough for this album before being replaced by Mac, before coming back yet again after the release of 'Dead Reckoning' in 2007. But, at the time of this recording the future was yet to unfold and although Glynn had done a good job, many fans (me included) were pleased to have Damian back as the frontman.

I think of all their albums, this is the one that takes the longest to make an impact and I have never been able to work out why, possibly most of the stronger songs are to the end? No idea. All I know is that each time I play it I start off by thinking that it is a 3* album but by the end I am convinced that it is a solid 4*, and that happens every time, and I hate to think how many times over the years I have played this. Maybe that's the point. I first heard and reviewed this album when it came out some 15 years ago and I still play it. True, I have just been sent this to review by Nuclear Blast which is why I am playing it so much at the present, but Threshold have never gone out of favour with me from the time I first heard 'Wounded Land'. By the time that was released I knew Karl from Shadowland and Strangers On A Train and Damian from his solo work and Landmarq, yet Threshold blew me away, and still do. The understanding between keyboard player Richard West and his guitar-toting colleagues is second to none, and bassist/backing singer Jon Jeary was an awesome presence during his tenure. Mostly more metal than prog, this is an album of different shades and colours and they all come together in "Forever" which is a ballad, a symphonic masterpiece, and a brooding metallic monster all in under five minutes.

By the time 'Clone' came out the following year Damian was gone, and this album gets somewhat overlooked by many, but if you want metallic prog with stunning vocals, great melodies, and musicianship then this is worthy of discovery.
Feb 2013

TOHPATI ETHNOMISSION
SAVE THE PLANET

I have no idea how many albums I have reviewed over the years, but it is well into the thousands, but I can honestly say I have not come across an album quite like this before. Although I have heard some of Tohpati's previous work with simakDialog, it hadn't prepared me for his debut work as a bandleader in his own right. He has brought together a group of traditional musicians and created a world/jazz/traditional fusion that is as deep in colours and context as it is broad. Indro Hardjodikoro (bass), Diki Suwarjiki (suling - Sundanese flute), Endang Ramdan (Indonesian percussion - kendang, gong, kenong) and Demas Narawangsa (drums, Indonesian percussion - rebana, kempluk) have combined with Tohpati to create something that is breathtaking in its' complexity, yet combine it with simplicity and traditional sounds to truly fuse together different worlds, not just of music and culture.

Tohpati can be as fluid as Holdsworth when he wishes, combining with Diki to provide a double hit of melody that is incredibly tight as they take flight, or can be in straight jazz areas with a band that is highly structured and rehearsed or then again can throw all the rule books out of the window with an amalgam of styles and textures that is all their own. This is progressive fusion in its' truest sense, played by masters of their craft.
Feb 2013

DEVIN TOWNSEND PROJECT
EPICLOUD

Back in 1998 I was sent an album to review called 'Infinity' which was by a Canadian who I knew had previously been with The Wildhearts and a metal act called Strapping Young Lad, but I hadn't actually heard any of his music. As soon as it started blasting out of the speakers I was totally blown away, and since then have tried to get hold of everything he has been involved with (if you have never heard SYL then grab 2005's 'Alien', I can promise that you won't regret it). The mad Canuck has many talents, one of which is that whatever style of music he is playing at the time appears to be the one he is born to play, combined with a very distinctive production style which is the closest thing you'll ever come across to a real wall of sound, whatever fans of Phil Spector may think.

After hearing "Ziltoid The Magnificent" I decided that nothing that Devin would do could surprise me anymore, but even I never expected the album to start with a short a capella number where he has again joins forces with singer Anneke Van Giersbergen (ex-the Gathering). She also takes the lead into the next number, with her pure clear vocals quite at odds with the force that Ryan Van Poederooyen (drums), Mike Young (bass) and Dave Young (guitars) bring to bear on the rest of the song. Devin moves between genres from one song to the next, sometimes all at once (he of course provides vocals, guitars and keyboards). There is an intensity in Devin's music that is often missing from bands who purport to be much heavier and aggressive than he, and the use of Anneke provides yet another dimension that adds light to a very dark place indeed.

This is a stunning album, and amazingly with the bonus demo songs (which don't really sound like demoes to be honest) it is nearly 100 minutes long with nary a filler in sight.
Nov 2012

TRAUMHAUS
DIE ANDERE SEITE
I recently received a copy of Traumhaus's third album, which reminded me that I really ought to get my ass into gear and review their second, which was released in 2008 (I haven't had it since then, honest!). At the time they were a trio of Tobias Hampl (guitars), Alexander Weyland (vocals, keyboards), Hans Jrg Schmitz (drums, percussion) with guest bassist Jordan H. Gazall. The album is sung in German, a somewhat unusual approach given that most German prog bands use English, but it really works. It reminds me at times of one of my favourite German prog acts, Grobschnitt, especially with their use of Mellotron as they have a very Seventies feel to the music. Also, the vocals are very much sung in a register where Alexander can concentrate on emotion, and only goes higher when there is a need instead of trying to sing high all the time.

The guitars have a strident edge, while the keyboards provide the layering, and Hans knows when to pummel the kit or when to just gently tap on a cymbal here and there. The result is a band who clearly understand the need for space within the music and while at times it can be almost overpowering in its' intensity, there are others when it is quite calming and soothing. The layers can be wound into and across each other so that they have strength or unwrapped and loose so that there is room for it all to flow and breathe.

It is an album of grace and passion, one that brings a smile to the face of this proghead every time I play it. If you missed this when it came out back in '08 then you owe it to your ears to get hold of it now.
Nov 2013

TRAUMHAUS
DAS GEHEIMNIS
The third album from Traumhaus shows some line-up changes, as only Tobias Hampl (guitars) and Alexander Weyland (vocals, keyboards) are here from the last one. They now have a new member in bassist Sebastian Klein, along with Stefan Hope who provides additional drum loops alongside guest drummer Jimmy Keegan (Spock's Beard). I have a major issue with these guys, and it has nothing at all to do with the music, but plenty to do with the artwork! Guys, this is what I expect from an

atmospheric Black Metal band, not a progressive outfit that has so many melodies and uplifting sounds (alongside plenty of atmosphere, but not nearly as much as is suggested by the artwork). It is hard to read the information inside the digipak and associated booklet as it is so dark, and I worry that people may see this in a CD rack and pass it by.

Now that would be a real shame as again Traumhaus have managed to produce a quite exceptional album, interesting in all facets as they move through melodies and styles. Jimmy has proved himself to be a real asset here, driving the music with plenty of rolls around the kit when the need arises, or just a gentle cymbal to provide the necessary accents. The music can be symphonic or simple, piano or swathes of keyboards, gentle background guitar or full-on riffs. The more I have heard from these guys, the more I am incredibly impressed by them. Lyrics are all in German, which allows me to treat the vocals as just another instrument, and yet again this really works for them, although Jimmy's drumming has lifted them into a new level.

Look past the cover art, and here is an exciting prog rock band who aren't afraid to throw in a 27 minute long epic, and why not indeed? It doesn't get much better than this, and the more I play it the more I find to enjoy about it.
Nov 2013

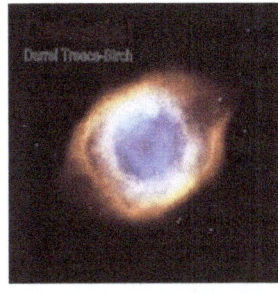

DARREL TREECE-BIRCH
CELESTIAL

Darrel is best-known for being the keyboard player in Ten and Nth Ascension, but here he is dabbling in solo waters and has made his debut album a free download! I came across this quite by accident the other night when messing about on the web, and I am truly glad I did as here we have a wonderful bringing together of Vangelis and 'New Age' Rick Wakeman with JMJ in a wonderful album that is perfect for late night playing. It is music which really brings the listener in and invites them to sit down and stay for the ride as it swirls and moves through melodies. It has just the right amount of edge to maintain interest, and it feels as if we are on a journey through space and time. It is an album that should be played at night, sat on the deck, with just the stars and a good wine in hand.

Like many rock fans I have a strong love for Ten, and have followed them since their debut album, but can honestly say that I never imagined any of those involved with the band to produce anything quite like this. Music as good as this deserves to be heard.
Mar 2013

TWELFTH NIGHT
MMX

Twelfth Night are a band I only discovered after they had broken up, and although I was lucky enough to interview Brian Devoil a few times it was always a source of frustration to me that I hadn't known about them in their heyday – especially as I was living in

 London at the time. I moved to New Zealand from the UK at about the same time that Clive Mitten returned from Australia to the UK, at which time rumours immediately started regarding reforming the band. Rick Battersby couldn't make it, although he gave his blessing and best wishes, and multi-instrumentalist Mark Spencer took his place. The shows were incredibly well-received, and it became obvious that another tour would be worth undertaking so in 2010 the band again hit the road. However, guitarist Andy Revell couldn't commit this time so instead TN drafted into two members of Galahad in guitarist Roy Keyworth and keyboard player Dean Baker. This meant that the band were a six piece for the first time and contained a few multi-instrumentalists, so they were able to perform songs that previously they hadn't been able to give full justice to.

When I played this the first time, I made the deliberate decision not to look at the track listing, so that I could enjoy the double CD as if I was there. As expected, they kick off with "The Ceiling Speaks" – one of my favourite songs, and here much more powerful than I have ever heard before. The new members fitted in seamlessly and it is hard to imagine that this band has been dormant for so long. Their last full album was in 1986, and the last new recording they had completed together was their appearance on the Geoff Mann tribute 'Mannerisms' in 1994. But if you listen to "We Are Sane" it sounds as if they have been playing it every night for years – it is incredibly tight.

The first surprise for me "Fur Helene I" which goes all the way back to their very first demo, 'Skan', in 1979. Clive has lost none of his touch over the years, his bass playing is still something to behold – absolutely incredible. I seriously could rave over every one of the 18 songs on this set, the way that the band are so tight, Andy's vocals, or the backing vocals from the enthusiastic crowd, but instead of doing that, let's just consider track 16. As I said, I didn't look at the track listing so when "The Collector" started my jaw hit the floor. One of Twelfth Night's longest songs at more than 18 minutes, this was never recorded during the actual career of the band although it was performed live. It was finally recorded for the 'Collector's Item' compilation in 1991 – one of Geoff's final sessions. All the power, the angst, the solemnity, the delicacy is here in spades. This set is worth purchasing for this one song alone.

Twelfth Night were sadly absent from the UK prog scene for way too long, and to my mind is the most overlooked band in the genre – if ever a band should have been major stars and weren't then this is them. They have influenced so many artists we all know and love today, and although I love their contemporaries Pallas and Marillion dearly – they are just not in the same league.

So now there is only question left to answer – are we going to see a new studio album? Until (hopefully) then, this will be a constant visitor to my player. Progheads – this is essential!
Oct 2011

The Progressive Underground Vol 4

TWELFTH NIGHT
LIVE AND LET LIVE – DEFINITIVE EDITION
At the end of the Seventies a band formed at Reading University, initially as an instrumental group and then with a female singer. Electra didn't last too long and after reverting to an instrumental outfit the band then recruited long-time friend Geoff Mann as singer and so the die was cast. All these years later I still can't understand why Geoff, Andy Revell (guitar), Clive Mitten (bass, guitar, keyboards), Rick Battersby (keyboards) and Brian Devoil didn't make the breakthrough they so richly deserved. In 'Fact and Fiction' they released one of the finest progressive rock albums of all times, but never managed to pass through the door recently opened by Marillion. By the middle of 1983 Geoff was starting to question his role in the band, and whether he should follow a different calling. Some of his lyrics had been Christian in nature, but few outside the band would have known just how important he felt his religion was to him. And so, he decided that he had to leave (and eventually became a C of E minister before passing away way too young) but in a totally amicable manner.

Everyone agreed they needed to record a live set, but also knew that they could only afford to record enough music for a single vinyl album, so 45 minutes. Certain epics would have to be included, so small instrumentals had to be played to get the timings correct. On 4th and 5th November 1983, they played their last two gigs with Geoff at the Marquee (massively sold out) and that was that. Originally it was to be released on their own private label, which would have had the catalogue number TN007 so hence the title, but during mixing (which took place the week after the gig – no overdubs), they were approached by MFN who then licensed it.

Although the band had paid only for certain songs to be recorded, the guys running the desk were so into what they were hearing that after the second gig they presented the band with a two-track recording of all the encores, and some of these were used when Cyclops reissued the album in 1996, but still it wasn't a complete record of what transpired.

Now in 2012, F2 Music have made available a double CD which uses all available sources to present what fans would have heard if they were there that night. This includes recordings from the gigs, soundchecks, VHS film and a version of "The Collector" that was recorded a month earlier. The whole lot was given to Karl Groom to work on the levels and place everything into the correct running order. So, although you may feel that you have heard this album before I can guarantee it won't have been like this.

If I had to choose a set list from this era of the band it would be pretty close to this. All of the epics are here, and even now hearing the whistle on "Sequences" sends a chill down my back as the band go over the top into no-man's land. It is strange to think that this already existed as an instrumental long before Geoff was involved as to me this is something he really owned. "The Collector" is one of the most visual of all their songs, and to hear it in this environment is just brilliant. It was never recorded in a studio when Geoff was in the band, but thankfully that was rectified when the compilation

"Collector's Item" was worked on in 1991. How about "Human Being" with the lines "If every time we tell a lie a little fairy dies, they must be building death camps in the garden" or the way that the crowd know all the words to every song, even to the introduction to "Fact and Fiction" or the way that "Love Song" is the fitting end. The final song Geoff would sing while a member of the band.

Of course, Twelfth Night didn't end there, Andy Sears was recruited, and more great music ensued before they called it a day. But the band are now active again and are gigging, albeit with a slightly revised line-up, have released some great archive albums, and have worked with Dave Robinson of F2 on some brilliant reissues, of which this is the finest. As well as the great music there is an extended booklet with details of what happened, all of the lyrics, wonderful photos etc. If ever anything was an essential purchase, this is it.

Disc 1
1. The Ceiling Speaks recorded 4 November 1983, first released on the original Live and Let Live vinyl album in 1984
2. Human Being recorded 4 November 1983, previously unreleased
3. The End of the Endless Majority recorded 5 November 1983, remixed from the original 16-track tapes, this remix version previously unreleased
4. We Are Sane recorded 4 November 1983, first released on the original Live and Let Live vinyl album in 1984
5. Deep in the Heartland recorded 5 November 1983 (soundcheck), previously unreleased
6. Fact and Fiction recorded 5 November 1983, first released on the original Live and Let Live vinyl album in 1984
7. The Poet Sniffs a Flower recorded 4 November 1983, first released on the original Live and Let Live vinyl album in 1984
8. The Collector recorded 27 October 1983, previously unreleased

Disc 2
1. Afghan Red recorded 4 November 1983, previously unreleased
2. Sequences recorded 5 November 1983, first released on the original Live and Let Live vinyl album in 1984
3. Creepshow recorded 5 November 1983, first released on the CD reissue of Live and Let Live in 1996, remastered from the original 2-track tapes
4. Art and Illusion recorded 5 November 1983, first released on Geoff Mann's Recorded Delivery CD in 2003, remastered from the original 2-track tapes
5. East of Eden recorded 5 November 1983, first released on the CD reissue of Live and Let Live in 1996, remastered from the original 2-track tapes
6. Aspidentropy recorded 5 November 1983, first released on Geoff Mann's Recorded Delivery CD in 2003, remastered from the original 2-track tapes
7. Love Song recorded 5 November 1983, first released on the CD reissue of Live and Let Live in 1996, remastered from the original 2-track tapes
Oct 2012

TWELFTH NIGHT
LIVE AT THE TARGET - DEFINITIVE EDITION
Shortly after the release of 'The Electra Tape', singer Electra departed which meant that the band had a recently released tape for sale which featured a vocalist but were now an instrumental outfit again so they needed to have some product available that featured this sound. This time they were going to move away from cassettes and instead release a record, and the decision was taken to record two gigs from The Target in Reading on 15th and 16th January 1981. From these tapes they would then select the best songs and that would be the album done and dusted. This 'Definitive Edition' release finds the original four songs on the first CD, with another nine on a second. To me the highlight is "Sequences", one the band's most powerful numbers. I only came to this album sometime in the Nineties having already been familiar with the vocal version and I was amazed at how the guys told an incredible story without the use of lyrics (and 20 minutes long to boot) and how little the arrangement changed when Geoff became involved.

The sound is really good, especially considering that here was a local band with little money doing everything on a shoestring budget, and it certainly doesn't sound as if this recorded more than 30 years ago. There is a vibrancy and power to their music that means that the listener becomes involved in their world. The bonus songs on the second CD add to the overall package, although there is some variance in the recording quality, and one of these is from as early as 1979. I have always loved "The Cunning Man" with its hypnotic keyboard passage, and the version here from 1980 is great. These days this album is often overlooked with people heading straight to the recordings featuring Geoff or Andy Sears, but this is well worth investigating.
Oct 2012

THE TWENTY COMMITTEE
A LIFEBLOOD PSALM
One of the major benefits of being involved with a site such as www.progarchives.com is that I am sometimes approached by a band that have seen some of my reviews, asking whether I would be interested in writing about their latest album. Such is the case with The Twenty Committee who was only formed in 2012 but have already released their debut album. Now, I am a recent member of the Crossover Team so wasn't involved when these guys were submitted, but I can see totally why my colleagues voted to include these guys in that subgenre, as they are mixing pop sensibilities (think Coldplay) with progressive (think Gentle Giant) with rock (think John Miles and City Boy).

The result is something that is complex, simple, yet stacked full of melodies and vocal harmonies that many bands would give their eye teeth for. I am always a sucker for a good key change, and the use of that technique in "How Wonderful" provides an added sense of drama that has already seen twin lead vocals, twin lead guitars, being driven along by piano with the whole band just firing. In many ways it reminds me of the first time I came across Salem Hill, with the same sense of constrained power that gives them a real edge. There are loads of nuances and frills just thrown in that add to the overall sound and feel, and the more I play it the more I like it. Although they don't contain the menace and angst of Discipline, they definitely have something in common with them in the way that a pure piano sound is so important to much of what they do.

In many ways it is quite commercial, and these guys definitely understand late Seventies melodic rock (without ever falling into the sappiness of mass AOR). Whatever song I am listening to is the favourite, and the main question to ask is given that they have delivered this so quickly what have they got left? I know that at the end of the year this is going to be sitting comfortably inside my Top Ten.
Aug 2013

VANGOUGH
MANIKIN PARADE
Like many other progheads, one of the sites that I visit regularly is Sea of Tranquility (as well as MLWZ, Silhobbit etc.). While I may not always agree with everything they write, it gives me an additional insight into the scene, and I know they are not prone to hysterical outbursts. But when they start an interview with the comment "Vangough is probably the best Progressive Metal band you'll discover in 2009" one must wonder on what basis do they make that comment? Well, I am currently listening again to the evidence and in all fairness, I have to agree with them. This is prog metal of the highest quality; it certainly doesn't sound like a debut as this is melody, musicianship and class all rolled into one – the result of which the only thing that the listener can do when it finishes is to hit the play button yet again.

Only one song can remotely be said to be lengthy, and that is not even ten minutes so in terms of the genre what we have here is short and punchy. The vocals are strong and the production clean with the music twisting and melding its' way through gentle piano balladry and harmonies while they can suddenly go into full on metal with the guitar riffing and the band in full flight. I have had this CD for a while and each time I play it I find something new here to enjoy. It is of no surprise to me that it is rated so extremely highly by sites such as Amazon, yet this isn't the latest release from ProgRock Records or InsideOut, but rather is an independent release. Singer and guitarist Clay Withrow has a strong vision that drives the band far beyond what one would normally expect from a debut. They claim they "spit fiery madness by drenching your ears with a purple sunrise of melodic cocaine and a not-so-subtle approach to reading you the story behind today's headlines."

And do you know what? They do all that and more. If you enjoy prog metal, then you need to have this CD. Nuff said
Oct 2009

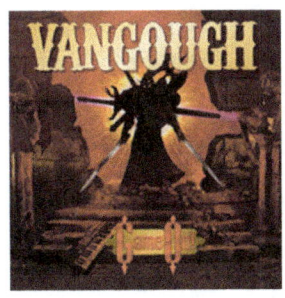

VANGOUGH
GAME ON!
In 2009 Oklahoma based prog metal act Vangough released their debut album 'Manikin Parade' and I like many others was totally blown away by it. There was certainly great acclaim for this album, but the band didn't feel that the time was right yet for the follow-up so instead went off on a complete tangent and recorded an homage to video games. The concept is a simple one, take all of their favourite video games and then record versions of the music that is present. To make it easier for the listener they have stated where every song is from, and a little bit of information about each. Now, there's only one slight problem about this for me – it has been pointed out to me many times (by children, staff, friends etc.) that I am old, and I never got into video games. I have always much preferred listening to music or reading (yep, now I am starting to feel old...) as opposed to video games. All my children are into Angry Birds and various others, but I don't even own an X Box – in fact I have never had a games station of any kind, not even a Nintendo. So, it means that I have never heard any of these songs in their original setting whereas most of the people this album is aimed at certainly will have.

But is that a problem? Not really. It means that I can take this album for what it is – a series of short instrumental pieces that need to stand in their own right, which they definitely do. I have been able to listen to this album without unconsciously making any comparisons – it matters not at all where the material is sourced from, it is whether it works in the current context. In a simplistic form it could be stated that this is a covers album, and every cover version must be valid – if a cover version sounds the same as the original what on earth is the point, and if it is very different (as it should be) then does it work without comparing to the original? "The First Cut Is The Deepest" has been covered many times by many different singers, but many will state that Rod Stewart's is the definitive and not that of the writer, Cat Stevens, or there again should it be PP Arnold? But younger listeners may not realise that it even existed before Sheryl Crow had a hit with it in 2003.

So, does the album work as a series of instrumentals to the listener who has no idea of the originals? The answer must be an emphatic "Yes!" This album is a joy to listen to, with wonderful interplay between the different musicians and some very lyrical guitar that is almost Jadis-like in its clarity and tone. I have really enjoyed listening to this album and can't wait to now hear the follow-up to 'Manikin Parade', 'Kingdom of Ruin'. This is a great band, one that all progheads need to discover.
Oct 2011

VANGOUGH
KINGDOM OF RUIN
The more I hear of Vangough, the more I am incredibly impressed. These guys just refuse to be pigeonholed into any one genre and if anyone deserves to be called 'progressive' in the truest sense it is this quartet from Oklahoma. Some would liken them to Dream

Theater, and while that is true in certain passages, there are times when they can be as gentle as they are bombastic, as simple as they can be complex, always melodic and bringing together a wealth of influences from bands as diverse as Muse, Porcupine Tree and even Coldplay (and the record label even references Pantera – I don't think they are quite that heavy, but I understand where they are coming from). This is Clay Withrow's band in that he writes all the music and lyrics, provides vocals, guitar and keyboards but the rest are far from being bit players. Brandon Lopez has an incredibly deft touch at the back and provides straightforward rock drumming when required to drive the music along but is more than happy to provide fills and nuances that Nick D'Virgilio or Mike Portnoy would recognize. Fully locked in is bassist Jeren Martin while Corey Mast has a wealth of styles and sounds at his fingertips.

For their third album the band decided to provide a simple set of songs in 4/4 time with lyrics about boy meets girl relationships. Okay, so I lied. To tie in with the prog/metal/acoustic/rock music it would only be right and fitting to have grandiose lyrics. What could be better than a concept album telling the story of a Rabbit Kingdom, by a man who is stepping through the veil of two realities. Through the course of the story, he begins to realize his link to this other world and has to come to a difficult decision regarding his role in it. Yep - must be prog after all.

This is a band that sound at home whether it is with acoustic guitars and piano, soaring prog or crunching the riffs. Well produced, and with a story that contains bunnies, surely this will get them even greater attention! Indispensable.
Aug 2012

VANGOUGH
ACOUSTIC SCARS
Even before putting this on the player one knows that it is going to be looking back at previous works as it combines the crow from 'Manikin Parade' with the rabbit from 'Kingdom Of Ruin' but what is somewhat unusual for a prog band is that this is fully acoustic, and also all the proceeds are going to charity (Heartland Rabbit Rescue in Oklahoma where band leader Clay adopted two rabbits himself). This has been put out there as a Vangough release, but only singer/guitarist Clay and bassist Jeren Martin are there from the last album, with Corey Mast (keyboards) and Brandon Lopez (drums) absent but that may well be due to the structure of this album as while there is a percussionist (Kyle Haws) the other musicians are Justus Johnston (violin) and Jose Palacios (cello).

The gentle introduction of "Leaving Bricolage" with the strings combining with the sounds of crows and a storm leads us into "A Song For Crows" and a nod back to the debut. This is a wonderful acoustic combination where Clay sings both emotionally and powerfully yet with control and restraint. It is easily one of the best songs they have ever done, just proving that numbers don't have to be bombastic to be effective. I have read that "Throne of Rusty" contains an acoustic version of a game song, but as with all of the songs on their second album I was too busy playing music to play video games so don't know any of the originals. What I do know is that here they have allowed the violin to take the lead in a wonderfully evocative number that to me feels like the perfect music to put alongside galloping horses. Then we move into "The Rabbit Chronicles" which is of course linked to the last album, where yet again Clay allows the strings to take centre stage. I particularly like the way that this one switches emphasis, and moves around. The final "The Road To Blighttown" brings back the crows and the storm as everything winds down.

This is only an EP but shows just how much the band have expanded their musical outlook in a very short period of time and I look forward to the next album with interest.
Feb 2013

VANGOUGH
BETWEEN THE MADNESS
Although it isn't that unusual for me to review an album more than once, normally years pass between the two. Yet here I am totally rewriting a review that I only completed yesterday. When I listened to the CD I was distracted by the mix, which I believed not to be correct, and said so in the review. But what I wasn't aware of was that the band also felt that the mix wasn't as good as it could have been, so pulled the complete run of CDs, remixed it, and then put new CDs in the digipaks. It was just those that had been sent out as promo's that weren't replaced. Clay then provided me with the new mix as a download and I have been playing it all day (when not in meetings – why does the work I get paid for get in the way of the work I want to do?). What I am now listening to is far more balanced, which has allowed me to get past my initial views and instead listen to the album as I should have in the first place.

Now, I have been a fan of Clay Withrow's music since I first heard 'Manikin Parade', and I have been lucky enough to hear everything they have released since, so when I became aware that a fourth full-length album was coming out, I was suitably excited. Jeren Martin was again working with Clay on bass, while they had a new drummer in Kyle Haws plus a few guests on additional guitar and strings (the additional guitarist, Jay Gleason, plays with Jeren in a death metal band!), Clay of course provides everything else. Here is an album that has seen the band grow, both in musical style and in stature. The harmony vocals are bang on, and the restrained use of falsetto here and there provides an additional edge, much as Roger Taylor used to do with Queen. There is music that rocks and belts along, or music that is way gentler and more refined, with a control that is breathtaking. Clay provides some breathtaking solos and runs, or crunching riffs, or acoustic, whatever is right for the song itself while Jeren seems to instinctively know what is required to lift the piece itself, either providing the bedrock, or additional back up melodies, or even not playing at all and allowing the space created to be used by others. Although it will be viewed by many as progressive metal, there are passages and even complete songs that are far more crossover in aspect than one would expect from the genre, and the result is something that has incredible depth and breadth.

This is music that refuses to be pigeonholed, with the band at times firing as a metallic monster (with Clay doing some wonderful James Hetfield style vocals) while at others it is way more restrained and thoughtful. There is a wonderfully delicate string section in "Separation" which really accents the guitar on either side, while the title track demonstrates a very different side of the band with Clay on acoustic guitar, supported by some wonderful violin and cello. From that we go into "Vaudeville Nation" which is as hard hitting a prog metal monster as one would wish, with some great interplay.

I gave their debut 5 *'s, and since then each release has had 4 (not too shabby), but I am pleased to say that this is back to top marks. It is easily the best they have done, and all power to the guys for pulling the original release and making this available.
Nov 2013

VOTUM
TIME MUST HAVE A STOP
I have been lucky to hear many Polish prog bands over the years, and this 2008 debut from Votum has brought another into my area of knowledge. Now, Poland isn't a country that many Western progheads would necessarily think of as being a hotbed, but over the years there have been some great bands (think SBB, Collage, Satelite to name just a few) and of course Riverside has made a huge impression on everyone. With this release, Votum deserve very much to be spoken about in the same sentence.
When one looks at the CD cover the impression is one of darkness and menace and isn't hard to imagine that the music inside is Black Metal, but instead we have one of the most atmospheric and interesting debuts from recent years that I have heard.

Yes, when they decide that the time is right, they can punch out the heavy metal riffs and give us some symphonic passages that wouldn't sound out of place with Therion or Nightwish, but often it is the 'menacing threat' that takes this forward. It is simply one of the most atmospheric albums I have heard, and while there are times when it sounds more like Negură Bunget than Pink Floyd or Porcupine Tree, it is also true that all these bands have obviously had an influence. The vocals are in English, and for the most part are melodic without too much of an accent.

This isn't going to be for everyone, as it straddles so many genres and sub-genres, but I urge anyone interested in hearing great rock music, whatever label people saddle it with, to search it out.
Jan 2012

VOTUM
HARVEST MOON
When I reviewed Votum's 2008 debut I managed to include references to bands as diverse as Therion, Nightwish, Negură Bunget, Pink Floyd and Porcupine Tree, as well as of course mentioning Riverside as these guys are also Polish. Back then I said that however you wanted to describe them, it was essential you search them out. A few years down the line and they are back with their third album, and with Millenium and Riverside also releasing superb works in recent months it appears that 2013 is going to be a bumper year for aficionados of the Polish prog scene. Somehow the band have managed to become even more diverse yet at the same time have brought in control and a restrained power that makes this a wonderfully rich album.

There are times when they bring in the power of Opeth, but move to RPWL and folk influences without even batting an eye. This is music that pointedly refuses to stick in any particular subgenre and is happy to meander all over the place wherever it needs to be. It is going to be appreciated by those who want their prog to have bite, and there is a section in "Cobwebs" where they are a straight out metal band, nothing more or less. But, for the most part it is the threat of darkness as opposed to a straight metallic attack that gives this the edge. Sure, they can be Dream Theater when they want to be, or they can be full on emotional Anathema, with harmony vocals and gentleness and picked guitars. Or not.

If you have yet to come across Votum then you need to increase your musical education as this is a great piece of work.
May 2013

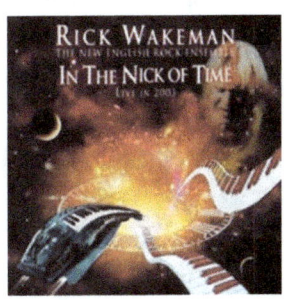
RICK WAKEMAN
IN THE NICK OF TIME
In 2003 Rick released a new album, 'Out There', with The New English Rock Ensemble. The line-up was his touring band of the time, so he was joined by drummer Tony Fernandez, bassist Lee Pomeroy, guitarist Ant Glynne and singer Damian Wilson. Now I have a few of Rick's albums (okay, most of them), and when I heard it I was just blown away and I rated it as one of my albums of the year. So, I was extremely eager to catch him on the tour to promote the album and it was a major surprise to everyone (including Rick) when Damian dropped out of the tour just a couple of days before it was due to start. So, the choice was to either cancel the tour or to find someone at extremely short notice who was familiar with at least some of the material. Step forward one Ashley Holt who of course had sung on both 'Journey' and 'King Arthur' among others. He has a very different vocal style to Damian, and of course knew none of the new album either, so there had to be a radical shift in the setlist (hence the album title).

So, everything was in place for this to be a disaster, but instead the show I saw was an absolute triumph with all the audience understandably annoyed that Damian wasn't there, but very pleased indeed that Ashley was the person who had stepped into the breach. The DVD was released in 2004, but for some strange reason it took until 2012 for this CD to be made available but at least it is here now. My biggest issue with it is that it is way too short at just over an hour, and while there are some songs on the CD that are not on the DVD it is also true the other way around so why not make it a longer album and more like the setlist?

But this is worth getting just for the version of "Out There" alone where Ashley doesn't attempt to hit Damian's notes but instead uses control and passion to make it his own while the rest of the band simply rock. Ant is a revelation here, as while he is content to provide the muscular support required by Rick, he is not adverse to moving to the fore when the time is right. And any album that contains versions of "Catherine Parr" and "Wurm" is going to sit well with progheads isn't it? Absolutely brilliant.
Jun 2013

ROGER WATERS
IN THE FLESH
What a bargain this was. Less than £5 equivalent for a triple CD and DVD set. Talk about value for money. Given the choice of seeing a Water-less Floyd or Waters himself I would probably plump for the latter, although in truth neither have managed to produce a great studio album without the other, but for me this was the man behind Floyd – the driving force. Although there are some songs from his solo albums (including one brand new), it is the Floyd numbers that many will know and love, and it is hard to pick fault with the track listing. There may only be one truly historic number here, but when it is a delicate and psychedelic version of "Set The Controls" it more than does the job. There are even some songs here from 'Animals', surely these days one of the most overlooked of the later period Floyd as everyone seems to talk about 'Dark Side', 'Wish' or 'The Wall' and seemingly forgetting this. Of course, they are well represented as well – it would be unforgivable if he had not performed "Shine On", "Time" or "Money".

He isn't a one man band, and it is interesting to note that Snowy White is still with him after all these years along with two more survivors from the Sixties in Andy Fairweather Low and PP Arnold. The DVD contains all the songs, plus a behind the scenes documentary, biographies, lyrics and so much more. If you can get this for anything like the price I paid for it then this is essential!
Sep 2007

DAMIAN WILSON
I THOUGHT THE WORLD WAS LISTENING 1997 – 2011
This double CD digipak is Damian's first compilation, with 31 re-mastered, re-recorded or previously unheard songs. I have long been a fan of Damian's, whether it be with

Landmarq, Threshold, Star One, Ayeron or Rick Wakeman (that particular album, 'Out There', is one of the finest prog albums ever in my humble opinion). The first time I met him in person was when I was queued outside the Marquee waiting to see Jadis and Shadowland on the 'Lurve Ambassadors' tour – and he was excitedly going up and down the line talking to everyone. That night he was a last-minute replacement for the extremely ill Geoff Mann, and he captivated everyone with his melodies and vocals. He has long been widely regarded as one of the finest singers to come from these shores, and I still feel that Iron Maiden would have been better choosing him instead of Blaze after Bruce's departure (I would love to hear the tapes of that audition if they exist), as he is much more of a singer than a shouter. He hits all the notes with a grace and elegance, a real performer as well as a showman which has enabled him to take a lead role in the UK National Tour of Les Mis as well as being an in-demand guest vocalist with different bands.

This album is extremely diverse, lots of acoustic and gentle stuff but also some that is much more in your face such as "Please Don't Leave Me 'Till I Leave You" which is a fun party song in direct contrast to the one that follows, "Never Close The Door" which is a sad ethereal joy to listen to with gentle guitars and violin. Whenever I think of Damian as a solo artist, the song that springs to mind is "She's Like A Fable" which is song 13 on CD1. It may be only just over three minutes long, but it belongs to the time of Cat Stevens in his prime, and in a better world would be a song known by all. Damian is a musician who has worked hard at his craft, and this compilation shows a very different side to the same man who came up with the lyrics and melody to the crushing and awe-inspiring "Sanity's End" (and if you don't know this classic from Threshold's debut 'Wounded Land' then you need to rectify that immediately if not sooner).

This compilation is a must for every lover of good music, and the digipak release and artwork does justice to what is contained within.
Dec 2011

STEVEN WILSON
THE RAVEN THAT REFUSED TO SING
If I go through my music collection there are numerous albums by Porcupine Tree, No-Man (even a compilation with a song by No Man Is An Island Except The Isle of Man), Blackfield etc., so it can be said with some confidence that I am no stranger to the music of Steven Wilson, and it could even be argued that I am a fan. I also love many of the albums he has been involved with remastering, so why do I feel so strangely indifferent to this? There is no doubt at all that there are some fine moments on here, and it opens with some superb bass from Nick Beggs (who I like to think of as ex-Iona as opposed to ex-Kajagoogoo), yet for all its' complexity and cleverness it somehow leaves me strangely cold.

As I write this it is the number one album of the year to date according to PA, yet I would much rather play number 2 (Big Big Train), 4 (Comedy of Errors) or 5 (Riverside), but why? I have puzzled over this and the only conclusion I can come to is that for some reason this feels false. It is as if Steven is writing a prog album because he can and knows all the buttons to press to ensure that it is raved over by fans and critics alike. There are wonderful harmonies, great swathes of keyboards, flute and Mellotron, all being brought together to produce some wonderfully complex yet flowing prog but to my ears it all sounds somewhat contrived. Having read numerous reviews I have found it interesting to see that I am not the only who feels this way, although it is obvious that we are very much in the minority.

What really irks me is that although I haven't enjoyed the album nearly as much as I wanted to, I can't bring myself to award it any less than 4 stars as it is such a clever piece of work. If only it contained a prog heart and soul, it could have been so much better; although I am fully aware that most progheads will welcome this with open arms I'm just not one of them.
May 2013

WINTER CRESCENT
BATTLE OF EGOS

Winter Crescent were formed in 2000 by guitarist Alexis Ktistakis, in Heraklion Crete, Greece, but it wasn't until 2008 that the band line-up became stable and they released this their debut EP in May 2009. Apparently it gained a lot of press at the time (Greek Metal Hammer named it Pick of the Month in September 2009) but it has only just come to my attention. It never ceases to amaze me at just how much good music is out there that we rarely get to read about, and here is another good example. Imagine Progressive Metal a la Fates Warning that also contains some Savatage influences then you may just get close to the mark. The feeling here is of a very strong unit, which is tight and heavy when they need to be but are also very aware of the need for light within the shade. There is a polish, an added gloss that provides a shine without taking away from any of the powerful riffs.

Complex twin lead breaks with an almost mathcore intensity lead into riffs that are tight and solid. It is hard to realise that this is a debut self-released EP (35 minutes with 7 songs), and not something from a major label as this shouts class from start to end. Apparently the guys have recently been in the studio working on their first full-length album but until that is ready I urge you to discover this further, as this really hits the mark.
May 2013

WOLFSPRING
WHO'S GONNA SAVE THE WORLD?
This is the second album from the side-project of Nemo singer/guitarist JP Louveton, where he is joined by Julian Clemens (vocals – importantly, unlike Nemo, the vocals are here provided in clear unaccented English), Guillaum Fontaine (keyboards, Irish fife), Max Moro-Sibilot on bass and Ludo Moro-Sibilot on drums. Now, I am a huge Nemo fan, but it is important to put any ideas of comparisons to one side as this is a very different offering altogether. They are often referred to as being progressive metal, and I understand why that would be the case, but I am not sure that I would always agree with that term as they move between 'normal' prog (if there is such a thing) in the vein of Porcupine Tree into something much heavier altogether which is more metallic than the prog metal tag would tend to indicate. JP likens the band to Sabbath, and if we are talking about the later post-Dio period of that band then I can see where he is coming from.

The production is superb, and while everyone has a key role in this band, particularly Julian, it is the guitar that really stands out. There are some fine solos, and at other times some crunching riffs, but this is JP's music. Unusually for a prog band, they close with a Sabbath cover, "Wheels of Confusion" which is from 'Vol.4'. It has been cleaned up and has a psychedelic edge which is fun, so although it doesn't contain the naivety of the original it is still extremely enjoyable. Makes a change from all the 'normal' Sabbath covers as well.

All in all, just because you love Nemo don't think that this is essential: this is a totally different band playing a different kind of music altogether. But if you want to hear some classic sounding riffs that feel that they have been brought straight from the Seventies through modern recording and production techniques into the present day then this is for you.
Feb 2013

XANADU
THE LAST SUNRISE
There are many great progressive bands coming out of Poland these days, and Xanadu can be added to that long list. The band came together in 2008 with the idea of performing ambitious music with a hint of melancholy – so I think it is safe to say they have achieved their aims with this their debut release (there was a promo album 'Violent Dream' released in 2010) which came out in 2011 on ProgRock Records. It is obvious that there are going to be comparisons with Riverside due to the fact that they are from the same country, but here the comparison is justified as musically there are quite a few similarities. This is a driving rock band and Hubert Murawski is key to the overall success of this album as here is a band that remembers how to put 'rock' back into the genre. Lyrics are in English, with not too much accent,

and the feeling here is of a band reaching for the heights and managing to attain them.

This is a prog album that demands attention of fans of Riverside, Votum and the like as they bring the power of neo-prog into an arena that verges on the metallic. Great stuff!
Aug 2012

YAGULL
FILMS

Yagull is an acoustic project that has been put together by Sasha Markovic (acoustic and electric guitar) together with Lori Reddy (flute), Sonia Choi (cello), Eylon Tushiner (sax) and Josh Margolis (drums). Now, I was already familiar with Yagull as they have a song on the Moonjune compilation that is available through Bandcamp, a wonderful version of "White Room" so when I was looking at the CD I checked out the song at #10 which took me completely by surprise.

Back when I was 11 or 12, I was around a friend's house, and we went into the den to have a look at his brother's records. Neither of had heard of any of the names, bands like Deep Purple, Atomic Rooster, Yes, Edgar Winters, Pretty Things etc. Of course, back then the covers and artwork were things of beauty and based on nothing else apart from what they looked like we chose two to play. The first was 'Free For All' by Ted Nugent, and the second was 'Sabbath Bloody Sabbath'. We were so enamoured with the latter that it was hard to get the title song off the player, and we even 'borrowed' the album to play the song in our music class at school. It is no exaggeration then to say that this one song had a huge impact on my musical enlightenment (and we then played every album his brother owned to expand our knowledge, much to his annoyance).

So, track 10, "Sabbath Bloody Sabbath". I was very good when I played the album first time in that I didn't go straight to it but instead played it all the way through but coming back to it time and again, I have to say that for me it is the standout song, probably due to my own relationship to the original. The first thought I had when playing it was "I never realised that it was so beautiful". Ozzy's vocals have been replaced by delicate acoustic guitars as have the rest of the band – this is a multi-tracked solo piece by Sasha that has to be heard to be believed. The original has been deconstructed but it is still there, instantly recognizable to the fan, but transformed into something quite different.

'Films' is a great title for this album, as it is very cinematic in feel and if I was to compare it to anything else it would have to be with the wonderful Karda Estra although the approach here is quite different and, in many ways, even more laid-back. The label describes this album as "next generation post-rock chamber music" and while I am not quite sure where they are going with that, if they mean that it is an acoustic album of depth and great beauty then they are bang on.
Feb 2013

ZEN ROCK AND ROLL
UNDONE

This 2011 release was the third from one man band Jonathan Saunders, who had previously been in the Led Zeppelin tribute band Dazed and Confuzed, who played a lot in Memphis and around the Southeast and even played at an outdoor festival in Winnipeg, Canada in 2003 along with Peter Frampton, Paul Rodgers and Joan Jett. He decided that he would never find anyone who wanted to play the music that he wanted to create, so released his debut as a one-man project in 2002, 'End of an Age', following it with 'The Birthright Circle' two years later. He has attempted to recreate the lighter forms of symphonic prog, bringing together Genesis and Yes, but from 1978 through the early Eighties as opposed to the soaring prog epics of the early Seventies. Strangely, although I am referencing two British bands, this does have a very American feel about it, with an almost power pop AOR sensibility coming in as well.

The result is an album that is interesting while being played, but not strong enough in terms of songs or vocal performance to really enthrall the listener and make them want to seek it out. But as I said it is pleasant enough but feels much more of being a starter as opposed to the main course. That being said, this isn't an album to be dismissed out of hand and does contain some nice passages.
Sep 2013

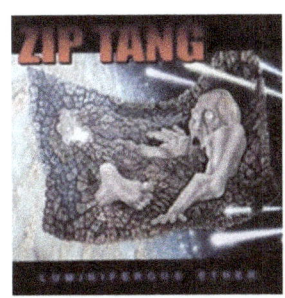

ZIP TANG
LUMINIFEROUS ETHER

Before even listening to the debut album from Zip Tang, which was released in 2007, I was mighty impressed. The artwork on the digipak is superb, and when one realises that this is a self-released album then there is the knowledge that someone has put a lot of effort into it. That feeling only intensifies when listening to what is on offer. The four-man line-up have all been playing music in bands for quite some time, and have come together with a love of wanting to provide something new and that they definitely do here. There are times when they are blasting out in good hard rock fashion, but even that is tempered by keyboards or sax, or they are bringing in healthy elements of Zappa and taking that on a journey with Proto-Kaw. One thing I found fascinating is their closing song, a cover of "Tarkus" that is treated both reverentially and deconstructed into a Zip Tang number.

This is powerful stuff, music that is truly progressive as it refuses to be pigeonholed into any particular area and is always driving forward. The proghead can only listen to this with a smile on their face as it hits so many bases. It is not often that prog music really defies categorisation or comparison but with this release these guys have done it. Intense and complex, at times simple and spacious, this is progressive music that demands to be heard.
Oct 2009

ZIP TANG
PANK
Pank is Zip Tang's second album, released in 2008 (so hopefully that should mean that there will be another one soon!). As with the debut, again we have a digipak with great artwork, and the same four guys kicking hard into music in a style that is their own. Yes, it is possible to bring in comparisons (this time possibly some elements of Mr. So & So?), but this is a world of their own creation where jazz, prog rock, hard rock and art rock collide. "It's In My Head" has moments of incredible intensity that is offset by far quieter passages, so that the listener is drawn in – not wanting to miss anything. I find it incredible that the band have yet to be signed to a fairly major label as there is no doubting their skills or abilities – what they need is to somehow get their name in front of more people because I can guarantee that if you are a proghead in the truest sense of the word, not someone who wants rehashed neo-prog time and again or prog metal, then you need to hear music that while very much of the current time also has its' feet truly set in the ideals of the golden age. Rick Wolfe, Perry Merritt, Fred Faller and Marcus Padgett have a lot to answer for. The main case against them is that they have released some of the most inspiring and true progressive music that one is likely to come across. All you have to do now is go out and discover it. Wonderful stuff.
Oct 2009

ZLYE KUKLY
STRANGE TOMORROW
One of the great things about living in such a small world is that it possible to uncover some great gems at times. Here we have an album by a Russian group, who reside in Israel, signed to an Austrian label, which was sent to me in NZ by a Polish friend to review! This was the band's first record label release, although all of these tracks (apart from two) were available on two earlier albums, taken from the albums 'Чужой небесный город' ('The Strange Heavenly City'), 2004 and 'На закате времен' ('At The End Of Days'), 2006. Although this is described as a band album, the impression is that of Fred Adra being joined by guest musicians as the need requires, whether that be violin, mandolin, additional acoustic guitar etc. as he provides guitar, bass, keyboards, vocals, percussion etc. I guess one of the questions is how to describe what I am listening to. I know I like it, am often captivated by its' honest beauty, but what genre is it? It isn't exactly folk, and certainly isn't heavy, but there are elements of the more ambient Black Metal bands, combined with the more whimsical moments of bands such as Negură Bunget. It is music that defies definition, music that is immediate and enjoyable but has huge depths. Some of that is due to the music, but also Fred sings in Russian which to me adds greatly to proceedings. Over the years I have been lucky enough to hear plenty of Eastern Europe music, particularly Hungarian, and is it very reminiscent of some of the releases from the Stereo Periferic label. It is the combination of so many elements – both cultural and musical - that makes this album such a joy.
Jan 2012

Various Artists

STABBING A DEAD HORSE EP

Knifeworld, The Fierce And The Dead and Trojan Horse are touring together at the end of October/beginning of November in the UK and to celebrate they have put together this EP which is available as a *free* download. They may all be on the cutting edge of the UK prog scene but these guys are all very different indeed. Knifeworld is the only band that I had previously come across as they contain guitarist Kavus Torabi (Cardiacs). It is great to see that they are keeping the spirit of pronk alive as they mix Chumbawamba into their sound and create something that refuses to conform to recognised norms yet is incredibly accessible and just great fun, albeit in a rather strange way. The Fierce and the Dead started off as a studio project by Matt Stevens but it has taken on a life of it's own and their instrumental "666...6" with fuzzed instruments and repeated riffs is simple yet clever and just cries out for the shaking loose of dandruff. Trojan Horse are quite different, with angular music that one feels will cut the listener, as if XTC are being taken to a new level as they bring in elements of PEH.

So, three very different bands, yet all with a lot to offer – a real breath of fresh air for the prog scene and given the price what are you waiting for? Download the EP, see them in concert and give them your support.
Oct 2012

The Progressive Underground Vol 4

PROGRESSIVE ROCK CHRISTMAS

No prizes for guessing what this album is about – yes, it's a Polish progressive rock compilation which brings together songs from many of Poland's top bands. The vast majority are sung in Polish, and musically don't sound very Christmassy but I can see 'Betlejem' in two of the song titles and 'Jezusowi', 'Jezu' and 'Jezuniu' in others so I am guessing that lyrically they must be. One of my favourite Polish bands of recent years is Millenium and they open the album, with an English language version of "Silent Night". To be honest I have always felt that this is one of the most boring carols imaginable yet somehow the guys have given it new life and have turned it into a nice little prog rocker. This album is very much a sampler for the groups involved, and the digipak contains a photo of each band along with line-up and a picture of all of their albums. It is quite a diverse mix, with Loonypark probably being the most interesting after Millenium with strong guitar lines and great vocals from Sabina Godlua-Zajac. Lynx Music continue to release good music, and the label is certainly worth checking, but the chances of progheads being allowed to put this on the family CD deck instead of 'Now Christmas' is probably quite remote..
Dec 2012

MOONJUNE 2001 – 2012

Leonardo Pavkovic, the man behind Moonjune Records, has decided that he is going to make all of the catalogue available digitally, and to assist in the promotion of this event he has put together a 60 song 7 hour long compilation which is available until 12th December, 2012, for just $1 US. Yep, you read that right, just one solitary buck. Okay, if you live in NZ like me then it is more than $1 NZD, but if you live in the UK it is well under 1 GBP – that in itself should be enough to get you all interested. I mean, if there was just one song you enjoyed out of all of this then it would still be a bargain, right? Having been through everything on the compilation I am amazed at just how diverse the catalogue has become, and if you even remotely like jazz then there is going to be something here for you, whether it is fusion or supreme guitar, ethnic jazz, free jazz, or even an astounding acoustic version of "White Room" by Yagull that has to be heard to be believed. D.F.A blow the mind, as does the one and only Allan Holdsworth while both Soft Machine and Soft Machine Legacy are simply stunning. And as for Boris Salvodelli's take on "Crosstown Traffic", well Zappa would be proud. Actually, he would enjoy this album immensely, and I think he would have been particularly taken by Copernicus who is a cross between Beefheart, Waits and Olivier. His spoken word command over the music is awesome – it is an acquired taste to be sure, but it is strangely compelling, and the compilation finishes with six songs of his taken from different albums. Then the master Elton Dean is here as well, and Hugh Hopper, and Phil Miller, and... well, you get the idea.

This has to be the best value for money set I have ever seen. This is quality music being

played by musicians who have a real love for the genre and a great deal to offer. By getting this, you are supporting someone who is doing what he is doing not for money, but to help these artists have their music heard.
Dec 2012

MR. MOONJUNE PRESENTS VOL. 1

Over the years I have met many people within the music industry who do what they do because they love music. I have to confess and say that I don't know any multi-millionaires, but I do know plenty of musicians who given up a great deal to follow their own musical path. Many of these can only tour in their work holidays as they have to have another job to pay the bills, or just scrape through – the one reward being that their music will be appreciated by a select few. But out of all of these, it is rare indeed to come across someone who isn't a musician who feels the same way. Step forward Leonard Pavkovic, who as well as running Moonjune has two other businesses that actually pay the bills. He loves jazz and jazz forms, and one of his regrets is that he can't release everything that he wants to so he has come up with a novel idea. Why not put together a series of compilations of albums that he wished that he had released when he was offered them?

As he says himself, "All the featured music represents in some way the philosophy of MoonJune Records - progressive music exploring the boundaries of jazz, rock, avant, ethno, and the unknown - and anything in between. In the world we live in, with its oversaturated music market, rapidly disappearing record stores, and a record business that ignores real musicianship, and with fewer and fewer outlets where quality progressive music can be exposed, it's becoming more and more difficult for artists to be noticed unless they have a well-known legacy or they tour frequently and intensively, which many are unable to do. This compilation (the first of many) is my tribute to these musicians and contribution to their cause. I hope that all who download and listen to this remarkable music can appreciate the artistry of these musicians and their determination to keep great music alive. Note that the tunes chosen for this compilation do not necessarily represent the best tracks from the featured CDs; they're purely my personal choice."

So, if you go to Bandcamp to investigate this and click on each track in turn you will discover that each comes with complete information about the artist and the album from which the tune was selected, and a direct link to the artists' sites where those albums can be purchased. This latter is the most important. Leonardo isn't making any money out of this at all – he has spent the time, effort and money in attempting to publicize artists that he feels deserve a reward for their efforts, with the full knowledge that someone may then purchase a CD from an artist as opposed a Moonjune release. All he is asking for is for the listener to spend time doing just that, then reading more about the artists that interest them and making an effort to buy one or two CDs to support them. Some of these names will be well-known (Jan Akkerman, Elton Dean, Allan Holdsworth, Chad Wackerman) while others are from left-field (Swedish act Nude Fox Ensemble for example). Personally I ought to mention John Sund Special Venture from Denmark where the guitar and glockenspiel is in total harmony while the bass and drums provide the perfect backing.

How many times do you have the opportunity to discover 25 artists with a playing time of three hours for so little? All he is asking is a donation of between $1 and $5 USD to cover costs, and in return you will have at your fingertips some incredible music.
Feb 2013

SKIN & BUTTER
One day on the PA Crossover Team Forum I discovered that one of my colleagues used to be in a band called Kel Loch & Gold. Being my normal unassuming self I asked for a copy of the album, but was told by Scott that he didn't have any left but would I be interested in a compilation instead? I know that this is listed as being by various artists, but of the 13 songs six are credited to Kel Loch & Gold and either Scott (Gold) or Andy (Kel Loch) played on all the rest, while 2 of the 13 are credited to Eddie Goicura who also appeared on the sole Kel Loch & Gold album, 1990's 'Men In Black'. So, there may be a few different names for the bands, but the two guys responsible for O-Zone, a MIDI controlled recording studio and production facility (which is why this is subtitled 'an O-zone assortment') had their hands in everything.

This 1992 album doesn't really belong in that decade, but at the beginning of the one previous, and includes a multitude of styles from IQ to Talking Heads and pretty much everything in-between. When they want to get a little heavier then do, or if they want a little funk in it comes, but to me this is all about serious music that doesn't take itself too seriously. I have never been a fan of programmed drums, but that aside this is an album that I found myself enjoying a great deal. But, it does have to be said that there is one song that is head and shoulders above the rest, one song that more than any other has its' birth in the world of Zappa. That song is of course "Fat Nick". Apparently an ape escaped a secret scientific experiment where he was being trained as a soldier, and recruited by the underground as a hitman. As it says "do not attempt to apprehend him for he is armed, dangerous, and has fleas". This sums the album up for me as it is infectious, is fully tongue in cheek, and is just great fun. I defy anyone not to sing along with this the very first time they hear it.
Nov 2013

Book Reviews

THE AUTOBIOGRAPHY
BILL BRUFORD
Anyone who is wishing to get a blow-by-blow account, in chronological order, of one of the UK's most respected drummers (whatever the genre) needs to find another tome as this isn't it. Bill Bruford decided that as of 1st January 2009 he was going to retire from the world of music, and part of that involved writing what is termed 'The Autobiography', but to be honest should more accurately be called memoirs. Yes, there are chunks of the book that are in some sort of timely order, but for the most part Bill moves backwards and forwards through his career: at times annoyingly skating over what to the outsider appears to be an important part of his career, while at other times we get the fullest detail. The end result is less of a book, and more of a one-sided conversation as the book almost seems to follow his train of thought as opposed to being printed words on a page.

In some ways I am reminded of Keith Emerson's 'Pictures of an Exhibitionist' in that we don't get the full picture, but in that instance, it was because the book basically finished with the release of 'Love Beach'. Here we have someone who has had an incredibly varied career working with three of the most important groups from the progressive rock movement and also driving forward the music of jazz and also the role of the drummer. Here is a person who was never content to conform to society's view of a drummer of someone keeping 4/4 time at the back and staying quiet, but rather a very intelligent individual plagued by self-doubt and a lack of confidence in his own ability. I enjoyed the book immensely and it has led me to re-evaluate especially his music with Crimson, as

well as seeking out some of his releases of which I was not aware. This may be too disjointed for everyone, but once you get used to the style it is absolutely enthralling.
Dec 2009

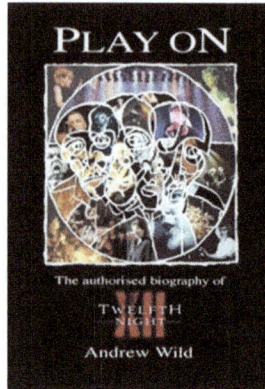

PLAY ON
ANDREW WILD
Everyone has some musical regrets, whether it is only discovering a band post their demise or never taking the opportunity to see someone in concert. I have many, from not seeing Thin Lizzy, Yes, Gentle Giant, King Crimson or Pink Floyd in their prime, but the one that rankles most is Twelfth Night. In 1985 I was living in London and attending many gigs, but I hadn't even heard about this group. Move forward some years and I was introduced to their music and couldn't believe that the group had existed and I knew nothing about them. I couldn't make a combined gig of Galahad and Geoff Mann but that was okay as I expected to see Geoff support Shadowland and Jadis. Sadly Geoff was too ill for that gig, his place being taken by Damian Wilson. After Geoff sadly passed away the band reformed to record "Piccadilly Square" for his tribute album, but no gigs were forthcoming. Clive was living in Australia; Andy Sears was in Spain and although I was in regular contact with Brian Devoil, interviewing him a couple of times, I really thought that was the end. But of course, just as I moved to NZ, Clive moved back to the UK and a reunion was on the cards, and although Rick was unable to rejoin the rest of the band went out and played some shows! This year Andy Revell has left, and the band have brought in Roy and Dean from some outfit called Galahad and increased to a six-piece line-up and are again going to be playing some gigs. I still haven't seen them as I am on the other side of the world! C'est la vie.

Anyway, while I am still missing out on seeing the band live, I and other fans have been spoiled with all of the reissues and live concerts that have been made available on CD. The 'Live In London' set has been released on DVD and there are going to be more shows and treats available soon. One of the real joys that has come our way is this book by Andrew Wild, which has to be one of the most complete and researched books about a band I have ever had the pleasure to read.

Andrew has interviewed everybody who ever had anything at all to do with the band and has been allowed unlimited access so that what we have here is an exhaustive and extensive tome that will satiate all lovers of the band. But it is much more than just a book about a criminally overlooked act, it is about how a group that was recording incredible music and playing to sell out crowds never got the rewards they deserved. If you turn the book over to read the rear cover it starts with "This is a cautionary tale: how a combination of industry pressure, bad timing, bad luck and bad decisions can negate almost 10 years of musical innovation, progress and sheer hard work". Remember, to many people this was ***the*** prog band that was going to succeed, and to my ears 'Fact and Fiction' is still one of the greatest albums ever released of any genre. But, only a lucky few have ever come across it – yet if you enjoy the genre your collection cannot be called complete without it.

The book contains details of every song ever written, every recording and every gig. It tells how the band started as a duo and what events led to their demise and in turn how they got back together. There is the tragedy of Geoff's death, and the delights and celebrations of the Reading Festival and getting the deal with Virgin. Simply put, it is one of the finest musical biographies that I have ever had the pleasure to read. But there's more!!! Along with the book there is a DVD which contains just about everything a fan could wish for! There are clips of archive performances on video, unreleased music, a complete set of all of their newsletters as PDF's, examples of merchandise, guitar tabs, interviews – it seems to go on forever. Without the DVD, I love this, but with the DVD this becomes totally indispensable to the fan. Incredible.
Mar 2010

DENNIS REA
LIVE AT THE FORBIDDEN CITY
I only became aware of Dennis earlier this year when Leo from MoonJune sent me some of his albums to review, two of which were with the band Moraine and one was a solo piece titled 'Views From Chiceng Precipice'. I really enjoyed all I heard, but was especially taken with his solo album which to me was an incredible piece of work which to my Western untrained ear seemed extremely authentic. It was only later I discovered that he had spent some considerable time in China, and in fact had written a book about his experiences. I mentioned to Dennis that I was intrigued by this and he kindly offered to send me a copy. So, I sat down not really sure what I was going to read and by the end I was still at a loss, but this time it was how on earth was I going to be able to convince others that this is an essential purchase and that anyone interested in China, travel or music, should read it?

I am a bit of a musical omnivore when it comes to reading, and so while I tend to buy books that concern progressive rock or metal, I will in fact read anything about musicians, especially if it has been written by the musicians themselves. But, in many ways this isn't about a musical journey, although that is the very theme that allowed the experiences to take place, but rather it is about travelling both physically and emotionally in a country that in many ways no longer exists.

At the beginning of 1989 Dennis and his fiancée Anne went to China to teach English at Chengdu University. Dennis describes himself as at the time being "an idiosyncratic guitarist with a modest niche in the tiny Seattle experimental music scene", so of course he took his guitar with him (although a taxi driver nearly smashed the instrument to pieces as he was dropped off). The book then tells the story of day to day life of Westerners in China, restrictions on their travel, the way that music was viewed etc. He and Anne are some of the few non-journalist Westerners who were in China at the time of Tiananmen Square, and he talks about the impact of those events and what it meant to the local students etc. In 1989 I was living in a flat in Exeter, and like many I felt affected by the events taking place, and so I purchased the poster of *that* photograph, and put it up in my front room and spent many hours looking at it. Now, here I am reading the words of someone who was in China at the time, living not in a sterile hotel but among the people and understanding the impact from a far closer perspective. It really made me think back to those days and understand the horror a little better.

But, the book is much more than being about just one event, as Dennis is encouraged to share his music and ends up playing with local pop royalty, and creating bands and arranging tours. It is an immensely powerful book, and one that really grabbed me from beginning to end. Even now, I have heard just three albums by Dennis, and we have never met (these days he is back in Seattle and I am in New Zealand), yet I found this book absolutely enthralling and highly recommend it to anyone interested in modern history, culture, travel or music. Absolutely essential.
May 2013

ANDREW WILD
ONE FOR THE RECORD
Some time back in 1991 I became aware of a band from Dorset called Galahad. Now, one thing led to another and over the years it is safe to say that I have done my best to review their music in a totally fair and objective manner, and have failed at every turn. I mean, Stu has stayed at my house, I'm pretty sure it was he who introduced me to Artur Chachlowski (who twenty years later is still one of my best friends) and I know for a fact that Stu was the person who suggested to Big Big Train that they send me their demo tape, which started me thinking that maybe I could approach bands to see if they would send me music to write about instead of buying it all the time. So, one way or another the band has had quite a considerable impact on my life. Galahad are the only prog band I have ever taken my wife to see, not that she had any choice to be honest as it was when we were guests at Stu and Lin's wedding. That is one of my favourite memories of the band, as I remember standing outside in the sunshine with Neil, Mark and Karl chatting about music and the scene for what seemed like hours.

That is what this book is all about for me. Memories. When it is mentioned about Spence falling asleep at a Suzi Quatro gig it reminded me of seeing him sprawled across three chairs at the side of the stage at Walthamstow when they supported The Enid, with Robert John Godfrey in full flow. I was told then that he would sleep anywhere, at anytime, and often did. Over the years I have reviewed everything they have released, and still have the single (and the Fatea flexi!) as well as tapes (including the Polish versions) and of course all the CDs. I still have the letter where Stu says that one day he will ask me to write their biography, but I'm so glad that they didn't as Andrew Wild has achieved something I know I could never have managed. Although he really only got to know the guys through the writing of the book and previously hadn't heard any of their music, he has captured an incredible story and has produced something that is absolutely compelling.

Nearly everyone involved with the band has been interviewed, and there is a feeling of a band that have been through a lot but are still having fun and enjoying themselves all these years down the line. While I write this I have the accompanying DVD playing in the corner of the screen, and the intro from Tim Ashton says it all (although I didn't recognise him to be honest!). The DVD contains concert clips from through the years, with the early ones fascinating for me as I didn't see the first incarnations while others transport me back through time, to when the prog scene may not have made anyone any money (does it now?) but boy was it fun as everyone knew each other and met up at all the gigs.

If you only buy one book about a prog band this year then make it this one, and if you buy two then get this one and Andrew's other essential tome, on Twelfth Night.

So there we have it, yet another totally unbiased review which is totally objective. When you go and buy this you will know exactly what I mean. Oh yeah, maybe I ought to mention that some of my reviews have been reproduced in the book as well, although of course that has no bearing on my giving it five stars…..
May 2013

Interviews

Roger Chapman, Sept 2006

Surely a performer who needs no introduction, Roger has been viewed as one of the UK's top singers for more than thirty years now.

What got you interested in music and who inspired you to become a singer?

Same as every other kid on the block, pop music and its heroes.

Have you ever tried to emulate any other singers or followed your own path?

That's why I started; I wanted to be like Elvis, Fats, Jerry Lee, Little Richard, Eddie Cochran, Gene Vincent etc....then became myself.

What were you musically trying to achieve with Family? What influenced the band's approach and how would you describe the music to someone who had not come across them before?

I think everybody in the band had a different idea of what they wanted but at the same time accepting other ideas. Anti-pop and anti business, that's the only way I can describe it and our attitude. Very anti... very insular, aggressively so. We did things just for the sake of not being accepted; we were fearless and didn't give a fuck. All influences, from Whitney's Beatles and west coast, to King's jazz and blues, Townsend's love of trad jazz, my sense of rock and roll and soul, and I suppose most of all we had lots of passion and belief in ourselves.

Why do you think that they weren't as successful as many feel they should have been?

Too varied for popular taste maybe? Not everybody liked my voice and attitude on stage but that was the way it was. But saying that, I would think all of us now, considering what we were about, would say we were very successful and proud of it. I certainly am, I hope they are.

What led to the demise of Family and how did Streetwalkers come about?

We fell into the trap of being dictated to by everything we used to hate.....then it got boring. Streetwalkers; CW and myself were still writing and Warners asked us to make an album of new songs so we did it. The album was called 'Streetwalker', then they asked us to promote it and all of a sudden we were back on the road with 'Streetwalker' the band.

If someone was to look to just one Streetwalkers album which one should they get, and why?

'Red Card'. The others were good but this one had a sense of direction which we never achieved before or after.

Why do you feel that you have been more successful in Germany than here in the UK?

Because Europe accepted me as a musician and the UK accepted me as an also ran, so I ran.....thankfully.

You have worked with some fine guitarists over the years. What do you look for when choosing a musician for your band?

Adaptability, must be on their toes, ready to try anything at the drop of a hat. Coming ready or not. Shit... loads of people. The last but one big musical event for me was being on stage with Georgie Fame in Bill Wyman's Rhythm Kings. George's always been one of my heroes and I'm glad to say he was superb with them. I always try to make a trip to see him when he's on somewhere, usually 'Ronnies', if and when I can. Another was being on stage with a 90-piece orchestra, at an outdoor classical fest in Halle, Germany, June 2006, wow! That's something I've never done before; scary shit but I enjoyed it.

You have been in the music business for over thirty years now. What inspires you to keep going?

To make good albums, always wanting to write a classic song, always trying to prove my critics wrong, lots Of reasons....

What's next?

New album, that's the most important thing for me now. I'm not interested in gigging until I get this fucker out of my system.

David Allen, May 2007

Carmen are a band I hold in very high regard and when I heard their albums were being re-released by Angel Air I was soon in touch with Peter Purnell, and a short while later I had the opportunity to put some rather fawning questions to David Allen, founder and guitarist of the world's greatest ever flamenco rock outfit.

What or who first inspired you to meld flamenco music with rock?

I've played flamenco guitar since I was 2 years old. I was trained to be a concert performer by my parents, who had all the connections in that field - but then the Beatles came along and changed everything for me

How did the band first come together, and how did John come to be in the US?

I was 19 when I started putting Carmen together - we were called Rose in the beginning. There were 7 of us to begin with including another guitarist and singer - both of which were changed a few times. Brian Glascock was our first drummer and when I couldn't find a bass player I was happy with, he recommended his brother. I flew John over and was so knocked out with him that he ended up living with my family for quite a while, in order to be able to stay in the country.

Why did you move to the UK and why did John's brother not come with you?

We moved to London because after two years of auditioning for the likes of Clive David, etc. no one in the music business in the States understood what we were doing. They all thought we were a great Las Vegas act! Brian didn't come because he had a family to support and the chances were fairly small that we'd get signed and supported in England. All the rest of us had less to lose.

How did you get involved with Tony Visconti?

We saw an interview with Tony on the Old Grey Whistle Test one night after signing with our manager, Brian Longely. The next day we called Brian and said we just found our producer, you don't happen to know how to get hold of Visconti, do you? He did. He knew his business manager, Roger, and through that connection we met and auditioned for Tony in his office and were signed to him and making our first album within a matter of a few weeks.

How would describe your stage show?

We put on a flamenco stage show to compliment the music we made. Angela and Roberto were world class dancers and had movie star looks to boot.

How important was the dancing to the overall performance?

The dancing was crucial because we used it as percussion. We had a special stage that went with us everywhere and was miked with barcus berry hotdots

Were there problems miking the stage to capture the stamping?

There were problems to begin with until we tried the hotdots, which changed everything and allowed us to create an immensely loud and powerful sound.

How did you get on with other bands, and who did you support aside from Bowie and Tull?

We got on well with most of the bands we worked with. Most touring bands have similar experiences of loneliness and aggravation along the way and it makes for a bond.
We supported Santana, Blue Öyster Cult, ELO, Golden Earring, etc.

Why was the third album only released in the States?

I have no idea. Mercury Records might have felt that, as we were in the process of breaking up, it was best to concentrate on the most lucrative market. Who knows.

Had the band already decided to split when John joined Tull or was that a contributing factor?

We had split when John joined Tull. He would never have left the group, otherwise.

What did you do after the band split up?

I hooked up with Jack Nietzche and Herb Cohen for a while. Played session guitar for Michelle Phillips solo album among other things.

And what other musical ventures have you been involved with?

Wrote two songs for Agnetha - of Abba fame - which were included on her first solo album. I've recently formed Widescreen, whose first album is being released along with 'The Gypsies' on Angel Air records.

Have you kept in contact with any of the others, and if so did they ever do anything else musically?

I'm in contact with all the remaining members. Paul Fenton heads the reformed T Rex; he knew Marc well and played with T Rex whenever Carmen wasn't touring. None of the others has had anything released commercially since, although Roberto remains active in Flamenco and as a producer.

Looking back, what legacy do you feel you have left behind?

It was a very youthful, passionate, and intense period of my life. We were the originators of flamenco/fusion world music.

Leonardo Pavkovic, Dec 2012

Before forming MoonJune Records what had you been doing in the music industry?

I was involved only peripherally with the music industry, and the year before starting MoonJune I worked with two other partners in a jazz label, but our investors left us dry in the last moment, focusing on something else. Before that I had been a partner since 1991 in the legendary graphic design and advertising parlor from New York City's Downtown, Studio T led by Brazilian designer and photographer Fernando Natalici since 1973. Half of our clients were in the music business: all music promoters, from small to giant, many jazz and independent labels, musicians so you can say that I have actively lived the New York "music scene" in 90's through graphics and advertisement. At one point we serviced almost 75% of the performing music business in the city, and among labels our clients were Blue Note, Dreyfus, Knitting Factory Records, Celluloid, Stern's Africa, and many others.

Why did you decide to form the label?

I am still asking myself the same question. It happened organically without precise planning, with no budgets, no distribution, no entertainment lawyer, no capital, simply, it happened and here I am, still alive after 11 years. While I am not making my living from the label, I do other things within the music industry.

What is your musical policy in artists?

Intellectual and artistic freedom, camaraderie, and music that I like. I have complex and multiple taste in music, and my label represents in part my taste.

What is the label's proudest achievement to date?
To be still around after 11 years and to have our 50th release next month in January (Marbin's new album 'Last Chapter of Dreaming'). Also, releasing Indonesian artists makes me proud and happy, exposing to the world some amazing musicians such as Riza Arshad of simakDialog, guitar virtuosos Tohpati and Agam Hamzah and soon, the Indonesian ultimate guitarist Dewa Budjana. Additionally, I am proud to be involved with Allan Holdsworth who is an extra-terrestrial guitar genius. I am his worldwide booking manager and one of his best friends.

What made you concentrate so much on Indonesia?

My love and passion for that country which I have visited 14 times, and where I have so many friends in so many different circuits, not just in the musical circuits. Indonesia is the 4th most populous country in the world, culturally and musically extremely rich and still, not so many people know about Indonesia. Also, the country is experiencing tremendous economy growth, becoming not just a regional economic power, but also able and capable to be a world class player in terms of economy and business, due also to its own potential, and parallel, the Indonesian culture and music is gaining a momentum and

Indonesia is about to happen, full time.

What's next?

Looking forward to celebrate my 100th release, which I hope will be in about 5-6 years, I plan to release 10-12 albums per year, but you never know, I might start releasing more. 15-20 of my next 50 releases should be Indonesian.

I hope you enjoyed the latest collection of my prog scribblings and that you will use this and the other books in the series to discover "new" bands and great music.

Remember, Prog never died, it just went underground.

Kev Rowland

Kev Rowland is a self-confessed music addict, who has never really been the same since he heard 'Sabbath Bloody Sabbath' in 1975. In the Eighties he spent quite a ridiculous amount of money on all things related to Jethro Tull and was asked by David Rees to write a piece on Carmen (the band including John Glascock, not the opera) for the Tull fanzine 'A New Day'. This simple request was life-changing, although neither realised it at the time.

Kev discovered he enjoyed writing about music and submitted reviews for the inaugural Mensa RockSIG newsletter, before becoming secretary himself in 1990. Over the next 16 years, the newsletter gained a name, and he put out more than 80 issues, many of them doubles, in excess of 11,000 pages. When he moved to New Zealand in 2006, he retired from the music scene, but was pulled back in – initially kicking and screaming until he accepted his fate. These days he can be found contributing to many magazines and websites, and is thoroughly enjoying the amazing music which can be found at the end of the world, saying the gigs remind him so much of what he used to attend 30 years ago.

When he isn't listening to music, writing about music, or thinking about music, then he can be found on his lifestyle block with his wonderful wife Sara, and their 8 cats, 6 dogs, chickens, sheep, lambs, calves and cattle. Oh, apparently, he has a day job as well.

Online:
http://www.progarchives.com/Collaborators.asp?id=5626
https://www.muzic.net.nz/articles/authors/35899

The Progressive Underground Vol 4

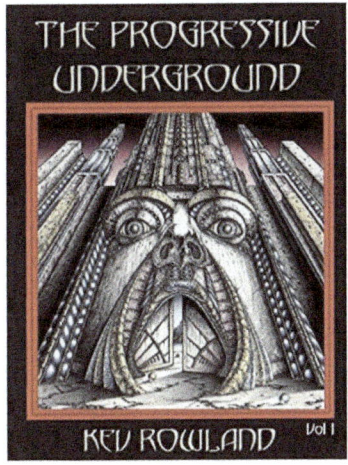  

Containing all of Kev Rowland's progressive rock reviews and interviews written between 1991 and 2006, the first three volumes of The Progressive Underground are essential for all lovers of the genre, but don't just take our word for it.

A book that will be quickly referred to as "a bible".
Daryl Easlea, Record Collector

Rowland is collecting his reviews in three volumes (in alphabetical order): their preservation for posterity is welcome. His writing is informative, intelligent, and generous. It certainly makes interesting reading... As Brian Appleton would put it, thank you Kev for your contribution.
Rychard Carrington, Rock n Reel

The third compilation of reviews from his Feedback fanzine is warm, honest and engaging. It is also, like the best underground writing, unvarnished and unencumbered by any expectations of PR; the reviews in The Progressive Underground Vol 3 are clearly done for no other reason than the love of the genre.
DE, Prog Magazine

This is best treated as a kind of guide to the neo-progressive genre. Thanks to this release, you can rediscover the wonderful albums of great bands and see that progressive rock has never really died, it just went from the mainstream to the underground.
Artur Chachlowski, MLWZ

All I can say is if you are a true proghead this book should be in your library of progressive rock literature. Because it's a great work. A book to be considered of superior or lasting artistic merit.
Henri Strik, Background Magazine

Chronic well-crafted, short and mostly written in order to develop the subject with ease...Simply relevant information, the essential and useful. Personally, I believe that many current columnists should emulate the writing of Mr. Rowland.
Fred, ProfilProg

Laying his fan card on the table, Rowland has brought all of these reviews together to create a veritable Encyclopaedia Progressivica in three volumes... the ultimate pan-progressive fanzine.
Peter-James Dries, Muzic.net.nz

There is still such a thing as alternative Publishing

Robert Newton Calvert: Born 9 March 1945, Died 14 August 1988 after suffering a heart attack. Contributed poetry, lyrics and vocals to legendary space rock band Hawkwind intermittently on five of their most critically acclaimed albums, including Space Ritual (1973), Quark, Strangeness & Charm (1977) and Hawklords (1978). He also recorded a number of solo albums in the mid 1970s. CENTIGRADE 232 was Robert Calvert's first collection of poems.

Hype   'And now, for all you speeding street smarties out there, the one you've all been waiting for, the one that'll pierce your laid back ears, decoke your sinuses, cut clean thru the schlock rock, MOR/crossover, techno flash mind mush. It's the new Number One with a bullet ... with a bullet ... It's Tom, Supernova, Mahler with a pan galactic biggie ...' And the Hype goes on. And on. Hype, an amphetamine hit of a story by Hawkwind collaborator Robert Calvert. Who's been there and made it back again. The debriefing session starts here.

Rick Wakeman is the world's most unusual rock star, a genius who has pushed back the barriers of electronic rock. He has had some of the world's top orchestras perform his music, has owned eight Rolls Royces at one time, and has broken all the rules of composing and horrified his tutors at the Royal College of Music. Yet he has delighted his millions of fans. This frank book, authorised by Wakeman himself, tells the moving tale of his larger than life career.

There are nine Henrys, purported to be the world's first cloned cartoon character. They live in a strange lo fi domestic surrealist world peopled by talking rock buns and elephants on wobbly stilts.

They mooch around in their minimalist universe suffering from an existential crisis with some genetically modified humour thrown in.

Marty Wilde on Terry Dene: "Whatever happened to Terry becomes a great deal more comprehensible as you read of the callous way in which he was treated by people who should have known better many of whom, frankly, will never know better of the sad little shadows of the past who eased themselves into Terry's life, took everything they could get and, when it seemed that all was lost, quietly left him … Dan Wooding's book tells it all."

Rick Wakeman: "There have always been certain 'careers' that have fascinated the public, newspapers, and the media in general. Such include musicians, actors, sportsmen, police, and not surprisingly, the people who give the police their employment: The criminal. For the man in the street, all these careers have one thing in common: they are seemingly beyond both his reach and, in many cases, understanding and as such, his only association can be through the media of newspapers or television. The police, however, will always require the services of the grass, the squealer, the snitch, (call him what you will), in order to assist in their investigations and arrests; and amazingly, this is the area that seldom gets written about."

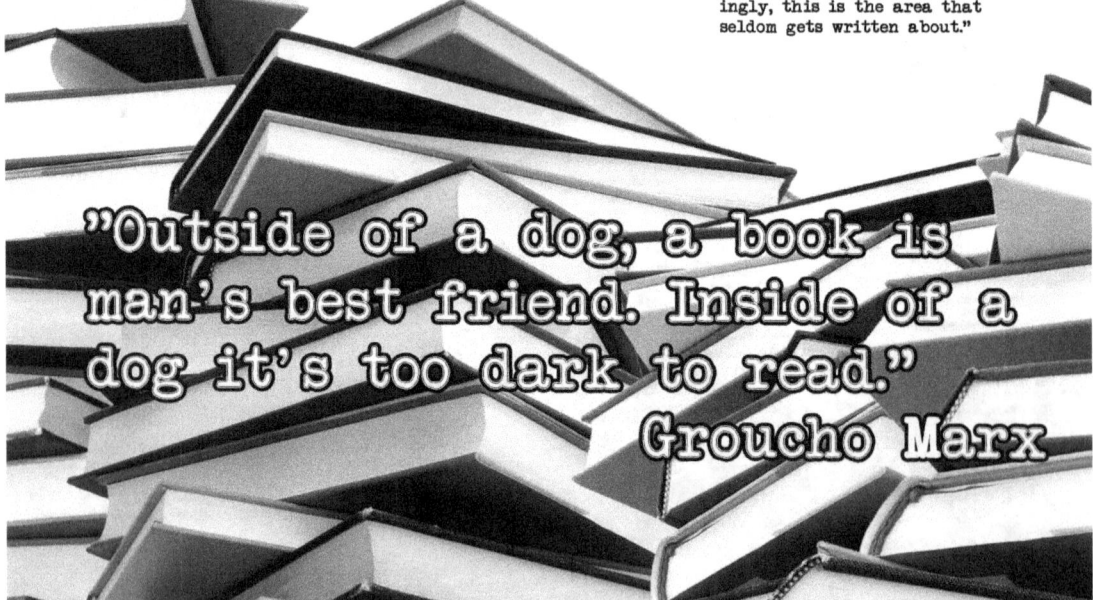

"Outside of a dog, a book is man's best friend. Inside of a dog it's too dark to read." Groucho Marx

Bill Harkleroad joined Captain Beefheart's Magic Band at a time when they were changing from a straight ahead blues band into something completely different. Through the vision of Don Van Vliet (Captain Beefheart) they created a new form of music which many at the time considered atonal and difficult, but which over the years has continued to exert a powerful influence. Beefheart re christened Harkleroad as Zoot Horn Rollo, and they embarked on recording one of the classic rock albums of all time Trout Mask Replica - a work of unequalled daring and inventiveness.

Politics, paganism and .... Vlad the Impaler. Selected stories from CJ Stone from 2003 to the present. Meet Ivor Coles, a British Tommy killed in action in September 1915, lost, and then found again. Visit Mothers Club in Erdington, the best psychedelic music club in the UK in the '60s. Celebrate Robin Hood's Day and find out what a huckle duckle is. Travel to Stonehenge at the Summer Solstice and carouse with the hippies. Find out what a Ranter is, and why CJ Stone thinks that he's one. Take LSD with Dr Lilly, the psychedelic scientist. Meet a headless soldier or the ghost of Elvis Presley in Gabalfa, Cardiff. Journey to Whitstable, to New York, to Malta and to Transylvania, and to many other places, real and imagined, political and spiritual, transcendent and mundane. As The Independent says, Chris is "The best guide to the underground since Charon ferried dead souls across the Styx."

This is is the first in the highly acclaimed vampire novels of the late Mick Farren. Victor Renquist, a surprisingly urbane and likable leader of a colony of vampires which has existed for centuries in New York is faced with both administrative and emotional problems. And when you are a vampire, administration is not a thing which one takes lightly.

"The person, be it gentleman or lady, who has not pleasure in a good novel, must be intolerably stupid."

Jane Austen

www.ingramcontent.com/pod-product-compliance
Lightning Source LLC
Chambersburg PA
CBHW082035230426
43670CB00016B/2666